Equipment of th

Following the D-Day landings in Normandy, some British and American jeeps were converted for rail use by removing their normal wheels and replacing them with flanged wheels that could run on the European standard gauge tracks. This opened up an entirely new transportation network through some of the more rugged parts of France and Belgium where cross-country travel was difficult.

by DAVID B. GORDON

PICTORIAL HISTORIES PUBLISHING CO., INC.
Missoula, Montana

. . . . .

i

LIBRARY OF CONGRESS
CONTROL NUMBER 2010931328

ISBN 978-1-57510-151-4

Originally Printed in April 2004 under ISBN 1-57510-107-6

Revised and Expanded Edition
First Printing: July 2010

Volumes in this Series:

Equipment of the WWII Tommy

Weapons of the WWII Tommy

Uniforms of the WWII Tommy

PICTORIAL HISTORIES PUBLISHING CO., INC.
713 South Third Street West
Missoula, Montana 59801
Phone: 406.549.8488   eMail: phpc@montana.com
http://www.pictorialhistoriespublishing.com

· · · · ·

Kurt Ahrens Mays
1 FEB 1965 – 1 MAR 2003
Oxfordshire & Buckinghamshire, L.I.
(British Airborne Reenacted)

Stephen Lee Huff
4 OCT 1966 – 1 MAR 2003
Le Maquis de l'As de Coeurs
(French Resistance Reenacted)

This book is dedicated to the memory of two good friends that died in a tragic automobile accident following the national D-Day reenactment at Camp Gruber, Oklahoma.

· · · · ·

Acknowledgments

Special thanks to the following individuals for making elements of their personal collections available to be photographed and/or for providing access to reference material and photographs from their private libraries:

Norman Bonney	Fred Ganske	Richard Horrell
Malcolm Johnson	Darryl Lynn	Michel Perrier
Mike Saffrey	David Sampson	Jim Teel

And to the following WWII veterans for their observations and feedback:

Nobby Clark   John Howard   Bill Millin
Hans von Luck   Wally Parr   Bill Vine   Jim Wallwork

Additional thanks to the Imperial War Museum, the Australian War Memorial and the Library and Archives of Canada for making their documents available and for the use of some of the period photographs in this book.

The information contained in this volume was derived from many sources collectively. While period records and training manuals were researched, they were not always considered to be the final word in how something was done during the war. Information gleamed from regimental notes and war diaries, combined with veteran accounts and period photographs provide the details that are often missing from the story. This approach is critical when considering the subject because a manual written in 1941 detailing a task might be completely different in its 1943 revision. Things changed and the simple Tommy adapted as he learned first hand how to survive while on the job in his hostile world at war.

Because needed resources were not always available and there were so many manufacturers for a given item, variations in color and material may be found when comparing two examples representing the same thing. Items made early in the war were sometimes replaced by later patterns as far as production was concerned but both patterns would typically co-exist in the field until they wore out. This book makes an attempt to cover some of the more common patterns of items available to the British and Commonwealth soldiers during the war. It by no means is a comprehensive reference to everything that was produced, but it's a good start.

· · · · ·

Table of Contents

· · · · ·

The original WWII period photographs used in this publication were assembled from a number of sources. Some came from previously classified military reports which were printed in such limited numbers that the actual photographs were

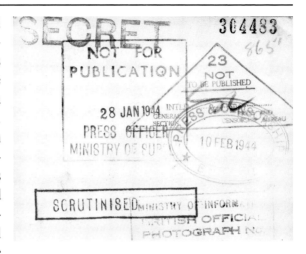

pasted directly onto the pages. Many were purchased through on-line auctions or made available from private collections. Whenever possible, the original caption or photographer's notes were printed with the photograph. In some cases, only the military censor and classification markings were on the back of the photograph and on others, there were no markings whatsoever. This is often the case when copies of a photograph were produced from the original negative over the past sixty years since the war. Due to the unusual circumstances that wartime photographers sometimes found themselves in, original

photographs are not always clear, centered or focused. The best shots were always selected when there was a choice but some topics have very little photograph evidence that they even existed.

. . . . .

Chapter 1 - Basic Webbing Equipment

Basic web equipment had to be sorted by type of item following the war as most of the army was gradually demobilized. The equipment would be cleaned and stored for issue in possible future conflicts.

. . . . .

The Pattern 1937 web equipment was designed for the most part as an improved version of the Pattern 1908 web equipment. The most notable difference is most straps were narrowed from two inches down to one inch in width. This helped to lighten the set and to reduce the surface area that would rub against a soldier while marching with a full com-bat load. Other changes were made to accom-modate new weapons and equipment that had been adopted over the thirty years between the two patterns. The only item that remained virtu-ally unchanged was the pack and its supporting straps. These were in-tended to hold the great-coat and other items that would be stored and transported from station to encampment in unit trucks. When the pack was worn, the haver-sack, also known more commonly as the small pack, was worn at the side suspended by the web equipment braces.

· · · · ·

For pattern 1937 web equipment, three sizes of the ***Web Equipment Pattern `37 Waist Belt*** were officially produced. These were: extra-large at 56 inches long; large at 50 inches long and small, which was sometimes marked with an "N" or the word "Normal", being 44 inches long. Unofficially a fourth size exists which was made in India and it is 42 inches long. Measurements are end to end which is longer than

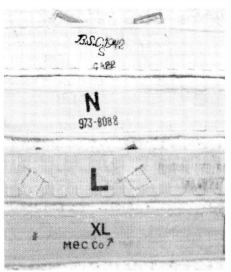

the effective waist size since the belts are folded over at each end and fastened with brass or steel hooks back onto themselves. All have a height of 2.25 inches with a hook and loop pattern brass clasp buckle in the front. Two brass or web material sliders are used to hold the folded over web belt ends together. A pair of buckles is sewn onto the back of the belt, they angle towards each other for attachment of the web equipment braces that cross in the back and go over the shoulders. The Web Waist Belt is the principle piece of equipment since all of the other basic web components fasten to it. A second Web Waist Belt was normally issued for dress or walking out purposes. This allowed the soldiers to keep their main equipment set together since it was a time consuming process to get everything properly adjusted. The second Web Waist Belt was worn without any other web equipment and the pair of brass buckles on the back was often removed for a smarter presentation.

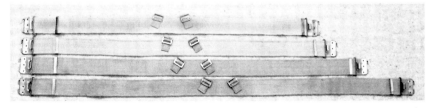

· · · · ·

Web Equipment Pattern `37 Braces were produced in left and right pairs. The left brace has a loop sewn onto it that the right brace slips through to form a cross on the back. This keeps the two braces together and prevents them from shifting around while marching. Official records indicate two sizes were produced. These were *normal* which had a length of 47 inches and *long* which had a length of 55 inches. The shorter length Web Equipment Braces can sometimes be found marked with an "S" as the

photograph at the lower right shows along with examples of the long and normal sizes which can also be marked as "L" and "N" respectively.

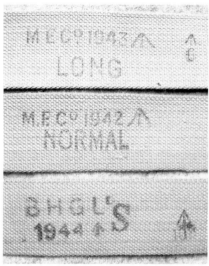

The wide portion of the brace is the section that rides on the shoulder. The narrow ends that are in the rear when worn are fastened to the pair of buckles on the Web Waist Belt. The narrow ends that are in the front when worn are fastened to the Basic Pouches. The ends that hang out on the left side of the wearer are used to connect the Water Bottle Carrier. The ends that hang out on the right side of the wearer are used to connect the Haversack when carried at the side if the Pack is being worn on the back.

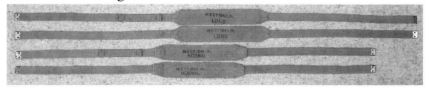

· · · · ·

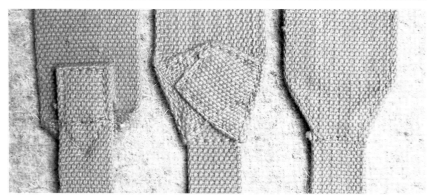

This picture shows the three most commonly encountered methods of Web Equipment Brace construction. These are variations in the manufacturing process and not an indicator of the country that produced them. In this case, all three of the pictured braces were made in the United Kingdom.

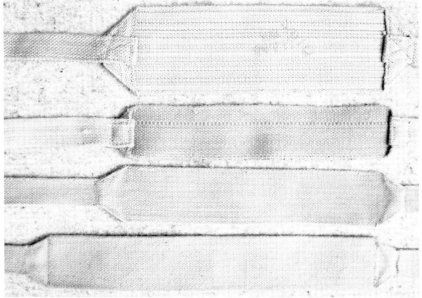

Examples of a few Commonwealth patterns of Web Equipment Brace which allows a comparison of shape and weave. Color variations unfortunately don't come through as noticeably with B&W photography. Top to bottom are the wide pattern Australian, Indian, British with a slightly longer shoulder area and a Canadian pattern with even longer shoulder area.

· · · · ·

Web Equipment Pattern `37 Brace Attachments were used to connect the ends of the Equipment Braces to the Web Waist Belt in the front when Basic Pouches and Cartridge Carriers were not worn. They are made with a metal rectangular fitting that is tall enough for the Web Waist Belt to fit through. A metal bar in the center of the fitting is free at the bottom so it can swing up and out of the way when the belt is pressed through from the back. Once enough belt has been pressed through the fitting to allow the bar to fold back down, the remaining belt is pulled back trapping the bar back down against the belt and the fitting. An economy version was also produced and it has no moving parts. The fitting has a solid bar in the center and the outer two sides have a gap in the middle for the belt to be slipped

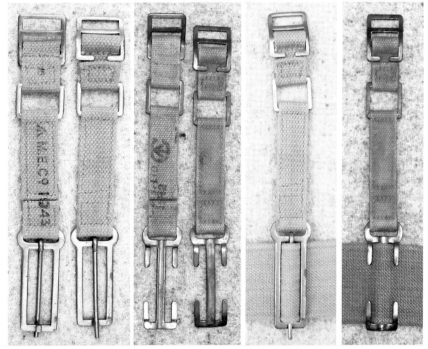

Standard production British-made (left) and Canadian-made economy pattern Brace Attachments shown from the front, the back and connected to a Web Equipment Belt for reference.

. . . . .

through. Typically these were part of the equipment issue for officers and NCOs that either carried no arms or just a pistol. The metal fittings at the top of the Brace Attachments are the same as found on the Basic Pouch and allow the Braces to attach as well as to provide a place for the Haversack Shoulder Straps of the Haversack to fasten.

Lieutenants Joseph Maurice Rousseau (left) and Joseph Philippe Rousseau of the 1st Canadian Parachute Battalion photographed at a transit camp wearing Denison Smocks and webbing equipment with standard production Brace Attachments. Both officers were killed in action in France during the fighting following the Normandy invasion, Philippe on 7 JUN 1944 and Maurice on 20 SEPT 1944. Near Down Ampney, England - 13 FEB 1944.

· · · · ·

Several patterns of **Web Equipment Pattern `37 Water Bottle Carrier** were produced during the war, including those that originated as components of patterns in service prior to the adoption of the 1937 pattern. All patterns worked with the Mark VI water bottle which was made out of metal that had an enamel coating and a felt outer cover. The cover helped to dampen the sound made by the water bottle striking an object and it also served to protect the enamel coating so it wouldn't become chipped and rust. The main patterns encountered are often referred to as skeletal and sleeve water bottle carriers. At least two patterns of each exist. The difference in the two skeletal patterns is the location of the snap fasteners and the length of the strap they are connected to. The difference in the two sleeve patterns is the height of the web material and how much of the water bottle they cover. All patterns have a pair of web tabs with brass adjustable buckles at their ends which are used to connect onto the ends of the Web Equipment Braces. The sleeve pattern water bottle carriers require less of the brace strap to be available since their buckles are higher up when compared with the skeletal pattern.

The water bottle is kept closed with a cork. This has a metal disk on one end which has a hole in the top for a threaded rod with an eye on one end to pass through. This rod passes completely through the cork from top to bottom and is kept in place by a nut. The eye on the rod is for a length of sturdy string to tie off to which is connected to the water bottle. This prevents the cork from getting lost when removed from the water bottle. Neither the threaded rod nor the nut is treated metal and they quickly rusted from exposure to water.

· · · · ·

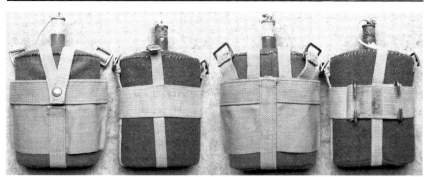

Front and back views of a 1940 dated carrier used by mounted troops and an Australian pattern that could be fastened to the web equipment belt or to the braces.

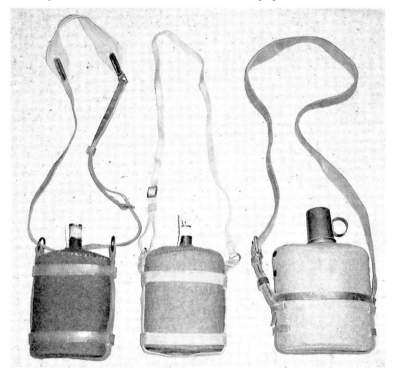

Pictured on the left is a 1942 dated Pattern 1903 water bottle carrier made from leather with integral leather and web sling. The center and right water bottle carriers are typical to medical orderlies with the one at far right being oversized and having its own cup.

• • • • •

Web Equipment Pattern `37 Basic Pouches were normally worn on the chest and were issued in pairs which were interchangeable. They are rectangular in shape and have an opening at the top that is covered by a hinged box lid that is kept closed by a single fastener in the center. A pair of brass double hooks in the rear is used to connect the pouch to the Web Waist Belt and a brass adjustable buckle at the top in back is used to connect to the end of the Web Equipment Braces. This buckle also has an extra slot in the very top for the hook on the Haversack Shoulder Straps to connect to. Several patterns of Basic Pouch were produced during the war, although some of these are not believed to have been issued before the war ended. The first design has come to be known as the Mark I. It is identical to the Mark II with the exception of the placement of the piece of webbing material on the back that holds the pair of double hooks in place. The Mark I pattern has the hooks on the back one inch higher than the Mark II pattern.

Fusilier Tom Payne of the 53rd Welsh Division wearing Battledress Serge and full webbing with Mark II Basic Pouches. 12 AUG 1944.

This places the pouch lower on the wearer when connected to the Web Waist Belt. The Mark II modification came about in June 1940 to raise the pouch to a higher position when worn and became the new standard production pouch. The Mark III pattern was developed after the Sten submachine gun came into issue. It has an increased depth of approximately one inch so the pouch can accommodate the stick magazines used by the new weapon. Basic Pouches were produced by many manufacturers in several nations including the United Kingdom, Canada, India

· · · · ·

and Australia. Several variations of each Mark exist including alternate types of metal and shape of the fittings. Early Basic Pouches produced in Canada and India have three web loops sewn into the inside of the lid for easy access to Ballistite or marking rounds. This feature was not carried over to the Mark III pattern used for Sten magazines. It also does not appear to have ever been a feature in British produced pouches. Mark I and Mark II Basic Pouches have dimensions of 8 inches tall by 5.5 inches wide by 2.625 inches deep. The later Mark III Basic Pouches have dimensions of 9 inches tall by 5.5 inches wide by 2.625 inches deep. To increase the load carrying capacity of soldiers fighting in jungle regions, Large Australian Basic Pouches were developed which had dimensions of 9 inches tall by 6.75 wide inches by 3.75 inches deep.

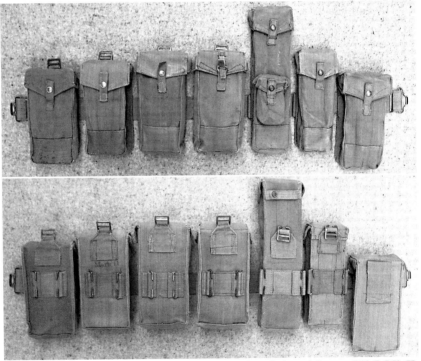

Examples of British-made WWII pouches from left to right are: Mk I, Mk II, Mk III, Mk III with quick release closure, Lanchester magazine pouch with dividers, Sten magazine pouch with dividers and a Motorcyclist and Driver's pattern pouch.

. . . . .

 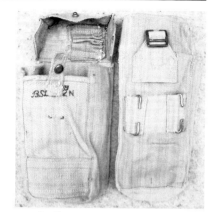

British-made Basic Pouch   **Indian-made Basic Pouch**

Australian-made Mark II Basic Pouches (above left) and Australian-made *Large Basic Pouches* shown for size comparison (above right) and worn by the Commonwealth soldiers in the photograph at the right.

• • • • •

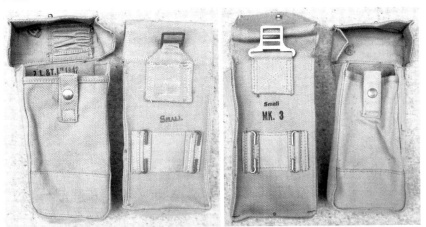

Canadian-made early pattern Basic Pouch (left) and later Mark 3 pattern.

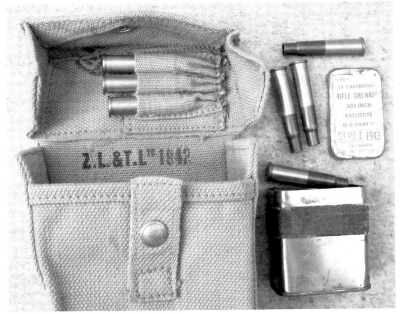

A close up of an early production Canadian Basic Pouch showing the loops found in the top of the flap for cartridges. Normally these were for Ballistite cartridges used when launching grenades from the Enfield rifle grenade cup launcher. They were also used to hold special marking rounds, either tracers or incendiary. These were used to help indicate a target to be collectively fired upon.

· · · · ·

13

In 1944, some Mark III pattern Basic Pouches were produced with quick release closures, also known as a hasp and staple. This modified method of keeping the lid closed was already in use on some patterns of the Sten magazine bandolier, Bren spare parts wallets and barrel holdalls as well as on both patterns of holster used with the Inglis Hi-Power. This Basic Pouch is otherwise identical to the normal Mark III pattern with snap closure. Consensus among consulted historians and collectors is this pattern Basic Pouch was not issued during WWII except for basic trials. No photographic evidence has been found so far to prove otherwise. This design was, however, produced and issued in the postwar period along side the regular pattern pouch with snaps.

Another Mark III variation developed in 1944 for drivers of AFVs and universal carriers is one without metal fittings on the back. It merely has a web loop sewn at the top for the Web Waist Belt to slip through

and hold it in place. This *Web Equipment Pattern '37 M.T. Drivers Basic Pouch* was intended for Sten magazines and one pouch was issued along with a pair of Brace Attachments. The pouch could be worn on the left or right side and placement was a matter of convenience when driving.

. . . . .

Machine Carbine Magazine Pouches with internal dividers were produced during the war for the purpose of each holding three submachine gun magazines inside. The dividers held magazines firmly in place even if the pouch was not full or if the flap were left open. They also served as sound dampeners so the bodies of the magazines wouldn't rattle against each other. The original long pattern was for Lanchester 50-round magazines. One pouch per pair featured an external pocket to hold a magazine loader. The shorter pattern was produced initially from cut down Lanchester magazine pouches for use with

Lanchester magazine pouches issued in left and right pairs with one having a pocket for the loader.

1941 dated pouches modified for use with Sten magazines.

32-round Sten magazines, and these had no external pocket. Newly manufactured Sten magazine pouches with dividers were also produced towards the end of the war which suggests that these were being issued and used by units since the modified pouches were not in quantities to meet demand. But since their size is virtually identical to the Mark III Basic Pouch, none todate have been identified in wartime photographs.

. . . . .

Web Equipment Pattern `37 Utility Pouches were issued in pairs to supplement what could be carried in the normal Basic Pouches. They were larger than the normal Basic Pouch and consisted of a left and right pouch that were connected at the top by a two inch wide web yoke designed to go over the shoulder. This placed one pouch on the chest and the other on the back of the wearer. One pouch had a long one inch wide web strap sewn to its back. This was passed around the wearer and through a loop on the back of the oth-

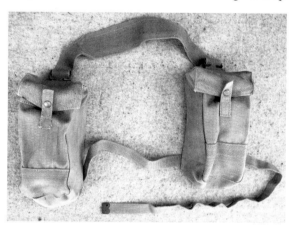

er pouch. It was then fastened back where it started to an adjustable brass buckle. This kept the pouches firmly in place so they wouldn't bounce around and beat on the wearer when marching or running. The Utility Pouch set was often issued to the Number 2 Bren Gunner with six filled magazines which he supplied to the Number 1 Bren Gunner when needed. Empty magazines were traded out for filled magazines carried by other mem-

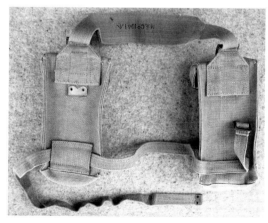

bers of the section who would refill them from bandoliers when they could. The pouches were also used by soldiers issued with the Boys Anti-Tank Rifle as a more convenient and comfortable method of carrying multiple 10-round bandoliers of ammunition.

· · · · ·

British infantry on patrol during Operation Epsom. Note the Web Utility Pouch set being worn loose around the neck for fast access. Outskirts of Caen - 26 JUN 1944.

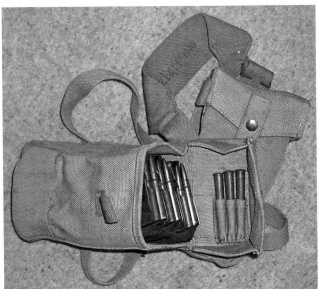

A Canadian-made example of the Web Utility Pouches with filled Bren Magazines. Note that these have three cartridge loops in the pouch flaps just as they are found on Mark II Canadian-made Basic Pouches.

· · · · ·

17

Special web pouches were introduced on 16 JAN 1942 that were designed to carry 20-round box magazines for the Thomson Machine Carbine. The ***C.M.T. Magazine Pouch*** was shorter and slightly wider than the standard Mark I and Mark II Basic Pouches but general construction was very similar. There were no provisions for attaching the pouch to a Web Equipment Belt and the single brass buckle at the top on the back had no second bar to allow the Haversack Shoulder Straps to attach. A non-boxed flap with a single snap in the center was used to close the pouch and each side near the opening had a short weather tab that could be folded on top of the magazines prior to the flap being secured. Little is known about how these pouches were carried but they could easily have been fastened onto the ends of Equipment Braces where they would simply hang at the hips of the wearer. The same List of Changes entry that introduces the pouches included an entry for a ***C.M.T. Magazine Pouch Strap*** and it was 30 inches long and 1 inch wide with tabs at each end. This would provide a means of attaching a pair of C.M.T. pouches together so that they could be slung over the shoulder or around the neck in a way similar to the Utility Pouches but with no provision to keep them from swinging around as there was no additional waist strap.

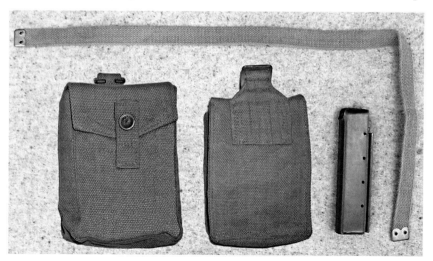

. . . . .

The web pouch pictured on this page was issued to some members of Home Guard units that had been issued with the M1918 Browning Automatic Rifle (BAR). The BAR was a 30.06 caliber lend-lease weapon from the United States. It was first produced during the Great War but continued to be manufactured and used well into WWII. It used a 20-round box magazine 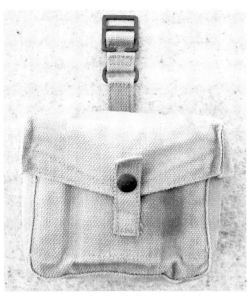 and the pouch could hold two when they were inserted sideways inside. Two small web loops are sewn to the inside of the front wall of the pouch for the oiler and cleaning accessories. Aside from this, the pouch is one large open area. The back of the pouch has a pair of belt loops sewn into it but has no metal fittings. It also has the same type of hanger as found with the 20-round .303 Cartridge Carriers so it could

 be used with the Web Equipment Braces. Of the pouches covered in this chapter, this is one of the hardest types to find today. Binocular Cases are sometimes used to represent them in films and television broadcasts pertaining to the Home Guard.

· · · · ·

When issued, ***Web Equipment Pattern `37 Cartridge Carriers*** were usually worn in pairs in place of the Basic Pouches. Each Cartridge Carrier consisted of two pockets covered by a flap that could be snapped into one of two positions. Each pocket could hold two 5-round .303 rifle chargers, also called stripper clips, giving a single Cartridge Carrier a capacity of 20 rounds. A one inch wide web strap is sewn to the back in the center of each carrier and it has a brass buckle at the end which is the same design found on the Basic Pouches. This provides a fastening point for the Web Equipment Braces. A brass loop sewn below the buckle allowed the brace strap to slip behind the carrier so it could be connected to other pieces of equipment. Like the Basic Pouch, a pair of brass fittings is sewn to the back so the carrier can be connected to the Web Waist Belt. Early production examples like the Canadian-made pair

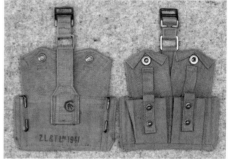

below feature an internal piece of webbing that prevents filled chargers from falling out if the flap of the pouch is open. This also made it harder to quickly remove a charger when needed and may account for it being omitted in later production.

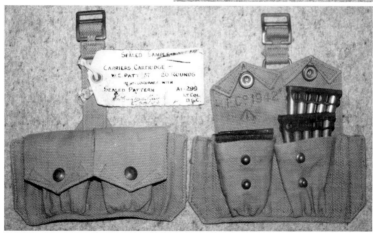

· · · · ·

Special Grenade Carriers were produced in the last year of the Second World War and were designed to hold two Number 36 fragmentation grenades. The design is similar to the Web Cartridge Carriers but there is no provision to accept the end of a Web Equipment Brace. The rear has a pair of brass fittings sewn to the back so the carrier could be connected to the Web Waist Belt adjacent to one of the Basic Pouches or over a Brace Attachment if worn. While the Number 69 Concussion and Number 77 Smoke grenades will not fit into the pockets, the American-made Mark II fragmentation grenade will.

The lower photograph on the facing page shows an example of a Cartridge Carrier tagged as being part of the sealed pattern. Pattern Room items like this were provided to web equipment manufacturers as a master pattern for them to copy when they began production.

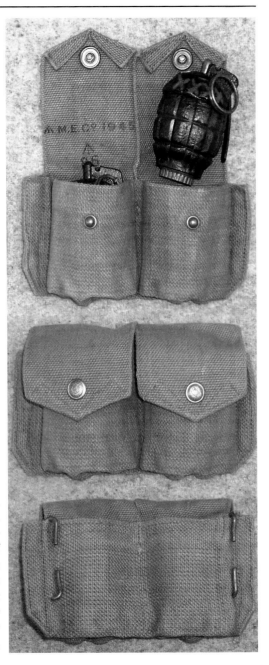

• • • • •

The ***Web Equipment Pattern '37 Binocular Case*** was made from two layers of material which had fibre board stiffeners between them help to protect the optics when carried inside. The box lid flap was held closed by a single centered snap. The back of the case has three double hook fasteners. Two are used to connect it to the Web Waist Belt. The third is situated at the top and it was used for connecting a Compass Pocket or Pistol Ammunition Pouch. The case was designed for the Number 2 prismatic 6x30 binoculars. These were issued with a ¼ inch wide web neck strap. It connected onto the mounting points by looping the strap through and back to small brass buckles.

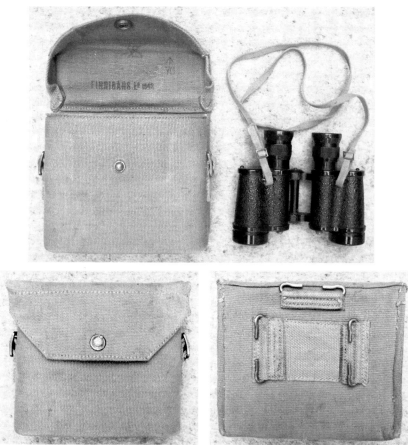

· · · · ·

An unidentified officer graduate of Number 33 Canadian Army (Basic) Training Centre (Canadian Army Training Centres and Schools) wearing a complete set of Officers' webbing. Ottawa, Ontario, Canada – JUN 1944.

The original design of the binocular case had no provision for being carried other than on an equipment belt. Initially a web skeletal carrier similar to the type used with a water bottle was produced which could be connected to a single web equipment brace and slung. In 1941, side buckles on web chapes were sewn onto newly produced cases and this eliminated the need for the special carrier. At this time, an A.C.I. was issued that allowed for earlier produced cases to be modified by the addition of side buckles on web chapes that were riveted on as can be seen in the photograph below and at the right.

· · · · ·

The primary ***Entrenching Implement*** issued to the individual soldier during WWII was the 1908 pattern that had been used during WWI. A Pattern 1937 web carrier was introduced for use with it and this was a new design. It had a main pocket for the head which consisted of a cast metal spade with a pick on the opposite end. A pair of loops is sewn onto the outside cover to hold the helve in place. The early war helve is identical to the WWI pattern which has a metal fitting on the end that fits snugly into place in a socket in the center of the head. In 1944 a Mark II helve was introduced that had an additional metal fitting to accept the Number 4 spike bayonet making the assembly more suitable as a mine probe. A longer web strap sewn into the top of the outside of the entrenching implement carrier was used to keep the head in its pocket, and was also intended to provide additional tension to hold the helve in place. The ***Entrenching Implement Carrier*** has a pair of metal adjustable buckles at the top that are fastened onto the ends of the Web Equipment Braces after they have passed through the buckles on the back of the Web Waist Belt. A common problem for soldiers during both World Wars was the helve of their entrenching implement working itself loose and getting lost. This was addressed at the end of the war in Europe

. . . . .

by a modification to the carrier. An additional web strap was sewn at the top on the side where the helve was inserted into the first loop that held it in place. The strap had a snap to connect it to the loop and thereby prevented the helve from slipping out. Very few were produced even after the war and these are sometimes sold as a rare airborne item by "creative" merchants.

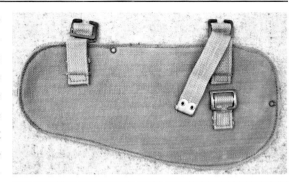

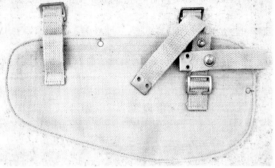

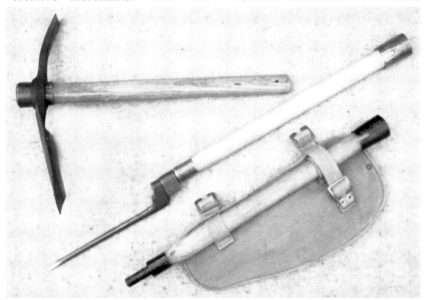

· · · · ·

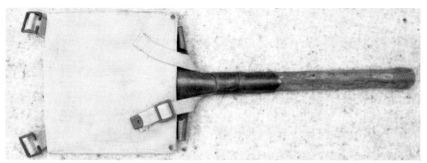

A second pattern of entrenching implement was issued in limited numbers to British commandos as well as to some Home Guard units during WWII. It was designed as part of the 1939 Pattern equipment and was based on the shovel used by the German army during the First World War. It featured a Linnemann style square blade with a short wooden handle. Most will have "BRADES" and the date of manufacture stamped into them along with the /|\ broad arrow. The web carrier for the entrenching implement covers the blade completely and holds it inside with a web strap that goes around the handle and connects to an adjustable buckle on the opposite side. Another pair of adjustable buckles is at the top of the carrier and they fasten to the ends of the Web Equipment Braces in the same way the water bottle was connected. The water bottle would normally be on the wearer's right side and the entrenching implement would be on the left side. The web carrier pictured on this page was made in 1939 by M.E.Co.

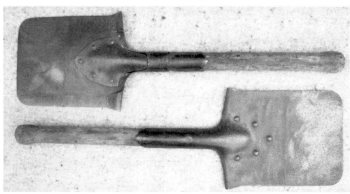

The front and back of the *1939 Pattern Entrenching Implement*.

· · · · ·

The ***Compass Pocket*** and ***Pistol Ammunition Pouch*** are virtually the same in construction and design. They each have a boxed shape with square lid that fastens with a single snap. The back has a pair of double hooks for connecting to the Web Waist Belt. Additionally they have a web fitting sewn to the lower back which accepts the double hooks on the Pistol Case. Lastly they have a web piece sewn across the back at the top for an Equipment Brace to pass through if the item is worn above the binocular case or other pouch in front. The only difference between the two web pieces is the Compass Pocket is felt lined and has fibre board stiffeners between the pieces of material to provide added protection for the compass.

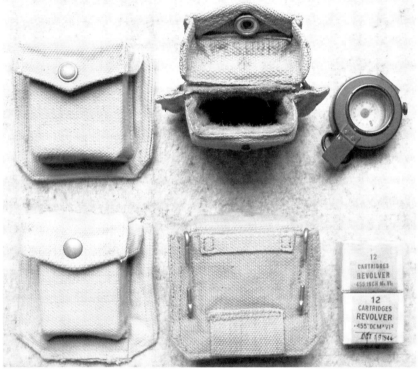

Pictured above are two Compass Pockets shown over two Pistol Ammunition Pouches. The items at the left side are filled with duplicates of the items pictured at the right for comparison. Two 12-round boxes of .380 or .455 ammunition will fit inside the Pistol Ammunition Pouch.

· · · · ·

The *Web Equipment Pattern `37 Pack*, a.k.a. *Large Pack*, as mentioned at the beginning of this chapter, is the only virtually unaltered item retained from the Pattern 1908 web equipment set. The pack itself has no internal dividers and was roomy enough to hold the Greatcoat, gloves, comforter and other small items to be transported with the unit baggage caravan. The back has a pair of web tabs at the top for attachment of the Haversack Shoulder Straps if it was to be

worn for a prolonged period of time. These would be removed from the Haversack which would be connected to the left side on the ends of the Web Equipment Braces. A pair of one inch wide *Web Equipment Pattern `37 Supporting Straps* is fitted so they cross the outside of the Pack and they can be used to hold the helmet in place when not worn. This can be seen along with the alternate method of wearing the Haversack on the second page of this chapter. The equipment straps can also be used as shoulder straps for carrying the Pack from the baggage caravan so the Haversack Shoulder Straps do not have to be removed from the Haversack. They are passed through a web loop on the bottom corners of the pack and pulled through their own buckle. The free end of the equipment strap is then attached to the small buckles at the top of the pack on the back.

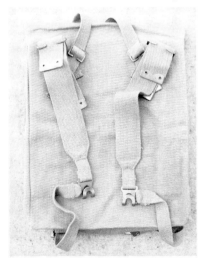

· · · · ·

The ***Web Equipment Pattern `37 Haversack***, a.k.a. ***Small Pack***, is a rectangular bag designed to be worn by the soldier when going on the line. They were often temporarily discarded for immediate action by a squad when assaulting a position or to present a lower profile while crawling across a field. The inside has two dividers

made of cloth. One crosses the inside of the pack length wise and the other crosses from the center of the first divider to the outer wall of the pack. This forms one large pocket and two smaller ones. The smaller pockets are sized to hold the water bottle when not attached to the Web Equipment Braces and the mess tins. Spare ammunition in bandoliers as well as rations and other comforts were kept in the larger space. Often the ground sheet is folded into a flat square and placed at the top of the Haversack under the flap when it is buckled down. This helped to keep the contents of the pack dry while serving as a convenient place to carry the ground sheet. Period photographs also show the common practice of attaching the drinking mug handle to one of the pack flap straps. This freed up more room inside the pack that would otherwise have been lost. As described previously with information on the Pack, the Haversack could be worn with a pair of Haversack Shoulder Straps or fastened to the ends of the Web Equipment Braces.

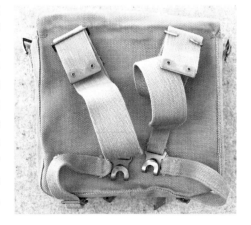

· · · · ·

Web Equipment Pattern '37 Left & Right Haversack Shoulder Straps were used with the Haversack and the Pack. These were issued in mirrored pairs so they would go around the wearer's side and hang properly when worn. Canadian-made examples will have right and left designations stamped onto the webbing as can be seen at the far right. The wide portion of the straps, 18 inches by 2 inches, is intended to fasten onto a web tab with a buckle found at the top of the Haversack or the Pack. The narrow portion of the straps, 13 inches by 1 inch, fastens to a buckle at the lower rear of the Haversack or onto the buckles of the Supporting Straps when used with a Pack.

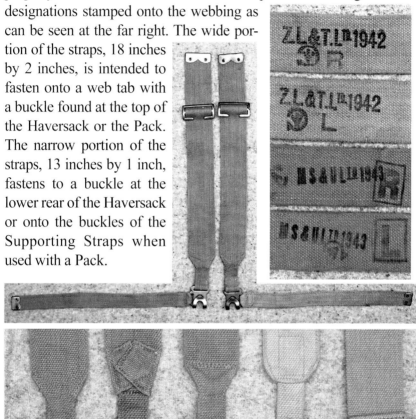

Five variations of Haversack Shoulder Straps produced during the war. Manufacturers used different construction methods and fittings based on textile equipment and resources that were available to them.

· · · · ·

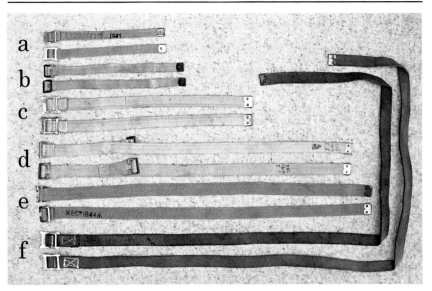

Web Equipment Straps were produced in several lengths for different purposes and a few examples can be seen in the photograph above. (a) 10.5 inches by .75 inch with quick release buckles (b) 12.5 inches by .75 inch with closed brass buckles (c) 18.5 inches by 1 inch with quick release buckles (d) 28 inches by 1 inch with double standard buckles. This was used as an extension for the pack or could be fastened into the Web Equipment Braces to hold the Rain Cape or Anti-Gas Cape when the Haversack was not worn. (e) 30 inches by 1 inch Web Equipment Pattern `37 Supporting Straps as used with the Pack with standard buckles (f) 56 inches by 1 inch vehicle and artillery equipment straps quick release buckles.

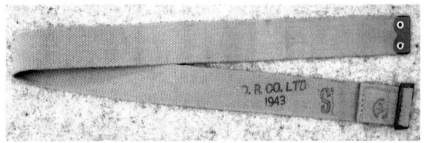

An example of a wartime produced Canadian made trouser belt at the right. These were available in sizes small, medium and large.

. . . . .

The ***Web Equipment Pattern `37 Officers Haversack*** has dimensions of 12 inches by 9 inches by 2 inches. It was designed to serve the purpose of a valise or small briefcase for the individual it was issued to. A pair of brass buckles is on the back at the top and these allow for the attachment of a single brace so the haversack can be carried slung. They can alternately be fastened to the ends of the Web Equipment Braces on the wearer's left side when used in the field with full webbing. A short one inch wide web strap is sewn on top between the two buckles and this serves as a carrying handle when webbing is not worn and it is not desirable to sling the haversack. The main compartment inside the haversack is divided by a cloth partition long ways for storage of maps, notepads and other larger items. Two pockets are built into the front wall of the haversack and each is closed by a small snap. One is 4 inches deep by 3.5 inches long and the other is 4 inches deep by 7.5 inches long. Their purpose is for pencils, rulers, protractors and other small items. The haversack has a web flap that folds to cover the opening on top and this is kept closed by a single web strap that attaches to a brass buckle on the front.

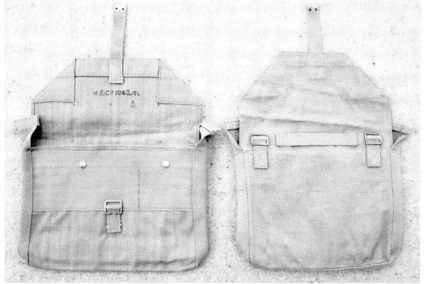

Front and back views of the Officers' Haversack shown without a sling.

· · · · ·

Web Anklets, often incorrectly referred to as Gaiters, were issued in left and right pairs as a replacement for cloth Puttees. Four sizes were produced during the war and they were numbered smallest to largest as 1 through 4. The difference in size between numbers was one inch in length while the height remained constant. Each Anklet has a pair of brass buckles that are used with a pair of either web or leather tabs to keep them closed around the lower legs and over the top of the ammunition boots. When worn, the buckles should be on the outside and the tabs should thread from front to back. Anklets should be tight enough to hold the bloused trouser legs in place but should not be so tight they are difficult to put on.

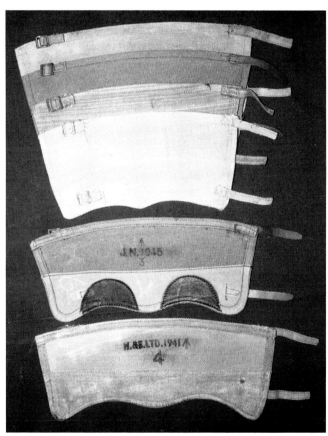

Examples of the four sizes of Anklets produced with the largest at the top and the smallest at the bottom. Color variations are a result of using Canadian, British, Australian and Indian made Anklets. Beneath these are examples of the inside of two different Anklets, one has leather reinforcements where the boot would rub.

• • • • •

The *General Service Map Case Number 1 Mark I* measured 16.5 inches by 13 inches. A metal hanger on a swivel mount, connected to the top on the back, allowed it to be hooked onto a Web Equipment Belt or suitable mount inside an AFV or Universal Carrier. A thin blued metal framework was riveted onto the back and this provided support for viewing a map while it was still in the case. The inside panel can be folded down and snapped to the base to expose the top half of the map contained within. This eliminates the need of removing the map for reference and makes it easier to place the map inside if removed. The photographs below show different views of a 1941 Canadian case (above) and a 1942 British case (below).

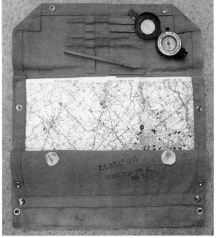

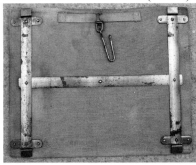

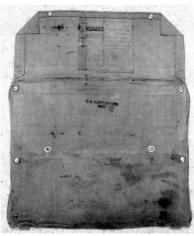

The two main patterns of infantry map case that were issued during WWII each had adjustable carrying straps and overall dimensions of 9.25 inches by 11.25 inches. The *General Service Map Case Number 2 Mark I* (left) consisted of a stiffening board made of *Tufnol*. A clear celluloid map cover along with an outer protective webbing cover was sewn onto the *Tufnol* board. The celluloid and map beneath were held in place by four brass swivels and

the webbing cover had two snaps to hold it down. The *General Service Map Case Number 2 Mark I Emergency Pattern* (right) was made entirely from webbing material with a clear celluloid panel sewn inside. There were no brass swivels and the Tufnol stiffener was removable. This was initially an economy design and it saved on vital brass resources and the *Tufnol* board could be omitted until shortages in materials were overcome.

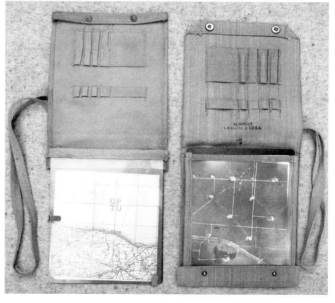

· · · · ·

Several sizes of large briefing map cases were produced and the one pictured is the smallest pattern. It measures 17 inches tall by 19.25 inches wide when closed. The next larger size is approximately 17 inches tall by 30.5 inches wide when closed. These have the same basic design with a large flap cover that has three web straps for closing it in the front. All have buckles in the rear with adjustable length carrying straps that can also be used to hang the map cases up. This particular example was made in 1941.

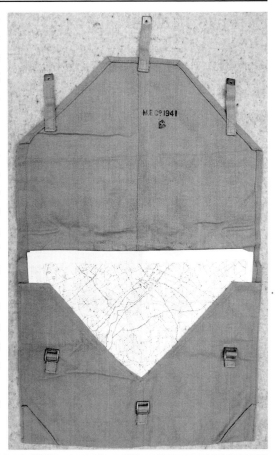

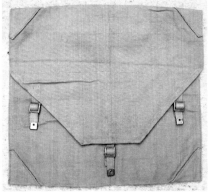

The map case often issued to airborne troops because of its small size has the same design originally issued to horse-mounted troops. It has a folded width of 5.5 inches and an open width of 16.5 inches. The height of the map case is 10.5 inches and it has a swivel at the top with a spring clip fastener for a carrying sling to attach. A piece of linen covers the center celluloid panel to prevent it from rubbing and damaging the two outside celluloid panels. This example is dated 1943.

 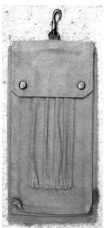

Protective linen strip folded and snapped down.

Linen strip folded back to view the map inside.

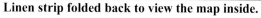

· · · · ·

The pouch pictured on this page was made to hold a flat tire repair kit. They were produced from the same web material as other Pattern 1937 webbing and had a width of 6.5 inches and a height of 7.5 inches. They are often misidentified as being for bicycles but bikes have their tools and repair kit in a leather pouch suspended beneath the saddle. This kit was actually part of the spares kept with larger vehicles with tires mounted on split rims, also referred to as combat rims. Vehicles that had split rims included jeeps, jeep trailers, some of the larger lorries and some motorcycles. This particular example was made in 1944. The contents include two squares of sand paper to rough up the inner tube, an envelope of rubber patches, a pair of scissors for cutting and shaping the patch, a tube of rubber patch cement, a small tin of chalk for helping to locate the hole and a small screwdriver for working the patch or for prying debris out of the tire.

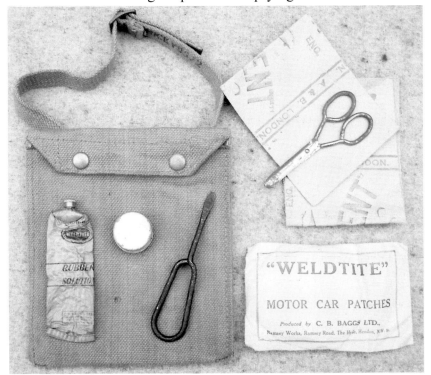

. . . . .

This large bag was used for transporting unit mail and confidential documents that were not classified or restricted. It conforms to the normal Pattern 1937 look and feel and this example was produced in 1942. Maker markings on the bag are H.H.C. & Company Limited and it is Broad Arrow marked. Inside there is a reinforced web section that has three metal rings fitted to it. These rings pass through embroidered button hole type slots in the front. A web strap with another

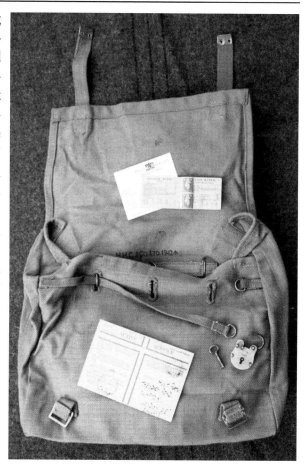

ring is passed through the three rings protruding through the button holes and this is then pad locked to a final metal ring on the outer edge of the bag. It certainly doesn't prevent the bag from being stolen or cut open but

the curious are kept at bay. A large web flap covers the security features of the bag and it has a pair of web straps that fasten to buckles in the same way as the normal Pack.

. . . . .

Another document case used to secure despatches until they could be delivered was produced in the UK along with a similar variation that was produced in Australia. These had the same basic shape and features of the Pack but were thinner and had a single adjustable shoulder strap built onto the rear. The closed dimensions were 15 inches wide by 13 inches tall by 1 inch thick. The flap was held down by two web straps and buckles that covered a corded security system which utilized a series of individual cord loops that were passed through metal

grommets and then laced to each other. A padlock at one end prevented the cords from being undone and ensured the confidentiality of enclosed documents. If the cords or the case were cut, it would be known that the information on the documents had been compromised.

A Despatch Rider hands urgent messages to a member of the Australian Woman's Army Service (AWAS) at the signals office of Grosvenor House where the AWAS headquarters is located. Melbourne, Victoria, Australia – 2 APR 1943.

The despatches case in the photograph above is a variation of the case described on the previous page. Physical dimensions are virtually the same but the flap of the case is held closed by the security device as opposed to being under a weather flap. The security device consists of a metal rod that has a loop on one end similar to a long pistol cleaning rod. This passes through three metal rings sewn into the case. A padlock is fastened to a hole in the end of the rod and the case cannot be opened while they are connected.

· · · · ·

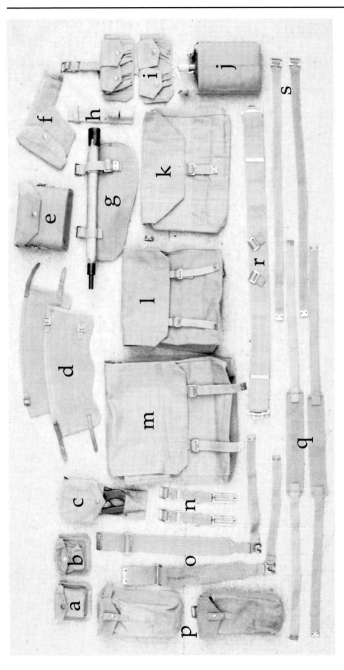

A sampling of Pattern 1937 Web Equipment laid out for size comparison of items including: (a) Compass Pocket, (b) Pistol Ammunition Pouch, (c) Wire Cutter Pouch, (d) Anklets, (e) Binocular Case, (f) .38 Revolver Holster, (g) Entrenching Implement Carrier, (h) Bayonet Frog, (i) Cartridge Carriers, (j) Water Bottle Carrier, (k) Officers' Haversack, (l) Haversack, (m) Pack, (n) Brace Attachments, (o) Left and Right Haversack Shoulder Straps, (p) Basic Pouches, (q) Equipment Braces, (r) Web Waist Belt, (s) Pack Supporting Straps.

. . . . .

42

Chapter 2 - Load Bearing Equipment

Infantrymen of the 1st Battalion, the South Lancashire regiment on the Queen White sector of Sword Beach. They were part of the first assault wave of the 3rd Division and were loaded down with everything they might need until reinforcements and fresh supplies could be landed. Normandy - 6 JUN 1944.

. . . . .

The ***Battle Jerkin*** was developed in 1942 and introduced in 1943. It was intended to be a substitute for the pattern 1937 webbing equipment, having pockets and features incorporated into it to handle most tasks the regular webbing was designed to handle. Several problems were found with the Battle Jerkin when compared with a webbing equipment set made up of individual components. Being a one piece item, you could not discard unwanted sections when they were no longer needed or when a lower profile for stealthy action was required. Troops often dropped small packs when going into an attack and this could not be done with the Battle Jerkin. It was also considered warmer than normal webbing, which was ideal for use in snow, but this was a disadvantage when worn in the desert, the jungle or in Europe during the summer. The Battle Jerkin was produced in three sizes; small, medium and large. The waterproof canvas duck material used to make the Battle Jerkin came in four colours; tan for desert and Mediterranean use, white for use in snow covered terrain, brown for spring and summer use in Europe and green for use in the Pacific. Tan and brown examples are the most common colours encountered today. Many tan Battle Jerkins have "For Training Only" stamped on the inside and were used during practice landings conducted in early 1944. The brown Battle Jerkins were issued to some assault troops of the 21st Army Group for the Normandy invasion but not many are evident in photographs of these troops in the months following the invasion. The Battle Jerkin pictured on the following two pages was produced in 1943. All of the pockets are described in the accompanying captions with the exception of a single inside pocket. This pocket is located at the left breast and is similar in design to the inside pocket on the Denison Smock and Battledress Blouse. Also not covered in the photographs is a pair of heavy strings situated on the outside of the front of each shoulder. These were used to tie on the rolled up rain cape which would then ride above the large main pocket on the back. A white Battle Jerkin was used for an example since they are so rare and because the brown versions are more often seen in other publications. It should also be noted that reproductions of the brown pattern exist and these are sometimes passed off as originals.

· · · · ·

44

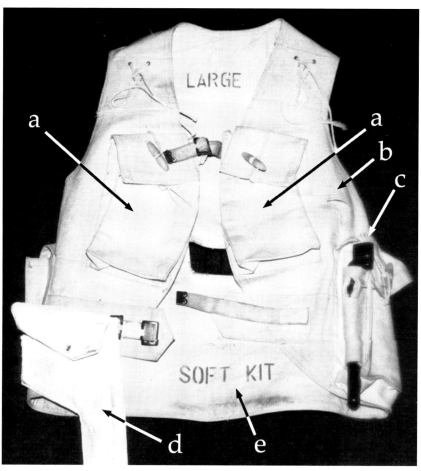

Pockets can obviously be used to hold anything a soldier requires but the layout of the Battle Jerkin was intended for: (a) A pair of pockets high on the chest designed to hold four Bren gun magazines, rifle ammunition in bandoliers or four 2-Inch mortar bombs. (b) Horizontal and vertical slots with reinforced edges designed for a fighting knife or the SMLE sword pattern bayonet. (c) Sleeve with a single reinforced slot at the top designed to hold the spike bayonet in its scabbard. (d) Holster {blancoed white in this case} for the .38 revolver. The brass tabs of the holster are fixed to a reinforced webbing tab sewn to the Battle Jerkin for this purpose. (e) Pocket sewn into the lower rear of the Battle Jerkin for storage of spare socks, shirts, sweaters or other items of "Soft Kit".

• • • • •

(f) Tapered sleeve designed for the helve of the entrenching tool. (g) Main pocket designed to accommodate anything typically carried in the small pack. This could include rations, spare water bottle, mess tin and utensils, personal kit and spare ammunition. (h) Pocket designed to carry the head of the entrenching tool. (i) Large waist pocket designed to hold the water bottle but can also hold four fuzed H.E. 2-Inch mortar bombs. (j) Sleeve {lower} with webbing tab with adjustable buckle {upper} designed to carry a spade based 2-Inch mortar or standard machete with leather scabbard. (k) Small waist pocket designed to carry hand grenades.

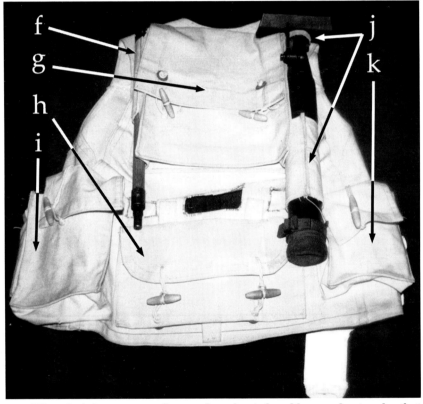

All pockets have canvas flaps and are kept closed by wooden toggles that pass through sturdy string loops. All strings are tied in a knot at one end and then are passed through a leather washer before being threaded through the canvas where they form a loop for the toggles. The knot behind the leather washer prevents them from being pulled out. A pair of one inch wide webbing straps with brass buckles keeps the Battle Jerkin closed up in the front.

. . . . .

Able Seaman Amand Therien of the Royal Canadian Navy Beach Commandos, armed with a Lanchester submachine gun with fixed bayonet. He wears standard Battledress with a brown Battle Jerkin which has had a pair of webbing pouches attached to the front. These were designed to each hold three 50-round magazines for the Lanchester. This type of submachine gun was adopted for use by the navy while the army adopted the Sten. England - 20 JUL 1944.

· · · · ·

In an attempt to lighten the Battle Jerkin, also known as the Assault Jerkin, and make it more functional for main line troops, a simplified pattern was introduced as the ***Skeleton Assault Jerkin***. This new Jerkin was made from the same waterproof canvas duck material as the Battle Jerkin and it featured the same type of pocket closures that used string and small wooden toggles. Known colours include the same brown and white as used with the Battle Jerkin. Tan was not produced since fighting in most desert regions had ended. It is probable that a green version was produced for jungle use in the Pacific but none have surfaced to date.

Two patterns were produced during the war. The first pattern features a pair of "Bren" magazine pockets high on the chest and they curve outward towards the shoulders. Like the Battle Jerkin, they could be used for 2-Inch mortar bombs or ammunition for other weapons as needed. A small webbing closure is provided at the chest and a thicker one is at the waist. These keep the Jerkin from bouncing around when on the run and prevent the carried load from shifting. A provision for either an SMLE sword pattern bayonet or a Number 4 spike bayonet

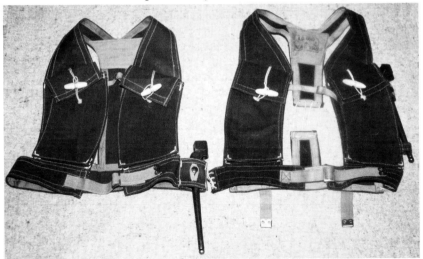

Front view of first pattern (left) and second pattern (right) Skeleton Assault Jerkins. This first pattern example was produced by H. & S. Limited in 1944 and this second pattern example was produced by W. & G. in 1945.

· · · · ·

is found on the left side of the waist. These Jerkins were produced in sizes small, medium and large, as also found with the Battle Jerkin.

The second pattern was a modification of the first. It also had a pair of large pockets high on the chest but they curved inward to the center. The provision for a bayonet on the waist was removed and a version that would only work with the spike bayonet was added to the side of the left hand chest pocket. A new feature was the addition of a pair of one inch webbing extensions designed to allow the entrenching tool to be carried. Probably the most significant change is that this pattern was produced in only one adjustable size. Brass eyelets were placed at breaks in the Jerkin at each side and at the lower back in the center of the waist. Sturdy string was used to lace the breaks together. This allowed waist size to be adjusted as well as to allow for troops of different heights to be able to use the Jerkin.

Rear view of first pattern (left) and second pattern (right) Skeleton Assault Jerkins worn over a snow suit for contrast. The strings for size adjustment can be easily seen on the back with only a partial view of the waist adjustments at the sides.

· · · · ·

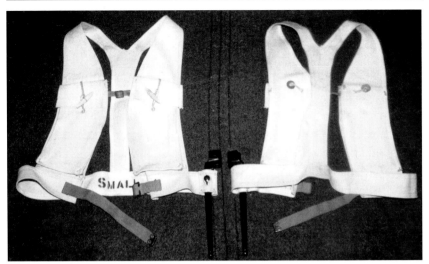

Front and back of a first pattern white coloured Skeleton Assault Jerkin.

One of the platoons in C-Coy, the 1st Canadian Parachute Battalion, photographed in the fall of 1943. Eight of the eleven men pictured are wearing first pattern Skeleton Assault Jerkins.

* * * * *

The **Wire Carrier** consists of a small tubular metal frame which has five 1 inch wide webbing straps bolted to the outer edges to form a cushioned back rest. The shoulder straps are standard webbing equipment braces fitted to special attachments at each end. One of these is a small loop of webbing with a buckle for the brace at one end and a metal swivel buckle connected to the frame at the other. The second type of fitting also has a loop of webbing with a buckle for the brace at one end and the other is connected to a flat piece of metal which has a key  hole and slot cut into it. This metal fitting connects to a metal stud at the opposite end of the frame and serves as an easy way to get into and out of the carrier straps. When worn, the braces are crossed high on the back and this helps to centralize the wire spool and prevent it from slipping off the shoulders. The wire spool is the same type used with the earlier heavy wooden side slung spool carrier. A hand crank is used to roll in excess wire and wire can be laid out by merely walking forward while the loose end is held at a stationary position. A length of cord with a metal ring is provided as a way for the layer to brake the rotating wire spool if needed.

· · · · ·

Two types of special ammunition carriers were produced during the war to carry the rectangular shaped ammunition tins. One had a single pocket and the other had a double pocket. The base size of the *Single Ammunition Carrier* is 9.25 inches wide and 15.5 inches tall. A small pad at the lower back measures 3 inches tall by 5.5 inches wide by 1 inch thick. A pair of left and right modified "L" straps serve as adjustable shoulder straps. The two primary differences

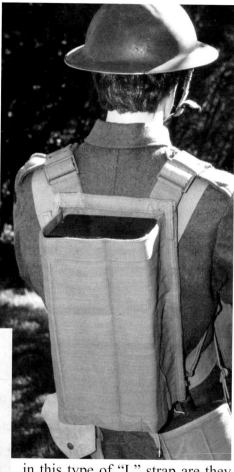

in this type of "L" strap are they had a webbing loop at the top to hold any excess strap after size adjustments have been made and the lower ends have brass hooks. These hooks clip into metal D-rings that are sewn into the bottom of the ammunition carrier. The top is completely open and the bot-

• • • • •

tom has two 1.5 inch wide straps sewn from front to back to prevent the tin from falling straight through. The pictured example was produced by R.P. Limited in 1945. The *Double Ammunition Carrier* is constructed along the same lines as the single ammunition carrier. The base size is 17.25 inches wide and 15.5 inches tall. A pad on the back at the top measures 12 inches wide by 4 inches tall by .5 inches thick. A lower pad measures 8 inches wide by 3 inches tall by 1 inch thick. The pictured example was produced by M.E.Co. in 1944.

The ammunition tin shown in the photo above being hand carried is one of the types used for cartons of 9mm ammunition.

· · · · ·

This next pack assembly is much less common than the other items covered in this section. Experts in the field of WWII British specialist equipment didn't have a name for this rig but say it was used for explosives, fuzes, detonators and other items essential to carry out a mission to blow something up. The upper pack measures 12 inches wide by 10.5 inches tall by 4.5 inches deep. It has a canvas flap that is secured by a pair of webbing quick release fasteners. The inside has three internal dividers that create four equal size chambers 3 inches wide and 4.5 inches deep running the full depth of the pack. A box shaped pocket on the outside of the upper pack measures 7 inches tall by 5.25 inches wide by 3.5 inches deep. It has a canvas flap that is secured by a single webbing quick release fastener. The lower pack is 7 inches tall by 10.5 inches wide by 7 inches deep and has a single undivided compartment. It has a canvas flap with quick release fasteners identical to those found on the upper pack. The upper pack has fittings at the top and bottom to accept a pair of standard "L" straps for carrying the complete assembly. It also has a 9 inch wide

by 4 inch tall by .5 inch deep pad at the top on the back. The two packs are connected to each other by a pair of 2 inch wide webbing straps that run down the outer sides of each pack and are fastened by adjustable brass buckles. By design, multiple lower packs can be assembled beneath each other as needed. Both sections of the pack assembly shown below were produced by H & S in 1945.

The tin sticking out of the small pocket holds 48 feet of Number 11 Mark II Safety Fuze.

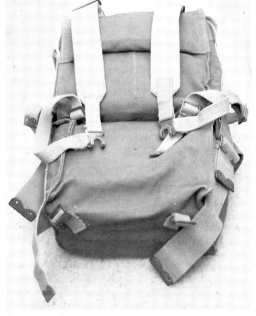

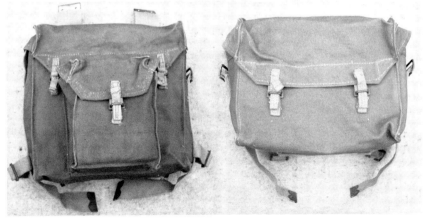

· · · · ·

When trucks couldn't get to the men, hot food, when available, was carried in special packs designed for metal insulated containers. Like the ammunition carriers, single and double pocket patterns were produced. The **Single Ration Canister Carrier** is 9 inches wide at the back and 15 inches tall. A fibre stiffening pad is inside the lining at the back of the pack as well as at the floor to help maintain the shape of the pack. Two pads are built into the back. The top one is 7 inches wide by 5 inches tall by .5 inches thick. The lower pad is 8 inches wide by 3 inches tall by 2 inches thick. Non-removable but adjustable length shoulder straps are sewn into the top at the back for carrying the pack. The lower ends have brass hooks that connect to metal D-rings sewn into the lower rear of the pack. An adjustable strap is provided in the front to keep the shoulder straps from being able to separate and thereby prevent the load from shifting. The pictured example was produced by M.E. Co. in 1942.

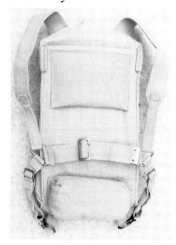

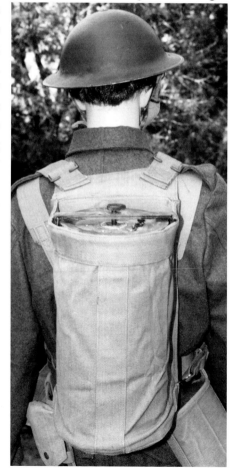

• • • • •

The **Double Ration Canister Carrier** is similar to the single pattern in having fibre stiffening inserts in the back and in the floor of the pack. The base size of the pack is 15 inches tall by 14.75 inches wide. A pair of pads at the top and bottom of the back is similar to those used on the single carrier with the exception of being longer. The front wall of the pack stops short of the top to facilitate

easier removal of the metal canisters when they are full. A webbing divider serves to form two pockets inside and this helps to dampen any sound that would be created from the canisters rubbing each other while carried. The single carrier had no top flap because the canister fits so snugly inside; however, a flap is needed with two canisters since the pack forms a boxed rather than rounded shape. This flap is closed with a pair of webbing straps similar to those found on the large pack. The shoulder straps for this pack are the same as found on the single carrier. This example was produced by M.E. Co. in 1940.

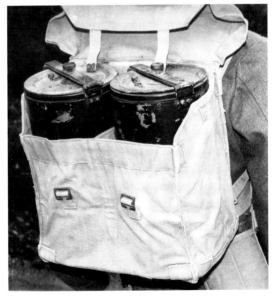

. . . . .

57

A pack intended to carry packaged dry rations was designed along the lines of a scaled up Large Pack. The boxed dimensions of this pack are 14 inches tall by 16 inches wide by 8 inches deep. At the top two sides, small flaps with webbing tabs can be cinched together in the center to provide added reinforcement to the outer sides of the pack if the contents are not packaged inside tins. The pack has a

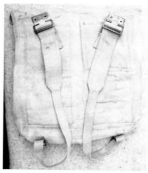

flap which is secured closed with a pair of adjustable webbing tabs. The shoulder straps are 2 inches wide at the top where they connect to brass adjustment buckles and they taper down to 1 inch in width where they connect to brass buckles at the bottom. An additional 1 inch webbing strap is fitted to the top outside on each side and allows the pack to be carried slung like a postal carrier's bag so rations can be issued out. The padding on the back of this pack is much simpler than the packs designed for carrying heavier loads. They consist of four square sections of triple thickness webbing material. Typically rations carried in this pack were packaged in light weight rectangular tins or in similar shaped cardboard boxes. This example was made in Canada in 1944 by Z.L. & T. Limited.

• • • • •

Pack Saddle Bags were also used for hauling supplies by men who had no beasts of burden. A pair of large canvas bags were connected at the top by joining their shoulder straps and additional webbing straps held them together at the lower sides. The man carrying them would wear one bag on his chest and the other on his back. This design was used more commonly in the Pacific for carrying water bladders, rations and camp type supplies as opposed to small arms ammunition.

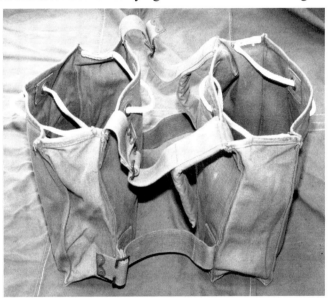

A Canadian soldier loads a Double Ration Canister Carrier that is being worn by another. The type of pack can be determined by the shape of the side walls and the flap. Normandy, France – JUL 1944.

• • • • •

The ***Everest Carrier*** consisted of a tubular metal pack frame with folding metal framed shelf at the bottom. The shelf itself is made of a double layer of canvas that is sewn around the frame. The back part of the frame is 17 inches tall and 13 inches wide at the base which tapers inward as you go up the frame to the top where it is 10 inches wide. The shelf is box shaped and is 13 by 8 inches. The shoulder straps and the thinner straps used to secure the load are made of leather and are adjustable with roller buckles. At the waist, the frame has a fold out section at each side where the hips are situated when the pack is worn. A wide leather strap runs behind the hips and provides added support to prevent the metal framework from rubbing the wearers back. A waist belt wraps around the front of the wearer to help hold the pack frame against the body so it can't bounce up and down on the shoulder straps. These are most recognizable as the framed carrier used by groups of commandos during the Normandy landings as well as often being seen mounted on the front of the folding bicycles when they had need of a pack.

Commandos with Everest Carriers mounted on bicycles during a kit inspection.

· · · · ·

The **Bergen Rucksack** had its origins in Norway before being adopted and produced in the United Kingdom during the war. It has a tubular metal frame that is 15 inches wide at the hips which then curves smoothly to the top where the shoulder straps are mounted and the frame is 5 inches wide. The high point in the center of the frame stands 18 inches tall. The actual rucksack is attached to the metal frame at the base where the hips are located when the rucksack is worn and at the top where it has a leather reinforcement that is slipped onto the frame. The shoulder straps are adjustable webbing, sewn to leather straps that connect to the frame at the top as well as the bottom areas where the rucksack is fastened to the frame. The rucksack has a massive central compartment with grommets at the top so it can be closed with a draw cord like a kitbag. A large flap covers the top to keep the contents dry. A small zipper closed map pocket is on the inside of the flap so it can be reached without opening the main bag. A large deep outside pocket with flap is on the left and right sides of the rucksack and a smaller long external pocket is on the lower rear. Webbing straps are provided at the top and bottom of the rucksack for fastening additional kit as needed. Many variations exist since the Bergen Rucksack was produced by several countries before and during the war. The example pictured on the previous page was made in 1942.

A heavily laden Commando with a Bergen Rucksack is part of a group relieving Airborne troops in a defensive position near Benouville, France.

· · · · ·

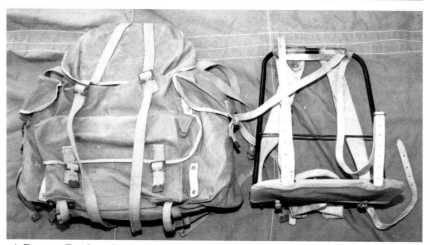

A Bergen Rucksack placed next to an Everest Carrier for size comparison.

While the Bergen Rucksack could carry a lot of equipment and supplies that fit within its body, there were still loads that had odd shapes and sizes that were better handled by an Everest Carrier.

. . . . .

The **Yukon Pack Board** was a heavy load carrier developed in the United States. It was used by the British and Commonwealth forces during the early part of the war. It was made of plywood with a hardwood frame and weighed a little over six pounds. Canvas was stretched over the framework on the inside and this served as a back support and pad. Shoulder straps were placed so the bulk of the load was carried on the shoulders and not as much by the hips which was the case with the Everest Carrier. This increased the weight a man could comfortably carry. In late 1944 a new pack board of British manufacture was introduced. This was known as the **General Service Manpack**

Carrier. It was made out of aluminum channels and

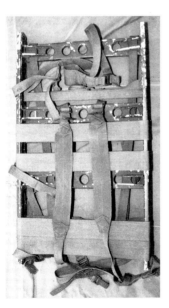

had a weight of roughly four pounds. A series of two inch webbing straps made up the back rest and the load was secured by one inch webbing straps. Most people associate this design with the Pattern 1944 webbing equipment because of the dark green coloured webbing and painted frame but it was in fact issued and used during the Rhine Crossing in March of 1945. It was not widely issued before the war ended because most units already had sufficient stocks of other carriers.

• • • • •

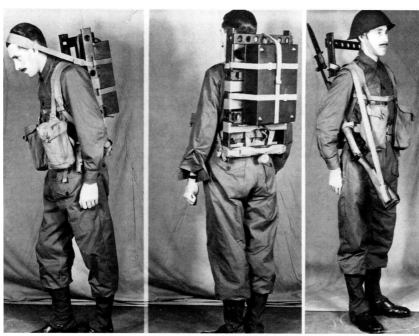

Wartime photographs showing the General Service Manpack Carrier.

. . . . .

The 3-Inch Mortar and its Mounting could be broken down into three loads and carried when needed with special harnesses. These were made of webbing with leather strengthening pieces and straps with each one being designed to fit over a man's shoulders. The Number 1 Mortar Harness was used for the barrel. The Number 2 Mortar Harness was used with the Base Plate. And the Number 3 Mortar Harness was used for the Mounting, aka Bipod. All of these Mark I pattern mortar harnesses were introduced in 1935. Ammunition was carried in special containers consisting of three cardboard tubes that each held a single bomb. These could be carried with an attached handle or suspended from a special load bearing harness. A webbing pack was also developed in 1937 and it could carry four bombs.

A pre-war British mortar section photographed prior to the adoption of Battledress. The Number 1 with slung mortar barrel without muzzle cover is in the center. The Number 2, seen at the right, has the base plate slung on his right side and six bombs in two carriers slung on his left side. The Number 3, at the left, has the bipod slung on his right side. All three men have shoulder strap pads on their harnesses.

· · · · ·

The ***Mortar Harness Number 1*** was designed as a sling to carry the 3-Inch Mortar Barrel. It consists of two lengths of two-inch wide webbing connected to each other with an adjustable brass buckle. This provided a way to adjust the length of the sling and also a way to slip on a shoulder pad if needed to help prevent the weight of the load from cutting into the bearer. A three inch diameter steel ring is permanently sewn to one end of the sling and this fits over the ball on the end of the barrel breech. The other end is sewn onto a two inch wide strap at a right angle. This sixteen-inch long strap is cinched around the mortar barrel, above the sight supporting bracket, which prevents it from sliding down towards the breech when the barrel is slung. A leather strap is sewn on near the end of this strap and it can be fastened to the leather extension strap of the barrels muzzle cover using the attached quick release buckle. The example shown above with an attached shoulder pad is dated 1942 and the one below is dated 1941.

· · · · ·

The ***Mortar Harness Number 2*** consisted of a pad and sling that were designed for use in carrying the base plate of the 3-Inch Mortar. The pad was covered in canvas and had an approximate size of 12 inches square by 3/8 inches thick. Sewn loops at the two top corners allowed metal spring swivel hook at each end of the sling to pass through so that they could fasten onto footman loops on the base plate. The sling itself was similar in construction to a web equipment brace and it had a length adjustment buckle near one end. The same type of shoulder pad used with the Mortar Harness Number 1 could be slipped onto the sling to offset the heavy weight of the base plate. When carried, the sling was slung over the shoulder with the pad hanging between the bearer and the top, flat side of the base plate. This prevented the raised retaining lugs of the breech ball socket from digging into the bearer's hip.

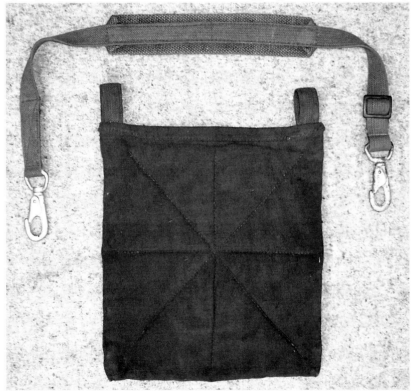

. . . . .

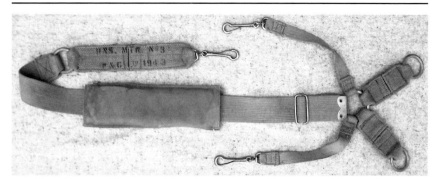

The ***Mortar Harness Number 3*** was a sling assembly used to carry the 3-Inch Mortar Bipod. The main sling was made from two-inch wide webbing in two sections. One section had a 2 inch diameter metal ring near the center and a metal spring swivel hook at the end. The hook end of the strap would be passed through the cradle of the bipod and looped back so it could fasten to the ring. The other sling section had five lengths of webbing sewn to a 2.5 inch diameter metal ring. The center section of webbing formed the second side of the sling by joining onto the previously described section using an adjustable buckle. The other four lengths of webbing were used in pairs. Two ended with metal spring swivel hooks and the other two ended with 2 inch diameter metal rings. One ring was placed over each of the metal spikes on the bipod legs. The straps with hooks were wrapped around the legs and leg stays on the bipod, and then fastened back to the rings. Like the Mortar Harness Number 1 and Number 2, this one could also accept a shoulder pad to offset the weight of the slung load. The example shown on this page was produced in 1943.

The Shoulder Pads used with the 3-Inch Mortar Harnesses were made from canvas that was sewn to form a long tube which the main harness strap could be passed through. A soft rubber filled pad was sewn to one side of the canvas and this would rest on the bearer's shoulder when used. Both sides of a shoulder pad can be seen in the photograph at the right.

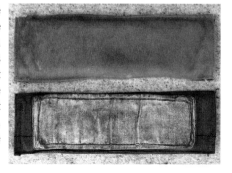

· · · · ·

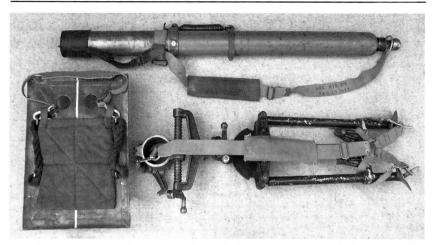

A webbing pack was designed for transporting 3-Inch mortar bombs. It has four pockets that are open at the top and closed at the bottom by individual 1.5 inch wide straps that are sewn into position. The back of the pack has a padded area 5 inches tall by 11.5 inches wide by .5 inches thick at the top where it would come in contact with the shoulders. A second pad that is 3 inches tall by 7.5 inches wide by 1 inch thick is situated near the bottom where the small of the back would be. The base of the pack is 17 inches tall by 13.5 inches wide. A pair of adjustable shoulder straps is provided and they are fastened to the bottom of the pack by a pair of brass hooks that connect to brass D-rings which are sewn into the bottom of the pack. This example is dated 1937.

• • • • •

With the expansion of the role airborne troops were to play in Operation Overlord and in operations that followed, new mortar and bomb carrying harnesses were developed in 1943. The standard infantry long carry mortar harnesses were used in a slung fashion by troops that typically had contact with other fighting and support units. Airborne troops could land by parachute or glider at a position that was many miles from where they would engage the enemy and needed to carry additional supporting weapons and equipment when they moved. The new airborne mortar harnesses were all worn on the back like a pack which made it easier for the bearers to also carry small arms and regular webbing equipment. While physical evidence of the items discussed on the following pages exist with wartime production dates, along with photographic evidence of their use by the airborne forces during the war, they were not officially introduced until June 1949. This was done in Amendment Number 1 to the *Identification List for Ordnance, M.L. 3-In. Mortar*, where they are referenced as only being available for use by the Parachute Battalions. At that time, the designations changed with the Number 2 now being for the Bipod and the Number 3 being for the Base Plate. Modifications were done to the webbing 4-bomb pack and it was thereafter designated as being the Number 4 which can be seen in use below by Polish troops that were part of the 1st Airborne Division during Operation Market.

This eight man section is lined up beginning with the base plate, the bipod, the barrel and then five men each with a 4-bomb pack.

· · · · ·

The *Equipment, Carrying, 3-In. Mortar and Bombs, No. 1* consisted of a webbing *2-Bomb Carrier* that was worn on the back with a *Neck Pad* which is described further in this chapter. The bomb carrier used a pair of straps with hooks on their ends so that they could fasten onto the buckles on the Basic Pouches in a similar way to the Haversack Shoulder Straps. No additional bombs were carried by this bearer since he would also carry the mortar barrel using the

General Montgomery inspects airborne troops prior to a field training exercise. The soldier on the right is wearing one of the 2-bomb carriers while the soldier to his left carries the bipod.

Mortar Harness Number 1 which is described earlier in this chapter.

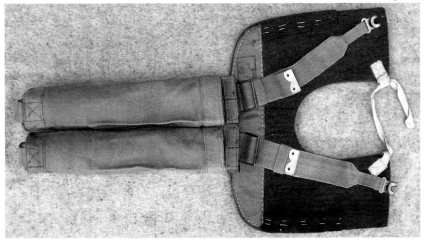

· · · · ·

1-Bomb Carrier pouches designed to hold a single 3-Inch mortar bomb were produced to help offset the load carried by the Number 2, Number 3 and multiple Number 4 soldiers in a mortar squad. The pouches were issued in pairs and are open ended at the top and closed at the bottom with a webbing strap as found with the mortar bomb pack. The pouches are 17 inches tall and the back is 3.5 inches wide. A

strap 1-inch wide is sewn across the top of the back side and a brass buckle is sewn to a web tab at the midpoint of the pouch. The shoulder strap of the Number 2, Number 3 and Number 4 mortar equipment carriers slip through the loop at the top and get fastened to the brass buckle in a similar way to securing equipment braces to a basic pouch. A 4.5 inch long by

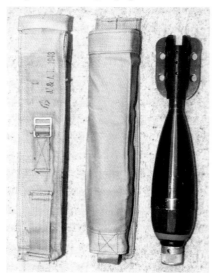

1.5 inch wide strap is sewn to the back of the pouch at the bottom and it is designed so the web equipment belt can be passed through it. This prevents the pouch from being able to swing around. By having the pouches merely slipped onto the web belt and not being fastened to any of the other standard webbing, the pair of bomb pouches along with the load connected to the mortar harness can be dropped off quickly when needed. The earliest examined examples were made in 1943.

· · · · ·

The ***Equipment, Carrying, 3-In. Mortar and Bombs, No. 2*** was used for carrying the mortar bipod. The assembly was made up of a *Neck Pad*, two of the *1-Bomb Carriers*, and a *Bipod Securing Pad.* This last item is a webbing back piece 12.5 inches tall and 13.5 inches wide. A

1-inch thick raised pad in the center comprises most of the area and it is what the cradle assembly of the bipod rests against. Four leather straps extending from the top and right side. The two straps on the right are used to pass through the cradle and worm gear to keep the bipod from shifting left or right on the pad. The two straps on the top are used to secure the legs of the bipod to the pad and hold it firmly in place. Each of the shoulder straps connects to a 1-Bomb Carrier pouch worn on the front of the bearer. This example is dated 1943 and it was produced by B.H.G. Limited.

· · · · ·

The *Equipment, Carrying, 3-In. Mortar and Bombs, No. 3* is similar to the previously described item but its purpose was to carry the base plate. This assembly had a *Neck Pad*, two *1-Bomb Carriers* and a *Base-Plate Securing Pad*. The webbing back piece of the Base-Plate Securing Pad is the same in size and function to the one used with the bipod. It has a long 1-inch wide webbing strap with an adjustable buckle sewn to the

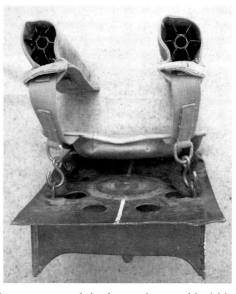

lower section of the pad and this goes around the base plate and hold it firmly against the pad. A pair of S-hooks is fastened to D-rings sewn to each of the shoulder straps. The S-hooks are used to connect the upper section of the base plate to the harness for carrying. Each of the shoulder

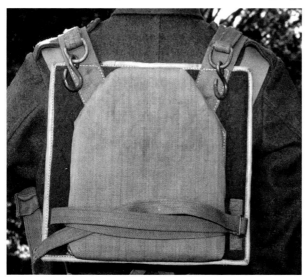

straps connects to 1-Bomb Carrier pouch worn on the front of the bearer. This example made by B.H.G. Limited is 1945 dated but photographic evidence of airborne troops with this equipment indicates it was issued as early as 1943.

· · · · ·

74

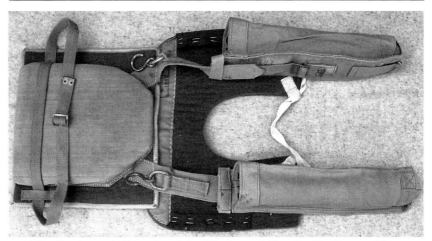

The Equipment, Carrying, 3-In. Mortar and Bombs, No. 3 as used to carry the 3-Inch Mortar Base Plate and two mortar bombs.

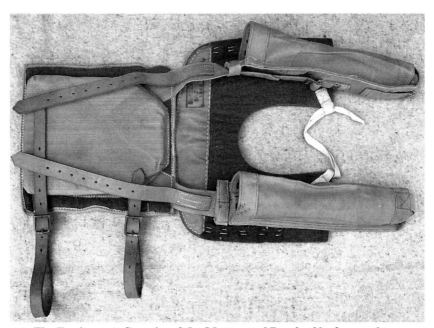

The Equipment, Carrying, 3-In. Mortar and Bombs, No. 2 as used to carry the 3-Inch Mortar Bipod and two mortar bombs.

. . . . .

The *Equipment, Carrying, 3-In. Mortar and Bombs, No.4* assembly was produced in the largest quantities compared to the first three assemblies that have been described for carrying the components of the 3-Inch Mortar. Anywhere from one to a dozen could have seen service with each mortar used by the Airborne Forces. These consisted of a *Neck Pad*, two of the *1-Bomb Carriers* and a *4-Bomb Carrier*. The 4-Bomb Carrier was worn on the back in a similar fashion to the first pattern bomb pack used by the infantry. The shoulder straps connected onto the 1-Bomb Carriers worn on the chest and then continued to loop back around where they clipped onto rings at the bottom of the pack. This prevented it from bouncing around and the assembly could still be easily discarded. The bearers issued with these assemblies would often make multiple trips hauling bombs to the mortar pit location. The normal rate of fire was 7 to 10 rounds per minute.

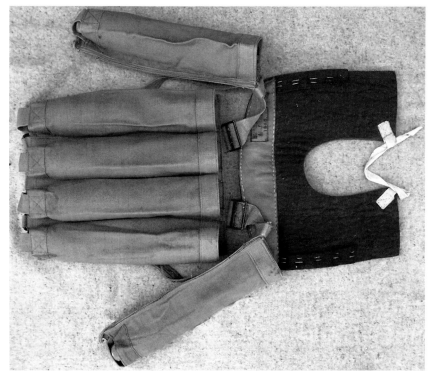

. . . . .

Neck Pads were issued to provide protection from shoulder straps and to add comfort to troops hauling heavy loads. They were normally made from heavy felt with leather reinforcements where items would rub. The head is placed though the hole so the pad surrounds the neck and covers the shoulders. Cotton ties in the front prevent the pad from being able to slip off when the load is mounted and dismounted during rest stops. The two pictured examples show the front and back of pads made by Bury Felt.

Shoulder Pads were produced to dampen the load of heavy or rigid items that were carried on one or more shoulders. They had a ½ inch thick rubber pad that had steel on top of it. This was covered in canvas with two adjustable 1-inch wide straps sewn onto the top. The straps could be lashed onto the item being carried so that it stayed with the load, making it easier to hand off in shifts for long carries.

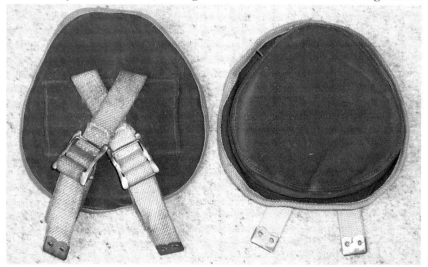

· · · · ·

This harness was designed to assist in the carriage of two mortar or P.I.A.T. bomb carriers. It could as easily be used to carry two five gallon water or fuel cans or any other pair of containers that had a handle on the top at a balanced location. The yoke of the harness is 2 inches wide and 7 inches long. It then branches out into four individual 1 inch wide webbing straps. Each has an adjustable brass buckle so it can be looped back on itself after being passed through the handle of whatever load is to be carried. This example was produced in 1945 by B.H.G. Limited. In recent years, post war production examples have surfaced on the militaria market and are normally offered as Bren tripod slings. By design, this harness will connect to the four sling mounts on the Bren tripod but it cannot be carried properly this way. The Bren tripod used a pair of standard rifle slings. More information on this can be found in the weapons volume that is a companion to this book.

The photo above illustrates this harness being used hands free to carry a pair of 3-Inch mortar bomb carriers with normal webbing.

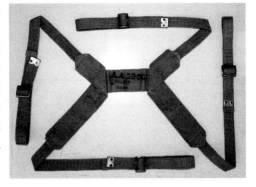

· · · · ·

78

A special load bearing system was developed in Australia that provided a means of carrying the 4.2-Inch mortar in three two-man loads. The base plate required two poles that would have been cut from local timber, four harness shoulder straps and four shoulder pads. Each end of the four harness shoulder straps was formed into a loop back to itself using the built in quick release rings. One end of each harness shoulder strap was slipped over the timber roughly two feet from the end of the timber. The straps would then be crossed over and the free ends would be slipped over the end of the opposite timber. Lastly a shoulder pad would be attached to the center point on each of the harness shoulder straps. The base plate resting across two timbers could then be carried by a pair of men and the weight of the load would be distributed across their backs and shoulders. The bipod and barrel each required a timber and two shoulder pads when carried. Each of these mortar parts would be lashed to an individual timber and a shoulder pad would be attached to each end of the timber. Two man teams would then carry each of these items which would rest on one of their shoulders on the shoulder pads.

Front and rear views of the front bearer carrying a 4.2-inch mortar base plate.

• • • • •

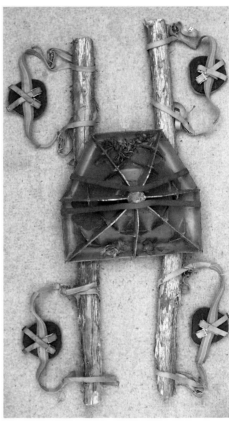

The three photographs on this page show how the component parts of a 4.2-Inch mortar can be carried by six men using the Australian load bearing system. The mortar barrel and bipod are lashed to their timbers in such a way as to allow them to hang beneath the timber once it is picked up and this ensures it is balanced when resting on the shoulders of the bearers. The harness shoulder straps attached to the timbers for the base plate would be crossed at the rear as the men stepped between the timbers and raised the straps and shoulder pads up and onto their shoulders.

· · · · ·

The British-made mortar and P.I.A.T. bomb carrier harness described on page 78 of this chapter was also produced in Australia during the war with a slightly modified design. In Australia it was known as the ***P.I.T.A. Bomb Carrying Harness (Aust)***. A strap was added to the front which joined the two front braces and this prevented the load from swinging

Side view of the front bearer carrying a 4.2-inch mortar barrel or bipod. (above)

around while on the move. And adjustment buckles were added to the rear ends of the braces which allowed them to be shortened on their own. This could only be done on the previous pattern by increasing the size of the loops where they attached to the items being carried. Larger loops would shorten the straps but would give the load more free play to move around which was unwanted.

· · · · ·

A metal carrier for three 4.2-Inch mortar bombs saw service with Australian troops fighting against the Japanese. The body of the pack is 13 inches by 4.5 inches with a height of 19 inches. It is divided into three cells that each holds one bomb. A wooden insert at the bottom provides support for the head of each bomb and holes in the wood provide a free space for each bomb's impact fuze. The last inch of the tail unit on inserted bombs will stick out from the top of the body of the pack and this makes it easier for them to be extracted when needed. The cap of the pack is slightly wider than the body which it fits over when put on. Reinforcements inside the cap prevent it from being pressed down too far and coming into contact with the bombs since they can be carried with both primary and augmenting cartridges already in place. The pack is carried with 2-inch wide webbing shoulder straps that meet at the top of the body in the center. The free ends have metal snap hooks that connect to rings at each of the lower edges of the body.

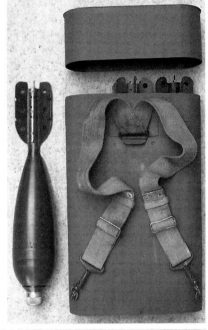

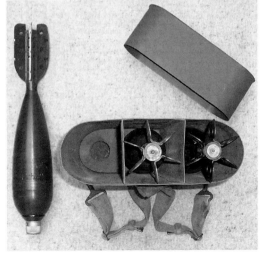

· · · · ·

82

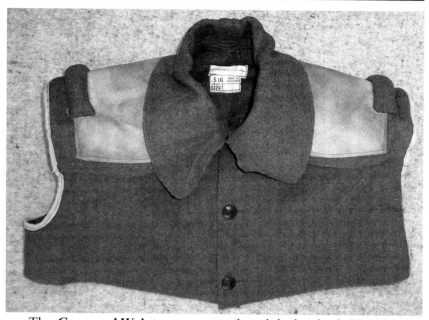

The ***Gunners' Waistcoat*** was produced during both World Wars for load bearing purposes. These were originally for the carriage of a Vickers Medium Machine Gun or the tripod, but the design was equally useful for carrying other bulky items. It consisted of a shortened other ranks Service Dress jacket which had thick leather pads sewn over the shoulder regions. Rolled wool was added to the outer edges of the leather to help prevent a carried item from slipping off the side

of the shoulder. The example shown here was produced in 1942.

Back view of the Gunners' Waistcoat.

· · · · ·

Special *3-Gallon Canvas Water Bags* were developed in 1942 for troop aerial resupply purposes using CLE Mark III drop containers. The canvas bags are 6 inches wide with a diameter of 13 inches. A 2-inch wide adjustable sling is sewn to the top of the bag at the sides across from the cap to keep it upright when slung and carried. These bags were originally produced in white canvas  but many were later dyed dark green as a means of concealing them from observation. Beginning in 1945, 3-Gallon Canvas Water Bags were produced from dark green material for use by troops who were to be issued the 1944 Pattern Web Equipment. These will be marked AF 0005. The original production bags have a VAOS code of 0050 and were classified as airborne equipment.

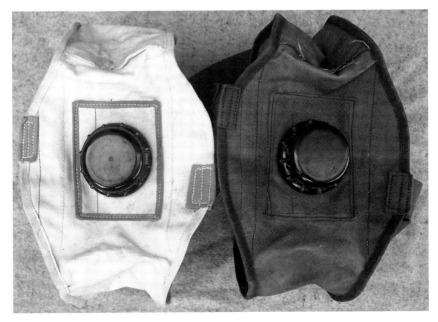

· · · · ·

The cap assembly is made from thick Bakelite in three parts. The spout has a wide base which is inside the bag and slipped through the square canvas reinforcement that was sewn to the top of the bag during production. A wider retaining ring screws onto the spout and traps the reinforcement canvas between itself and the base of the spout. The actual cap then screws down on the spout until it is tight against the retaining ring. The outside diameter of the retaining ring is 3 inches and the internal opening of the spout has a diameter of 1.25 inches.

The two bags shown on these pages were made by R. Burns Limited. The white bag

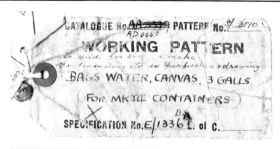

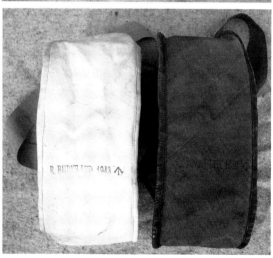

is 1943 dated and the bag dyed green is 1942 dated. A 1945 dated bag produced from green material can be seen in the chapter covering 1944 Pattern Web Equipment.

· · · · ·

The airborne *Lightweight Trailer* was a small single axle wagon constructed of thin sheet metal. It had an A-frame towing arm that could be fastened to a pair of mounting points at both ends. Each had three angle adjustment settings to compensate for being pulled by soldiers on foot or various heights of towing vehicle trailer hitches. Two hooks were welded at each lower corner beneath the towing arm mounts and these served as attachment points for toggle ropes. This allowed the trailer to be pulled by men with ropes while being pushed by others using the towing arm. The wheels were wire spoke motorcycle type and the trailer had no suspension. These trailers were used as ammunition carts and were intended to be expendable during combat. They were transported by and were typically added to gliders that were not already at their maximum takeoff weight. This ensured the maximum amount of ammunition would be loaded and taken into combat and the trailer provided a simple and effective method for the troops to transport it with them until it was needed.

Airlanding Brigade troops of 1st Battalion, The Border Regiment, with folding bicycles and lightweight trailers move off from the landing zone and head towards Arnhem.

· · · · ·

Airlanding Brigade troops load lightweight trailers (above) into an A.S.51 Horsa Mark I glider during an assault exercise. A cased mortar plotting board is attached to the front wall of the handcart and a 3-inch mortar barrel is fastened to the frame. The mortar base plate and bipod were carried inside the handcart. They quickly unload (below) and head to their staging area.

• • • • •

Trolleys were produced in two formats that were each constructed from metal tubing and canvas. The larger rigid framed pattern was introduced first for general service, followed by a smaller lightweight collapsible pattern that was designed for airborne operations. The rigid framed pattern had a pair of handles at each end. It could be used by one man in the same way as a wheelbarrow or by two men as they would carry a medical stretcher. This also made it easy for two men to run with it while filled. They could lift it over rough terrain and use the centrally located set of wheels to take the weight off the load when crossing flat terrain. When parked, one set of handles is lowered to the ground. The contents of the trolley will remain slightly off the ground since the handles stick out past the triangular framework that holds the canvas.

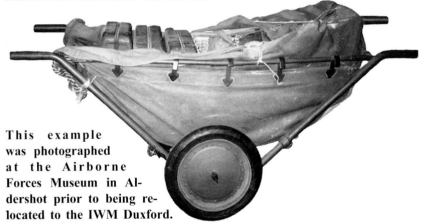

This example was photographed at the Airborne Forces Museum in Aldershot prior to being relocated to the IWM Duxford.

The *Lightweight Collapsible Trolley* was constructed from tubing sections in the shape of a conventional wheelbarrow with a canvas body. This consisted of two folding side frame rails that each had a handle at one end and a wheel with a rubber tyre mounted to it. Tubing crossbars slipped through sewn loops in the canvas body and rested in open fittings welded to the side frame rails. These could be locked together by tightening knurled knobs on to threaded studs at the ends of the crossbars. There were a total of

· · · · ·

Webbing straps with quick-release fittings helped to secure loaded items inside the lightweight collapsible trolley.

eight adjustment points. Hinged crossbars that were part of the folding side frame rails were positioned to serve as horizontal supports that ensured larger items such as ammunition crates or weapons transit chests would not be able to come into contact with the wheels when loaded. The lightweight collapsible trolley could be used by one man or by a combination of men in a similar way to the lightweight trailer.

One or more men could balance and push the handles while others pulled from the front by attaching toggle ropes. This piece of equipment could be delivered by parachute and required no tools for assembly which only took a few minutes to do.

· · · · ·

Two parachutists assemble a lightweight collapsible trolley on the drop zone.

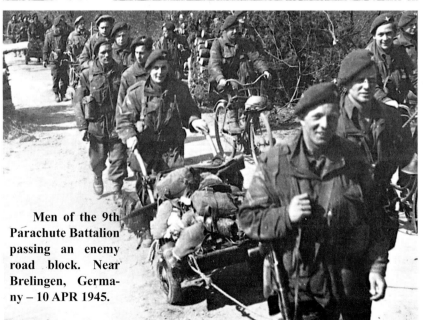

Men of the 9th Parachute Battalion passing an enemy road block. Near Brelingen, Germany – 10 APR 1945.

. . . . .

Chapter 3 - Personal Effects

Trooper Fred Beale of Brisbane shows his metal shaving mirror which prevented his becoming a casualty. He was carrying the mirror which was pierced by a shot fired by a Japanese sniper during the Papuan campaign on 26 JAN 1943.

. . . . .

Each solider was issued a ***Holdall*** for his personal toiletries. These were made from white linen material and were approximately 17 inches long by 8 inches wide. There was a series of loops sewn into the center for holding individual items and a larger pocket at one end where the shaving mirror and bar of soap could be stored. Before rolling the Holdall up, the long sides are folded in and this keeps the contents from falling out. A pair of cloth ties keeps the Holdall closed when not needed. Issues of tooth powder, bathing soap, razor blades and shaving soap were drawn monthly from company supplies.

The Holdall in the photo was made in 1942. A bar of lye soap which was commonly issued is at the right above a more refined bar of Lifebuoy soap. Working to the left is a 1943 dated shaving brush lying on a metal shaving mirror. A bar of shaving soap is next with a 1944 dated metal safety razor and British made blades in their individual packages. Bakelite safety razors of the same pattern were also very common. The toothbrush is a late war 1945 made nylon version with a comb and private purchase tweezers next to it. The safety blades at the far left are of U.S. manufacture.

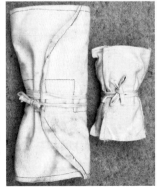

. . . . .

The ***Housewife Holdall*** was issued so minor mending of uniform parts could be done in the field when necessary. These were typically made of white or khaki linen with a single large pocket that was closed up by a flap with cloth ties. The pictured example was made in 1942 and has a small piece of wool tacked to the flap for safe keeping until needed for patching an article of battledress. The two gray balls at the left are for darning socks. A thimble, packet of needles and a card of thread are included in each kit along with brass and plastic replacement buttons. The piece of material at the right is green denim for use to repair jungle green uniform parts. The single button in the center is the type used with the denim utility coveralls and uses a metal ring to keep it in place on the uniform. This type button was removed from the uniform before laundering and replacements were often needed when they were lost. The Shaving and Housewife Holdall were kept in the small pack when in the field.

· · · · ·

An example of a wartime Canadian military issue shaving set produced by Gillette in Canada with Minora safety blades made by Dowd Blade Company Ltd of Canada. In addition to the blades and three part metal safety razor, a small metal mirror 1.75 by 3.75 inches wrapped with protective paper is included. The folding storage case has five fibre stiffeners covered in fabric with pockets and slots to accommodate the contents and the flap is held closed by a pair of snap fasteners.

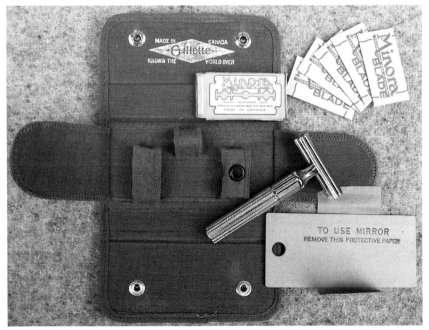

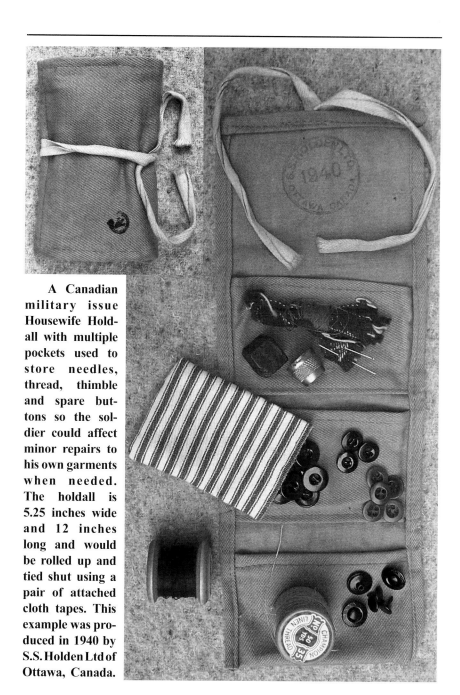

A Canadian military issue Housewife Hold-all with multiple pockets used to store needles, thread, thimble and spare buttons so the soldier could affect minor repairs to his own garments when needed. The holdall is 5.25 inches wide and 12 inches long and would be rolled up and tied shut using a pair of attached cloth tapes. This example was produced in 1940 by S.S. Holden Ltd of Ottawa, Canada.

• • • • •

The webbing pouch pictured was an item issued to officers as a convenient way to keep track of their essentials when separated from their full kit. It is 6.5 inches tall by 4 inches wide by 1 inch deep and has an adjustable carrying sling fixed to the sides. Inside is a long pocket with a series of loops for pencils and small tools on its front side. The pocket is made to hold the shaving mirror and a smaller pouch that is connected by a piece of twine. This smaller pouch is designed to hold the safety razor and blades and closes up to keep them clean. These are known to have been produced in the United Kingdom, Australia and India.

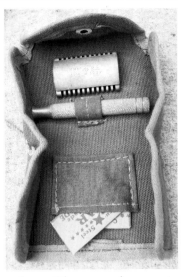

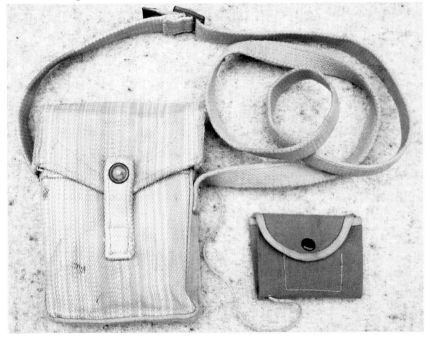

· · · · ·

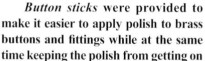

Button sticks were provided to make it easier to apply polish to brass buttons and fittings while at the same time keeping the polish from getting on the material of the uniform. Numerous patterns were produced and the type a soldier was issued depended partly on what regiment he was in. Button sticks were made from several materials and examples made from pressed fibre board, brass and bakelite are pictured above left.

Four styles of WWII dated British issue *Brushes*

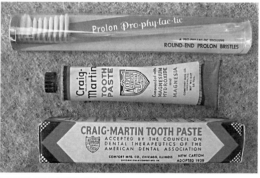

Canadian private purchased 1941 packaged *Tooth Brush* and 1939 packaged *Tooth Paste*.

Pictured at the far left is an example of a tin of *Brass Polish* with a tin of *Boot Polish* to its right.

· · · · ·

Blanco came in both solid and powdered forms and was produced in several shades of dark and light green, khaki and white. It was used to clean webbing in the sense that it covered stains and gave the equipment a consistent color and appearance. Blanco also helped to further waterproof the webbing by sealing seams and this extended the useable life of the gear. The process of cleaning the webbing started with brushing off any dried dirt. Soap and water could be used to help remove stains and embedded mud from the webbing but sufficient time had to be allowed for it to completely dry before proceeding. The application of Blanco began by rubbing the block with a damp sponge which was then wiped over the webbing. An even coating should be applied and it should be worked into the seams and joints. After the Blanco has been applied, it should be left to dry. The webbing could be lightly brushed after drying to remove any loose or built-up Blanco. New and heavily soiled webbing often required two applications for a complete coating to take. Normally only the outside of the webbing was treated, this being the side that did not come in contact with the uniform. This kept the Blanco from rubbing off and possibly staining the uniform.

Examples of British, Canadian and Australian produced Blanco in both solid block form and powder in sprinkle containers.

· · · · ·

Pictured above are three British military issue tins that hold 1.75 ounces of *Foot Powder*. The tall one at the left has a flat oval shape, the central can is rectangular and the one on the right has a cylindrical shape. Foot powder was an essential issue to soldiers and was used to help keep their feet dry to prevent fungus and infections.

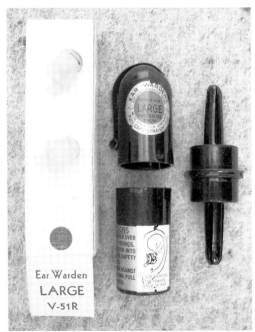

Ear Protectors were issued to all soldiers to help protect their ear drums from the blasts of exploding bombs and the sharp report from other weapons. These were made from rubber during the early years of the war and from cotton wool which was tucked into the ears later in the war due to the shortage of rubber. The "Ear Wardens" pictured at the left are of Canadian manufacture and had a bakelite storage housing designed to keep the plugs separated and clean when not in use. A metal clip on the container allowed it to be worn on a uniform epaulet for easy access.

• • • • •

99

A large variety of battery operated *Electric Torches* (flashlights) were in use by Commonwealth military personnel during the Second World War. The long shaft type (far left) was used in gliders and bombers. A belt clip is at the rear near the battery compartment cap and it was powered with four 1.5 Volt BA-30 dry cell batteries. This example was produced by Eveready and has a 1940 date with Broad Arrow mark. The torch to its right is an American-made TL-122-A pre-focused, right-angle two-cell spotlight and they were favored by the British and Canadian airborne troops. The "A" model was originally made before the war from brass and then later from steel. In September 1943 a plastic TL-122-B model was introduced and it featured a spare bulb in the battery compartment cap. The TL-122-C was introduced in April 1944 and it was very similar to the "B" model but with greatly improved seals to make it waterproof. The TL-122-D became available near the end of 1944 and used more durable plastic lenses instead of glass. Spare colored filters were stored with the spare bulb and the angle head had an extension that accepted one of the filters in front of the normal lens. These American torches each used two of the 1.5 Volt bat-

teries. The torch at the right is a British-made Number 5 Electric Lamp. Construction and features are similar to the TL-122-A with the exception of not having an angle head. The two torches at the bottom of the photograph are both small wartime civilian models that were often kept and used by soldiers owing to their being small and lightweight. The shaft type has a fisheye lens similar to a design manufactured in Germany but this model is marked "British Make" on the battery cap. The torch beneath it was manufactured by Philips in the Netherlands. These generated power for the bulb by repeatedly pressing a handle on the top, so it required no batteries. Wehrmacht marked examples were also produced during the German occupation.

· · · · ·

Five views of different variations of the Number 1 Electric Lamp are shown in the photograph above. All of them feature a swivel handle at the top where the on/off switch is mounted. Pulling the ends of the handle out of the housing allows the upper portion of the body to be removed giving access to the battery compartment. The bulb is accessed by unscrewing the lens cap in the front. Some variations have lugs mounted to the side of the body which hold a movable blackout hood over the lens and others feature a rotating shielded lens cover along with colored filters. All variations have a mounting clip on the rear.

The Electric Lamp Number 2 (above) is a simpler design with similar features to the Number 1 pattern. It has four feet on the bottom so it can stand on its own or can be hooked to a belt or bicycle mount by using the metal clip on its back. The Electric Lamp Number 4 (above) takes its design from a pattern used by the German military forces during the war. It has colored lenses that are put in place by sliding one of the two levers on the lower body. A leather strap on the back helps to hold it on a belt when needed.

· · · · ·

101

The item shown above is an Electric Spot Lamp with an integral helmet clip. The thumb screw on the clip is designed to be tightened down against the rim of the standard infantry helmet once inserted into the slot on the housing. A pair of long wires allows the battery compartment to be placed on a table or to be worn from a belt to minimize the weight on the wearer's head while being used. The battery compartment has the same general characteristics as the Number 1 Electric Lamp.

Four Lieutenants of the British 6th Airborne Division's 22nd Independent Parachute Company synchronize watches before emplaning on the eve of the Normandy Invasion. Note the angle head American TL-122-A torches visible on two of the men. The model can be identified by the blackened lens and battery compartment caps and from the shape of the battery compartment cap.

· · · · ·

There are many variations of time pieces that were issued to troops that had a need to know what time it was. These individuals included radio operators and observers that had to record and broadcast their sightings. Issue was free to Other Ranks but Officers had to purchase their own. Wrist watches that were government property will have the Broad Arrow mark; normally on the back side of the case along with the engraved letters "ATP" which is short for "Army Time Piece". Larger pocket watches will typically have "GS/TP" engraved on their cover which stands for "General Service Time Piece".

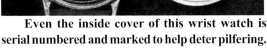
Even the inside cover of this wrist watch is serial numbered and marked to help deter pilfering.

· · · · ·

Tools of the trade used by Military Police and Provost Units.

Men of the Independent Provost Platoon demonstrate their method of arresting a drunk. Alice Springs, Australia – 29 DEC 1942.

Military Police and Provost Units were responsible for keeping drunk and disorderly soldiers in line as well as for assisting with the processing of prisoners of war. Here a field security officer interrogates a prisoner captured during a raid. 21 SEPT 1942.

· · · · ·

A Japanese prisoner of war under the control of an Australian M.P. awaits interrogation by intelligence officers at the headquarters for the 11th division where he was flown to. Dumpu, New Guinea – 19 APR 1944.

A concentration of enemy prisoners being held by a provost unit. The apparently casual attitude of the men in the provost unit was explained by the fact that the prisoners were Italians and therefore very well behaved. Middle East – 21 SEPT 1942.

A member of the 11th Division Provost Company standing outside a Japanese sentry box at an intersection in the Rabaul township. Troops of the 4th Infantry Brigade are occupying the area following the surrender of the Japanese. Rabaul, New Britain – 14 SEPT 1945.

. . . . .

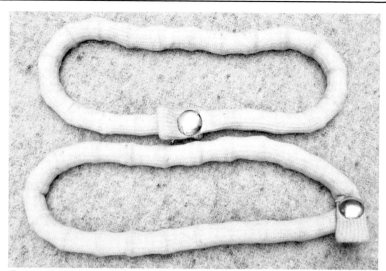

Leg weights were homemade or sometimes private purchase items some soldiers used to keep their trousers looking smart. They were used to pull the bloused trouser legs down and hold them over the very top of the web anklets. They normally consisted of a small tubular case filled with a light weight chain or lead shot.

Water purification tablets were on hand for use by the troops when drinking water had to be drawn from questionable sources. Each *Sterlizing Outfit* contained a bottle with 50 sterilizing tablets and another bottle with 50 Thio tablets. The later were used to help eliminate the bad taste that was created by the first tablet. Treatment took 30 minutes.

• • • • •

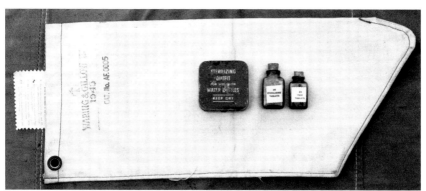

The bag pictured above was used as a means of primary water filtration. The sterilizing outfit was still required to purify the water since the purpose of the bag was merely to help remove mud and slime before treatment. The bag was squeezed underwater until it was saturated and then it was filled up and hung from the metal grommet at the top. Once the water level had lowered to a mark on the side of the bag about one third from the top, the water bottle could be placed beneath the dripping bag and allowed to fill. This process was expected to take five minutes.

Most awards, with the exception of medals for gallantry, were applied for by soldiers once the war was over. The photo above shows the form where an individual applied for the Defense Medal on the right and his approval note along with the award and the box it was mailed to him in on the left.

· · · · ·

Goggles with clear and tinted lenses came in several forms and were an issue item for Despatch Riders and crew members of some of the light armoured fighting vehicles and tanks. Most of these could be folded in the center and the sides had pieces of wire inside that allowed them to be compressed for storage in a smaller container when not needed. The outer edges of the goggles had a piece of leather or padding of another type that blocked the glare from the sides and these also kept the wind and dust out of the wearer's eyes. Wire framed glasses with polarized lenses were also available and these were an issue item to some snipers. The darkened glass helped to relieve eye strain and prevented fatigue from the arduous task of scanning for potential targets. These also had leather sides to block the light from entering.

Brigadier Murphy, 1st Canadian Armoured Brigade, visiting the forward Headquarters of the Calgary Regiment to make rush plans to cut off Germans paratroops that are withdrawing. Aquino, Italy – 23 MAY 1944. Note the soldier sitting in the foreground wearing Number 3 Tinted Spectacles. (above)

Women workers in England sort out and pack cigarettes into 50-count tins for Allied prisoner of war parcels.

· · · · ·

Reading and writing was one way to relax and focus the mind on other places and times. Maintaining a diary was a common practice for the time. One example of personal expression is the poem at the right that was part of the personal effects of a British Captain serving with the Royal Artillery and stationed in West Africa from 1942-1943.

Drinking was another favorite pastime and a trip to the N.A.A.F.I. for a shot of liquid courage was often the order of the day. The stoneware jugs below are marked S.R.D. which stands for *Supply Reserve Depot* and they were used to store rum as well as other small quantities of liquid. The troops referred to the initials as *Service Rum Diluted, Seldom Reaches Destination* or *Soon Runs Dry*. When rum was stored in the jars, it was pure and undiluted. The "Rum Ration" was only watered down if the recipient preferred to have "Grog".

WEST AFRICAN NIGHTMARE

(A TONE POEM)

BosoMs, bosoms, bouncing bare,
Down the Bush-paths, everywhere,
What fantastic hand or eye
Framed your frightful symmetry?

Row on row of naked chests,
Glands mammalia, bosoms, breasts;
Bosoms brown and bosoms black,
Bosoms firm and bosoms slack,
Bosoms bashful and bosoms bold,
Bosoms pendulous and cold,
Bosoms glossy, bosoms dim,
Bosoms dainty, bosoms grim,
Bosoms huge and bosoms tiny,
Bosoms moist and warm and shiny;
Sugar plums and acid drops,
NAAFI teacups, razor-strops.

What a nightmare in the nude,
Overpowering—rather rude;
Oh! to see again one fair
Damsel in a brassiere.   KEATS.

Three examples of the stoneware jugs used for rum and other valuable liquids.

• • • • •

110

British soldiers relaxing in the trenches in France during the Phoney War period in the early months of 1940.

Company Sergeant-Major Irene Roy distributing a rum ration to infantrymen of the Royal 22e Regiment, who are in weapon pits along the main road between Gildone and Campobasso. Central Italy - OCT 1943.

· · · · ·

A British
Highland Divi-
sion stops their
Bren Carrier at
a N.A.F.F.I. in
Egypt. 16 SEPT
1942.

Men of the
Royal Scots
Greys Regiment
at a N.A.F.F.I.
in Egypt along
with the crew
of an M3 Grant
tank which is
pulled up in the
foreground.

Australian
army and air
force person-
nel being served
tea at a com-
bined Comforts
Fund & Salva-
tion Army Red
Shield mobile
canteen. Noem-
foor, New Guinea
– 14 DEC 1944.

· · · · ·

Men of the 1st Battalion, the Oxfordshire & Buckinghamshire Light Infantry, part of the 53rd Welsh Division, at a mobile N.A.F.F.I. canteen in Germany towards the end of the war in Europe.

The tail of a German ME110 fighter resting on a pair of 44 gallon drums serves as bar for an allied squadron. Western Desert, Libya – 5 JUN 1942.

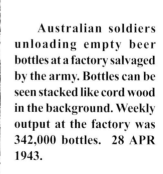

Australian soldiers unloading empty beer bottles at a factory salvaged by the army. Bottles can be seen stacked like cord wood in the background. Weekly output at the factory was 342,000 bottles. 28 APR 1943.

· · · · ·

Card games, decks of playing cards and dice traveled with the troops everywhere they went as a means of relieving long stretches of boredom. Board games and darts were also on hand at the comfort stations and rear areas where the troops took leave.

The Alexandria wharfs immediately after troops landed on 28 APR 1941.

· · · · ·

114

Luminescent Discs were issued to some British and Canadian pathfinders, paratroopers and reconnaissance patrols during the war. They consisted of a brass disc 1.5 inches in diameter with a pair of holes at opposite sides so it could be tied to the back of the helmet or other piece of equipment. The central section was filled with a radioactive substance that would glow after being charged with a flashlight and this made it easier for troops to follow each other when cover-

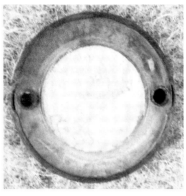

ing ground in total darkness. The example at the right is American-made and has the words "Poison Inside" stamped into the back.

Another luminous disc produced during the war by Radium Luminous Industries of Toronto, Canada is shown at the left and below with its brown suede storage pouch. This example is the same size as the American-made disc but features a pin for clipping it onto a uniform in addition to the pair of holes for tying it on.

Toggle ropes were issued primarily to airborne and commando units but they were also available to other troops when needed, as was the case for some of the assault groups during Operations Overlord and Varsity. They consist of a length of rope 6.5 feet long with a diameter of ¾ inch as shown at the bottom of the photograph on the right to 1 inch in diameter like the one at the top of the photograph. A spliced loop is at one end and a wooden toggle is at the other. They were a general purpose item that could be used for pulling vehicles and artillery piec-

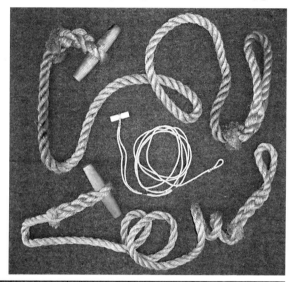

es or for making scaling ladders and rope bridges. The thin toggle rope in the center of the photograph is an 8.5 foot *Life Line*. These were used to connect troops or seamen to one another while in the open ocean following a ship sinking or aircraft ditching. This prevented them from drifting apart due to wave action or weakness and made it easier for search aircraft to locate them in groups.

Two examples of British military issue cotton *Trouser Braces* or suspenders. Each pair has a metal adjustor for setting the length of the straps in the front. The pair at the top has leather tabs for fastening to buttons on the trousers while the lower pair is an economy pattern with cotton tabs.

• • • • •

116

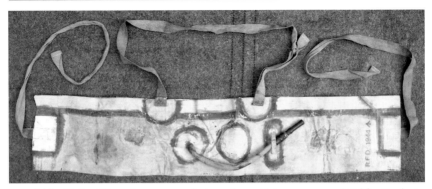

Life Belts like the ones pictured on this page and Life Jackets shown on the following pages were produced for issue to the British and Commonwealth soldiers to be worn during the invasions and while crossing major water obstacles like the Rhine River during Operation Varsity. They were also issued to airborne troops in the Parachute Regiments and the Airlanding Brigades in the event of a water landing while enroute to their objectives. The 1944 dated example above had to be manually inflated by means of a flexible nozzle on the front.

Captain S. Mendelsohn of the Royal Canadian Artillery (R.C.A.) briefing Canadian soldiers aboard a Landing Ship Tank (LST) en route to the Normandy beachhead, France. English Channel - JUN 1944.

. . . . .

117

Life Jackets were larger by design than Life Belts and they provided greater buoyancy while also maintaining a head up and back position for the person wearing it. The early airborne pattern with a heavy denim covering can be seen on the facing page while the later and more common pattern made from rubber can be seen in the photograph below. Both of these patterns were meant to support a soldier in the water for an extended period of time, much like an aircrew *Mae West*. Life Belts on the other hand were intended to assist a soldier who was either moving ashore and loaded down with equipment or who abandoned a landing craft and was swimming ashore.

A Canadian infantryman wearing a Life Belt, eating a meal aboard ship en route to the Normandy beachhead, France, 6 JUN 1944. (above)

British 6th Airborne Division RAMC Parachute Field Ambulance personnel wearing life jackets relax with RAF crewmen wearing *Mae Wests* while awaiting the order to enplane for the Normandy crossing.

· · · · ·

A Parachute Regiment corporal models a special airborne life jacket which was equipped with toggle operated CO2 cylinders for fast inflation. An inflatable bladder with a secondary manual inflation tube was inside a heavier protective denim cover worn underneath the parachute harness. Due to the weight of equipment and need to get out of harness following a water landing, paratroopers required a self inflating life jacket. It was essential for the paratrooper to unfasten his parachute harness prior to activation of the automatic inflation device as the rapid expansion could cause broken ribs if restrained. An example of an internal inflatable life jacket bladder is shown at the bottom of this page.

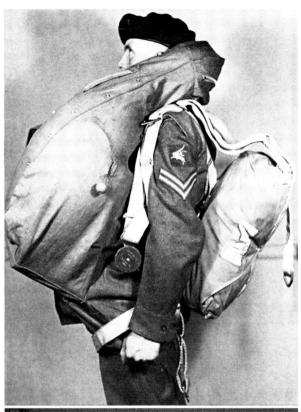

. . . . .

A three-piece eating utensil set was issued to each soldier along with his mess tins and drinking mug. The primary sets issued during the war consisted of a separate knife, fork and spoon but the knife was not always carried in the field as a space and weight saving measure. Additionally the troops were rarely served food in the field that required a knife to cut it and they had an issue clasp knife if one were actually needed. Today war dated examples of the knife utensil tend to be harder to find when compared with forks and spoons from the period. Most general service utensils were produced from nickel silver or nickel stainless and will be appropriately marked on the back, usually along with the maker name or initials and sometimes the date. Many patterns were produced and issued owing to the vast number of manufacturing firms and a large percentage of Australian and South African military issue utensils were made in England.

Examples of British, Canadian and Australian wartime three-piece cutlery sets. The British set has a matching 1944 dated spoon and fork with a 1943 dated knife. The Canadian set features a large stamped "C" on each item. The Australian set is marked "Allbrite" on the back and features the AMF crest on the front.

· · · · ·

Towards the end of the war, a new lightweight stackable set of utensils was designed but few sets were issued and they are considered part of the Pattern 1944 equipment intended for use in the Pacific after the war in Europe ended. These three piece sets are made from stainless steel. The spoon has a fold out clasp at the end of the handle that holds the set together when they are stacked. Australia also produced a lightweight knife, fork and spoon set for issue to troops serving in tropical areas outside of Australia. These were designed to be as light as possible without impairing their serviceability and to be short enough in length to fit within the rectangular mess tin set. Each item is 6 inches long and the fork and spoon are made from nickel silver. The knife blade is made from cutlery steel with a die-cast aluminum handle. The set had a weight of only half that of the traditionally issued cutlery set.

· · · · ·

Wartime *Mess Tins* consisted of a pair of shallow rectangular pans with folding handles at one end. The smaller pan was 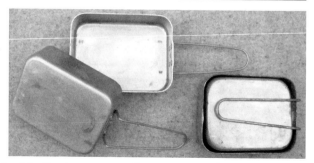 designed to stack inside the larger pan for storage. The earliest pattern was produced from aluminum but this was changed to tin plated metal for economic reasons in 1940. Aluminum was readopted again in 1945 as a weight saving measure intended for issue in the Pacific. Several changes were made to the basic design over time and these included a reduction in the depth of each pan, rounding the corners of the rectangular pans, adding reinforcement crimps to the top edges of each pan and adding a reinforcement groove on the long edge of the large pan and an inward groove on the long edge of the small pan.

Progression of mess tin styles as seen from the side. Top to bottom are the early style aluminum with smooth sides and smooth top edge, early tinned steel with smooth sides and crimped top edge, mid-war tinned steel with reinforcement side groves and crimped top edge, Indian-made tinned steel using multi-part construction and end of the war aluminum with smooth sides and smooth top edge.

· · · · ·

The photograph above shows the bottom of four styles of mess tins. Top to bottom are the original rectangular aluminum design, tinned steel with rounded edges, Indian-made with soldered together pieces and lastly the return to aluminum at the end of the war with rounded edges.

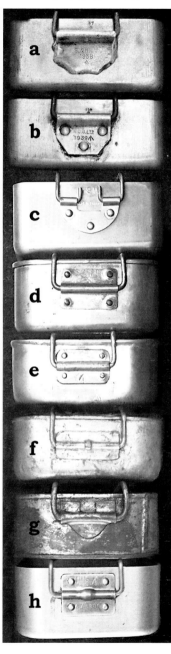

(a) British-Made S&H Ltd 1938 /|\ Aluminum with welded handle plate

(b) British-Made N.C.J. Ltd 1939 /|\ Aluminum with riveted handle plate

(c) Canadian-Made G.S.W. Aluminum with riveted handle plate

(d) British-Made REGICOR 1941 /|\ Tinned steel with riveted handle plate

(e) British-Made MB2 1942 /|\ Tinned steel with riveted and soldered handle plate

(f) Australian-Made WILLOW D/|\D Tinned steel with soldered handle plate

(g) Indian-Made Metal Box Coy Bombay 1941 Tinned steel with separate side and bottom parts soldered together

(h) British-Made MMS 1945 /|\ A.F. 0225 Aluminum with riveted handle plate

· · · · ·

123

Drinking mugs were issued to the individual soldiers because their water bottle had no cup. These were made from enameled metal with a handle cast into the side. There were several patterns owing to the wide range of manufactures but they all held one imperial pint. Early war issues tend to be white and later war issues were dark brown or dark green. It was common practice to carry the mug on the outside of the small pack with one of the flap straps being passed through the handle of the mug. This made it easy to get to for tea and made more room for other goods inside the pack.

British issue 1944 and 1945 dated enameled metal drinking mugs.

· · · · ·

A liquid fuel tent lantern was in issue during the war and it was housed in a steel can. The top portion unscrewed from the base about an inch from the bottom. The base held the fuel and it had an adjustable wick area built into its top. A metal bar on one side had a hole in the top edge so the lantern could be hooked onto a nail. A reinforced wire screen contained the flame and this also helped to intensify the light. This lantern also served as a small heater which could double as a light duty stove for heating water in a mess tin half or drinking mug. The closed up can had a diameter of 3.25 inches with a height of 5 inches.

• • • • •

A cooker in the form of a folding tripod was also on issue so the individual soldier could heat rations or make tea in the field. These typically used a small can filled with wood alcohol or jellied petroleum as a source of heat. The three legs served as the platform for

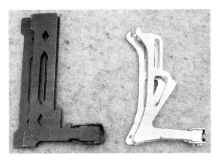

the cooking pan once the canned fuel was placed between the three legs and ignited. These stoves folded flat and were easy to store when not needed.

Pictured above on the left is a Canadian made tripod cooker with a private purchase version made by the Sterno Company pictured on the right with its canned heat and a small aluminum pot that everything can be packed into.

At left is an example of a tent lantern being used to brew up a pint of tea in an issue enameled drinking mug.

• • • • •

In addition to tea, cigarettes were one of the most important comfort items available to the troops at the front. They were a part of the issued rations and were often used like money for wagers in card games and as payment for favors. The main packaging formats were 10 pack boxes and 50 pack tins. Boxes of 20 were also available but these were not as common in the field. Lighters were a private purchase item but boxes of matches were normally on hand for lighting a cigarette. Pictured below are samples of some of the types of filter-less cigarettes and matches that were available during the war. Many other brands as well as filtered cigarettes also existed and could be purchased at local canteens or the mobile Navy, Army, and Air Forces Institutes (N.A.A.F.I.).

* * * * *

An officer's air travel kit bag is pictured in the background with a white coloured sea kit bag leaning on it and a normal khaki coloured army kit bag in the foreground. All were made from canvas and had metal grommets around the open end which would be closed by a draw cord or kit bag handle. The traveling allowance weight for officers' kit was forty-four pounds. The standard soldier's kitbag had a circular bottom with a 10 inch diameter and a side wall height of 28 inches. These originally had 12 grommets around the opening but a later Mark II pattern reduced the number to 8. It was normal for the name and army number to be written onto the side of all patterns of kit bag for easy identification.

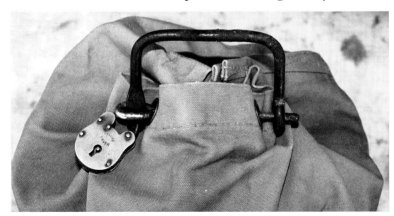

A kit bag handle locked in place after it was passed through the grommets in the end of the bag. This convenient device made it easier to carry the kit bag while providing security for the contents.

• • • • •

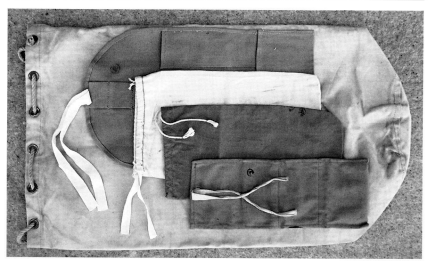

Five standard issue Canadian-made canvas and cloth bags that were each produced in 1940 are shown above for size comparison. From top to bottom they are a sewing kit housewife holdall, a rations bag, a mess tins bag, a shaving kit holdall, and a Mark I pattern army kit bag.

Captain C. H. Davis welcoming an incoming draft of soldiers to No. 1 Canadian Armoured Corps Reinforcement Unit. Each is wearing their full webbing equipment set and holds their kit bag with service rifle slung. Woking, England - 8 AUG 1944.

• • • • •

The British *24-Hour Ration* was packaged in a small wax-coated card stock box measuring 6 inches by 4.5 inches by 2.5 inches. The contents were small individually wrapped portions of items that could be eaten cold or dissolved in water and heated. These included dried meat, both neutrally flavoured and sweetened biscuits, vegetable soup powder or bouillon cubes, oatmeal, tea, salt, hard candy referred to as boiled sweets, chewing gum, vitamin enriched chocolate, jam, pasteurized cheese and powdered milk. Cigarettes were provided in 50-count tins which were an individual soldier's ration for a week.

The contents of a British wartime 24-Hour Ration.

Airborne troops each drawing two 24-Hour rations prior to D-Day.

· · · · ·

The ***Canadian Army Mess Tin Ration*** was a compact ration similar to the British 24-Hour Ration. It was packed in a box 7.375 inches by 4.75 inches by 3.375 inches and it had a weight of 2 pounds, 15 ounces. A small folding tripod stand was issued along with a container of sterno canned heat which was adequate for cooking six meals. The meat component of each ration contained 3.5 ounces of sardines, 3 ounces of spiced beef and 3 ounces of prepared pork in sealed tins. Three 3-ounce packages of neutral flavoured biscuits, 1.5 ounces of foil wrapped cheese, 1.5 ounces of jam, 2 ounces of butter, and 2 ounces of powered pea soup made up the rest of the food staples. Tea, soluble coffee, a skim milk sugar mixture, and a chocolate with vitamins packet made up the drinks. Three lumps of sugar, a 2-ounce chocolate bar, hard candies, gum, iodized salt, ascorbic acid, 10-pack of cigarettes, 20-count matches, can opener, and a wooden fork and spoon finished out the issue.

British soldier's receiving two 24-Hour Rations, two compact tinned emergency rations, one water sterilization outfit and one tinned cigarette ration.

· · · · ·

131

The *Australian Operation Ration* was originally produced as an Emergency Flying Ration. These were packaged in a sealed tin that was opened using a turnkey similar to the type found on a tin of sardines or tin of spam. The tin was painted green and was completely waterproof allowing for bulk supplies to be safely buried if needed. The ration contained three separately packaged meals making it adequate for twenty-four hours like it's British and Canadian counterparts. The original meat components for each meal consisted of meat and vegetable stew, meat and vegetable hash, and meat and beans or corned beef hash. After June 1944, the meat components were changed over to more solid processed meats such as Hampe, Meatreat and Corned Beef Loaf. Other food components included wholemeal biscuits, carrot biscuits, peanut butter, barley sugar rolls, chocolate, Blackcurrant spread, cheese, caramel bars, lime tablets, sugar, tea, skim milk powder and salt. By design, the meals could be eaten cold and without the addition of water, with the exception of the drinks.

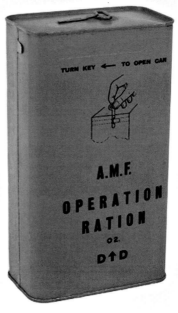

Three soldiers examining the new Australian Military Forces Field Operational Ration that was being issued. Each one contained three meals that were wrapped separately. This was equivalent to the British 24-Hour Ration but had a more durable waterproof container to protect the contents. Guy's Post, Faria River area, New Guinea – 8 NOV 1943.

. . . . .

A small white linen bag was provided to the troops to hold non-packaged rations. This included dried beef and pork, bread, biscuits and tobacco when available. The British-made example shown is 1942 dated and 7 inches by 12 inches with a pair of cloth tapes at one end to keep it closed. While the two piece mess tin will fit inside the bag, this was not its intended purpose. Mess tin bags made of cotton drill material had been issued during the first few years of the war but this was abolished in 1941 and existing bags were to be reissued as ration bags. This decision was reversed in 1945 and mess tin bags were once again issued. They were made from dark green cotton drill material and intended for use in the Pacific.

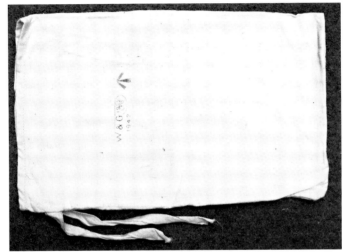

A signalman with a fighting patrol uses Canned Heat to warm a meal in his mess tin during a rest break. Bougainville - 31 MAY 1945.

. . . . .

133

The different individual rations pictured on this page are each 4.25 inches long by 3.25 inches wide by 1 inch thick with the exception of the Australian emergency ration shown open and closed at the bottom of this page which is 4.25 inches wide by 5.75 tall by .75 inches thick. The lids have no hinge and lift completely from their containers. In the case of the British Emergency Ration and the Horlicks 24 Hour Ration, the lid has a rubber gasket inside to help it seal and stay fresh. The picture at the top right on this page shows the vitamin enriched chocolate that makes up the standard British Emergency Ration. It's not very appetizing after ageing for sixty years.

· · · · ·

134

An example of a WWII Canadian Royal Navy lifeboat ration assembled and distributed by W. Clark Ltd is shown sealed, open but packed and again with contents laid out. These were issued as supplemental emergency rations to some units from 1943-1945. The tin was manufactured by General Steel Wares Ltd and is 3.75 inches wide by 2.5 inches tall by 1.75 inches thick. Contents included 12 biscuits produced by Harrison Brothers Ltd, 2 small chocolate bars produced by Fry-Cadbury Ltd and 12 concentrated milk chocolate tables packaged six per roll which were produced by Dominion Packaging Ltd. All five of these firms operated facilities in Montreal, Canada during the war.

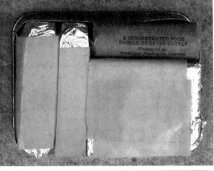

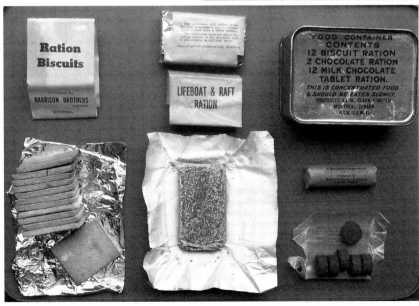

• • • • •

135

Red Cross parcels were sent out to troops in hospitals and prisoner of war camps. They usually contained tea, cocoa, sugar, chocolate, oatmeal, biscuits, sardines, dried fruit, condensed milk, jam, corned beef, margarine, cigarettes or other tobacco products and soap.

Contents of a gift parcel provided to hospital patients by the Australian Red Cross Society on Christmas of 1942.

Chapter 4 - Camp Equipment

An armoured column stopped on a narrow forest trail in the Reichswald. The soldier at the left against the embankment is setting up a Number 2 Safety Cooker. The fuel tank has already been removed and is in his hand while he sets the burner grate back in place.

· · · · ·

Before the outbreak of war, officers in H.M. Forces were obligated to purchase campaign furniture for their own use in the field. But with the rapid expansion of the army following the German invasion of France, newly commissioned officers found themselves in need of campaign furniture for personal use while still in the United Kingdom, due to the necessity of living in temporary quarters or tent cities that were otherwise unfurnished. Items such as chairs, stools, tables, bedsteads, trunks and valises could be purchased from commercial outfitters or through the military quartermasters. Like most privately purchased equipment, a wide range of variation in materials, styles and colour exist but they generally conform to a government approved pattern. Overall quality for individual items was largely based on the officer's means since they not only had to purchase campaign furniture, but also their uniforms, personal hygiene items and baggage for carrying all of their kit. Examples of several pieces of wartime economy folding campaign furniture are shown on the following pages as a basic reference. And an overview of a higher end set of campaign furniture can be seen below.

General Sir Bernard Montgomery (eighth from left) talking with Lieutenant-General Guy Simonds (ninth from left) and other senior officers of the 2nd Canadian Corps at Corps Headquarters. In the Normandy bridgehead, France - 20 JUL 1944.

. . . . .

The ***Officers' Folding Camp Chair with Detachable Seat*** is composed of a wooden framework with canvas seatback and seat section. The seat has two wooden supports with a section of canvas fastened to them. Each support has a pair of holes which connect onto dowel ends on the main chair framework. When assembled, the base of the seat is 19 inches above the ground with a 15 inch by 15 inch framework. The canvas tapers towards the rear so that it clears the wooden seatback upright supports. The canvas seatback has dimensions of 14 inches by 10 inches. A basic folding camp stool was also produced and in use during the war.

· · · · ·

The *Canvas Camp Basin* and *Canvas Camp Bath* each consisted of a folding wooden frame with a waterproof canvas liner. The folding frame was the same for both items but it remained taller and narrower for the basin and lower and wider for the bath. A short metal folding towel bar 7 inches long was mounted onto the frame at the top of one leg and it could be moved in-line with the leg so as to be out of the way when not needed. The canvas liners had reinforced hangers sewn into each corner and these served as the mounting points for the four ends on the folding frames. A tapered pocket was built into one side of the basin to provide a holder for soap or shaving gear to keep it out of the water when not being used. The bottom of the basin was unsupported since it didn't hold much water. But the bottom of the bath rested on the ground. When set up, the top of the basin was 30 inches above the ground and its liner was 14 inches by 14 inches having a depth of 6 inches. The bath was 28 inches by 28 inches with a depth of 8 inches.

Baths, Camp – Canvas,
with Stands, Wood

· · · · ·

Basins, Camp – Canvas, with Stands, Wood

. . . . .

141

The *Canvas Bedstead* consisted of a folding wooden frame with metal supports, wooden end pieces, folding wooden side supporting rails, a canvas top and a canvas storage bag. The folding frame has a handle on one side to assist in expanding the accordion-like structure. Each of the upper ends of the wooden legs has a metal tip which connects onto a metal bracket on the wooden side supports after they have been slipped through reinforced channels on the long edges of the canvas top. The ends of side supports are tapered down to dowels which fit into holes at each end of the wooden end pieces and these are what maintains the bedsteads tension and prevents it from folding up when a person sits or lays down on it. When fully assembled, the top of the bedstead stood 19 inches above the ground with a width of 27 inches and a length of 78 inches.

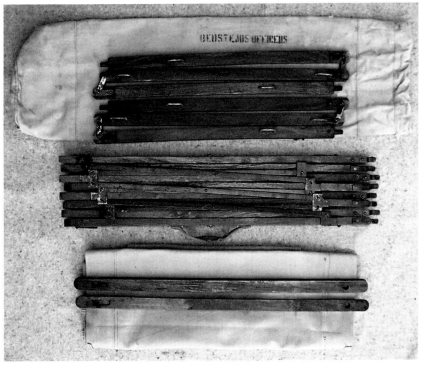

The component parts of a folding bedstead with canvas bag.

· · · · ·

The folding bedstead shown assembled from the top and from the side.

Commonwealth troops seen resting on lend-lease folding cots beside their lorry in the desert under the stars in August 1942.

· · · · ·

The **Camp Table with Folding Legs** was another lightweight and portable canvas and wood furniture item produced during the war. The top was made from a piece of canvas which had a series of twelve wooden slats connected to it on one side. A stabilizing slat was riveted to opposite corners of each side and these could be rotated 90 degrees and locked in place under the edges of the slats to create a flat and rigid surface. When the stabilizing slats were rotated back in-line with the surface slats, the entire top could be neatly rolled up for transit. The folding leg assembly is similar in construction to the pattern used with the camp basin and camp bath but has notches at one end which help to hold the table top from shifting around when it is placed on them. Once assembled, the top of the table is 26 inches above the ground with a useable surface area 30 inches by 24 inches.

An assembled table top with legs folded.

· · · · ·

144

Trooper Ernie Tester of the 12th Manitoba Dragoons lying on a collapsible cot in back of a T17E1 Staghound of a Canadian armoured regiment. Near Caen, France - 19 JUL 1944.

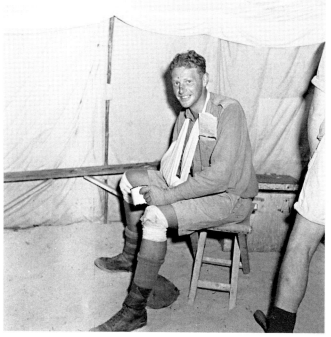

A wounded soldier seated on a folding camp stool inside a medical tent after being treated in AUG 1942. A 6-gallon container insulator and a folding wooden bench are in the background against the wall of the tent.

. . . . .

145

Primus stoves were invented in 1892 by Frans W. Lindqvist in Sweden and they were one of the first soot-less kerosene stoves available. There are several designs that came about as the product evolved and many were in use by the armed forces of both the Allied and Axis nations during the Great War and the period that followed. During WWII, the British produced their own pattern for military issue based on the Primus

design. The three legs making up the tripod for the burner grate are welded to the sides of the fuel tank unlike most commercial models. The brass grate can be removed for cleaning and for access to the actual burner. The example pictured here is /|\ 1943 dated on the top of the fuel tank along with maker markings but has no reference to Primus or their patents. The diameter of the burner grate is 8.5 inches and the over height of the stove is 9 inches.

· · · · ·

A jeep trailer being used to transport equipment needed for a field kitchen.

The good life for two well outfitted officers eating in the back of a lorry in the North African desert during the summer of 1942. Their cooking pan is sitting on a pair of Primus pattern stoves and they would appear to have a stockpile of rations including a large jar of jam in the foreground and several cases of Rheingold Beer which was brewed in New York.

· · · · ·

147

Two patterns of compact British made stoves produced during the war were the *Safety Cooker Number 2* and *Safety Cooker Number 3*. These were both fueled by leaded gasoline. The basic design of both stoves is essentially the same. They each have a single burner housed in a metal box measuring 9 inches by 9 inches by 4 inches. The lid on each pattern hinges upward and has a second fold out panel that serves as a wind screen. Metal legs hold the lid of the box closed for transit when folded up. They can be folded outward and under the box for supports and to hold the box off the ground. Vents in the lower side of the box draw air for the burner. The main difference in the two patterns is the fuel tank. On the Number 2, the fuel tank is stored loose inside

Soldiers of the 7th Canadian Infantry Battalion cooking supper with a Safety Cooker Number 2. Normandy, France - 9 JUL 1944.

· · · · ·

the box. When the box is open, the burner grate is lifted up and the fuel tank is removed. It then is fixed to the front of the box on the outside and a fuel line connects it to the burner. On the Number 3, the front wall has a handle which can be pulled outward if the lid is open and the burner grate has been removed. The fuel tank is connected to the burner and this entire assembly will slide outward placing the fuel tank outside the box and the burner in the center. Both patterns were issued to tank and armoured fighting vehicle crews since they normally stayed with their vehicles at the end of the day when in the field.

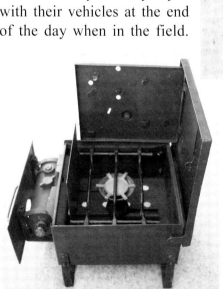

Two photographs of the Number 3 Safety Cooker set up and ready for use. The photograph at the left shows the folding legs locked in the lower position. The photograph above shows tools issued with each stove. These include a metal funnel for filling the fuel tank, a double sided open wrench, a box wrench with blade style screwdriver at one end and three tools with needle ends for cleaning the jets on the stove's burner.

• • • • •

The **Petrol Cooker Number 1**, also known as the *Hydro Burner* or *Hydro Cooker*, was introduced in 1939. They were typically issued to mobile units on the scale of one cooker per 120 men. The cooker consisted of a metal housing with interlocking vented plates on top which could hold cooking pots or frying pans. This was connected to a two-gallon pressurized fuel tank with a burner unit and a foot or hand pump. A pressure of 20 pounds was needed to push fuel into a pre-heater which was ignited while the fuel flow valve was turned off. Once the burner warmed up, the tank would be manually pressurized to 50 pounds and then the fuel flow valve could be opened up again and the flame could be adjusted. Fuel pressure needed to be maintained at 50 pounds while cooking and a gauge on the top of the tank made this possible to monitor. The fuel tank and burner were mounted to a common base and were separated by a heat shield. A carrying handle was situated in the centre to make it easier to lift, especially when still hot.

Men of the British Expeditionary Force photographed cooking for their unit with a Hydro Burner in France. A wide range of mobile kitchen items can be seen including three 6-gallon container insulators in the background on the right side of the photograph. The three 6-gallon containers from the insulators and a single Dixie are on the burner. More of the Dixie sets along with other pans can be seen in the background on the left.

· · · · ·

A unit cook checking the status of the fire inside the wood burning stove he is using to prepare a meal. Tripolitania, Libya – 17 FEB 1943.

A Hydro Burner being used to cook food in a 6-gallon container while keeping prepared food hot in a pair of Dixie sets. The man in the upper right corner of the photograph is using a foot pump to pressurize the petrol tank on the Hydro Burner.

Men of the 4th South African Armoured Car Regiment prepare a meal on their petrol stove beside their vehicle. Egypt – 8 SEPT 1942.

. . . . .

British ***Dixie Sets*** were large tin plated metal pots used for boiling water and cooking food. The pots are oval shaped and have a level capacity of 15 quarts. A heavy gauge metal handle at the top provides a way to hang the pot over a fire pit for heating and also a means of carrying the pot to the serving area. The pot has a flat pan style lid that has two handles on the sides. It fits over the top of the pot for storage and to keep debris out when cooking. The low walls on the lid are adequate for it to be used as a serving tray. The Dixie sets were being used by the army before the Great War and continued into the post WWII years. The only difference is the tin plating was abandoned and replaced by aluminum for health reasons. The example pictured on this page was made in 1943. Large rectangular 6-gallon steel containers with removable lids were also known as Hay Boxes and these had a separate removable frame. They were kept in large insulated boxes for transport or to keep prepared food warm until it was served.

· · · · ·

Infantrymen of The Highland Light Infantry of Canada cooking a meal aboard H.M. LCI(L)-306 of the 2nd Canadian (262nd RN) Flotilla en route to France on D-Day, 6 JUN 1944. The ship was transferred to the United Kingdom under terms of the Lend-Lease Act on 2 APR 1943 and then later transferred to the Canadian Navy and re-commissioned HMCS LCI(L)-306 on 29 SEPT 1944.

British officers inspecting a mess hall facility and its German cook inside a warehouse that had been converted into a German prisoner of war camp. United Kingdom – 1939.

. . . . .

Insulated boxes made from galvanized steel were used to hold rectangular 6-gallon containers of food. These had an outside dimension of 20.75 inches long by 14.75 inches wide by 18 inches tall. The hinged lid was held closed by a pair of rotating hasps on the front. Insulated panels were on the inside walls of the box and these were help in place by round-head screws. The insulated panel in the lid was 1.5 inches thick while those on the side walls were 5/8 inches thick. A carrying handle can be found on each end and two rings are mounted on the back for strapping the box down when vehicle transported.

· · · · ·

The **6-Gallon Container** that was used with the Insulator on the facing page has measurements of 12.75 inches by 16 inches with a depth of 12.25 inches. These were produced from quality stainless steel and had an empty weight of

just over 13 pounds. The heavy handle on the top can be pivoted all the way down for storage moving it one direction. When rotated the opposite way, it will stay elevated two inches above the container body. This prevents it from heating up when food is being prepared. The thin removable lid is also made from stainless steel and has a centrally located handle for lifting it off the container. The pictured example was Canadian-made by General Steel Wares in 1941.

A 6-Gallon Container shown beside a Dixie Set for comparison.

· · · · ·

Soldiers of the Regina Rifle Regiment having lunch during maneuvers. England - 18 DEC 1941.

Lance-Corporals S. L. Stout and J. E. Wamboldt, and Sergeant H. E. Jantz of the Support Company, Saskatoon Light Infantry (M.G.), placing turkeys in roasting pans which are on top of insulated containers. Italy - 15 SEPT 1943.

. . . . .

Collapsible buckets made from canvas were the standard during both World Wars and several patterns had come and gone. At the outbreak of the Second World War, the British standard pattern was the **Canvas Water Bucket Mark V.** This consisted of a bucket made from rotproofed

canvas with a rope handle spliced onto two reinforcement loops. The upper edge of the bucket was rolled over and sewn back to itself to make a tunnel, and a length of rope inside it helped to form a rim. Like other canvas goods designed to hold water, they work best when saturated prior to being filled and carried.

A selection of WWII period canvas water buckets that are filled with water (above) and then shown collapsed (below). The far right example is a 1939 dated British Mark IV bucket and the pair at the far left are American-made as provided with Lend-Lease vehicles. The other two buckets are European patterns that could have been encountered and used by the troops during the war.

Thermos flasks were issued to flight crews and were available to airborne troops while on aircraft and to AFV crews inside their vehicles. They were used to keep tea, coffee and soup warm and fresh until needed. Pictured above are a large size thermos with its padded case and two of the smaller types often found in gliders and tanks. They all used a cork as a stopper and had a lid that doubled as a cup.

Men of the British 6th Airborne Division with a padded thermos carrier making the Channel crossing on the Eve of D-Day, 5 JUN 1944, in a Mark IV Short Stirling bomber converted for parachute operations.

· · · · ·

Two types of padded carriers were produced during the war to help prevent damage to insulated flasks when used under rough conditions. The smaller type was made of leather which was sewn in the form of a cylinder. It had a leather cap which was held down over the top of a thermos by an adjustable strap. Another leather strap mounted on one side served as a handle to aid in carrying the container. The larger size carrier was designed for airborne use and it had a canvas outer shell with a lid that used a press stud to keep it closed. The inside had several layers of padding which were glued together around the circumference of the canvas cylinder and to the lid which was slotted to accommodate the carrying handle on the thermos. The smaller thermos shown on this page has no carrying handle or brackets as they would obstruct loading into the leather carrier. It is marked "Thermos Reg. Trademark 1944"on the bottom. The larger thermos is marked "Thermos (1925) Limited" 1944 London /|\" on the bottom.

. . . . .

Kerosene was invented in 1846 by Abraham Pinero Gesner of Nova Scotia as a process to extract a liquid fuel from coal. The intent was a cleaner and cheaper substitute for Whale Oil which was the fuel of choice at the time for wick lamps. Coal Gas was already being used in pressurized street lamps and Kerosene came to be known as Coal Oil. Robert Edwin Dietz, an American, began selling Whale

Oil lamps in 1840 and with the advent of Kerosene, designed the modern flat wick oil lamp in 1859. With increased demand for Kerosene, an alternative manufacturing process was developed using petroleum in place of coal. The word Kerosene is commonly used for the fuel oil in North America, Australia and New Zealand, while the word Paraffin is used in the United Kingdom and South Africa.

Four patterns of kerosene wick lamps. The example at the far right has blackout shields with directional stencil cutouts in the form of arrows and Xs in the hooded windows. It was used to mark lanes as an aid for troops moving at night.

· · · · ·

Pressurized hurricane lanterns that used paraffin (kerosene) as a fuel had their origins in the early 1800s with the gas street lamps that graced many of the larger cities in England, Europe and America. Small portable camp lanterns had been widely used during WWI and were produced by Petromax in Germany and by Tilley in England. These became commercially popular during the interwar years and a number of other companies including Primus, Stanley Lamps of London and American Gas Machine Company in the USA entered the market to provide lanterns to both civilians and the military. Because of the large scale of issue during the Second World War, the trade name Tilley became synonymous with pressurized hurricane lanterns in the United Kingdom and Tilley became the generic name for kerosene lamps in many regions of the world with historical ties to the British Empire. Vapalux Limited was a pre-war subcontractor for Tilley Lamp and they were awarded their own lantern manufacturing contract by the British Government in 1939. Vapalux was later absorbed by Willis and Bates, another English lamp manufacturer affiliated with Aladdin of Greenford, England. Two major advancements in lamp technology were kerosene lanterns with pre-heater ignition systems, introduced under the trade name Petromax Rapid in 1936, and later designs by Petromax and Coleman of Wichita,

Kansas having lanterns that could be operated with gasoline or diesel fuel.

Examples of paraffin lamps produced by (left to right) Tilley, Petromax and Primus.

· · · · ·

A small wooden cased, battery powered desk lamp was produced in Australia and issued for field use during the Second World War. The base had an on/off toggle switch and featured a clamp to fasten onto a desk top or lid of a crate. The arm assembly had four joints ending at a hooded light bulb housing making it highly adjustable in terms of light placement. Power was supplied by a Type "Y" Dry bat-

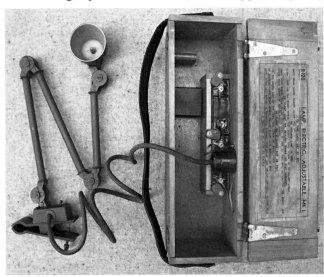

tery. A holder was built into the case for two batteries which allowed for one being a spare or it could be hooked up in parallel to allow the lamp to run longer without changing out batteries. A small container at the bottom of the case held spare light bulbs. Dimensions of the wooden case are 5.5" x 6.5" x 17" and it has a short leather strap to aid in carrying it.

· · · · ·

The ***ground sheet*** was made of water-proofed canvas which was normally produced in a khaki colour. Some were dyed dark green or black at some point in time following manufacture, probably to make them less conspicuous in the open. Early war examples will have metal grommets around the perimeter while later war examples merely have holes punched into

them. Their purpose was to make it easier to fasten cords to the edges when using the ground sheet like a rain cape or when making a shelter. The 1941 dated example in the top right photo measures 3 feet 4 inches wide by 6 feet long. The 1942 dated example to its right measures 3 feet wide by 6 feet 4 inches long. The dimensions only differ slightly but this gives the earlier war ground sheet a 144 square inch larger surface area.

· · · · ·

The ***Mattress Case***, also known as a *Palliasse*, essentially served as thin sleeping pad when filled with straw, dry grass or sawdust. These lightweight bags were economical to produce when compared with traditional mattresses of the time and they could be emptied and folded or rolled into a compact size for easy transport when needed. A 1943 dated khaki/green cotton Canadian-made example is 72 inches long and 31.5 inches wide when empty and flat. These dimensions will be somewhat reduced depending on the amount of stuffing that gets added to the inside. A 3.5 inch wide end flap is used to prevent the stuffing from coming out of the palliasse and three pairs of cloth tapes are used to tie it closed. Another example produced during the war in India is made from light grey colored denim and used two pairs of cloth tapes for closing the end. It has an empty width of 26.5 inches and a length of 79 inches. With filling 3.5 inches deep, this pattern has measurements of 24 inches by 78 inches. A British-made 1945 dated example is constructed from khaki/brown cotton and uses four pairs of cloth tapes to close the end. In a long-term encampment, soldiers typically drew fresh filling materials once a week.

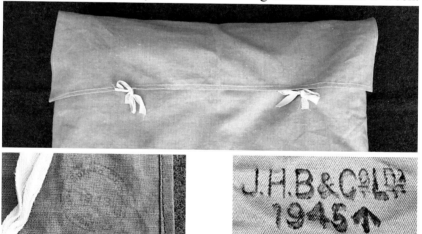

The end portion of a filled Indian-made Palliasse showing the closing ties along with photographs of the markings found on Canadian-made and British-made examples of the Palliasse.

. . . . .

Field pillows during WWII were virtually identical to the pattern produced during the First World War. They were empty cloth bags with an opening on the top which was closed with two pairs of cloth ties. The soldier stuffed the bag with his own clothing or with dry grass or hay if available. The pictured example bears the Canadian C/|\ mark.

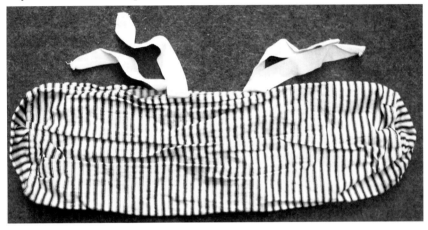

Linen towels were standard issue for drying off after a wash. The pictured example is a British military pattern produced in 1943. It measures 26 inches by 29 inches and has a cloth loop in the center so it could be hung up to dry when not in use.

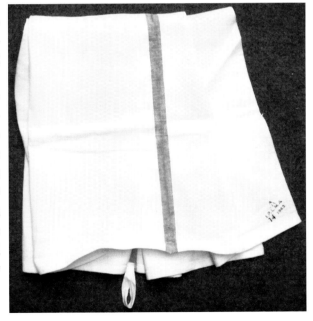

. . . . .

The early war production **Rain Capes** were made from a lightweight rubber coated canvas. They are heavier than the oilskin anti-gas capes and offer excellent rain protection to covered areas. Like the early ground sheet, they have metal grommets running around their perimeter. Late war produced rain capes are made from rubberized canvas which can leak once it becomes saturated. Instead of grommets,

punched holes will be found as with the late war ground sheets. The rain cape can double as a ground sheet when needed and it has a base rectangle of 33.5 inches wide by 6 feet 2 inches long. Buttons are used to close up the front and a hook and eye combination for added strength is at the neck.

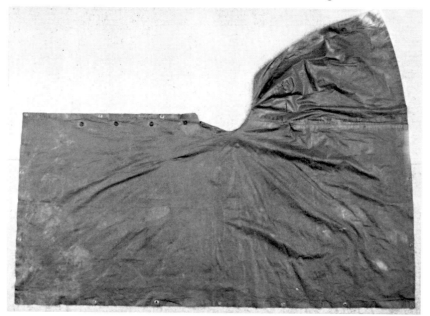

. . . . .

Examples of British WWII pattern rain capes. The one on the left was made in 1941. The one in the center was made in 1944. The one at the right was made after the war when production of the early pattern resumed. The only apparent difference between the early war and post war rain cape is the better and heavier rubber coating found on the post war example.

The five sleeping bag photographs on the next two pages come from a British WWII study which compared their effectiveness. The Denison pattern sleeping bag is referred to as an airborne bag. There really is no comparison between the two bags as they were made for different purposes. The captions would indicate flaws were found in the airborne bag due to its not closing up around the occupant but this was part of the design. The airborne bag was made bigger and had flaps to wrap around the occupant who could be inside fully clothed. By opening the flaps, he could easily and quickly get out, ready for action. The lightweight bag was made in the traditional sense of a sleeping bag and more snugly covered the occupant for sleeping in more secure surroundings.

• • • • •

167

The lightweight bag (left) and airborne bag (right).

Showing the lightweight bag with occupant.

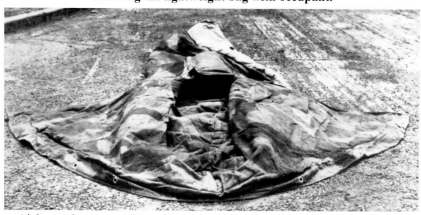
Airborne bag opened showing flaps and part of the canvas underlining.

• • • • •

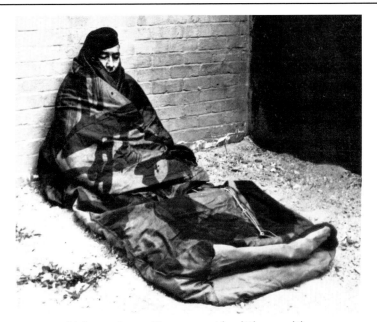

Airborne bag with occupant in sitting position.

Showing gap left by the flaps around the occupant's shoulders.

· · · · ·

169

British and Commonwealth *General Service Blankets* produced during the Second World War were made from 100 percent wool. This maximized their warmth potential even when wet and wool proves to be more fire retardant than most other compositions used for producing blankets. While some examples will have small manufacturer tags sewn near one corner or a government proof mark ink stamped somewhere, the method of identifying the item as military issue is the continuous pattern printed or stitched on both sides of the blanket. Generally the colour will range from light grey to dark grey and they are 48-50 inches wide and 74-78 inches long. Some examples that are shown on this page can also be seen in the colour section of this book since some of the patterns don't come through when converted to black & white images. Two British-made examples are shown at the top of the blankets photo-

graph on this page. The topmost is a charcoal grey colour with three red thin red stripes running the length of the center. The next Brit-

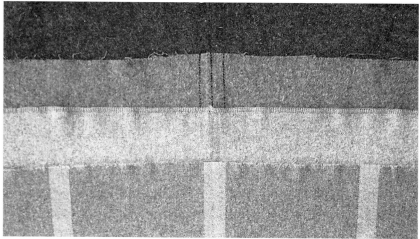

· · · · ·

ish-made example is a lighter grey colour with three black stripes located as described with the previous blanket. An even lighter grey coloured Canadian-made blank is next in the stack which features a light green 7/8" wide stripe running down the center. The short edges of the blanket are edged with this same colour to prevent it from unraveling. This was also done on some British and Australian produced blankets. This example has a Canadian Broad Arrow ink stamp which is 2.5 inches across. The final example shown is Australian-made and it is grey with three blue stripes. One stripe is in the center and then another is on each side 11 inches away. Each stripe is 1 3/4" wide and each of the outer stripes has a red lining stitch on the inside edge. This example has raw short edges and a production tag from 1944. Other examples tagged from 1942 and 1943 have blue edge stitching on the short edges.

Wounded British soldiers on stretchers covered with dark wool blankets, waiting to be loaded onto trains after being brought home from France on a British hospital ship. NOV 1939.

· · · · ·

171

A wide range of tents saw service with the British military forces during the Second World War. These were generally made of waterproof canvas but some lightweight mountain and arctic tents were made from nylon. While not widely used during the war, nylon had been patented by DuPont in 1935 and introduced as a commercial miracle fibre in 1938. In terms of tent nomenclature, the word single indicates one layer of material while double is two separate layers which provides additional insulation from the cold and offered greater protection from wind and rain. Examples of this are the ***Tents, Marquee, General Service, Single*** which had a floor space of 31 feet by 16 feet, and the ***Tents, Ridge, Double, Large*** which had a floor space 14 feet by 14 feet. Examples of the latter can be seen in the photograph below. The front and rear flaps are open for ventilation.

British soldiers running out of a ridge tent at their camp in the desert near Cairo. Maadi, Egypt – JUL 1940.

Circular Tents, also known as Bell Tents, are one of the earliest forms of British military campaign tents. The last pattern produced was officially listed as ***Tents, CS (Circular Single) Mark V***. This had a floor space 13 feet 6 inches in diameter and was made obsolescent in 1946. It used a two-section central pole that was 9 feet 9 inches long and could be used with a Mark III wooden floor that was assembled from four quarter-circle sections. The tent required an area 20 feet in diameter due to the rope lines and used 47 small sized wooden tent pegs.

· · · · ·

Circular Tents were produced in white coloured canvas before the war and in shades of light khaki to dark brown during the war. Accommodations were as follows:

Generals, colonels and C.O.s	1	per tent.
Other officers	3	per tent.
Warrant officers	5	per tent.
Serjeants	7	per tent.
Men	15	per tent.

Scottish troops in a temporary overflow tent city consisting of Circular Tents on the perimeter of a permanent base camp.

The mountains of Mourne by moonlight near Ballykinlar, Northern Ireland.

· · · · ·

173

A Ford GP parked in front of a Circular Tent encampment of the 1st Airborne Division. Note the steering wheel which has been cut down on this early pattern jeep, to allow it to be loaded into a glider. 29 AUG 1942.

The *Tent, Officer's, General Service* could accommodate one or

two officers. It had a central ridge that was supported by 6-foot tall uprights at each end. The floor space was 6 feet six inches long by 6 feet six inches wide.

· · · · ·

An attempt was made during the war to standardize tents into classes and eliminate a number of the specialized tents that were in service. This had been done in the United States with the General Purpose (G.P.) small, medium and large series of tents. The ***Tents, 80-Pounds, General Service*** (small) had a floor space of 8 feet by 14 feet with a central ridge beam and 7-foot tall uprights at each end. This tent could accommodate 8 British soldiers or 10 Native soldiers. It replaced the ***Tents, Shelter, Royal Artillery*** that had a floor space of 9 feet by 7 feet, the ***Tents, Shelter, Royal Engineers*** that had a floor space of 4 feet by 10 feet, the ***Tents, Telegraph*** that had a floor space of 10 feet by 7 feet 6 inches and the ***Tents, Wireless Station*** that had a floor space of 7 feet by 6 feet 6 inches. The ***Tents, 160-Pounds, General Service*** (large) had a floor space of 14 feet by 14 feet with a central ridge beam and three 7-foot tall uprights with one at each end and one in the middle. This tent could accommodate 16 British soldiers or 20 Native soldiers. It replaced all patterns of ***Circular Tents***, the ***Tents, Ridge Double, Small*** which had a floor space of 10 feet by 10 feet, and the ***Tents, Ridge Double, Large*** which had a floor space of 14 feet by 14 feet. These General Service tents were made from water resistant canvas with colours ranging from khaki to dark brown and had an additional fly that was stretched over the top to make them waterproof and to help reduce heat from the sun.

Front view of a General Service 80 pound tent.

· · · · ·

Marquee Tents had a high roof for increased air circulation, supported by a short central ridge beam with a pair of 15-foot tall uprights. The canvas slopes from the beam to a perimeter of shorter 5-foot tall uprights at the outer walls. These were often used in association with field hospitals and could accommodate 16 healthy British troops or 8 sick or wounded troops. The **Tents, Marquee, G.S. Double** had a floor space of 29 feet by 14 feet and the **Tents, Marquee, G.S. Single** had a floor space of 31 feet by 16 feet. The **Tents, Operating** had a floor space of 20 feet by 14 feet.

A Voluntary Aid Detachment at the 1st Australian General Hospital driving in a tent peg which was loosened by heavy rain. Gaza, Palestine – 25 DEC 1941.

General view of the tented wards of the 2/11th Australian Field Ambulance at El Alamein. Western Desert, Egypt – 22 JUL 1942.

. . . . .

The *Tent, Indian Pattern, 40-Pound* had a floor space of 7 feet by 6 feet. It featured a central ridge beam that was held upright by a 7 foot tall pole at the front and rear. This was used to house 1 British or Indian Warrant officer or N.C.O., or 4 Indian soldiers.

The *Tent, Indian Pattern, Privates*, also known as the *Tent, European Pattern, Indian Personnel* were very heavy and had a floor space of 18 feet by 18 feet. The central ridge beam was 12 feet 6 inches high and the side walls were 5 feet 6 inches tall. Like the 160 pound General Service tent, this was used to house 16 British soldiers or 20 Indian soldiers. The photograph above shows two examples that were brought back to Australia from the Middle East by the 2/1st Australian General Hospital. Guildford, Western Australia – SEPT 1942.

· · · · ·

Several patterns of *Bivouac Tents* were produced during the war and they were intended to each accommodate two men. They were a one piece design unlike the types utilized by German and American soldiers. This made setting up the tent a little quicker and easier while also eliminating buttons that could be pulled off and lost which would create gaps in the walls. The **Tent, Bivouac, Mosquito Proof** had a floor space of 7 feet by 6 feet and had 3-foot long wooden poles at the front and back. Each end had a pair of flaps that could be laced together when they needed to be closed for wind or inclement weather. The flaps on the front hang straight down so it is easier to get into and out of the tent. The flaps at the back form a triangle as they slope outward and down to the ground. Tents produced early in the war were made from various shades of khaki and brown cotton with a fairly porous weave of 30 x 40 strands per inch, and this helped them to breathe in temperate climates. This also meant they would leak initially when it rained. Water droplets would strike the outer surface and splatter through the cloth until the material became saturated and swelled up. The **Tent, Bivouac, Sandfly Proof** was identical in every way with the exception of having a heavier 120 x 120 strand per inch weave. They offered superior protection from the rain and from the tiny biting Sandfly or Midge, which is about the size of a pinhead, but these heavier tents were prone to being extremely hot. The trade off wasn't worth the fifty percent increase

· · · · ·

in production costs per tent and this pattern was made obsolescent before the end of the war. A dark green version with insect netting at the ends was produced very late in the war and this seems to have prevailed into the post war years. The netting was

Captain W. A. Dargie, official Australian War Artist at his camp. Veve, Greece - 7 APR 1945.

often torn out though because it got in the way while trying to quickly exit the tent and it restricted air flow which could make the tent hot.

The *Tent, Bivouac, Mountain, Light*, pictured below, had a floor space of 5 feet by 6 feet and was designed to withstand high winds and blizzard conditions. It had a weight of 13 pounds including the oversized, sewn on ground sheet. The front had two poles which were joined at the top and sloped to the outside lower front corners. This ensured a quick entry or exit through the unobstructed vestibule. A single vertical pole held the roof up at the back.

Parachutist Fred Swinford about to enjoy his weekly beer ration.

. . . . .

British infantry on the slopes facing Mount Sole on the 5th Army sector of the mountain ridges before Bologna are supplied with food and ammunition by an Italian Mule Pack Company. The mules are stabled in a disused railway tunnel at the foot of the hills just outside the village La Quereia. The journey to the forward positions takes 1 ¾ hours and the infantry are relieved after every 48 hours in view of the bad weather and living conditions. November – 1944.

Private Albert Vincent, Royal Canadian Ordnance Corps (R.C.O.C.) emerges from his tent north of Ortona, Italy. 15 FEB 1944. Note that his tent has been raised and he used crates for lower walls.

. . . . .

A series of tents that were assembled from pinned together sections of metal tubing were known as portable shelters. These had individual side and roof section panels that were hung on the tubing framework. One example is the **Shelters, Portable Number 5** which had a floor space 40 feet by 20 and this was used for supply units. Another smaller example is the *Shelters, Portable Number 12* which was known as the *Airborne Shelter.* These could be broken down to fit into a C.L.E. Mark III drop container for aerial deployment. These saw service with men of the Royal Army Medical Corps while attached to the 1st Airborne Division during the fighting for Arnhem in September 1944. The wall panels had a disruptive pattern painted on the sides as can be seen in the photograph below.

Signalmen of the 1st Airborne Division have a game of cricket. Lance Corporal M. A. Bate is at the crease. Fulbeck, Lincolnshire, England - 31 JUL 1944.

. . . . .

Troop tents at a British Army camp near one of the Great Pyramids. Giza, Egypt – JUL 1940. (above)

A Mobile Bath Unit sets up a portable shelter tent with Rutherford Type W oil burner and water boiler. England - 1940.

Lieutenant W. M. Robb of the Australian Army Education Service, Headquarters, 1st Australian Armoured Division issues a library book to Trooper R. A. Jackson. Walebing, Western Australia - 13 AUG 1943.

. . . . .

An office tent erected across an Australian 3-Ton Chevrolet Lorry.

An office tent erected across an Australian 3-Ton Chevrolet Lorry. (rear view of above vehicle)

Another office tent erected across an Australian 1-Ton Ford truck.

A Signals tent erected across an Australian 15-CWT truck.

• • • • •

A *Dugout* is a temporary shelter created from a hole or depression in the ground, which has some form of protective cover over the top. The cover can vary depending on what it is intended to protect the soldier from while in the field. For protection from the elements, the cape or ground sheet could be used with the edges being covered with soil except for where the entrance was located. For protection from shrapnel, bomb fragments or other falling debris, logs or a piece of tin or lumber were often used and then a thick layer of soil was added to the top. This wouldn't help for a direct hit but made a big difference with a near miss. In temperate regions, sleeping dugouts were built with netting covers since biting insects tend to feed at night. A tightly closed up tent provided protection but no ventilation.

An example of this last type can be seen in the diagram on the facing page. And a cross-section of the netting that was used can be seen below on a 1945 dated net. The central top area consists of dark green coloured netting with cloth reinforcements spanning it in several places. The lower perimeter is made of lightweight dark khaki coloured linen which has sand pockets sewn on midway between the bottom edge and the netting. When the sand pockets are filled, they weigh the lower edge of the netting down so the remaining linen skirting will lie on the ground when the central netting is elevated using either poles or ropes depending on the site selected for the Dugout. The Mosquito-proof and Sand-fly-proof Bivouac Tents also have sand pockets sewn onto the lower skirting for this same purpose.

· · · · ·

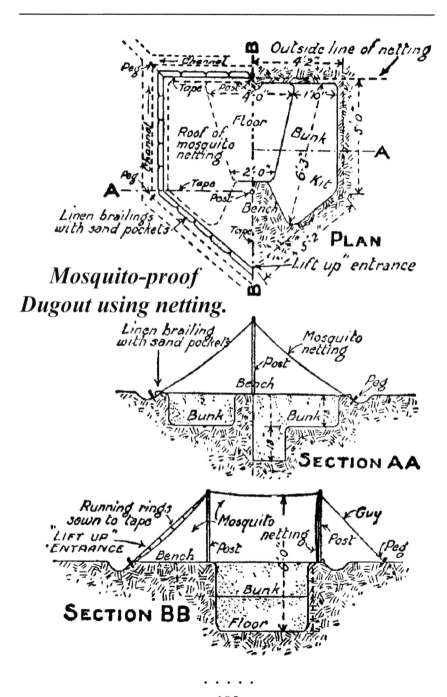

PLAN

Outside line of netting
Peg
Channel
Tape
Post
Floor
Roof of mosquito netting
Bunk
Kit
Bench
Tape
Post
Peg
Channel
Tape
Linen brailings with sand pockets
Lift up" entrance

4'2"
4'0"
1'10"
5'0"
2'0"
6'3"
5'2"

Mosquito-proof Dugout using netting.

Linen brailing with sand pockets
Mosquito netting
Post
Bench
Peg
Bunk
Bunk

SECTION AA

Running rings sown to tape
"LIFT UP" ENTRANCE
Mosquito netting
Guy
Post
Post
Peg
Bench
Bunk
Floor

SECTION BB

· · · · ·

185

The Australian Military Forces introduced a new Cape-Shelter in June 1945 which was intended to cover all needed situations a soldier might have for a personal shelter. It was similar to the German Zeltbahn in being a sheet of rubberized fabric with a closeable opening in the center. This new pattern was 6 feet 6 inches by 5 feet 4 inches. It could be used as a waterproof cape by pulling it over the body with the head passing through the central opening. Or the central opening could be closed

using a drawstring and then it would serve as a groundsheet or as a half-shelter. Two Cape-Shelters could also be joined to form a two-man bivouac by means of press studs along the edges in a similar way to the U.S. pattern shelter half.

Royal Canadian Engineers (R.C.E.) Sapper Joe Iaci of the 6th Field Company coming out of his dugout. Normandy, France - 3 JUL 1944.

· · · · ·

A web *Arms Rack* was used in tents by soldiers issued with rifles. This consisted of a short leather strap that had twelve web loops riveted to it. The strap had a roller buckle and could be cinched around the central pole on a Circular Tent or one of the thicker pattern uprights used on the Marque Tents. For use, the muzzle of a rifle was simply slipped through one of the loops and the rifle butt would rest on the ground.

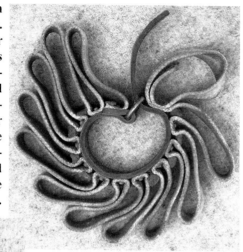

The *Mallet, Tent Mark II* with a wooden head 6 inches by 3.25 inches and an Ash oval handle that was 1 foot 7 inches long. It was issued for use with all of the various types and sizes of British tent pins used during WWII. Much larger wooden mallets were also produced as tools used for pile-driving and other heavier work. They will work to drive tent pins but at increased risk of splitting them in the case of wooden patterns. Different types of *Tent Pins* were issued for use with the various patterns of tents. Most tended to be the wooden large 20 inch or wooden small 13 inch pattern. Metal tent pins had been used more often in the pre-war years. These included steel 3 foot and galvanized iron 8 inch, 10 inch, 12 inch, 15 inch and 18 inch patterns. In addition to tent pins and mallets, tent pin bags and tent valises were also issued with the tents.

• • • • •

Lunchtime in a desert fighting hole. Tobruk, Libya – 1 SEPT 1941.

A Royal Australian Engineer having lunch on a bridge rests his back against a Japanese bridge post. The red shield of a Salvation Army sign can be seen in the background. Dumpu, New Guinea – 3 APR 1944. (left)

A Lieutenant of the Australian Independent Company eating lunch from his field operations ration. Ramu Valley, New Guinea – 20 OCT 1943. (right)

· · · · ·

Daily bread delivery. Western Desert – 1942.

The British military issue tin opener. (above and below)

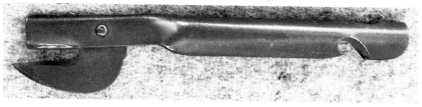

Three sizes of British wartime biscuit tins. The plain flour biscuits were a component of many of the daily meals.

Biscuits 25 lbs.

W.G. CLARKE & SONS 1929 L.TD

Packed 5/41

E. 11/42

67 Pkts. at 6ozs.

WELFARE BISCUITS

KEARLEY & TONGE L.TD

PACKED 7 43
Number of Biscuits per tin 32
Weight in Tin 15 lbs.
Moisture Content not more than 4 %

Biscuits – 7½ lbs.

P.F. & C.º L.TD

Packed 12/43

• • • • •

Men of the Australian Armed Forces stack bulk supplies at a service depot. 14 OCT 1942.

Members of the 2/22 Supply Depot Platoon loading rations on a food storage depot truck for transport to a stores issue depot. The unit holds bulk supplies including rations, petrol and ammunition for the entire 6th Division.

Breaking up rations into company lots in the ration store of the 25th Infantry Battalion. 9 AUG 1944.

Staff Sergeant L.W. Pentecost, C Company, 9th Infantry Battalion, sorting tinned rations for distribution to individual platoons. Torokina Area, Bougainville - 30 NOV 1944.

. . . . .

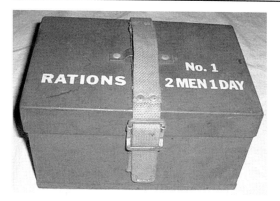

1942 dated British survival ration issued to crews of armoured fighting vehicles. This example was intended to sustain two men for one day.

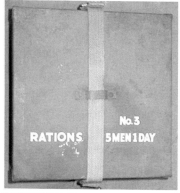

British 1942 dated tank crew survival ration intended to sustain five men for one day. The metal box measures 10 inches by 10 inches by 6 inches.

Trailers of the 29th Infantry Brigade loaded with rations being towed by a tractor, float across the Ogorata River which was flooded due to heavy rainfall.

• • • • •

The standard liquid carrying container in use by the British military forces at the beginning of the war was the *2-Gallon Can* made from pressed steel. They were often called *POW Cans*, short for *Petrol-Oil-Water*. The design was a simple metal box that had a screw on cap near one corner and a flat carrying handle that was diagonal to the cap to make it easier to pour. These had already been in service before the First World War and were readily used by civilian and commercial entities as well. A wide range of funnels were available for this pattern can since it could be used for so many things. 1-Gallon cans were also produced and these are virtually the same as the larger 2-gallon cans with the exception of their volume. They have the same height but are half the width as if one of the larger cans were simply cut in half. The arrangement on the top with the handle and cap are also the same as found on the 2-gallon can with the cap having the same size but the handle being shorter.

A few examples of 2-gallon cans can be seen above. Top left is a British military 1939 dated can, top right is a galvanized metal Australian military can, bottom left is a Canadian military 1944 dated can and the bottom right is a commercial can dated 1937.

· · · · ·

Examples of three types of funnel that were used with the 2-gallon cans during the WWII time period. The long curved version is flexible and has a built in vent near where it attaches to the can to help it burp while pouring. The pattern at the bottom of the page was useful for petrol when the contents of the can needed to be completely emptied. The short pattern at the right has a chain soldered onto the base and an s-clip to keep it with the can when not being used.

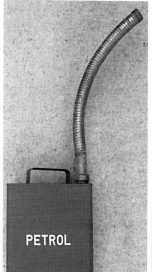

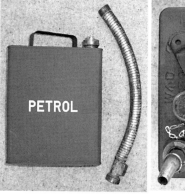

A 200 gallon Bedford M.W.C. 15-cwt water bowser provides a source of clean water for men of the RAMC 10th Field Hygiene Section who are filling 2-gallon cans. Normandy - 12 JUN 1944.

The 2-Gallon Can was commonly used with the Vickers Medium Machine Gun as a water condenser can. An example of one type of condenser can is shown on the left in the photograph above with spare asbestos string wrapped around the carrying handle. This was used as waterproof packing when a barrel needed to be changed out. The 2-Gallon Can on the right in the same photograph is fitted with a WWII Australian 2-Gallon Can Carrier. The Roko buckles at the top on the can are used to secure it in the carrier. The Roko buckles on the facing side are used to fasten the carrier to a soldiers Web Equipment Braces in the same way a water bottle would be worn.

· · · · ·

Filling a water tank on a truck from a standpipe at the El Imayid water point. Water for the troops in the forward area had to be transported more than 20 miles from this point. El Imayid, Egypt - 17 JUL 1942.

The scene at the El Imayid watering point. The water tins being filled were originally two-gallon petrol tins. El Imayid, Egypt - 17 JUL 1942.

A captured Italian water tank pressed into service by the Allies. Troops are seen drawing their ration of water from the water truck operated by a British Royal Army Service Corps unit. Tobruk, Libya – 1941.

. . . . .

The *4-Gallon Can* was another liquid container that was available in large quantities and these were pressed into service during the early war years. This was the case particularly in North Africa, where they were brought in filled with petrol and then reused for holding water since this commodity wasn't readily available at times. These cans came in several similar designs that were usually made from tinned iron. They were not very durable, especially once they had been opened and needed to be used again. And they tended to split at the seams if jostled around, dropped or simply had too much pressure applied to them which was often the case when stacked inside the hold of a ship or in the back of a lorry. As such, they were commonly known as *Flimsies*. Some had filling lids that were press sealed on and then had to be punctured to pry the lid out to get to the contents. Others had lightweight metal caps since they were not originally designed to be reused. A heavier duty pressed steel version also saw limited use and these had a proper screw cap. They tend to be a British military pattern with War Department markings and were mostly used in the United Kingdom and in France at the outbreak of the war.

The watering point at Ain Dalla, situated in the Western Desert of Egypt. Men of the Long Range Desert Group are filling 4-gallon *flimsies*.

· · · · ·

British WWII *5-Gallon Can* was copied from the pattern developed by the Germans. They are all marked on the side near the top with W /|\ D over the date and have the maker's mark, logo or initials in the center. Some cans had the word WATER pressed into the lower sides in an attempt to dedicate them to that purpose. These appear to be very rare today, probably because most never had fuel

or oil inside to prevent them from rusting out. Most of the *Jerry Cans* were used to carry whatever was needed at the time regardless of markings and original purpose.

· · · · ·

Four different wartime production British-made cans are shown above for size comparison. From left to right, they are a C.L.E. Drop Container 5-Gallon Cylinder and the standard 5-Gallon, 2-Gallon and 1-Gallon pressed steel cans.

The Central Landing Establishment (C.L.E.) had developed a range of drop containers for the purpose of safely delivering weapons and supplies by air with parachutes. Special 3-Gallon canvas bags had been developed for delivering water but they were not adequate for use with petrol or oil. So a new type of canister needed to be created that could survive a rough landing while maximizing the use of available space in one of the existing patterns of drop containers. 5-Gallon cylindrical containers with a corrugated body for strength were approved and three of these could be placed inside a *C.L.E. Type C Container.* The top was flat and tapered in at the edges and this could fit into the recessed bottom of another of the cylinders when packed into a drop container. Two patterns of filler caps exist, the type found on German and British 5-Gallon cans and a flat round cap which was in use on the heavier pattern 4-Gallon cans. All known examples of both patterns were produced in 1943 and quantities would seem to be limited as not many are known to exist today.

· · · · ·

A British sergeant in Italy, sits on an air dropped 5-gallon petrol cylinder while attempting to clean mud from his boots. Two U.S. pattern 5-gallon fuel cans can be seen beside him at the right.

The tops (below) of a 5-Gallon Cylinder and a standard 5-Gallon Can.

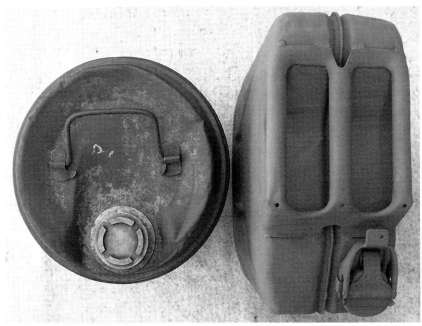

. . . . .

Petrol and Oil 4-Gallon drums stacked at the Eastern Command's bulk issue depot.

A German petrol dump captured during the 8th Army's advance. Libya – Nov 1941.

A team of pack mules is lead by British troops from a supply point loaded down with ammunition and water in five gallon fuel cans.

• • • • •

Chapter 5 - Tools and Instruments

Forward observation post of "B" Battery, 1st Field Regiment, Royal Canadian Artillery. (L-R): Gunner Chuck Drickerson (Rangefinder), Gunner Jim Tulley (Field Telephone), Regimental Sergeant-Major G. Doug Gilpin (Binoculars), Captain George E. Baxter (Map Board) ands Gunner Hugh Graham (Radio).

· · · · ·

Optics

A wide range of optics were manufactured and issued in several patterns and magnifications during the war. These included binoculars, monoculars, telescopes, stereoscopic telescopes and rangefinders. In general optics are rated by their power which is the magnification expressed as a number followed by an "X", and the diameter of the objective lens measured in millimeters. The objective lens is the larger of the lenses on an optic and it collects the light needed to project the image through internal prisms and out of the ocular at the eyepiece and into the view's eye. In the case of binoculars, six main British military patterns were introduced over the years from 1907 through 1936 and these were the Number 1 (8x20), Number 2 (6x30), Number 3 (6x20), Number 4 (5x40), Number 5 (7x50) and the Number 6 (4x24). While many of these were still in service, only the Number 2 and Number 5 patterns were in widespread production and issued to the army during the Second World War. Many other sizes of binoculars and monoculars continued to be produced for special purposes including low power night glasses and high power field glasses but these were in limited numbers.

Three British soldiers with binoculars, spotter's telescope and range finder, assigned to the U.S. Fifth Army, looking out their farmhouse observation post window down into a valley as they pinpoint the aim of artillery on German patrols while an African American 92nd Infantry Division "Buffalo Soldier" relays information to gun batteries. Italy – APR 1945.

· · · · ·

The *Number 2 Prismatic 6x30 Binoculars* were the standard general service optics in use by the British and Commonwealth army during the Second World War. There were three patterns produced by a number of manufactures including Ross, Kershaw, Watson & Baker, Bausch & Lomb, Taylor-Hobson, and Research Enterprises Limited (REL) of Canada. The Mark I pattern had plain eyepieces while the Mark II and Mark III patterns had graticule markings in the focal plane of the eyepieces which were ½ degree apart with heights of ¼, ½ and 1 degree. In addition to the graticule markings, the Mark III pattern also had four ports, closed with round-head machine screws, that provided for nitrogen filling. This kept the optics fog-proof and also provided a way to dry out the internal parts if the binoculars were immersed in water. Focusing for all patterns was done by rotating the eyepieces individually. The web equipment 1937 pattern and 1944 pattern binocular cases were designed to hold a standard pair of 6x30 binoculars.

A squadron leader photographed in 1941 posing with 6x30 binoculars beside his armoured car. Note the early pattern binocular case he wears which has no provisions for attaching a shoulder strap at the sides.

· · · · ·

Two pairs of 6x30 Number 2 binoculars made by Kershaw and Watson-Baker.

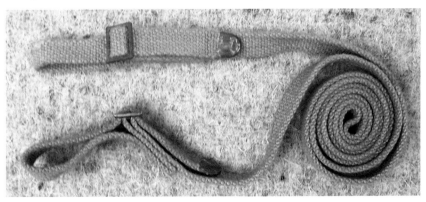

Most wartime military binoculars were issued with a leather or webbing neck strap. In the case of the webbing straps, the length was 32 inches between the adjustment buckles found at each end and the width was 5/16 of an inch. The adjusting ends had an additional five inches of webbing for forming a loop back to itself after being threaded though built in hangers on the bodies of the binoculars.

· · · · ·

The two 6x30 binoculars above show the difference between Kershaw 1943 produced Mark II (top) and Kershaw 1944 Mark III (bottom) examples. The four screw-plugged gas ports can be seen on the Mark III binoculars. Nitrogen purging of the housings eliminated oxygen that could fog up the inside of the prisms and lenses. Moisture in the air could also start fungal growth inside the housings under tropical conditions which greatly reduced the functionality of the binoculars and was difficult to remove. This gas port feature can be found on late production Number 5 binoculars in the same locations.

Typical markings found on wartime produced Number 2 pattern binoculars.

· · · · ·

205

The British *Number 5 pattern 7x50 Binoculars* were first introduced in 1935 and progressed through five Marks by the time the war ended. With a length of 8.5 inches, these were considerably larger than the standard issue Number 2 pattern binoculars which had a length of only 4.75 inches. Makers included Ross, Barr & Stroud, and Northern Light Industries (NLI). These higher power optics were primarily issued to artillery and armoured units but were often seen with higher ranking field officers as well. The progression of features advanced parallel to those seen with the Number 2 pattern binoculars. This included graticules marked with increments ½ degree apart and later war production models having ports for nitrogen gas filling and internal drying to keep them fog proof which came about in 1944. As with most other wartime produced binoculars, the eyepieces are individually focused. When not in use, the binoculars were carried in their issue leather case that was usually marked "BINOCULARS PRISMATIC NO. 5 CASE Mk.1." on top of the lid.

· · · · ·

Sergeant I.F. Chase with a pair of British 7x50 binoculars photographed cleaning his mess tin while sitting in the side of a General Motors T17E1 Staghound armoured car of the South Alberta Regiment. Bad Zwischenahn, Germany - 29 APR 1945.

Major-General Richard Gale, commander of the British 6th Airborne Division, photographed wearing a full-length zipper opening Denison smock and a pair of British 7x50 binoculars.

• • • • •

A more compact 7x50 binocular was produced by at least three companies in North America for use by the British and Commonwealth forces. These were Bausch & Lomb and Optical & Film, both based in the U.S.A., and Research Enterprises Limited (REL) of Canada. This base design was already being produced by several other optical firms for the U.S. army as the M17, and for the U.S, navy as the M28. The binoculars were 7.25 inches tall and had coated optics which helped to make them less reflective. The main housings had a black vinylite covering which made them easier to hold when wet. This also reduced the amount of sound they made when coming into contact with other hard objects. Focusing was achieved by rotating the individual eyepieces in or out as needed.

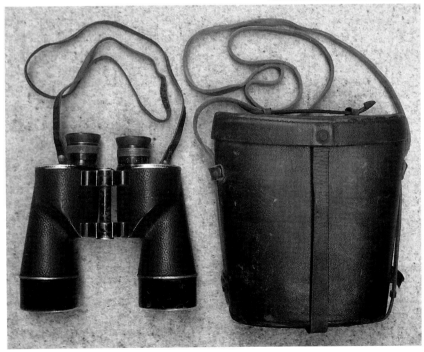

. . . . .

The top pair of 7 x 50 binoculars shown on this page was produced by Bausch & Lomb in the United States during 1941. The lower pair was produced during 1944 by Research Enterprises Limited in Canada. The example shown on the facing page was produced in the United States by Optical & Film Supply Company of New York. These binoculars are all focused by individually rotating the eyepieces in or out as needed until a clear image can be seen.

The leather case shown with the binoculars on the facing page has an adjustable shoulder sling as well as a carrying handle on the lid. It was manufactured by Bausch & Lomb.

· · · · ·

Monoculars proved to be a good economical solution to providing optics to the military during periods where shortages in equipment existed. This was particularly true during the early years of the war considering the tremendous amount of equipment that was abandoned, lost or destroyed following the evacuation of the B.E.F. from Dunkirk which began on 26 May 1940 and continued for nine more days. Wartime monoculars were simply half of a pair of binoculars as opposed to being a small fixed length tube telescope that is common today. Some examples had their origins as binoculars which were disassembled for salvage when it wasn't practical to make repairs to one side and others were produced through the elimination of the assembly steps at the factory where the left and right optics would have been joined together as binoculars. Factory-made monoculars also existed before the war on the civilian market and they were popular among hiking and camping enthusiasts due to their being small and lightweight. Many of these monoculars made their way into military service and will be Broad Arrow marked while others were simply private purchased by individual soldiers.

The 10x and 6x monoculars at the left were produced from cannibalized binoculars while the cased 6x monocular above was purpose built by Barr & Stroud.

· · · · ·

A leather cased set of moderating lenses was issued with binoculars to soldiers fighting in North Africa and other regions where the sun make the environment very bright. Their purpose was to  reduce the viewing size of the eyepieces and thereby restrict the amount of light that passed through the binoculars and into the eyes. The leather case had loops on the back so it could be connected to the neck strap of the binoculars. The case was velvet lined and had slots to hold four lens covers which simply fit snuggly over the eyepieces on the binoculars when needed.

Pictured at the left is a prewar German monocular produced by Carl Zeiss which feature a British government Broad Arrow. The leather case they were issued with was produced by Ross Ltd. Opticians of London.

Night glasses are binoculars that provided optical passive night vision capability without the aid of fragile electronic light amplifiers or a supplemental source of light as found with modern night vision starlight and infrared systems. For optimal results, night glasses require large objective lenses in the front as well as large ocular lenses at the eyepieces and a relatively low magnification in relation to the objectives. The ratio between the size of the objective and the magnification is typically seven or more.

When exploring physics, the objectives gather and intensify the light optically and project it into the eyes. The intensity of light falls off at a rate equal to the inverse of the distance squared. Essentially an object appears darker by a factor of four each time the distance viewed is doubled. This explains why an object viewed at night appears to lose focus and eventually disappears when you move away from it. The

· · · · ·

correlation to this is a lens gathers four times the light each time its size is doubled. A 50mm objective lens has a light gathering ability 52 times greater than the unaided human eye. But passive optics cannot make an object brighter than it actually is regardless of the size of the objective lens because a percentage of the light collected is used to brighten it. And magnification also requires a percentage of the collected light. This is why standard field glasses that work well in the daytime produce a dim image when used at night.

Lieutenant-General Browning photographed wearing a pair of night glasses that he used during Operation Market Garden (above). The pictured WWII night glasses on this and the facing page were produced in 1944 and are 2.5x50mm giving a ratio of 20. The maximum power magnification for minimal night vision capability would be 7x with a 50mm objective, so while this pair of optics had limited benefits during the daytime, they excelled when used at night. Note that these have a central focus dial that moves the eyepieces forward and backward when rotated to achieve a crisp image. A feature found on almost all modern non-automatic focusing binoculars today.

· · · · ·

213

The device pictured on this page is an example of one of the world's first infrared receivers which was produced for use by special units within the British military during the Second World War. In modern terminology, this item would be classed as a Zero Generation Night Vision Monocular. It had the capability of electronically collecting infrared radiation and forming an electron image on a phosphor screen. Civilian development of see-in-the-dark technology began in 1939 and the first British military devices were in use during 1943. These early production receivers were not used as one might first think to find enemy sentries in the dark. They were actually used to detect signals that were transmitted using lamps equipped with infrared filters since they would otherwise be invisible and undetectable by the naked eye. An example of use would be

· · · · ·

Royal Marine Commando SBS troops equipped with infrared receivers being able to locate and approach a designated beach landing site that had been marked with an infrared beacon. They could likewise receive securely transmitted infrared signals from a naval submarine or ship that was to pick them up upon completion of an operation.

The infrared receiver had a pattern number O.S. 960 G.A. and its signals equipment code was ZA 23119. The device had a weight of approximately 3.5 pounds and was issued with a leather case marked O.S. 1606A. The housing for the electronic components and a large battery was produced from dark green painted metal and the end caps were soldered on to ensure waterproof operation. To make the device easier to hold when wet, a khaki canvas wrapping was glued around the center of the housing. The device was activated by pressing a single button on the side of the housing.

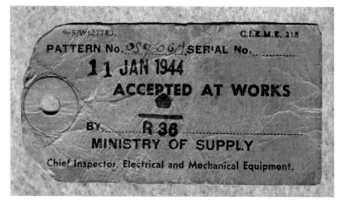

. . . . .

The first non-admiralty pattern telescope adopted by the British army was the **Signaller Telescope**, which was introduced before the First World War and progressed through seven Marks. The Mark VI "TEL. SIG. (Mk VI) ALSO G.S" was introduced early in 1926 and saw active service during the Second World War. These telescopes were considered a general service instrument and were used by signalers, artillery spotters and snipers. The average length closed was 11.5 inches and they had an extended length of 33.5 inches. A sunshield fitted to the end of the body could be extended a further 3.5-4 inches to block the sun from shinning directly on the objective lens. The sunshield and main body of the telescope were wrapped in leather and there were three tapered sections which could be drawn from the body until the telescope was fully extended. These telescopes typically had a two-inch objective coupled with low and high

A British forward observation post in operation in the mountains overlooking a valley during the 8th Army's advance toward the Sangro River in Italy, 12 OCT 1943.

• • • • •

power oculars providing 15x and 30x magnifications. The ocular not being used would be stored in a separate leather case. A Mark VII pattern telescope was introduced in August 1939 featuring a vulcanized rubber cover on the main body and the sunshield. Production was limited since the Signaller series of telescopes was superseded by the *Scout Regiment Telescope* '"TEL. SCT. REGT." that same year. This new line of telescopes was produced in two marks during the war and they were a lighter design that featured a swivel dust-cover on the eyepiece as well as a filter. Only one ocular was used with these telescopes and it had a 22x magnification. A hard leather case completely enclosed the telescope when not in use and this helped to better protect it when carried in the field by sniper teams.

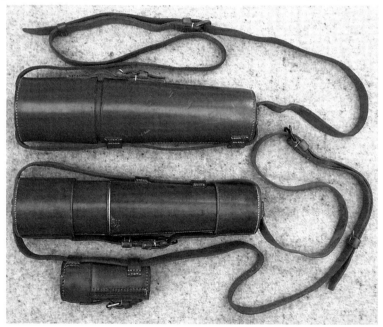

The Signals and G.S. Telescope (bottom) was issued with hard leather end caps. These were connected to each other with a short leather strap to hold them in place on the collapsed telescope. A leather carrying sling was fastened to each end cap as well as to the case for a second eyepiece. The Scout Regiment Telescope (top) had a hard leather carrying case that completely enclosed it to protect it in the field.

• • • • •

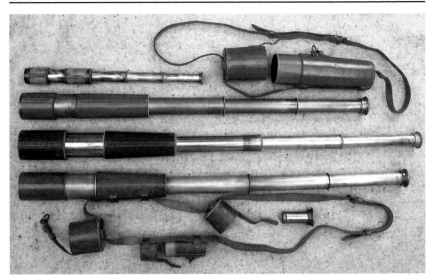

A grouping of telescopes, cases and accessories for size and feature comparison. The small 15x magnification telescope (spyglass) at the top has an objective with a 1.25 inch diameter. The fully extended length is 16.25 inches including the sunshield, with a length of only 5.5 inches completely closed. This example is marked B.C. Ltd & Co. 1942. The open case for a Scout Regiment Telescope is beside it. Beneath them is a wartime Scout Regiment Telescope produced by H. C. Ryland & Son Limited. The next telescope, which is the longest shown, is an Admiralty & Ordnance pattern produced by Stanley. And the last example is a Signaller and General Service Telescope produced by Negretti & Zambra of London with end caps and spare eyepiece case. The high power eyepiece is installed in the telescope and its spare low power eyepiece is shown out of the case beside it.

Pre-war commercial Ross-pattern 20x magnification two draw telescopes like the one shown above were favored by some of the Highland snipers including those in the Lovat Scouts. These were shorter, lighter and less bulky when compared to the official Scout Regiment Telescopes.

· · · · ·

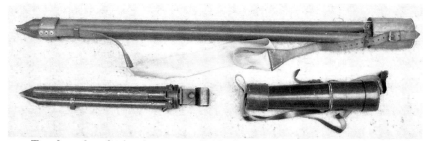

Two lengths of tripod were available for the scout telescopes, a standard length and a modified pattern that was shortened to present a lower profile. The length of the legs on the standard pattern was 33 inches and the shortened pattern had legs that were 14 inches long. The shortened pattern was favored by sniper teams and forward observation posts. A canvas sling was provided for carrying the tripod. A loop at one end was made to fit around the three folded legs to keep them together. An end cap was at the opposite end of the sling and it fit over the telescope mounting clamp.

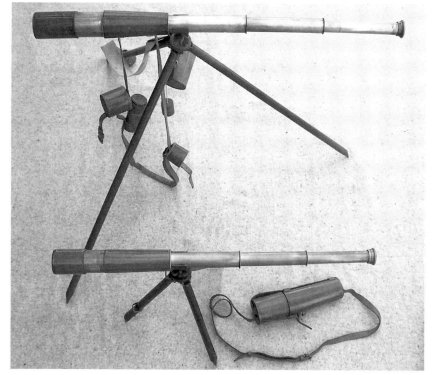

• • • • •

Stereoscopic Telescopes were also known as Trench Binoculars, Rabbit Ears and Donkey Ears. They consisted of a pair of angled tubes with hooded objectives at the top which joined together at the base where two eyepieces were situated. The tubes could be spread apart to increase the field of view and this also increased the clarity of viewed objects. Eye strain was minimal compared to using a single tube telescope for prolonged observations since both eyes remained open during use. These optics were favored for observa-

tion posts since the observer could use them from a more concealed and protected position when compared to traditional in-line optical devices. The Stereoscopic Telescope mounted onto a platform base which

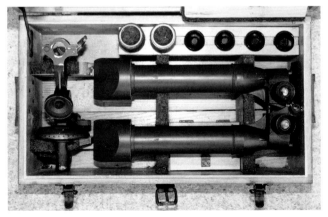

in turn could be placed at the top of a tripod. These devices were produced during both World Wars in the United Kingdom, Canada and Australia.

· · · · ·

Troops comparing observations of an enemy position made with telescopic optics to a compass oriented map to determine coordinates for an artillery barrage.

Range Finders

The *Infantry Range Finder* was used to more accurately determine the distance to a given location. This was critical for machine gun emplacements because they could not ascertain where they were hitting when shooting at extreme ranges. The instrument can be mounted on a tripod or it can be held using a pair of short folding handles. Eyepieces are located in the center of the tube and a rubber facepiece fits over them. Windows with removable covers are situated at each end of the tube and these provide the image seen when looking through the eyepieces. The image displayed is split in half horizontally and one half is upside down. By rotating a dial known as the working head, the images will line up. When they come together exactly, the range can be read from a scale that is superimposed inside one of the eyepieces over the image. Typically several range readings are taken for a given position and these are averaged to get a best range to target.

The photograph at the left shows the range finder with a removable facepiece in place.

This particular range finder is unique in that it was a Barr and Stroud (Scotland) design that was licensed to Research Enterprises Limited (Canada) to produce so they could provide them to China as part of the Mutual Aid Act . The dials and column headings for the range tables all have Chinese characters.

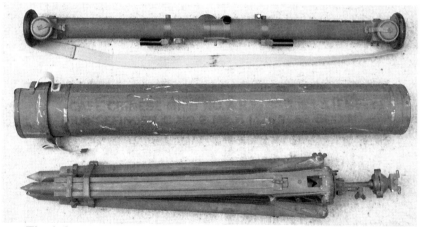

The infantry range finder has its own carrying sling that connects to mounts on each end of the tube. This one was provided with a metal transit tube that has a carrying handle in one end and provisions for a carrying sling on the sides. The tripod pictured below the transit tube was made by R.E.L in 1945 and has adjustable folding legs which are kept closed for transit by a leather strap.

• • • • •

The ***Pocket Periscope*** is a collapsible steel framework with a mirror mounted inside each end. When expanded to a maximum length of 24 inches, it allowed for concealed observations to be made in the same way that boxed trench periscopes were used during the Great War. When collapsed for carriage in the brown canvas case, the periscope is 4.5 inches long, 4.25 inches wide and 2 inches thick. The case has a flap that can be snapped shut in two positions. One was used when the periscope was stored inside and another when the case was empty to make it flatter. The case has a single belt loop on the back. This D /|\ D Mark I example was produced in Australia in 1942 but others have been seen dated 1943 and 1944.

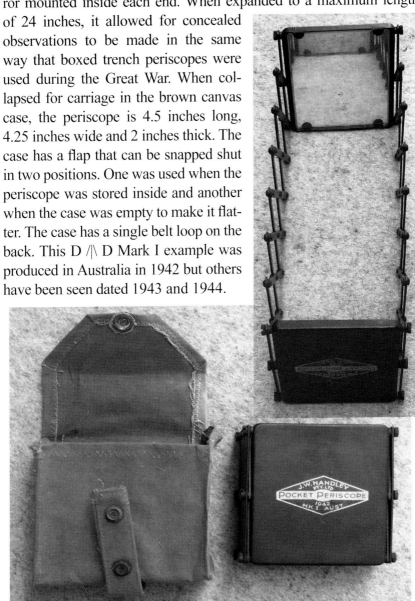

The ***Sun Compass*** is a navigational instrument that was used by the British military forces primarily in North Africa, India and in the Middle East as it required the light of the sun to work. It consists of a circular bearing plate with 0-360 degrees indicated in reverse order around the dial. A time plate in the form of a second circular disk is placed on top of the bearing plate. A vertical rod known as a *Gnomon* is in the center and the two disks rotate around it. The instrument must be firmly held or mounted to a vehicle and then leveled using the attached spirit bubble. Following this, the compass can be oriented based on a published table that includes latitude and date. Shadow angles in half-hourly increments are also published with their corresponding bearings. The shadow from the *Gnomon* is used to determine direction once everything is calibrated.

· · · · ·

The British army **Prismatic Marching Compass** had a housing made of brass with a glass cover. These were filled with oil which was used to dampen the dial made of Mother of Pearl. This was used as an alternative to radium and helped illuminate the markings on the dial at night for ease of reading. The adjustable prismatic lens folds over and was used as a sight and to simultaneously get a sharper reading from the scale around the bezel. The cover has a glass insert with a fine sight hair in the center. Some examples also have the addition of a brass frame on the lid to protect the glass. The thumb screw on the side of the housing is used to tighten the rotating bezel on top so it won't move once it is adjusted.

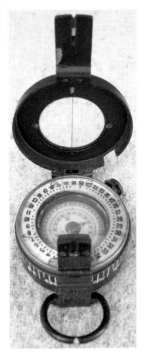

· · · · ·

The *Mark I Marching Compass* was made of bakelite and had an undampened luminescent needle. All markings are in white as are sight reference lines on the housing and below the slot in the mirror inside the lid.

COMPASS,
MAGNETIC, MARCHING, Mk. I.
INSTRUCTIONS FOR USE.
A. To march on a given bearing by day or night :
Rotate ring until given bearing is over luminous arrow. Hold compass level and move it so as to keep luminous needle tip between the two dots on the ring. March along the luminous line on the lid.
B. To read the bearing of a given object :
Hold the compass level and aim the centre line of the lid at the object, tilting the lid as required. Allow the needle to come to rest. Rotate the ring until the luminous needle tip lies between the two dots on the ring. Read the required bearing off the ring at the luminous arrow directly, or by reflection from the mirror in the lid.   Part No. 56005.

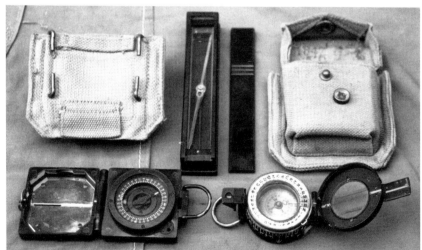

Pictured are both sides of a compass pocket with a British military 1932 dated surveyors compass in between. An escape compass is on the pouch to the right and a bakelite Mark I Marching Compass is at the bottom at the left with a brass Mark III Prismatic Compass besides it.

• • • • •

227

The British made leg compass shown above has a folding cover and it was used primarily by members of the Royal Air Force and Army Flying Pilots. The adjustable leg strap is 21 inches long.

The compass above was produced in 1941 by Short & Mason Ltd of London and has their company name, date, Broad Arrow and a serial number engraved on the back of the case which has a diameter of 1 ¾ inches.

Wrist compasses like the one at the left were issued to some elements of the airborne forces. This example has a bakelite body and thin leather strap.

• • • • •

228

Escape compasses took many forms, such as traditional types in miniature being hidden in something, to wooden matches containing magnetized pieces of metal that would point north when floated in water. Early in the war miniature compasses were concealed inside brass service dress and greatcoat uniform buttons. These buttons were not a part of the battledress blouse so in some cases, special buckles with a compass needle built into the back were available as were normal pressed buttons that could be removed and used as a compass. In each case, the compass needle was balanced and would rotate to indicate north.

The compasses pictured above and at the left are approximate to their actual size. Normally they were issued to S.O.E. agents, reconnaissance units, aircraft pilots and some airborne troops that were often behind enemy lines and potentially at risk of being captured.

Pictured at the right is a British made officer's private purchase pocket compass. The design is similar to the U.S. WWI military pattern but it only has a diameter of 1.375 inches.

· · · · ·

Various patterns of British military stopwatches and interval timers were issued for tasks that required split second measurements. Artillery crews were timed during gun drills, tests were conducted and timed to verify feet per second burn rates for fuzes, glider pilots performed turns based on flying a specific heading for a given number of seconds, etc. The stopwatch pictured at the top of this page was produced by Smiths in England and measures time in 300ths of a second. One full sweep of the main watch hand is three seconds and the inner dial measures elapsed seconds up to 90. The stopwatch at the bottom of the page measures half of one minute per sweep of the hand while the inner dial indicates minutes elapsed up to 15 which would be 30 sweeps. Several patterns of traditional stopwatches were also is-

sued which record one minute per sweep of the main hand and up to thirty minutes on the smaller inner dial. The example shown on this page was produced by Waltham Clock Company in the United States under contract for the British army. They also produced Admiralty pattern anti-submarine stopwatches that were used in conjunction with the *Asdic Apparatus* to plot data needed for depth charging U-boats. This stopwatch is marked "1/5 Sec T.P." on the case back. As with British military issue pocket watches and wristwatches, these all have the broad arrow engraved on the back of the case to indicate government property. All of these timers work by pressing down the crown stopper at the top. The first press activates the timer. A second press stops the timer. The third press resets the timer.

· · · · ·

Calculators and Measuring Devices

Thomas Fowler was an English banker who was born in 1777 and died in 1843. He developed several types of early adding machines which lead to the development of analog pocket calculators that were used by engineers, draughtsmen, and scientists. These first came out around 1898 and were still in use through the mid 1950s. The *Fowler's Calculator* pictured here was used by a Royal Engineer that took part in the Normandy landings and it is a variation of a circular slide rule. There is a printed disc on each side which has multiple scales printed on them. The knob on the top rotates the circular scales that are printed on the disc and the knob on the side positions a black radial line or cursor for taking readings. A second red fixed radial datum line crosses the 12 o'clock position. The scales are based on the properties of logarithms and enable multiplication to be performed by addition and division by subtraction. In addition to multiplication and division, other calculations can be performed including square roots, cube roots, percentages, proportions, cosine and tangents.

Fowler's Calculator with protective case made in Manchester, England.

· · · · ·

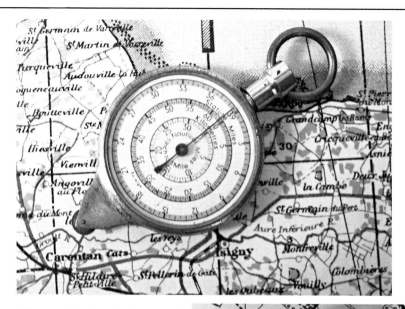

The tool pictured above and at the right is a mechanical **Curvimeter**. The small wheel on the bottom is placed on a map at the designated starting point and then rolled along the path to be traveled to the ending point. As the small wheel turns, the sweep hand on the dial rotates to indicate the distance traveled. This example was used by the Royal Engineer that owned the Fowler's Calculator on the previous page. It can measure up to 39 statute miles or the equivalent number of kilometers or nautical miles depending on the scale you read from on the dial.

· · · · ·

The small British military issue tape measure has a brass case made by Chesterman of Sheffield, England in 1942. Its cloth tape is on a spring loaded reel which winds up when a stud on the back is moved. The larger tape measure has a leather case with a manual winder in the center and was produced in 1939. The tape itself is 100 feet long with markings of inches and feet on one side and links, poles and chains on the other, which used to be common forms of measurement for surveyors. Under this system, 25 links equals 1 pole which is 16.5 feet. 100 links equals 1 chain which is 66 feet.

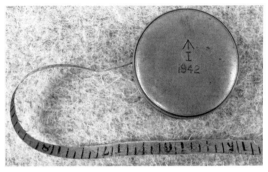

. . . . .

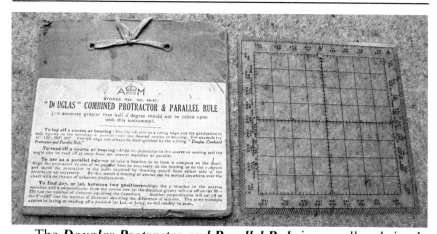

The ***Douglas Protractor and Parallel Rule*** is a small and simple navigational instrument invented by Vice-Admiral Sir Percy Douglas while he was part of the surveying branch of the Royal Navy. It was five inches square and made from clear acrylic with black silkscreen markings. The outer perimeter has a graduated scale marked off in 1 degree increments from 0-360 to replicate the face of a compass. A grommet hole in the center allowed for rapid determination of a heading needed to get from a known point on a map to an intended destination. The map and protractor both need to be aligned with north edges while the protractor is placed on the map with the grommet over the present or estimated position. The heading needed can be read from the protractor where a line from its center to the intended destination strikes the edge. That heading is then followed using a normal compass. Other navigational features that this tool was used for include: determination of magnetic course, bearing from true north, plotting a reciprocal course and plotting current position from two or three bearings. Since the useable space inside armoured fighting vehicles, tanks and aircraft was very confined, this tool became standard issue during the war along with maps and compasses. The Douglas Protractor was issued with a pressboard case to protect it from warping damage in the sun. Basic instructions were printed on affixed labels on each side of the case. This wartime example is Air Ministry marked.

· · · · ·

Test Equipment

The device on this page is a **Demolition Test Set Mark I** made in 1944. It was used for checking resistance and continuity in circuits. The appropriate OHMS are dialed in on the three knobs at the bottom, one for 100s, one for 10s and one for 1s. When the item to be tested is wired to the test set, deflection can be read on the galvanometer. Items missing from this example that would be stored in the compartment on the left side include guncotton, primers, electrical "J" cable and rectifiers. The rectangular 1 ½ volt battery pictured would normally be inserted in a hole on the left side of the case that has a wooden removable cover. The closed box measures 16 inches by 6.5 inches by 7.5 inches.

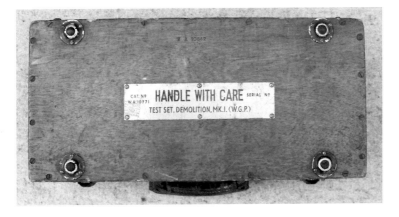

. . . . .

Exploder Dynamo Condensers were used for initiating electrical demolition charges. The type pictured on this page is the heavier Mark II pattern. The device

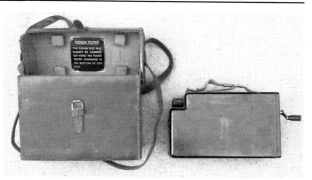

uses a rotating hand crank to generate a charge which is stepped up by an autotransformer. When sufficient power has been generated, a small neon lamp will illuminate on the top of the bakelite housing. The built up charge is stored in an internal large capacity condenser. Wires to

the charges being used are connected to a pair of mounts on the front of the exploder. When ready, a *"fire"* button is pressed on the side of the box. The maximum voltage the exploder can produce is 1500 volts which is sufficient to fire a number of detonators connected in series. The exploder has a webbing handle on its top. When not needed, the exploder is stored in a protective leather case which has a carrying sling. The case has a false bottom where three

extra generator handles are safety tied and stored. A fusion tester is also stored there along with the primary generator handle which is loose for easy access.

· · · · ·

Multimeters like the one pictured on this page were used for testing electrical devices for reliability and for checking the charge of batteries. This was very important in the case of wireless equipment and electrical demolition sets. A multimeter combines the features of several other instruments into one neat package. These include an ammeter which measures current, an ohmmeter which measures resistance and a voltmeter which measures the potential difference in voltage between two points. Switch settings on the cabinet are used for testing A.C. and D.C. power. Wire probes are connected to the appropriate positions before their opposite ends are connected to the device being tested. Instruments like this are available today but like most other electronic items, they have been greatly miniaturized.

This 1944 dated example was made by R.E.L. in Canada and the schematic on the inside of the lid is marked *Secret*. The closed box is 9.5 inches square with a depth of 5.25 inches. A leather carrying handle is on top and a latch is on each side to keep the box closed.

. . . . .

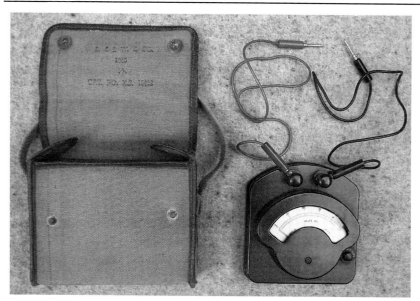

A 1945 British-made D.C. volt meter having 0-5 and 0-100 measuring scales.

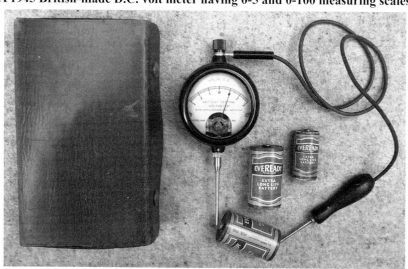

A Canadian military issue battery tester produced during the war by Weston Electrical Instrument Corp in the U.S.A. The wartime Eveready Extra Long Life Type "C" and Type "D" batteries in the photograph have "Best Use By" dates of 1942 and 1945 but they still have a small charge.

· · · · ·

Wire Cutters

Several patterns of wire cutters were available to the troops for cutting rolled wire used with field telephones and for working with barbed wire. These were needed for laying defensive works and for cutting through enemy strung wire. The longer handles on the folding patterns allowed a greater amount of leverage to be applied when cutting heavy wire. The blades only open a small amount even when the handles are separated all the way. Pressing them back together closes the blades slowly due to the way the handles are pinned together which provides a compound action to assist in cutting.

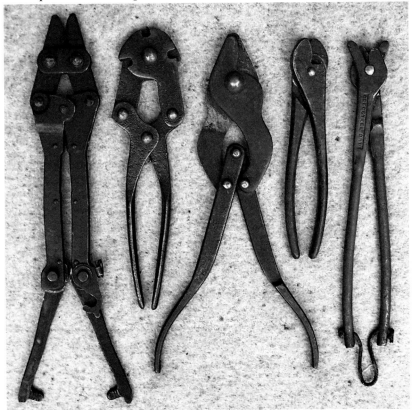

WWII produced examples of wire cutters. The first four sets are British and the last set (far right) is Australian. These were all made in 1944 with the exception of the second set from the left which was made in 1940.

· · · · ·

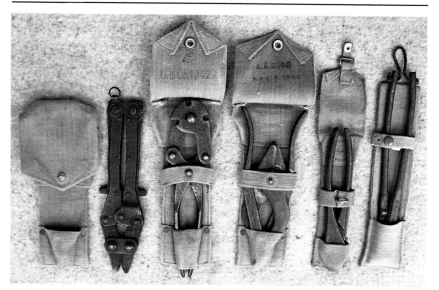

Pictured above are the five wire cutters from the facing page along with their web equipment frogs. Each of these has a sewn loop built onto the back so

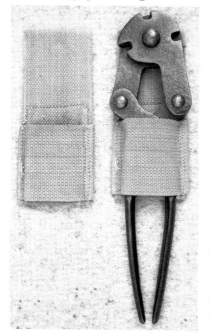

it can be carried on a belt. The Australian pattern (far right) also has a pair of brass double hooks so it can connect to the Web Waist Belt in the same way as a pair of Basic Pouches or a Binocular Case.

Pictured at the left is a webbing material frog made to hold large pliers or wire cutters. A loop is sewn into the back at the top so it can be worn suspended from the webbing waist belt. Most wire cutters and pliers had either a hole punched into one of the handles or had a ring mounted onto them for connection of a string lanyard. This prevented the tools from getting lost if they worked their way out of their case or were laid down and forgotten.

· · · · ·

Pioneer Tools

Hand Axes were standard equipment on bombers and the wooden gliders used by the airborne forces. They were intended to assist the troops in cutting holes in the fuselage after landing in the event the exit doors were damaged or if equipment shifted and needed to be removed from where it became lodged on impact. Pictured above are two war dated patterns with different shaped heads. Overall length on these is 14.5 and 15.5 inches. They each have a rubber coated handle which makes them safe to use for cutting through electrical cables and for smashing wireless equipment.

Commandos digging in after advancing from Sword Beach to link up with elements of the 6th Airborne Division on the edge of one of the glider landing zones.

. . . . .

Highlanders advancing inland from the Normandy coast towards Caen. At least four of the eight men in file are carrying infantry spades.

The three photographs of the lend-lease jeep on these two pages show various views of a British signals line laying conversion. The men have titles indicating Royal Corps of Signals and Polar Bear flashes designating them as part of the 49th (West Riding) Division.

The spare tire had to be removed from the rear of the tub and was mounted on a special fitting on the hood to make room for cable reels.

• • • • •

A pair of brackets was added to the rear of the tub on the passenger side to hold a pick/mattock pry bar combination. This tool was useful for digging very thin trenches in the ground for laying cable. It was also handy for clearing rocks, gravel and other obstructions out of the ground.

In addition to a spade and axe mounted to the driver's side of the tub, a special fitting was added to the driver side fender to hold a large sledge hammer.

• • • • •

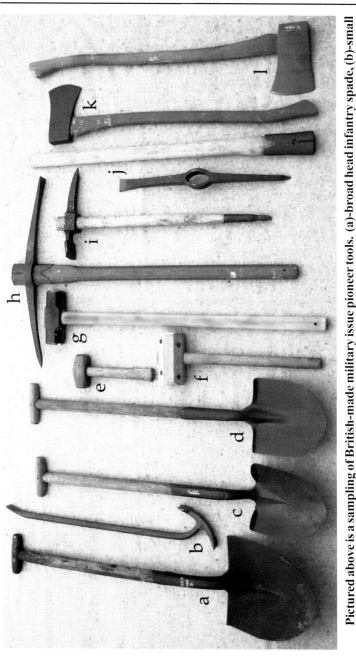

Pictured above is a sampling of British-made military issue pioneer tools. (a)-broad head infantry spade, (b)-small pry bar, (c)-small head spade with curved neck for vehicle mounting, (d)-small head infantry spade with straight neck, (e)-3 pound hammer, (f)-wooden mallet used with tent stakes and posts, (g)-8 pound sledge, (h)-standard pick, (i)-small pick/mattock and pry bar, (j)-standard pick shown disassembled, (k)-small head axe for vehicle mounting, (l)-large head axe. Typically the date, broad arrow /|\ and maker's name or marks are found on the metal parts of the tools.

· · · · ·

245

One of the primary *Field Saws* issued for use by the front line troops was a type that required two men to operate. The coarse jagged blade was ideal for quickly ripping through lumber or timber. It was made up of a series of metal segments that each had a small jagged blade in its center. A longer jagged blade was attached to each end and these were used to connect the segments together. The formed saw blade was flexible down its entire length and has a slight bow when opened all the way. Being flexible, it could be rolled up for storage in a small leather hip pouch. Rings at each end of the saw blade were intended to hold wooden handles that could also be stored inside the pouch. The design for this saw originated during the Great War and a Pattern 1944 pouch was developed after WWII so the same saws could be used during the post war period. These saws are often associated with commandos and airborne troops but they were in fact a regular issue item to any unit requiring them.

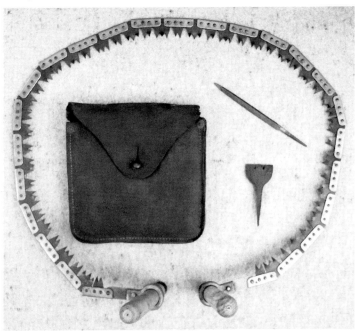

The pictured saw was made in 1943 in Sheffield, England. It has a length of 46 inches including the rings when completely unfolded.

. . . . .

246

The following photographs show examples of basic hand tools from the war years that have the British government acceptance markings on them. In most cases, little has changed in their designs.

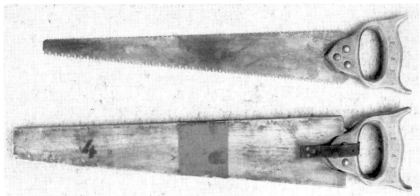

This hand saw (top) has coarse teeth on one side and fine teeth on the other. It has a wooden sheath for storage to protect the blade. This particular example has initials stamped into the handle indicating it was issued to one of the Auxiliary Fire Service units.

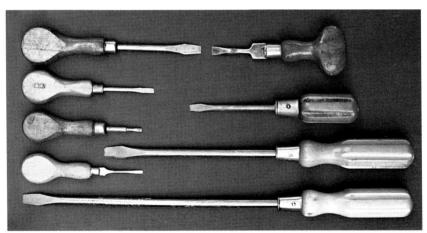

A grouping of wooden handled British and Commonwealth screwdrivers is shown in the photograph above. The three round-handled examples at the lower right side are Australian-made and have D /|\ D markings on them. The longest one has a length of 18 inches and was used for removing the buttstock on Enfield rifles.

· · · · ·

Open-ended spanners had two standardized patterns in the United Kingdom and Commonwealth during the war. These were British Standard Whitworth (BSW) which is sometimes referred to simply as Whitworth (W), and British Standard Fine (BSF). The markings on spanners refer to the diameter of a bolt the tool is used with rather than the distance across the flats

(A/F) of the bolt head or nut and this can vary between BSW and BSF. American-made open-ended wrenches produced during the war and issued with lend-lease vehicles are marked with a fractional measurement indicating the A/F size of the bolt head or nut they are used with. Several examples of British-made spanners are shown above with American-made wrenches shown below.

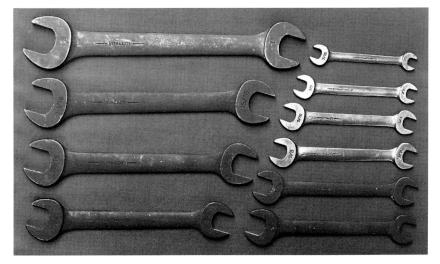

· · · · ·

A group of ball-peen hammers, also known as machinist's hammers, can be seen at the right. These are usually referenced by the weight of the head. Examples of small arms armoury point-peen and chisel-peen hammers can be seen upside down at the bottom of the photograph.

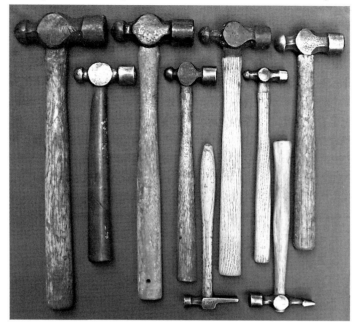

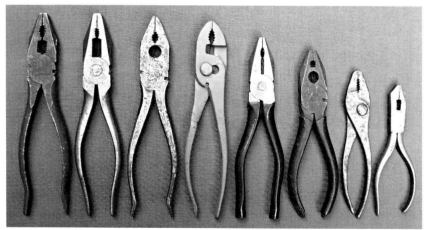

The photograph above shows variations of British-made and Australian-made WWII pliers with fine wire cutters built in. The examples with insulated handles are for electrical work. Some have a screwdriver blade built into one side of the handles.

· · · · ·

The tools shown above are an assortment typically found in use for WWII small arms repair. These include a small backsaw and pair of slick and butt chisels that were used for repair or outright fabrication of wooden grips and stocks on rifles and handguns. The Vernier Calliper seen at the far right can measure internal dimensions with one set of jaws and external dimensions with the other set. A depth probe at the bottom can provide accurate measurements of the depth of a grove or screw hole. And a selection of punches and files are pictured above a small clamp in the center of the photograph.

. . . . .

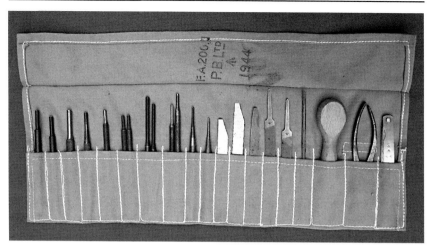

A 1944 dated armourer's tool roll with items used for small arms repair. It contains punches, files, cutting blades, gauges, a pair of small pliers and a small screwdriver.

A selection of British-made adjustable spanners is shown at the right. These are sometimes referred to as Monkey Wrenches.

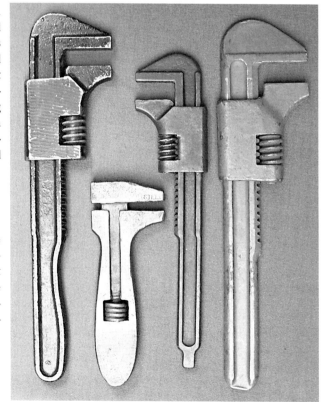

· · · · ·

Heavy Repair Base Sections and ***Mobile Repair Workshops*** of the Royal Army Ordnance Corps, Royal Engineers and the Royal Army Service Corps existed within British formations before the war but by 1941 it was realized that they were not adequate to support the large scale repair operations that were needed once the

army began deploying. The Corps of Royal Electrical and Mechanical Engineers were formed on 1 OCT 1942 specifically to assume the task of maintenance and repair of weapons and equipment.

. . . . .

Mobile Field Workshops were created so that repairs to vehicles, weapons and equipment could be carried out as close to the front lines as possible. These facilities typically consisted of trucks and vans equipped with mills, drill presses, forges and a wide assortment of hand tools. Petrol powered generators created electrical current needed to operate belt driven tools, grinders and sanders.

· · · · ·

253

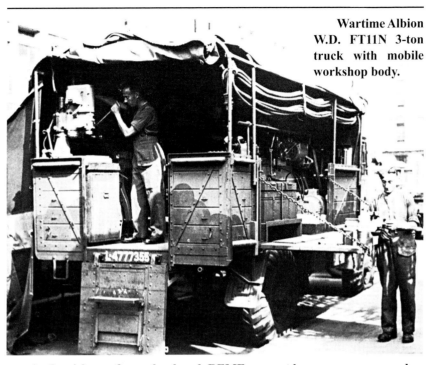

Wartime Albion W.D. FT11N 3-ton truck with mobile workshop body.

As the airborne forces developed, REME support became necessary and so their personnel took to the air in gliders that carried basic repair facilities on jeeps

and trailers. An airborne mobile workshop jeep is shown at the left equipped with a reel of generator power-er cables on the front bumper and a cylinder of compressed air on the hood. The bumper markings read "City of Bath".

. . . . .

Examples of air deployable REME equipment include the airborne lightweight machinery trailer shown above and the airborne electric arc welding generator trailer seen in use below.

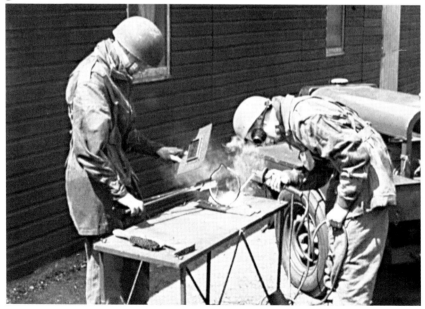

· · · · ·

A Royal Engineer with the British 8th Army photographed during February 1944 in Italy holding a light sledgehammer which he has been using to drive spikes into wooden sleepers on a railroad bed that is being repaired.

A British-made wartime tool valise and two large tool rolls are shown in the photograph below. The example at the right was originally intended for use with the Polsten gun.

· · · · ·

Chapter 6 - Knives and Bayonets

A trooper of Number 3 Commando inserts a First Pattern Fairbairn-Sykes fighting knife into its sheath which is strapped to his lower left leg.

· · · · ·

Spike Bayonets

The ***Bayonet, Number 4 Mark I*** was officially approved for British service on November 15, 1939 along with its tapered Number 4 Mark I steel scabbard. The bayonets design featured a cruciform blade running the length of the shaft which tapered to a sharp point at the end. These bayonets were made exclusively by Singer Manufacturing and only 75,000 were made. In addition to the cruciform blade, they can be identified by the maker markings "S.M." or "S.M.C." and the model markings "No. 4 Mk I". In December of 1941, a simplified form of the bayonet was put into production. It eliminated the milled cruciform blade in favor of a smooth steel spike that was flattened at the end on two sides and shaped into a point at the tip. This pattern was made to help speed up production while lowering the unit cost. The new model was designated the ***Bayonet, Number 4 Mark II*** and it is the most commonly found of the four patterns produced during the war. The Mark II was produced by numerous companies in the United Kingdom as well as in the United States by the Stevens Savage firearms company and in Canada at Canadian Small Arms Factory Ltd. located at Long Branch, Ontario. Bayonets produced in the United Kingdom will typically be marked with a code number for the company that manufactured it. This will be an Arabic number with a prefix of "N" for Northern, "M" for Midlands or "S' for Southern regions of the United Kingdom. U.S. lend-lease bayonets will have either a plain "S" or an "S" in a square representing Stevens Savage. Bayonets manufactured in Canada will have the letter "L" with a smaller letter "B" inside it indicating Long Branch.

Left to right are the No. 4 Mk III, No. 4 Mk II*, No 4 Mk II, No 4 Mk I

. . . . .

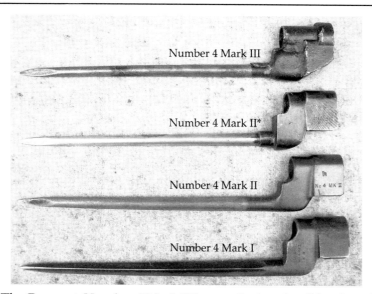

Number 4 Mark III

Number 4 Mark II*

Number 4 Mark II

Number 4 Mark I

The ***Bayonet, Number 4 Mark II**** was a further simplification of the original Mark I design. It had a two part design and the spike blade was brazed into the end of the socket. The last main pattern produced during the war was the ***Bayonet, Number 4 Mark III***. Most were produced by the Joseph Lucas Limited Company and had roughly fabricated sockets with the spike welded in place. Trials were held at the end of 1942 with production beginning early in 1943. Fewer than 200,000 units of this pattern were produced. All four spike bayonet patterns have an overall length of 10 inches with an 8 inch long spike. They are all compatible with the Number 4 series of rifles as well as with the Sten Mark V submachine gun. Combined production exceeded 2.5 million with only a small percentage of these being the first and last patterns.

Examples of a few maker marks from top to bottom: Long Branch, Stevens Savage, alternate markings for Stevens Savage, early Singer Manufacturing and the later code markings for Singer Manufacturing.

· · · · ·

Four main patterns of scabbard were produced during the war for use with the Number 4 series of spike bayonets. The **Scabbard, Bayonet, Number 4 Mark I** was approved for use on November 15, 1939. It is formed from an 8.125 inch long tapered steel tube. A raised metal stud near the top is used for attaching the scabbard to a bayonet frog. A mouthpiece made of steel or zinc is fitted into the end of the scabbard along with a metal guide designed to help hold the bayonet securely in the scabbard without a lock and release. Both of these parts are kept in place by a pair of small screws. The tip of the scabbard is shaped like a ball and it has a drain hole in the end.

The picture above shows the mouthpiece, metal bayonet guide and screws used for securing everything to the inside of the Number 4 Mark I and Mark II bayonet scabbards. An example of the top of one of the bayonet scabbard mouthpieces is shown at the right.

At the end of 1940, an easier to fabricate, alternative scabbard was put into production as the **Number 4 Mark II Scabbard**. It was made from plain straight tubing with one end capped off. It utilized the same mouthpiece, metal guide and screws as found on the first pattern scabbard. There is a small drain hole in the capped off end and the length, less mouthpiece, is 8.25 inches. A new plastic pattern with an alloy mouthpiece was put into production in July of 1943. Although not official, this became known as the **Number 4 Mark III Scabbard**. The end has a slight taper with a drain hole molded into it and the stud near the top end for holding the scabbard to the frog has an oval shape when compared to the first two patterns. Length of this scabbard without the mouthpiece is 8 inches.

· · · · ·

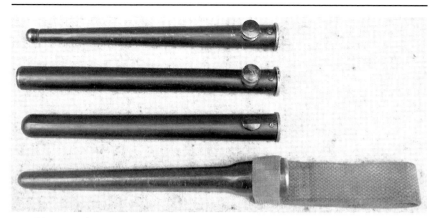

Pictured from top to bottom are the Scabbard, Bayonet, Number 4 Mark I, the Number 4 Mark II Scabbard, Number 4 Mark III Scabbard, and the Scabbard, Bayonet M5 which has the integral webbing frog.

In early 1943, a lend-lease bayonet scabbard was accepted for British Service. This was known as the ***Scabbard, Bayonet M5,*** produced by Beckwith Manufacturing in the United States. A more common name for this pattern was the *Victory Plastics* scabbard and they will have a logo incorporating a "V" and "P" on the back. The scabbard is completely different from the other patterns in having a flat backside and a webbing bayonet frog riveted to the top. A metal mouthpiece and internal guide are also in place at the top and these are held in place by a pair of smaller rivets. Overall length of this scabbard, not including the frog, is 8.375 inches. All four patterns of Number 4 spike bayonet, plus the special version produced for the Sten Mark II, are interchangeable in any of the bayonet scabbards covered on these two pages.

 This Victory Plastics logo is normally found on the backside of the lend-lease bayonet scabbards produced by the Beckwith Manufacturing Company.

· · · · ·

261

Three types of frog used with the Number 4 series of spike bayonets. The leftmost and center frogs are modified patterns of the type used with the sword pattern bayonets. Each has a slice across the upper webbing band for the scabbard securing stud. One has a button hole embroidered around the slice while the other has reinforcement stitching left and right of the slice. The rightmost frog requires the leather keeper to be looped over 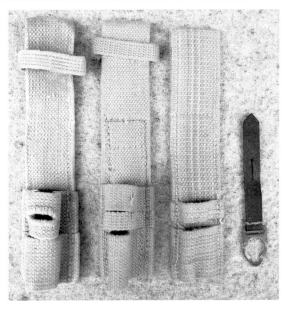 the upper webbing band and it must be fastened to the securing stud of the scabbard so it will not fall out through the lower webbing band.

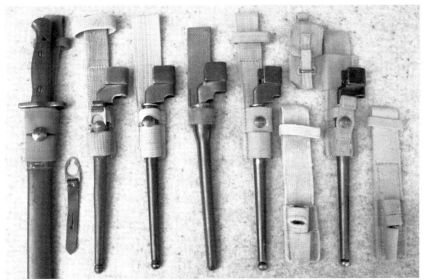

A few variations of the webbing pattern bayonet frog produced during WWII.

· · · · ·

The bayonet frog was designed to be worn on the equipment belt and was held there by a loop hanger built into the back. An unofficial alternate method of wearing the bayonet with frog was on the chest by threading it to the end of an equipment brace. Two wartime photographs on this page show this being done by men of the 6th Air-landing Brigade as well as static shots of the equipment from the front and the side to show how they did it.

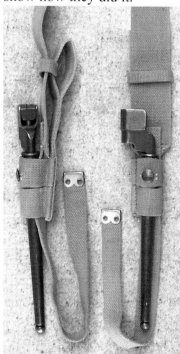

The *Sten Machine Carbine Bayonet Mark I* was approved for production in September of 1942 for use with the Sten Mark II submachine gun. Less than 76,000 were produced and few are thought to have been issued. Most were reduced to scrap metal after the war and the number that survived is unknown. The overall length of the bayonet is 12 inches with 8 inches of spike protruding past the mounting tube it is welded to. To use the bayonet, slip the mounting tube over the end of the barrel on the Sten. Compressing the leaf spring allows it to fit inside the barrel nut on the Sten which holds the barrel in place. The barrel nut has a series of ventilation holes and the small tab at the end of the leaf spring will lock into one of them and hold the bayonet in place. To remove the bayonet, pull forward on the curved part of the leaf spring at the spike end of the mounting tube and it will draw the locking tab down and release. Since the spike on this bayonet is the same length as found with the Number 4 series of bayonets, they can share the same scabbards. Markings on the pictured example include "B&J.S.L" on the mounting tube and leaf spring and "N.152" following the maker initials on the mounting tube.

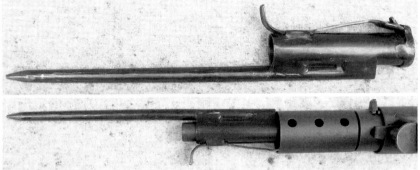

The barrel nut on the Sten has three groupings of three holes making a total of nine for cooling the barrel. The tab on the bayonet can be locked into any one of the three on the outer edge. The only thing you have to avoid is placing the tab into a hole that lines up with the very top of the Sten. This is because the curved release tab on the bayonet mounting tube will interfere with your sight picture. You can still line up the foresight with the rear peep hole but the bayonet release tab would obstruct your view of the target.

· · · · ·

Two paratroopers working together to get their Welbikes over a barbed wire fence while on maneuvers. The second Welbike is not visible in this photograph. The soldier with the Sten is wearing a sheathed Sten Machine Carbine Bayonet on his left hip. Bulford Camp, England – 9 JUN 1943. (right)

A British paratrooper of the 6th Airborne Division photographed holding a Sten Mark II with bayonet mounted during an airborne assault exercise. The webbing item he's laying on is an airborne pattern two-inch mortar leg case (AA.5380) which was declared obsolescent in 1943.

· · · · ·

Edged Bayonets

The **Bayonet, Number 1 Mark I** was officially known as the *Sword Bayonet, Pattern 1907 Mark I* prior to 1926 when the "Number and Mark" nomenclature changes were first adopted by the British military. The bayonet had a 17 inch long blade with an overall length of 21.75 inches. More than 5 million were produced including those made in the United Kingdom, Australia and India. These bayonets were used with the Number 1 series of service rifles from before WWI through the early 1940's since the Mark III* pattern rifle was still being produced and issued. It was also used with the Lanchester submachine gun issued to the Royal Navy as an alternative to the Sten. During WWII, the scabbard issued with this bayonet was the leather Number 1 Mark II pattern which used a separate webbing material frog to secure it to the equipment belt. The two piece slab grips were made from wood and had a pair of screws to keep them in place.

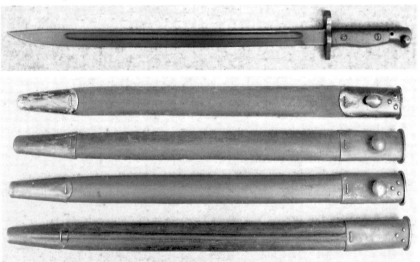

Examples of variations in Number 1 Mark II Pattern 1907 Scabbards. The topmost scabbard is an earlier production type with an oval frog stud which was later replaced by the type with a round frog stud as pictured below it. These scabbards were all interchangeable with the 1907 and 1913 pattern sword bayonets and have an overall length of 17.875 inches. The number 1 Mark I Pattern 1907 Scabbards have the chape, the metal tip at the end, on the inside of the leather.

· · · · ·

In the years preceding WWI, a new service rifle was planned to replace the Number 1 series but this never happened due to the efforts required to retool and the sudden large demand for rifles when war broke out. This rifle was the Number 3 Mark I Pattern 14 and it could not use the existing pattern bayonet. This resulted in a new bayonet design, the Sword Bayonet, Pattern 1913, which was changed in 1926 to the **Bayonet, Number 3 Mark I**. While not produced during the Second World War, the rifle was still in service with the Home Guard and a sniper version was still in use with some active infantry units at the beginning of the war. The bayonet is very similar to the Number 1 Mark I bayonet and uses the same leather scabbard. The primary differences between the two designs are the Number 3 Mark I had a slightly smaller diameter muzzle ring and this was also further away from the blade. The wooden grips are grooved in the center and this might have been done as a quick method of telling the two patterns apart. These bayonets all have the pattern year 1913 stamped into them on the ricasso while the Number 1 Mark I pattern bayonets have 1907 stamped into them.

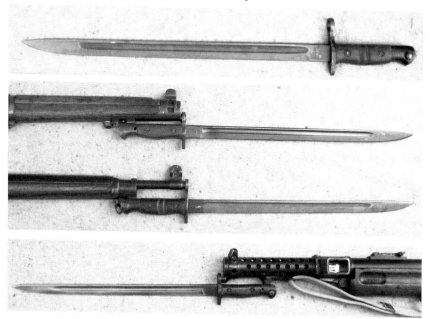

. . . . .

Beginning in 1941, India altered the design of their Number 1 Mark I bayonets. The length was reduced to 12 inches and a 2-inch long false edge was ground into the top of the blade at the end. Bayonets which were converted to the new design already had a long fuller which extended through the point of the now shortened blades. New made short bayonets were produced and these were known as the ***Bayonet Number 1 Mark II***. They had a blade with no fuller and were 12 inches long giving an overall length of 16.75 inch-

es. A later design using the same blade, but with a squared pommel, was known as the ***Bayonet Number 1 Mark III***. Most of these later bayonets were marked with the Mark II stampings but the pommel makes them easy to identify.

A Ford T-16 Universal Carrier in Indian Service. Note the short Indian pattern bayonet worn by the rear man.

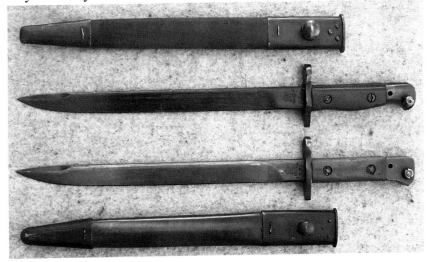

· · · · ·

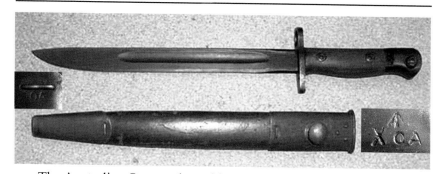

The Australian Owen submachine gun was not originally built with fittings to accept a bayonet when it was introduced into service in December 1941. Talks that Owen guns should have the capability for attaching a bayonet lead to trials being conducted in 1942 and 1943 with short blades that fitted directly onto the weapon's muzzle compensator. There was no mounting bracket to provide further support and the design was not adopted. A new shortened and lightened rifle bayonet was being trialed in early 1944 that was similar to the short Indian pattern and based on the standard Number 1 Mark I bayonet. This lead to the introduction of the *Owen Mark I Bayonet* in 1944 which fitted onto a bayonet bracket that was added to existing Owen gun barrels beginning in 1945. These new bayonets had a blade length of 10 inches and an overall length of 14.75 inches. Unlike the Indian Number 1 Mark II, the Owen pattern featured a 5 inch long fuller. But like the converted Indian bayonets, existing Australian-made bayonets which were shortened will have a fuller running through the end of the blade. The ricasso on Owen bayonets is stamped with a Broad Arrow, the bend test proof mark "X" and the production facility mark "OA" which indicates the Orange Rifle Factory in New South Wales. The wooden grips will be marked "SLAZ" which indicates Slazengers of Sydney. The short leather bayonet scabbards were converted from existing Number 1 Mark I bayonet scabbards and were produced from leather supplied by Mangrovite Belting of Sydney. These will be stamped on the back with MANGROVITE and a two digit year of production. The chape will also be marked "OA"

· · · · ·

The **Bayonet, Number 5 Mark I** was designed specifically for use with the Number 5 Mark I "Jungle Carbine" rifle and production began sometime in early 1944. The muzzle ring is larger than found on other bayonets because of the flash cone at the end of the rifle barrel which it had to fit over. The Bowie knife type blade is 8 inches long and the overall bayonet is just short of 12 inches. The two-piece wooden grips have a pair of screws to hold them in place. Very early production bayonets only had a single screw in the center for this purpose. The scabbard used with these bayonets was the Number 5 Mark I and Number 5 Mark II which are both made from sheet steel.

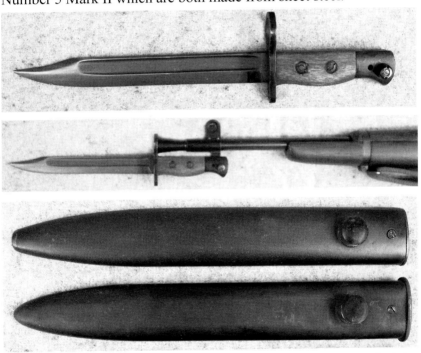

An example of the *Scabbard, Number 5 Mark I* shown above the later pattern *Scabbard, Number 5 Mark II*. Both are interchangeable for use on Number 5 and Number 7 bayonets as well as on the post war Number 9 and L1A1-L1A4 series of bayonets. The mouthpiece on the Mark II pattern scabbard has an extended rim around the opening and the tip is rounded where the Mark I pattern is blunt. Each pattern has a drain hole in the end.

· · · · ·

The ***Bayonet, Number 7 Mark I*** was originally designed for the Sten Mark V but it works equally well on the Number 4 Mark I service rifle since they both have the same bayonet lug on their barrels. This new design was approved in January of 1945 and it features the same blade as found on the Number 5 bayonet. The two piece composition grips were most often molded in black but the colour can vary to shades of brownish red. A unique feature of this bayonet is its rotating pommel. A latch is positioned roughly where the thumb would be if you held the grips properly. It is spring loaded and allows the pommel to swivel when pushed forward. Once the pommel has traveled 180 degrees it can be locked in position again. This action is required to fit the bayonet onto a firearm.

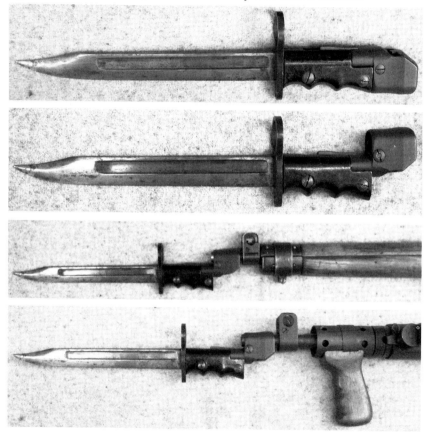

· · · · ·

Fighting Knives and Utility Blades

The classic Fairbairn Sykes fighting knife that is associated with British commandos and airborne troops was first designed in 1940. Captain William Ewart Fairbairn and Captain Eric Anthony Sykes worked with Wilkinson Sword Company to produce what became known as the F-S knife. While there are many variations of F-S knives, they are generally broken down by collectors into three basic patterns. The first pattern knives were only produced by Wilkinson Sword Company. They featured a flat square ricasso, an "S" shaped cross guard and a knurled grip. Production started in late 1940 and continued into 1941. These knives had a brass hilt and cross guard that was usually nickel plated. A very limited number of these knives had a 3 inch long cross guard which was later reduced to 2 inches. To speed up production, the second pattern knives adopted a flat cross guard which was 2 inches long, they retained the knurled grip but discontinued the flat square ricasso. Wilkinson Sword and a small number of other cutlery companies produced this pattern during 1941 and 1942. A variety of finishes exist such as blued overall, nickel plated overall, or a blued hilt and cross guard with a highly polished blade. The third pattern design was introduced in 1942

A soldier from Number 3 Commando holding his fighting knife between his teeth. Largs, Scotland - 2 May 1942.

. . . . .

in an effort to reduce per-unit cost and further increase production. This pattern is still in production today. These knives were produced by Wilkinson Sword and more than 100 other cutlery companies. Due to the large number of manufacturers, there are several styles of pommel nuts that were used to secure the hilt to the tang but few other variations. The knives feature a cast alloy ringed hilt that is copper plated to more easily take the blued finish. A small number can often be found on one side of the hilt which represents the casting number of its mold. The straight cross guard on early production knives is the same as found on the second pattern but this was reduced in thickness over time. These knives are usually blued overall.

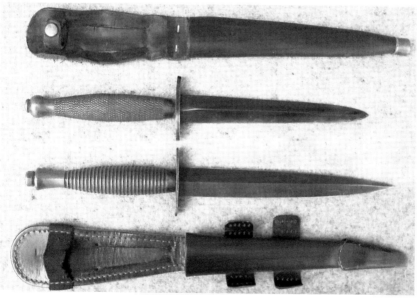

The knife pictured at the top is a Second Pattern which has had the tip reshaped after being cut down. This was done if the tip became damaged or to strengthen the blade for heavier use. The knurled grip is a carry over from the First Pattern that was made in limited numbers. Note the difference in thickness of the straight cross guard of this knife when compared to that of the Third Pattern knife below it.

· · · · ·

Wilkinson Sword Company produced all three patterns of F-S knives and they marked both sides of the ricasso. There were several variations of each design but one side featured the company's name with crossed sword logo and the other side had the F-S designation. These markings were wax templates on small pieces of paper that were pressed onto the knife ricasso prior to being etched. This left the metal beneath the wax template protected and slightly raised. While other cutlery companies produced F-S knives, none of them marked the blades.

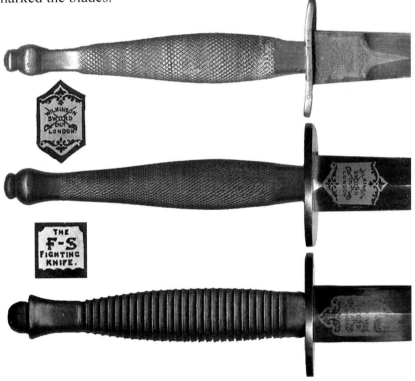

Pictured above are wartime Wilkinson Sword Company produced examples of all three patterns of F-S knives. The knives are shown with the company marked ricasso side facing up and the opposite side ricasso on each is marked with "The F-S Fighting Knife". Examples of the wax templates used during blade etching can also be seen.

· · · · ·

Sheaths were made from black or brown dyed leather and had a nickel plated or blued metal chape. Early production models used a pair of leather tabs with press-stud fasteners to secure the knife. This was later changed to an elastic strap sewn to the scabbard for economic reasons and because the knife could be withdrawn more silently. Leather tabs known as wings were also added to later production scabbards halfway down as a means to sew them onto clothing or equipment.

The leftmost soldier wears a 2nd Pattern F-S knife with the scabbard wings sewn onto his right side trouser leg. He is in the process of removing a PIAT from a drop container.

Airborne soldiers using a manually operated grinding wheel to sharpen the double edged blades of their F-S knives.

· · · · ·

The F-S knife blades were drop forged and those produced before 1943 were hand drawn and ground, which means the length will vary slightly (plus or minus ¼ inch) from one to another. On average, the blade has a length of 6.75 inches with an overall knife length of 11.75 inches. Hand ground blades have a V at the base of the blade where it meets the cross guard. This is a result of the grinding wheel overshooting the tang during its process of being shaped for the cross guard to fit. Machine ground blades used a more precise method for grinding down the tang and so no part of the actual blade became flattened out. The machine ground process was introduced towards the end of the second pattern, so late made examples exist with machine ground blades just as early third pattern examples exist with hand ground blades.

An example of a hand ground F-S knife blade and the flat "V" that results on the ricasso. The Broad Arrow over a "7" is an inspection mark and not an indication of manufacturer.

Several non-standard variations of F-S knife hilts also exist which all used the regular style flat 2 inch long cross guard. These were produced in limited numbers throughout the war and include a fatter and coarser knurled second pattern, a reverse knurled second pattern, a very tightly ringed pattern, a roped and ringed pattern that has groups of tight rings separated by thicker grooved rows, and a beaded and ringed pattern that has groups of tight rings separated by a row of beads. An example of this last style (on display in the Juno Beach Centre) is shown above.

· · · · ·

The knuckle dusters pictured here are unusual items and several variations exist. The handles are made of brass with a hole for mounting the spike from a Number 4 bayonet or the tang of a knife blade. While undoubtedly based on something fabricated for trench warfare during the Great War, it is my belief that these are fantasy items made up for collectors during the years following WWII. Fake specialty knife designs like this are also commonly encountered with German WWII militaria and buyers should beware.

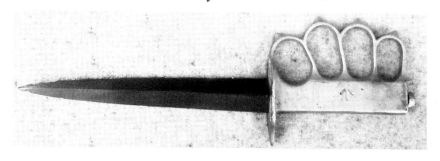

. . . . .

The photographs on this page show a few of the main patterns of clasp knives that were issued to the British and Commonwealth forces. Each type pictured was produced by numerous manufacturers and there are many minor variations. Any that were produced during the war will have the broad ar-

row /|\ format for the Commonwealth nation that produced it along with the date of manufacture and maker name or initials. The knives with the folding marlin spike were generally issued to airborne, commando and naval personnel. The purpose of the spike was to make working knots in rope or parachute lines easier to loosen and untie. Common features to all patterns are a main single edged cutting blade, a slotted type screwdriver found on one end of the frame assembly of the knife and a lanyard ring at the opposite side. With the exception of the larger navy pattern clasp knife at the far left, all patterns had a separate blade that served

as can opener. The pattern second from the left has flat metal slab sides and is a wartime production item that is generally considered part of the Pattern 1944 equipment. This design was retained at least in British service for many years following the war.

• • • • •

The British gravity knife was developed during the Second World War for parachutists and aircraft aircrew as they could easily find themselves in a situation where only one hand was available to retrieve and open a knife, if their parachute came down in a wooded area and they were left hanging by their suspension lines. The knives were a virtual copy of the German gravity knife which had wooden grips and featured one cutting blade, a manual folding Marlin Spike and a lanyard loop. The British-made gravity knives differ from the German design by having black Bexoid checkered grips. The unique feature of gravity knives is they require only one hand to open or close the main blade but they are not spring operated like switchblade and stiletto automatic knives. Rotating a thumb-lever 180 degrees while the knife was pointed downward released the blade and allowed it to slide out of the handle to the extended position. When fully extended, it could be locked in place by rotating the thumb-lever back to its original position. The blade could be retracted back into the handle by repeating this process while holding the handle in an upward direction. Length of the closed knife was 7 inches. The cutting blade had a length of 4 inches and the Marlin Spike had a length of 3.5 inches. Known examples are either sterile of markings for SOE and OSS issue, or have the George Ibberson & Company of Sheffield marker marking along with their trademark violin icon and a code of C.O.S.D./2194 on the main blade.

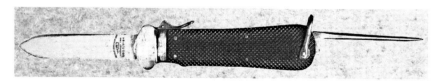

. . . . .

Examination of wartime photographs indicates that clasp knife hangers were available and in use by both straight leg infantry and airborne troops alike. No official records have been found to document them but several variations have been observed. These items were most likely private purchase, produced by firms that manufactured other military webbing, and sold through the NAFFI and civilian outfitters. It would appear that they were most often worn suspended from the trousers belt which would keep the clasp knife with the individual regardless of webbing being worn or not. The hanger itself would thus be partially obscured from view when the battledress blouse was worn and the clasp knife could neatly hang at the side or slip into a trousers pocket. Two examples are shown in wartime use on the facing page and two variations are shown on this page. The version with the shorter hanger features a loop of adjustable webbing so it could be worn with a trouser belt or webbing equipment belt if desired. The clasp knife is held by a shorter non-adjustable length of webbing by a snap fastener. The second version shown has a non-adjustable webbing belt loop and the clasp knife is held by a swivel snap hook. There are no markings on either of these examples.

· · · · ·

Canadian personnel digging a slit trench during Operation Spring. Note the clasp knife hanging from the trouser belt. South of Ifs, France - 25 JUL 1944.

British glider trained infantry being inspected prior to an assault exercise. Note the clasp knife hanger being worn by the individual in the foreground.

· · · · ·

During WWII, the British and Commonwealth soldiers were often issued a machete as opposed to an ax or smaller hatchet for field use. This even applied to military vehicle issue where you don't often see axes included with the pioneer tools, particularly with the airborne troops. The machete, also called a machet, was easier to carry and was as effective for most tasks short of chopping down large trees. Most machetes used during the war by Britain, Canada and Australia had a standard fixed blade that was 14.75 inches long with an overall length of 20 inches including the hilt. While the blades typically had the same shape and weight, the hilts seem to vary by country of origin. British-made machetes have smaller straight black Bakelite grips which are held by four or five rivets. Machetes produced in the United States for Canadian use have grips made from black plastic which is shaped to fit the hand more securely when compared to the British pattern. The end of the grips is also wider and extended to prevent it from slipping from the wielders' hand when wet. Australian-made machetes tend to have grips produced from wood with a similar shape to the American/Canadian machete grips. Scabbards tend to be made from heavy leather with a belt loop formed at the top. A small two-piece strap with a stud on one side provided a means of securing the machete by the hilt when not immediately needed.

Major General Eric Bols and Brigadier James Hill shown in the 6th airborne divisional commander's airborne jeep. A machete with leather scabbard can be seen in the passenger side rifle mounting clips.

. . . . .

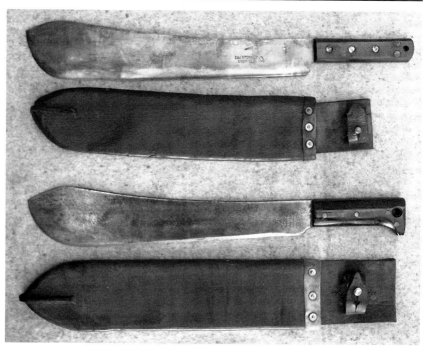

Two examples of standard wartime machetes. The top one is British-made with the blade marked S&J Kitchin Ltd., Sheffield and features a Broad Arrow and 1945 date. The scabbard is marked B.H.G. with a Broad Arrow and 1944 date. The machete below is Canadian issue, manufactured in the United States by Collins & Company in 1940. All of the Collins machetes with this design have a model number of 1250 and will be trademarked Legitimus. The scabbard is marked RobCo Ltd., Montreal, and has a Canadian Broad Arrow with 1943 date.

An example of the black plastic grips found on some 1944-1945 Australian-made machetes which have the same blade design as British machetes.

. . . . .

A folding machete with origins in the United States was produced for the Royal Air Force and the Royal Australian Air Force during the war and these found their way into the Pacific with the infantry. It was an official issue Survival Machete that was first made for the U.S. Army Air Force by Camillus, Case, Cattaraugus, Imperial and likely other cutlery companies. In 1945 a modified pattern with a lanyard ring was manufactured for the British and Commonwealth by several cutlery companies in Sheffield, England including George Butler and Joseph Westby. The folding blade had a light metal cover in place of a scabbard. And the blade locked in place when open using the same type mechanism found on lockblade folding pocket knives. The grips are smooth slab-sided black Bakelite that is held in place by rivets. The folded length of the machete is 11 inches, the blade is 10 inches long and the overall length when unfolded is 15.5 inches.

The R.A.F. Survival Machete shown folded with the metal blade guard held securely in place by the grips until released when opened.

Broad Arrow markings are found on the blade and Bakelite grips of this example.

· · · · ·

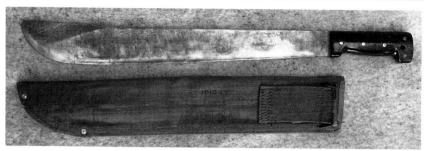

A late war machete design that was part of the Pattern 1944 equipment featured a webbing scab-

bard with U.S. pattern wire loop hangers designed to work with the grommets found on the Pattern 1944 waistbelts and haversacks. The blade was 17.5 inches long and the overall length was 22.5 inches. Grips are black plastic and will be marked with a code AF 0100 along with a Broad Arrow, maker name or mark and the date. At least six British manufacturers produced this pattern during 1945.

A Bren Gun team moving into position in the hedgerows of Normandy. Note the machete worn by the individual in the center of the section.

· · · · ·

Square-ended machetes were produced in great numbers during the Second World War by India for use by the Indian Infantry Divisions and for Major-General Orde Wingate's multinational Chindit Special Forces units. While most have similar blades, there are many variations of hilt designs. These ranged from crude wooden slab sides, to more refined wooden bayonet grips, to heavier wooden wedges as found on the Kukris. Some of the machetes were produced in the U.S.A. and have the standard black plastic grips found on Canadian and American issue machetes. More likely than not, these started out as normal allied pattern machetes with curved ends which were square cut to accommodate the Indian pattern sheaths. The pictured example is a U.S. made machete produced by Collins & Company in 1944 with the blade being marked Legitimus and featuring the hammer held over a crown logo. The blade has a length of 13.5 inches, a width at the grip of 1.5 inches and a width at the end of slightly over 2 inches. The Indian-made brown leather scabbard has a production date stamp and Broad Arrow acceptance date stamp of 1944. It has a non-adjustable belt loop at the top and a strap with stud for securing the machete inside when not in use. As the scabbard tapers towards the top, one side is open with the exception of the last three inches to allow quick removal of the machete.

A shorter version of the square-ended machete was produced with blades ranging from 8.5 to 10.5 inches in length. In place of a belt loop hanger, they feature a pair of leather straps and buckles so the machete can be worn on the leg.

· · · · ·

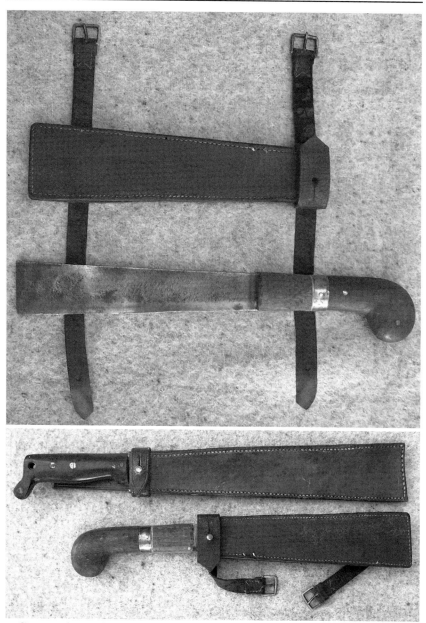

Comparison shots of the short and long square-ended machetes.

. . . . .

The Smatchet was a large and heavy edged fighting weapon that resembles the classical Roman short sword which was known as the Gladius. The large leaf-shaped blade was sharpened for the entire length on one side and halfway on the opposite side. The blade on the Smatchet is 11 inches long and the overall length of the weapon is 16.5 inches. Wooden grips were secured by rivets and the pommel was made of brass with a steel cross guard. Examples available to members of the OSS appear to have had an alloy pommel and a white metal alloy cross guard. Webbing sheaths were produced by Mills Equipment Company and known examples are dated 1942 and feature the Broad Arrow proof mark. Leather sheaths that are sterile of markings and likely intended for SOE and OSS use were also produced and have black leather that is stitched over a wooden former in the same way found with the Kukri. In both cases, a belt loop is attached at a slight angle on the back so that the Smatchet will hang diagonally from a waist belt making it easier to draw.

Armed to the Teeth: **A British Commando photographed in 1942 armed with a Smatchet in his left hand, 2nd pattern FS fighting knife, 1907 sword bayonet and machete.**

. . . . .

288

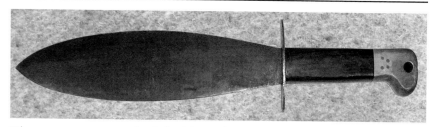

They were worn on the left side and cross-drawn with the right hand. Virtually all of the wartime photographs showing British soldiers armed with the Smatchet are posed and very few of the weapons are thought to have made it into combat as there were much more practical weapons available for issue. No production information has

ever been found but the Smatchet made its appearance sometime after the first pattern F-S knives became available. They were featured in Fairbairn's two personal hand-to-hand combat books titled *All In Fighting* and *Get Tough* in 1942 when the second pattern F-S knives were being produced. The Smatchet would seem to be one of the many wartime ideas that simply didn't become accepted. Weight of the Smatchet in its scabbard is two pounds three ounces.

· · · · ·

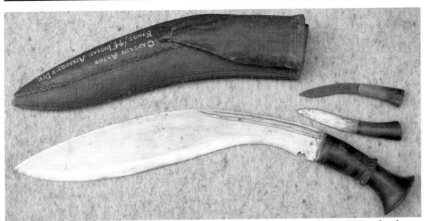

The Kukri is the national weapon of the Gurkhas from Nepal where it is officially spelled Khukuri. They have been used by the Gurkhas for hunting, chopping wood, opening cans, clearing trails and killing their enemies since the 1600s. Gurkhas serving with the British and Indian regiments carried the Kukri as did many of the British and Australian soldiers that fought in India and the Pacific Theatre. The size of the main blade can vary but typically they have a length of 12-14 inches. The blades on the quality fighting versions are forged from salvaged spring steel and railway rails. The scabbards are made from wood that is covered in leather. Some have two pockets which are used to hold a pair of small tools. One is known as the Chakmak and it is a thick blunt piece of steel with a wooden handle used for sharpening the main blade and for use with flint for starting fires. The other is known as the Karda and it resembles a penknife which can be used for skinning game and other light utility tasks. The scabbard pictured on this page has the addition of a third outer pocket made to hold a piece of flint.

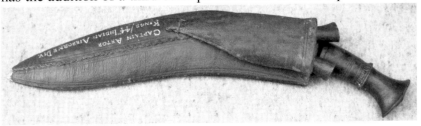

· · · · ·

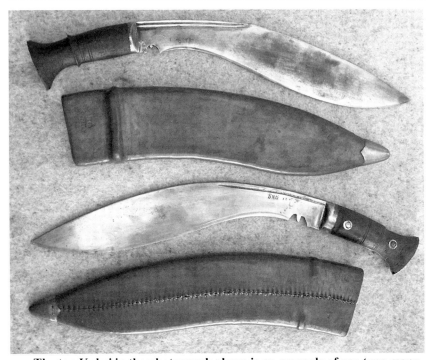

The top Kukri in the photograph above is an example of one type manufactured during the interwar years. It has a 13.75 inch long blade with an overall length of 17.75 inches. The grips are one piece of carved wood which flares out towards the end with a raised section near the center to provide a comfortable slip-free grip. A metal ferrule strengthens the hilt but the grips are not capped off on the opposite end. There are twin fullers on each side which are called "aunlo bal" on a Kukri. The only visible marking on the blade is a Broad Arrow. The bottom example was produced during the war and has a 13.25 inch long blade with an overall length of 17.75 inches and a single fuller on each side. Left and right side sections of the wooden grips are held to the tang by a pair of rivets. A metal ferrule where the blade meets the hilt provides added strength for the grips and a metal butt plate protects the back end of the grips. This plate is held on with a pair of heavy crude nails. The blade is marked SNB 41 with a Broad Arrow. Both of the scabbards shown are 1944 dated and constructed from brown leather sewn over a wooden former. The raised section near the open end is to hold a frog from slipping off but it also provided a means for the scabbard to be worn simply slipped between the body and a belt.

· · · · ·

291

A member of the 4th Indian Division of the British 8th Army holding a curved knife known as a kukri. North Africa – 1943.

Knife wielding Gurkha soldier emerging from a foxhole while serving in a unit attached to the British 8th Army somewhere in the Ortona sector during the Allied push to oust German troops from Italy. Near Ortona, Italy – January 1944

• • • • •

An RAF flying officer sitting next to a Mosquito on a 500-pound bomb manicures his nails with a Gurkhas Kukri in Kumbhirgram, Assam, India on 7 JAN 1945.

British troops crossed the border into Belgium following the German invasion on 10 MAY 1940. The soldier on the left is wearing an unknown private purchase hunting knife.

A flight lieutenant eating a lunch of canned cheese on the end of a jungle knife following the allied landing on Noemfoor Island, Dutch New Guinea on 2 JUL 1944. The knife appears to be a U.S. Marine Corps Ka-Bar fighting knife.

. . . . .

The left side of this page shows four photographs of WWII bayonet training. During 1940-1942, this included intensified training in battle practices using the 1907 pattern Enfield sword bayonet. Later in the war the basic drills involved the Number 4 spike bayonet.

Pictured above are crew members of the destroyer HMAS Napier undergoing weapon drill on the ship's deck. The men are armed with Lanchester submachine guns fitted with Lee Enfield bayonets. The pouches they wear are designed to hold three of the 50-round magazines for the Lanchester. Of note is the fact that this is an Australian warship and that Lanchester submachine guns were only carried on ships commissioned in the United Kingdom.

• • • • •

A grouping showing some of the knives and bayonets found in this chapter for comparison of their relative sizes.

An NCO of Number 5 Commando directing a Bren gunner with drawn Kukri.

· · · · ·

This page has photographs of a 1944 dated Number 4 Mark II spike bayonet, a cast nickel 1942 dated Fairbairn/Sykes fighting knife and a 1909 dated pattern 1907 sword bayonet which still retains the hooked quillon. Their main features are marked and identified below the photographs and these terms will apply to other similar style knives and bayonets.

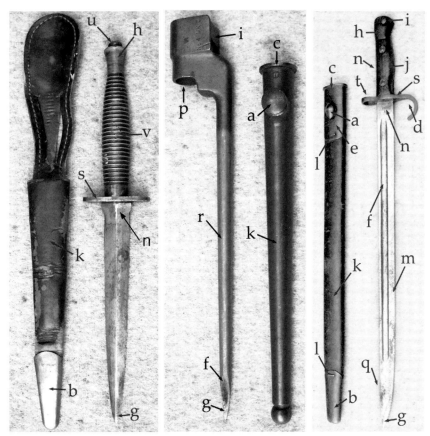

(a) frog stud, (b) chape, (c) mouth piece, (d) quillon hook, (e) locket, (f) fuller, (g) point or tip, (h) pommel, (i) locking bolt, (j) grips, (k) scabbard/sheath, (l) wire lace, (m) true edge, (n) ricasso, (o) hilt, (p) socket, (q) false edge, (r) spike blade, (s) cross piece, (t) muzzle ring, (u) pommel nut, (v) handle

· · · · ·

Chapter 7 - Signals Equipment

A Royal Air Force forward air controller works with an officer of the Queens Royal Regiment to call down an air strike during the Normandy campaign.

· · · · ·
297

Communications during the war were carried out in a number of ways and the method selected was often dependant on distance, terrain, security, reliability and what was available at the time of need. Methods ranged from basic carrier pigeons, runners, field phones, heliographs and wireless sets. Runners were suitable for short distance two-way communications but they could not always be relied upon since they were at risk of being killed or captured. This could mean anything from failure of a message being delivered to its possibly being captured and battle plans being compromised. Pigeons were a fairly dependable method of one way communication and they were used throughout WWII. There are lists of notable examples of pigeons being used for delivery of important messages during WWII. Many were from downed R.A.F. crews, S.O.E. agents working with Maquis units in France or from the Dutch Resistance in Holland. A few notable pigeons that actually received decorations, the Dickin Medal of Gallantry, for their service with the Army Pigeon Service include:

Beach Comber – Delivered the first news from the Canadian troops fighting on the beaches at Dieppe in September of 1942.

GI Joe – Was sent from the British 10th Army Headquarters in Italy to deliver a message to recall allied bombers that were enroute to bomb an area that British troops had succeeded in taking. The flight was 20 miles and the message was delivered in 20 minutes, arriving just in time to prevent a costly friendly fire incident from occurring.

All Alone – Flew a distance of over 400 miles to deliver an important message in August of 1943.

Gustav – Delivered the first news of the Normandy Landings on June 6, 1944 after being sent from a ship just off the beachhead.

William of Orange – Was sent from Arnhem in September of 1944 with an important despatch from the British airborne troops fighting there. The flight was 260 miles, much of it over the sea, and took 4 hours and 25 minutes to reach its destination.

Scotch Lass – Delivered 38 microphotographs across the North Sea from Holland while injured in September of 1944.

· · · · ·

A series of wartime photographs showing carrier pigeons, lofts, messages being prepared and the message tubes that were attached to the legs of pigeons. The pigeon at the bottom of the page was called "Aussie" and is a *blue checker cock* pigeon which returned to RAF Station Mount Batten with an SOS message from a ditched Sunderland aircraft on 16 SEPT 1944. The photograph of the jeep shows a despatch rider that has just picked up a basket of pigeons on 9 JAN 1945. This was done daily so birds could be redistributed to the divisions and messages could be carried back to HQ.

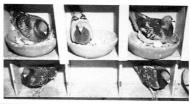

· · · · ·

299

A Royal Signal Corps soldier in service with one of the Parachute Regiments showing the method of parachuting with a basket of carrier pigeons. The basket was lightweight and connected to the parachute harness in the same way an airborne kitbag did when it was worn on the chest for jumping with fragile equipment.

Two members of the Royal Signal Corps attached to Number 2 Commando Brigade prepare to send a message by pigeon. The wicker basket holds several other pigeons until they are needed and a message pad can be seen resting on its top.

. . . . .

Morse Code and Phonetic Alphabet

	Morse Code 1835-Present	British Army/RAF 1924-1943	Allied Forces 1943-1955	NATO Forces 1955-Present
A	. _	Ack (Ac)	Able	Alpha
B	_ . . .	Beer	Baker	Bravo
C	_ . _ .	Charlie	Charlie	Charlie
D	_ . .	Don	Dog	Delta
E	.	Edward	Easy	Echo
F	. . _ .	Freddie	Fox	Foxtrot
G	_ _ .	George	George	Golf
H	. . . .	Harry	How	Hotel
I	. .	Ink	Item	India
J	. _ _ _	Johnnie	Jig	Juliet
K	_ . _	King	King	Kilo
L	. _ . .	London	Love	Lima
M	_ _	Monkey	Mike	Mike
N	_ .	Nuts	Nan	November
O	_ _ _	Orange	Oboe	Oscar
P	. _ _ . .	Pip	Peter	Papa
Q	_ _ . _ .	Queen	Queen	Quebec
R	. _ .	Robert	Roger	Romeo
S	. . .	Sugar	Sugar	Sierra
T	_	Toc	Tare	Tango
U	. . _	Uncle	Uncle	Uniform
V	. . . _	Vic	Victor	Victor
W	. _ _	William	Whiskey	Whiskey
X	_ . . _	X-Ray	X-Ray	X-Ray
Y	_ . _ _	Yorker	Yoke	Yankee
Z	_ _ . .	Zebra	Zebra	Zulu

1 . _ _ _ _	2 . . _ _ _	3 . . . _ _	4 . . . . _	5 . . . . .
6 _	7 _ _ . . .	8 _ _ _ . .	9 _ _ _ _ .	0 _ _ _ _ _

. . . . .

Heliographs

The ***Heliograph*** is a communications tool using reflected light and was invented by Sir Henry C. Moore, a British scientist and engineer. It was used successfully for the first time during the second Anglo-Afghan war, 1878-1880. The Heliograph in its most basic form consists of a mirror with a sight hole in the center allowing the person sending a message to sight on the person receiving the message. The mirror required sunlight for sending a series of long and short flashes using Morse code. Early tripod mounted mirrors used a Morse key to transmit and this controlled the mirror moving or *nodding* as it sent the message. Ranges of over 50 miles were easily achieved in desert regions and the devices were widely used in India and in the Middle East.

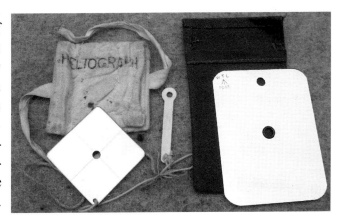

Pictured above on the left is a small Heliograph with separate sight and case. These were commonly packed inside the survival kits or life vests issued to British pilots. To its right is a 1945 dated Heliograph mirror and case that was part of the 1944 Pattern equipment that was issued to individual soldiers.

A group of Jat warriors native to India operating Heliograph units in Iraq.

· · · · ·

Pictured above are the leather cased contents of a Mark V Heliograph. They include sighting rods with movable vanes, the sight arm, main signaling mirror, a duplex mirror, and the main body holding the Morse key and beat regulating hardware. A pair of spare mirrors in a protective circular tin along with small tools is also part of the set.

Two British soldiers stationed in Cyprus photographed operating a Mark V Heliograph set. Both men are wearing early war Bombay Bloomers.

· · · · ·

303

The photograph at the right shows a Mark V Heliograph with a sighting rod attached to the sight arm for use when signaling to a station while facing towards the sun. The photograph below shows the same Heliograph with its duplex mirror installed which has a sight vane in the center of the disc. This configuration is used when signaling to a station while not facing towards the sun.

· · · · ·

Battery Powered Heliograph devices with Morse keys were produced during WWI and WWII. These had a small tube with a cross hair mounted to the top for sighting in on the intended receiving station. Because the units were used during the daytime and the flash is focused on a specific target, the signal is almost impossible to intercept unless you are very close to the recipients location. Coloured lenses were provided for nighttime signaling so the beam of light could not be seen as easily by others. This was not as secure for sending a message but it still proved to be very reliable. A similar method of sending messages is employed on ships when radios are not used during communications blackouts.

· · · · ·

305

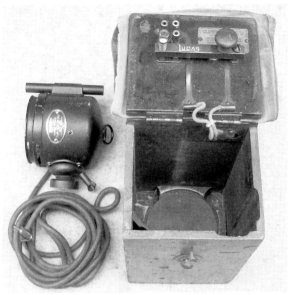

The Heliograph at the top of this page is a WWI pattern while the one below it was produced during WWII. The latter has a three section metal rod it can be mounted on when a tripod is not available. A standard tripod for use with both types of Heliograph is at the bottom of this page.

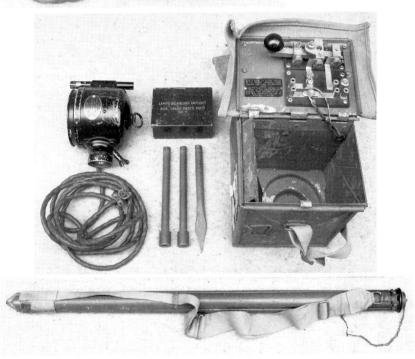

· · · · ·

The *Aldis Lamp* is another form of Heliograph. It is battery powered and has two triggers that are used for sending messages. One trigger turns on the high power light bulb inside the main housing. The other trigger is used for nodding a large mirror that is inside. If the light were triggered on and off to send messages, it would quickly burn out. The movement of the mirror is what actually sends the flashes of light as they are reflected towards the recipient using Morse code. A tube sight and a bracketed sight are both situated on the top for lining up on the target for transmitting. Aldis Lamps were a standard item at most facilities handling aircraft. They were also issued to some S.O.E. and Resistance units for signaling aircraft from the ground for supply drops. The example pictured on this page with its case and a pair of coloured lenses was made in Canada in 1942.

• • • • •

Still images from the British wartime produced airborne training exercise documentary *Airborne Assault*. The top photograph shows a soldier signaling to a landing craft with a battery powered Heliograph and the lower photograph shows the Navy signaling back with a hand-held Aldis Lamp.

· · · · ·

The ***Signaling Beacon Lamp*** is another large handheld battery powered lamp with a high intensity bulb. Like the Heliograph and Aldis lamps, it has a pair of sights along the top edge and a trigger to activate the light. But this device has no Morse key or second trigger for nodding. It was designed to be aimed and turned on for a specified duration, followed by a duration in which it is turned off. This sequence would be repeated and served the same purpose performed by a permanent, fixed-beacon type light house. For operational purposes, Commandos used these beacons to mark a designated point on a beach for nighttime seaborne landings or retrievals. Airborne Pathfinders and S.A.S personnel working with local Maquis or Partisan groups also used these beacons to identify troop or supply drop zones to inbound aircraft. The 200 watt bulb operated off a 12-volt battery and a pair of shielded 50 amperes capacity Crocodile clips provided a quick means of hooking it up.

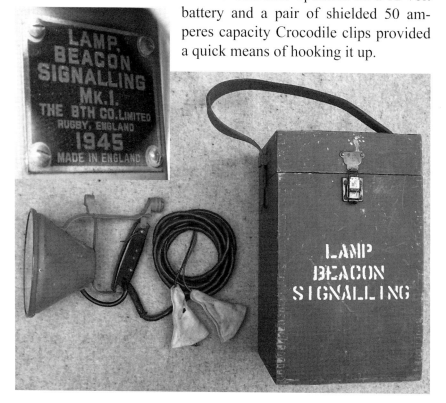

· · · · ·

Semaphore and Loudhailers

Flags were used for semaphore and Morse signaling but the distance they could be employed was fairly limited due to being subjective to lighting conditions and the background of the signal station. Range could be increased if the station being signaled to had the aid of a telescope, but this was still limited to around three miles with ideal conditions. The flags were two feet square and used in matching pairs. These were typically

either white with a horizontal blue stripe or they were all blue. This is represented on the Qualified Signaller and Signalling Instructor badges and an example is shown on this page. A chart showing the Semaphore positions can be found at the end of this chapter.

The *Loudhailer*, aka megaphone or bullhorn, used by the military forces during the Second World War was a portable, handheld, cone shaped device for directionally concentrating and amplifying the human voice. They were made of tin and had a handle on one side of the body. An indentation at the narrow end of the cone provided clearance for the nose when the operator held the device right up to their mouth. These were commonly issued to Vickers, mortar and artillery units for close pit-to-pit communications.

· · · · ·

A badly beaten up Loudhailer shown being used by a soldier of the 1st Airborne Airlanding Light Artillery in Italy.

· · · · ·

Field Telephones

Field Telephones consist of pairs of portable self contained units that allow two-way voice communications. They typically have a metal case that protects the main unit and houses the hand set inside. A hand crank is used to generate A.C. power for the ringer which is sent down the lines to the receiving set and sounds a bell announcing an inbound call. The transmissions are voice powered on some models and are D.C. powered by 1.5 or 3 volt batteries. The early WWI patterns used a single wire to connect a pair of sets and used an Earth ground for the return. Transmissions could be intercepted by other Earth induction sets if they were close enough to each other and this presented a problem in maintaining secure transmissions. The initial solution was to use paired wire between field telephone sets and this kept the signal secure as long as the lines were not tapped by the enemy.

Pictured is a pair of British WWII Type "H" Mark III Field Telephones and the user instructions located inside the lid of each set.

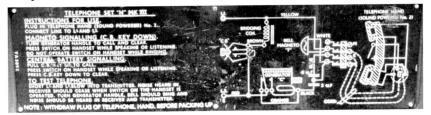

. . . . .

A wartime British signals relay station in the desert. The individual seen in the photograph is at the central location of five fighting positions. He has four wired field phones and can communicate with any single station at a given time. Messages from one station to another must be passed through this central station. As a backup, he has an electric torch and a loudhailer resting on top of a large empty wire reel.

Field Phones being used by a Canadian officer directing mortar fire. May-sur-Orne, France - 9 AUG 1944.

· · · · ·

Fullerphones

The ***Fullerphone*** was the invention of then Captain A.C. Fuller in late 1915. It was a D.C. powered Morse telegraph system with a signal that was virtually immune from being intercepted. The first patterns were used for secure transmissions during the remainder of the Great War and the Mark III was in use during the years between the two wars. The Mark IV Fullerphone was adopted for British service in 1939 and by mid war the Mark V was introduced. A Mark VI tropicalized pattern was produced for use in the Pacific and it featured a waterproof case. The basic Fullerphone is housed in a wooden box that has a double hinged lid that can be folded back once unhooked. Inside is the main unit which has a compartment for batteries and a Buzzer-Chopper which can be tuned to filter transmissions. A Morse key for transmitting is built into the base at the side of the main unit and a pair of sockets in the front are for the plugs of two separate headsets. The Fullerphone was capable of sending and receiving clear transmissions over a distance of 20 miles using normal rolled army wire and greater ranges could be achieved using telephone lines. As good as the Fullerphone was, it still required land lines of one form or another which could be cut by explosions or enemy soldiers, rendering the device useless.

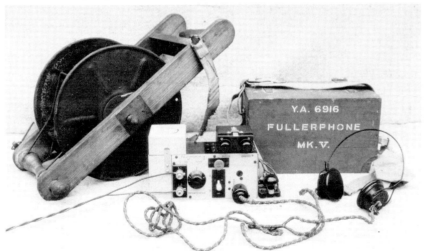

An example of a WWII British Mark V Fullerphone with carrying case.

. . . . .

There were several patterns of ***Signal Pistols*** in use by the British and Commonwealth forces during WWII; some were left over from the First World War and others were new designs that had been developed during WWII. The majority of these that were issued to the infantry and airborne forces used the 1.0 calibre very cartridges. Larger signal pistols that used the 1.5 calibre Very cartridges were more typically issued to aircrews and were kept on hand at the control towers of airfields for emergencies. Most WWI and early production WWII signal pistols were made from brass. The Number 1 Mark IV was an experimental pattern made from a zinc alloy in an effort to save on metal. They seem to have been produced in large numbers but later in the war, new designs were made from steel. Early war and pre-war models typically have wooden grips while later production models had black composition grips. Service revolvers also went through this same change with their grips.

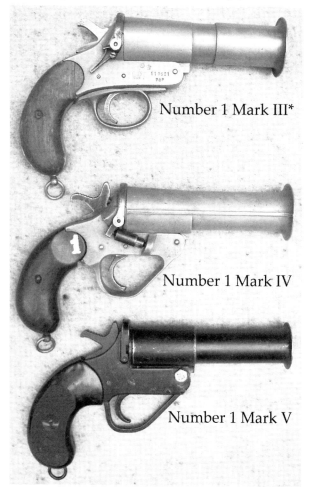

Number 1 Mark III*

Number 1 Mark IV

Number 1 Mark V

Patterns of both 1.0 and 1.5 calibre signal pistols were produced which have short barrels, and do not have the *blunderbuss* flared end found on regular models. They will normally have one or more squared lugs that project from the side of the barrel. These were made for use by the crews while they were inside tanks and airplanes. The barrel is pressed through a hole in the aircraft or tank which has key slots that match the lugs on the barrel of the signal pistol. Once inserted, it is rotated to lock it in place for firing. This ensured that fired Verys stayed on the outside of the vehicle so they couldn't start a fire on the inside. It was standard procedure for aircraft with wounded on board to fire Verys to alert the ground crews and to indicate to other aircraft in the formation that they needed priority.

Signal pistols were often used to coordinate attacks. One colour of very might indicate the start of a mortar or artillery barrage while another colour signaled for a halt to the barrage so the infantry could begin their advance. On airfields, a Very was normally fired to let formations of aircraft on the ground know that they should begin their roll out to take off.

Number 2 Mark V

Number 4 Mark I

• • • • •

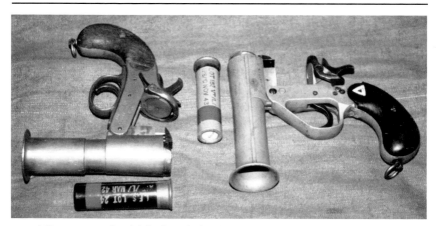

All patterns of British signal pistols have a top break action for loading. As with the revolvers using this type of action, the shell extractor extends on opening and pulls the cartridge from the chamber. For safety, signal pistols can only be fired single action which requires that they be manually cocked before pulling the trigger. The photograph above shows two 1.0 calibre signal pistols open for loading while the one below shows a 1.5 calibre signal pistol with a cartridge in the chamber and another beside it.

Holsters were produced for the signal pistols from leather and from web material as used on the normal 1937 pattern equipment. Each pattern has an adjustable shoulder sling. The holsters are slightly larger than the type used for the .455 Webley revolvers and will have a rounded end to accommodate the blunderbuss muzzle on the standard pattern signal pistols. A special web equipment brace was made during the war which had an integral square pouch sewn to it. This pouch has a flap that

closes the top and is held in place by a single web tab and buckle. The pouch will hold four of the 1.0 calibre Very cartridges.

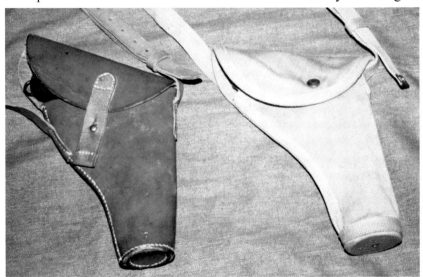

. . . . .

To assist with nighttime identification of what the colour a very was before firing, some manufactures milled grooves into the brass rim of the shell case. One quarter of the circumference of the head was milled on yellow Verys. White Verys were milled for half of the circumference. Red Verys were milled all the way around and green Verys had no milling at all. WWI and early WWII produced Verys tend to have completely brass cases. Later WWII produced British Verys have a brass head with a cardboard hull as found on shotgun shells of the time. Lend-lease cartridges from the United States tend to have a shorter case which is made of aluminum.

Variations of the 1.5 calibre Verys are shown at the left and a mixture of U.S. and British made 1.0 and 1.5 calibre Verys are shown below.

· · · · ·

Two types of tin that British-made Verys were packaged in. Each held six Very cartridges. With them is the special web equipment brace with integrated pouch for carrying four loose Very cartridges. This example was made in 1941.

Four pairs of the more common types of Verys produced during WWII.

This box for Verys was mounted on some Bren carriers and scout cars. The lid was colour coded to indicate where red, white and green verys could be drawn from.

· · · · ·

A signal pistol being fired during training exercises in the early months following the formation of the airborne forces in the United Kingdom. The men still carry Enfield Number 1 Mark III* rifles fitted with Number 1 Mark I 1907 pattern bayonets.

Tommy expressing himself to a pair of German prisoners in North Africa.

This "Up Yours" gesture originated as a taunt to the French by English longbowmen in 1415 during the Hundred Years' War. The French had threatened to cut off the bowstring drawing fingers from the right hand of any captured archers.

· · · · ·

Number 38 Mark II Wireless Set

The *Number 38 Wireless Set* was a transceiver introduced for infantry and airborne use in 1942 following a series of trials. The Mark II pattern became the standard short range set during WWII. It was developed during 1941 by the Signals Experimental Establishment (SEE) with the intent of creating a light weight and easy to operate wireless set for small unit communications. The aerial consisted of "F" type rods which were each four feet in length. The thinnest rod could be used alone with the Number 38 set and this provided a range of roughly half a mile. Alternately three sections could be fitted together to produce a 12 foot long aerial that could achieve a maximum range of 2 miles under ideal conditions. The reliable range was only considered to be 1 mile with the 12 foot aerial but this was normally adequate since it was a platoon level wireless set. Walking around with a 12 foot aerial was not always a safe thing to do in combat since it drew attention to the operator and the command element of the platoon. A 45 foot long aerial made from insulated wire was developed as a low profile solution to the problem and it was laid out behind the wireless operator on the ground when needed. Using it reduced the range of the set but this was a justifiable price to pay for not being as conspicuous on the battlefield. The "F" type aerials were carried in a web case with shoulder sling designed to hold four of the sections.

· · · · ·

The 38 set used dry battery HT/LT Number 1 which provided approximately 20 hours of operational life. The Number 2 battery could also be used with the 38 set and it could provide 35 hours of operational life. The drawback to this battery was it had a limited shelf life and could prove to be unreliable in the field if it was old. Batteries were carried in the small pack along with the junction box. The Junction Box used with the 38 set is the Number 2 pattern. It has a four point plug that connects directly to the battery. A socket in the center has six points and the cable from the wireless set connects into it. Two sockets located at the top are designed to receive the plugs from the throat microphone and the headphones. They each have unique plugs so they cannot be inserted into the wrong sockets. The throat microphone made the 38 set virtually hands free to operate. This allowed the operator to still carry arms while not restricting his movement. It also enabled him to wear a respirator and still work the set if needed.

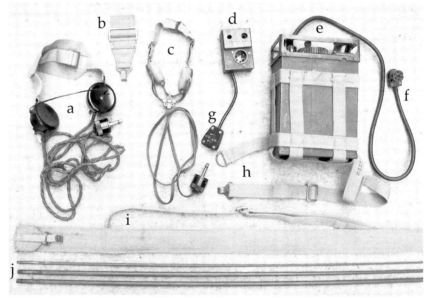

(a)-Headset, (b)-Brace Hook, (c)-Throat Mike, (d)-Junction Box, (e)-38 Set Main Unit, (f)-Cable from 38 Set to Junction Box, (g)-Cable from Junction Box to Battery, (h)-38 Set Web Carrying Harness, (i)-Aerial Case, (j)-Type "F" Aerial Sections

· · · · ·

A Number 2 Junction Box shown above with everything connected on the left and alone on the right.

Case for Spare Valves

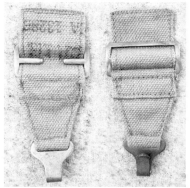

Pictured above is a pair of the special brace hooks used with the 38 set. The strap is buckled into the shoulder of one of the equipment braces and the wireless hangs from the metal hook.

Spare valves, pictured at the right, were stored in their own protective metal case which was carried in one of the Satchels Signals haversacks along with the throat microphone and headphones when not needed.

· · · · ·

A soldier of one of the Airlanding Brigades makes adjustments to a Number 38 set he carriers on his chest.

General Richard "Windy" Gale inspecting an airborne soldier equipped with a Wireless Set Number 38. He has an aerial quiver slung over each shoulder. No doubt he enlisted well before the war began as he has six good conduct chevrons on the left sleeve of his battledress blouse.

• • • • •

WEAR THE MK. 2. LIKE THIS—

[AND WEAR YOUR RESPIRATOR
AND HAVERSACK AS USUAL!]

CHECK YOUR KIT WITH THIS LIST

W.S. Set 38 Mk. 2	1
W.S. Set Carriers No. 2	1
Mic., Throat, Nos. 1 or 2	2
Phones, DLR, Nos. 1 or 2 (with canvas headband and mic. support strap.)	2
Batteries, dry, HT/LT Nos. 1 or 2	2
Aerial Rods F, Section 1	1
Do. Section 2	1
Do. Section 3	2
Cases, Aerial No. 3	1
Hooks, brace (1 spare)	2
Satchel, Signals	1
Junction Boxes No. 2	1
Working Instructions card	1

CANVAS STRAP
METAL BANDS
STRAP & HOOK
MIC.
WEAR YOUR PHONES AND
MICROPHONE LIKE THIS

CARRY IT AS UNDER WHEN NOT
IN USE

1. IN AERIAL CASE
The 4 aerial rods.

2. IN YOUR HAVERSACK
In place of water bottle:
1 batteries, dry (in use)
1 Junction Box.

3. IN SATCHEL SIGNALS
2 mics. and 2 phones. (1 set for officer)
1 Batteries, dry (spare)
1 Hooks, brace (spare).
AND THIS CARD.

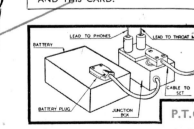

P.T.O.

326

W.S. NO. 38 MK. 2, WORKING INSTRUCTIONS

1. IMPORTANT—See that 'phones, microphone, and battery are plugged into their proper sockets in the Junction Box in the Back Haversack.

2. **AERIALS** (Rotate socket cover to select desired socket).
   - (a) Normal Signals. Use thin 4 ft. section inserted in small aerial socket.
   - (b) Weak Signals. Use 12 ft. rod (3 sections) in large aerial socket. Never use fewer than 3 sections.

3. **CHECK**
   - (a) Put on 'phones and microphone.
   - (b) Switch to "Send," and press rubber test button.
   - (c) Lamp should light and flicker when you speak.
   - (d) Your voice should be heard in the 'phones.

4. **TO SET UP A "NET."** In most operations a group of sets will be used, one as the "Control" and two or more as "Out Stations." All stations in one "net" must be tuned to the same frequency, and the "net" is set up in the following way:—

   (1) CONTROL
   - (a) Set TUNING Mc/s dial to allotted frequency and lock.
   - (b) Send tuning call for specified time so that out stations can identify you and tune their sets accurately. Then announce termination of call.
   - (c) One minute after termination call group.

   (2) OUT STATIONS
   - (a) Set TUNING Mc/s dial to allotted frequency. Switch to "Receive" and tune-in tuning signal. Adjust TUNING Mc/s dial as accurately as possible to centre of signal and lock. After locking, rock dial slightly to see that tuning is accurate. If it is not, readjust without unlocking.
   - (b) Await call from Control to check "net."

   IMPORTANT NOTE.—If the "net" is set up with the stations close to each other the out stations must remove their aerial rods while setting up.

5. **BATTERY REPLACEMENT.** When the indicator lamp ceases to glow while you are speaking, with the set switched to "Send" and the test button pressed, the battery may need replacement. Switch off before replacing.

6. **DO'S AND DONT'S**
   - (a) ALWAYS wait at least 3 seconds after switching to "Send" before speaking.
   - (b) ALWAYS end each message with the word "OVER," and switch to "Receive" immediately.
   - (c) ALWAYS switch the set to "OFF" when not in use.
   - (d) ALWAYS keep the set clean—particularly the aerial connecting ends and sockets.
   - (e) NEVER touch the dial while locking it.
   - (f) NEVER overtighten the dial lock.　　　　　P.T.O.

ZA.14284

· · · · ·

Number 18 Wireless Set

The *Number 18 Wireless Set* was the standard set used during WWII for communications between Battalion and Company headquarters while in forward areas. First production was in 1940 and they saw service in North Africa and the European and Pacific Theatres of Operation. It was a short range completely self-contained wireless that was designed to be man-packed. The main cabinet housing the wireless contained the transmitter, receiver and the primary battery which provided HT and LT power. This could be supplemented by an external battery or portable generator. The operational range for the set was considered to be 10 miles but this was subject to terrain and atmospheric conditions. The aerial was assembled from a series of type "D" rods which were hollow tubes approximately 12 inches long with tapered ends so they could be connected to each other. The mounting point for the aerial was on the left outer side of the cabinet as viewed facing the open set.

· · · · ·

The cabinet for the Number 18 Wireless Set is the same size as found on the Number 22 and Number 19 Wireless Sets. A metal loop at the top on the back provides a mounting point for the top of the shoulder straps and the lower ends clip into the back of the cabinet. A web waist belt similar to the pattern worn during WWI is attached at the bottom of the cabinet to allow the hips to bear most of the weight of the set.

The two sockets in the upper unit are for a pair of headphones. The square socket in the lower unit is for the microphone and a socket to its right is for connection of a Morse key. The cable at the bottom of the set plugged into a socket in the floor going to the internal battery. This lead can be pulled out and extended from the cabinet for connecting to a Number 5 Power Supply.

· · · · ·

The Type "D" Rods used to assemble the aerial are stored in the sides of the cabinet and small clips hold them in place. Additional storage areas are on the back of the cabinet and can be seen in the photo showing the load bearing harness on the previous page.

A waterproof cover is attached to the outer edge of the cabinet to protect the components from the elements when not in use. Metal braces hold it open when folded out and this creates an umbrella to shelter the set while being used.

An unidentified corporal and signaller of Le Régiment de Maisonneuve operating a Number 18 Wireless set while on guard duty. Somewhere on the southeast coast of England - 13 JAN 1942.

. . . . .

Private Harvey Lalonde and Signalman Raymond Gosselin of "D" Company, Regiment De Maisonneuve, with a Number 18 wireless set. Cuyk, Netherlands – 23 JAN 1945.

Airborne troops with a Number 18 Wireless set on an assault exercise.

· · · · ·

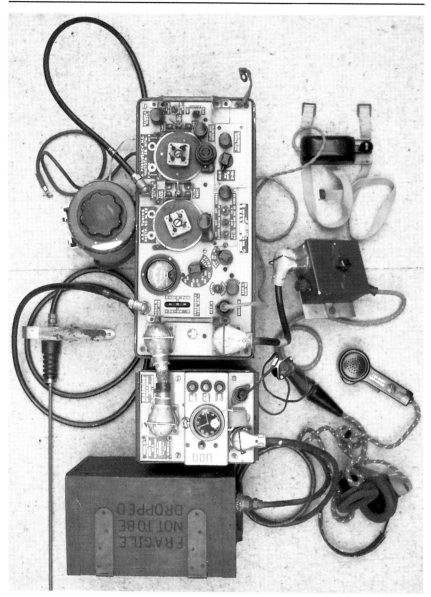

A complete Number 19 wireless hooked up with wooden boxed battery for power. The only item not pictured is the main aerial which would be connected to the loose lead coming from the variometer.

• • • • •

The **Number 19 Wireless Set** was a transceiver first developed in 1941. There were three Marks produced during the war and they were manufactured in the United Kingdom, Canada and the United States. Originally they were designed for use in tanks and armoured fighting vehicles. As the war progressed, they became the general purpose wireless set used in trucks, some command jeeps and for ground stations. Two sets are actually incorporated inside the main cabinet. The "A" set operated from 2-8 megacycles and used 4-foot long Aerial Rod "F" Sections in combinations dependant on the terrain and needed operating range. An 8 foot long aerial gave an effective range of 10 miles. This range could be boosted to 45 miles when the set was used with the Number 2 Amplifier. The "B" set operated on 230-240 megacycles and used a much shorter Type "G" Aerial Rod which had a range of ¾ of a mile. Its purpose was for command and control communications between moving vehicles in the same formation and it was limited to light of sight transmissions. The "B" set on Mark I and Mark II sets was also used for inter-vehicle intercom communications between crew members through a switch

An unidentified infantryman of the Calgary Highlanders servicing a Number 19 wireless set. Paghem, England – 20 JAN 1943.

· · · · ·

on the control box. The later Mark III set had an economy mode where individual A-Set, B-Set and/or Intercom components could be turned on or off as needed. Many of the later production Number 19 wireless sets have panels that have English and Cyrillic markings on them since they were also provided to the Russians via the Lend-Lease Act. The complete Number 19 set had dimensions of 27 inches long by 10 inches deep by 13.25 inches wide. The combined weight of the main unit with power supply was 88.25 pounds.

A Number 19 Mark II Wireless Set manufactured under a 1944 contract in the United States.

Canadian Number 19 Mark III Wireless Set produced in 1945 by RCA Victor.

• • • • •

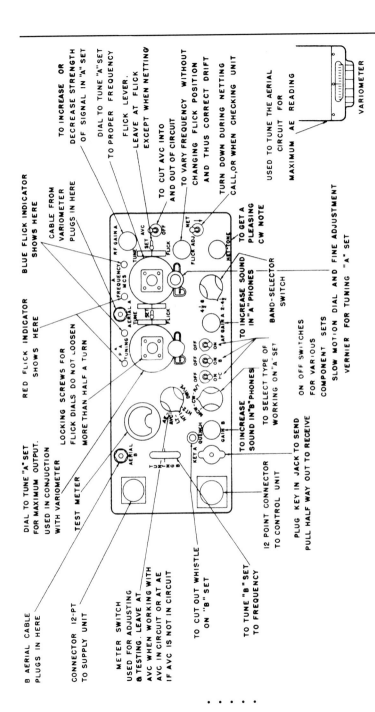

WHAT ARE ALL THE KNOBS FOR?

A diagram extracted from the manual

WORKING INSTRUCTIONS: WIRELESS SET (CANADIAN) No. 19 Mark III

TO INCREASE OR DECREASE STRENGTH OF SIGNAL IN "A" SET

DIAL TO TUNE "A" SET TO PROPER FREQUENCY

FLICK LEVER. LEAVE AT FLICK EXCEPT WHEN NETTING

TO CUT AVC INTO AND OUT OF CIRCUIT

TO VARY FREQUENCY WITHOUT CHANGING FLICK POSITION AND THUS CORRECT DRIFT

TURN DOWN DURING NETTING CALL, OR WHEN CHECKING UNIT

USED TO TUNE THE AERIAL CIRCUIT FOR MAXIMUM AE READING

VARIOMETER

CABLE FROM VARIOMETER PLUGS IN HERE

BLUE FLICK INDICATOR SHOWS HERE

RED FLICK INDICATOR SHOWS HERE

LOCKING SCREWS FOR FLICK DIALS DO NOT LOOSEN MORE THAN HALF A TURN

RF GAIN A

SET AVC

FLICK

OFF

MET

FLICK ADJ

NET-TONE

TO GET A PLEASING CW NOTE

TUNE

FREQUENCY MCS

AERIAL A TUNE

SET

FLICK

P A TUNING

AF GAIN A 2-4½

BAND-SELECTOR SWITCH

TO INCREASE SOUND IN "A" PHONES

ON OFF SWITCHES FOR VARIOUS COMPONENT SETS

SLOW MOTION DIAL AND FINE ADJUSTMENT VERNIER FOR TUNING "A" SET

DIAL TO TUNE "A" SET FOR MAXIMUM OUTPUT. USED IN CONJUCTION WITH VARIOMETER

B AERIAL CABLE PLUGS IN HERE

TEST METER

CONNECTOR 12-PT TO SUPPLY UNIT

AERIAL B

METER SWITCH USED FOR ADJUSTING & TESTING. LEAVE AT AVC WHEN WORKING WITH AVC IN CIRCUIT OR AT AE IF AVC IS NOT IN CIRCUIT

KEY A QUENCH

GAIN B

TUNING B

TO CUT OUT WHISTLE ON "B" SET

TO INCREASE SOUND IN "B" PHONES

TO SELECT TYPE OF WORKING ON "A" SET

TO TUNE "B" SET TO FREQUENCY

12 POINT CONNECTOR TO CONTROL UNIT

PLUG KEY IN JACK TO SEND PULL HALF WAY OUT TO RECEIVE

• • • • •

336

The *Supply Unit* is the device that provides the required power to the Number 19 set. It is operated off of either a 12-volt or 24-volt external battery. A toggle switch inside the chassis must be placed in the appropriate position to correspond with the voltage of the battery being used. The Mark I Supply Unit was introduced with the Number 19 set in 1941 but it was quickly replaced by the Mark II Supply Unit which became the standard model used for most of the war. An improved Mark III model was introduced late in the war and it greatly extended the life of the external batteries. The Mark III used a vibrator to produce needed power for receiving transmissions and a dynamotor produced the H.T. voltage required for transmitting. When the dynamotor was engaged, the Supply Unit made a humming noise as it generated power and drew down the battery. This later model allowed the Wireless to be operated with the Supply Unit set to economically produce power in the vibrator mode but the dynamotor would automatically engage when the pressel, also known as the Send/Receive Switch, is depressed on the microphone for transmitting. A three position switch on the chassis allowed selection of mode to be used for instances where the operator wanted the dynamotor to remain engaged. The earlier Mark I and Mark II Supply Units simply had an on/off switch.

Supply Unit Mark II made in 1944

Supply Unit Mark III made in 1945

• • • • •

337

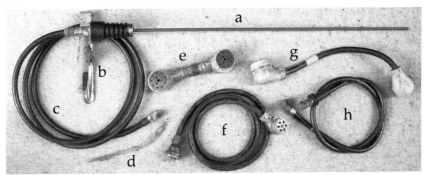

(a)-Aerial Rod "G", (b)-Aerial Base 9 with special fitting for mounting in airborne jeeps, (c)-Aerial Lean Number 2, (d)-Auxiliary Ground Cable, (e)-Power Supply Cable (Dog Bone), (f)-Power Cable to Battery with 6 Point Connector, (g)-12 point to 12 point Control Box Cable, (h)-RF Cable with Two Pye Connectors

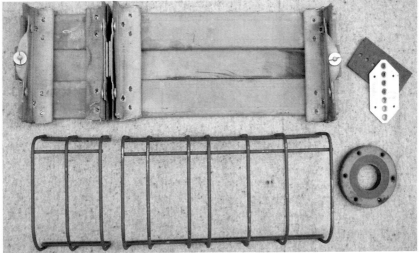

Pictured above is the *Carrier* with clamping straps needed for mounting the Number 19 set with Supply Unit onto a vehicle. Insulating pads rest under each of the components to absorb shocks and offset the cabinets from the metal carrier. Each has a wide strap with metal fittings with studs designed to match slots of the cabinets. Once locked in place, a thumb screw is tightened up on each end to prevent the wireless equipment from shifting around. Below the Carrier is a pair of *Brush Guards* used to protect the front panels on the Supply Unit and Number 19 Set main unit. These clip on to the front of the cabinets for each of the devices and lock firmly in place. To the right of the Carrier and Brush Guards are mounting plates for the Variometer and Number 8 Aerial Base.

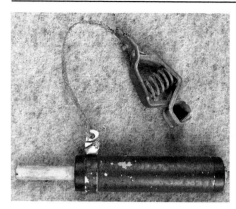

Dummy Aerial Number C1 (ZA/CAN 0677) used to prevent damage to wireless equipment while it is being tested without live aerials so no signal goes out.

Pictured below is a Number 9 *Key and Plug* assembly that can be used for CW (Morse) transmissions with the Number 19 Wireless Set. It is normally stored in the Spare Parts Case.

Operator Lamp Number 6 (ZA 11521) was used to extend the point where either power indicating lamps were mounted or to relocate the lamp that illuminates when transmitting. The cable screws into place where the desired light bulb needing to be relocated is situated. A clip on the housing allows the newly extended lamp to be fastened to something else to prevent it from swinging around.

. . . . .

Close up shot showing the markings on a 20 foot telescoping steel vertical mast and one of its insulated guy lines used to support it once extended.

Shown above are four 4-foot long *Aerial Rod "F" Sections*, a 20 foot telescoping steel vertical mast which would be topped with "F" Sections, four insulated guy lines and a grounding spike that would use an earth lead to connect it to the base of the mast.

The *Variometer* is used with the tuning dials to adjust the aerial to the frequency that is needed. It has two scales on the dial which is adjusted by rotating the large knob on the front of the device. The lower frequencies are adjusted on the scale ranging from 0-100 and the higher frequencies are adjusted on the scale ranging from 200-100. The back of the housing has a mounting point for a cable that leads to the Number 8 Mount used for the "A" set aerial.

. . . . .

Aerial Gear Bags were issued as part of the wireless kit allotment for Number 19 sets installed in trucks and used as ground stations. They were intended to hold items used with the 20 foot and 34 foot telescoping steel vertical masts. These included insulated guy lines, grounding spikes, earth leads, aerial leads and associated connectors. Several variations of the bags were produced during the war. The one shown in the photograph above is a Canadian-made version in leather. Two additional versions are shown below. The one at the top of the photograph is British-made from webbing material. The one below it is Australian-made from waterproof canvas material. The bags have a length of 42 inches with a 6.5 width and a 6.5 inch height. The leather version has handles built into the sides while the webbing and canvas versions each have a single adjustable shoulder strap for carrying the bag.

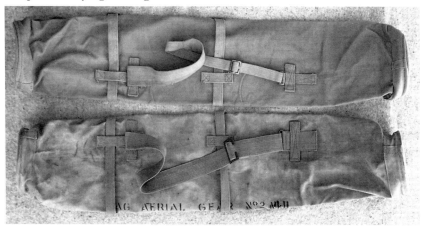

. . . . .

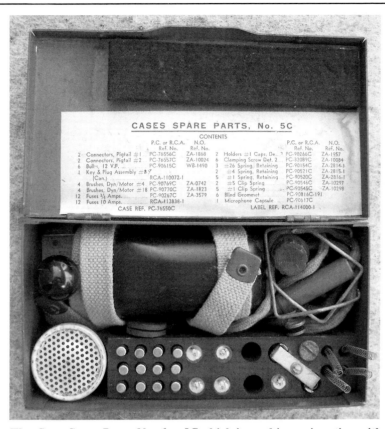

CASES SPARE PARTS, No. 5C

CONTENTS

	P.C. or R.C.A. Ref. No.	N.O. Ref. No.			P.C. or R.C.A. Ref. No.	N.O. Ref. No.
2 Connectors, Pigtail ≠1	PC-76556C	ZA-1868	2 Holders ≠1 Caps, De.. ?	PC-90266C	ZA-1957
2 Connectors, Pigtail ≠2	PC-76557C	ZA-10024	6 Clamping Screw Det. 2	PC-32089C	ZA-10084
6 Bulbs, 12 V.F.	PC-90615C	WB-1490	3 ≠26 Spring, Retaining	PC-90154C	ZA-2814-1
1 Key & Plug Assembly ≠9			2 ≠4 Spring, Retaining	PC-90521C	ZA-2815-1
(Can.)	RCA-110072-1		5 ≠1 Spring, Retaining	PC-90520C	ZA-2816-1
4 Brushes, Dyn/Motor ≠4	PC-90769C	ZA-0742	2 ≠5 Clip Spring	PC-90546C	ZA-10297
4 Brushes, Dyn/Motor ≠18	PC-90770C	ZA-1823	5 ≠1 Clip Spring	PC-90545C	ZA-10298
12 Fuses ¼ Amps.	PC-90267C	ZA-3579	6 Blind Grommet	PC-90816C-191	
12 Fuses 10 Amps.	RCA-113838-1		1 Microphone Capsule	PC-90617C	
CASE REF. PC-76550C			LABEL REF. RCA-114000-1		

The *Case, Spare Parts, Number 5C* which is used in conjunction with the Number 19 Wireless Set. It contains spare brushes, fuses, replacement lamp bulbs, the Number 9 Key set and other small parts needed to maintain the wireless and supply unit. These cases were typically bolted to the cabinet of the wireless set for convenient access. Airborne jeeps fitted with 19 sets had a special carrier frame designed to hold the case and it was bolted to the jeep's rear tub.

• • • • •

A metal case designed to house *Spare Valves* (radio tubes) was provided with each Number 19 Wireless Set. It had a hinged lid with a carrying handle made of web material on top. Inside the case there is a removable housing with sockets made to match the individual valves it was intended to carry. The housing is removable because some of the valves are stored underneath the main platform. A cloth tape is fitted to the housing to assist in pulling it free from the case.

· · · · ·

Remote Control Units

The ***Wireless Remote Control Unit*** was a device that worked with the Number 19 Wireless Set. It provided a means to relay a message back to the host wireless set from as much as three miles away. A pair of Remote Control Units were required. The one located near the wireless set was known as the *Nearby R.C.U.* and the distant unit was known as the *Remote R.C.U.* These were connected together by a paired ground wire known as the *Control Wire.* The remote Control Units has a carrying sling to make it easier to

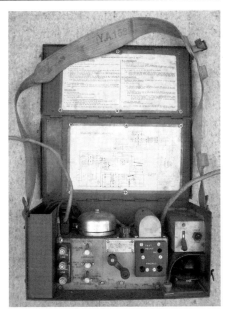

transport by foot to its intended destination. They had a weight of just over 22 pounds and were powered by dry cell batteries that were stored inside the cabinet. The idea behind using a Remote Control Unit was the wireless set could be situated in a more secure area away from the front lines where transmission requirements were needed to report enemy observations.

• • • • •

The ***Crystal Calibrator*** is an oscillator used for testing and more accurately fine tuning the "A" set of the Number 19 Wireless Set. This enabled a series of sets to be exactly tuned to the same frequency so they would be matched to each other and ensure reliable communications while netting. It also allowed the exact frequency to be determined when a wireless set picked up transmissions from an unknown station. The reason for the Crystal Calibrator being introduced for service is the tuning knobs on the 19 set didn't allow confirmation of an exact frequency being dialed in unless you already knew someone was transmitting on that frequency and you monitored for a signal while tuning. Once the

station was found, it would be locked in as a known station regardless of what the dial indicated. The Crystal Calibrator generated its own radio signals at equally spaced frequency intervals which served as accurate frequency markers. By selecting the needed range, frequencies could be identified at 1000, 100 and 10 kilohertz.

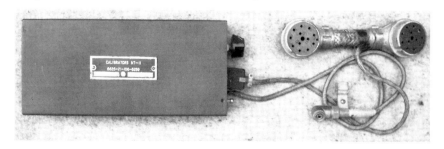

· · · · ·

Generators and Batteries

Wireless sets were dependant on D.C. power to operate and batteries were provided to supply it to them. Batteries were heavy and had a limited operating life. This was a concern for extended operations under combat conditions where communications were vital and supplies and equipment had to be carried. Portable man-powered generators were designed to overcome this problem and they could be used to slowly recharge drained batteries as well as to generate power for transmitting. The ***Number 5 Power Supply Unit*** was one such device and it worked with the Number 18 and Number 38 wireless sets. It was housed in a cabinet similar to the one used with the Number 18 wireless set complete with shoulder straps and waist belt for an individual to carry. Two sockets were built into the side of the cabinet for connecting the power cords for the wireless sets when they needed auxiliary power to supplement or replace their own batteries. A hand crank on the opposite side needed to be turned continuously to generate power.

· · · · ·

The *Batteries* for the Number 18 and Number 38 wireless sets could be carried in small packs worn on the back or at the side. This was not the case for the Number 19 and Number 22 wireless sets because they had a greater input need. In some cases the wireless set was hardwired into the power supply of the host vehicle it was mounted in which had its own generator so long as the engine was running at a high enough speed. Many of the airborne units with this type of wireless set preferred to have separate batteries and this helped to ensure their vehicle would still start when needed. Spare batteries were carried on airborne jeeps in baskets mounted on the wings and at the rear of the vehicle. The wireless set would be connected to one of these and when the battery ran low, it could be swapped out for a fresh one. The batteries were housed in wooden boxes that had handles on the top or at the side. A socket built into the front or side was used to connect the power cord from the wireless set.

Batteries in carriers on an airborne jeep at the rear near the aerial and on the wings.

Three other types of larger 6 volt battery boxes.

· · · · ·

347

In addition to the wooden boxed battery carriers, a pattern produced from webbing was also in use during the Second World War. They were only large enough to accommodate the smallest wireless six and twelve volt batteries but these still proved to be invaluable during some of the airborne operations in Europe as well as for jungle penetrations in the Far East where the troops we isolated and needed to maintain mobility.

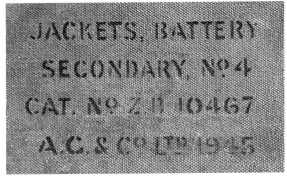

Size and weight of some of the more commonly used wireless batteries during the war.

Volts	Amp Hours	Dimensions	Weight
6	40	10 x 5.75 x 10.5	33 pounds
6	85	12.75 x 7 x 9.25	56 pounds
6	125	16.5 x 8 x 11.25	76.5 pounds
6	170	16 x 7.75 x 13	112 pounds
12	14	8.75 x 6.5 x 8.25	23.5 pounds
12	22	12.5 x 6.25 x 10	37.5 pounds
12	75	16.5 x 11.75 x 8	77.5 pounds

· · · · ·

348

A member of the Royal Corps of Signals attached to the 1st Airborne Division with a portable generator. This type folded up so it could be carried on the back with a frame similar to the one used with the Everest Carrier. One of the smaller type wooden battery boxes normally carried on the airborne jeeps is also on the individuals back.

The generator completely set up and showing how it would be hand cranked to charge a battery or to provide power for transmitting. These generators could also be pedaled if the operator had something to sit on.

. . . . .

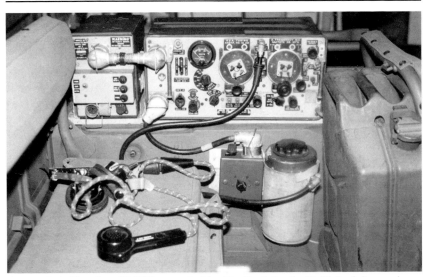

A complete Number 19 WS mounted inside the tub of a British airborne jeep.

Examples of the main type of plugs found in use with British signals equipment.

The 70 foot (left) and the 250 foot long Number 1 (right) wire aerials used with the Number 19 and Number 22 wireless sets.

· · · · ·

350

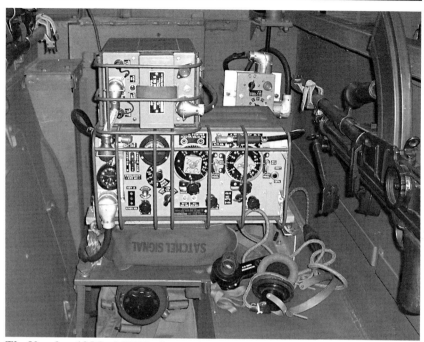

The Number 19 Mark II Wireless set installed in a Ford T-16 Universal Carrier.

On-going daily operations at a Canadian general signals office during 1941.

• • • • •

Several patterns of **Satchels Signals** haversacks were produced during the war. Some were intended for specialized applications while others served a generic purpose. Most will have the signals identification markings that begin with "ZA" so they can be easily identified from other web haversacks. The haversack pictured on this page was designed to hold microphones and headphones for the Number 18 and Number 38 wireless sets. It has a single internal compartment and a web carrying sling that attaches to the outer edges so it can be worn at the side. The flapped lid has a single web tab that buckles in the front to keep it closed. Unlike most haversacks, the lid folds back further on the back of the bag to allow for cords to be passed so they will be trapped underneath and will stay closer to the wearer and not slip around to the front when stored in the haversack while still connected to the wireless set.

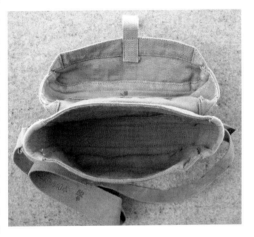

· · · · ·

The Satchels Signals haversack pictured on this page was intended for use with the Number 38 Wireless Set but it could also serve generic applications as needed. It is constructed along the same design as the Small Pack. Internally it is divided into two cells instead of three as found on the Small Pack. The dry cell battery for the 38 set was carried on one side and the junction box and metal case containing spare valves was carried in the other side. Like the Small Pack, it could be worn slung at the side by a web strap attached to the outer edges or be worn on the back via a pair of "L" Straps.

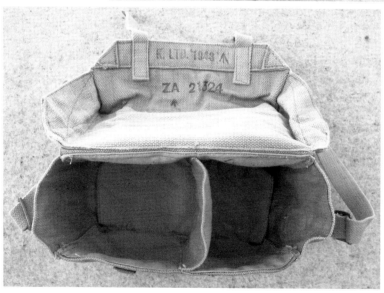

· · · · ·

Semaphore Alphabet and Numeral Signs

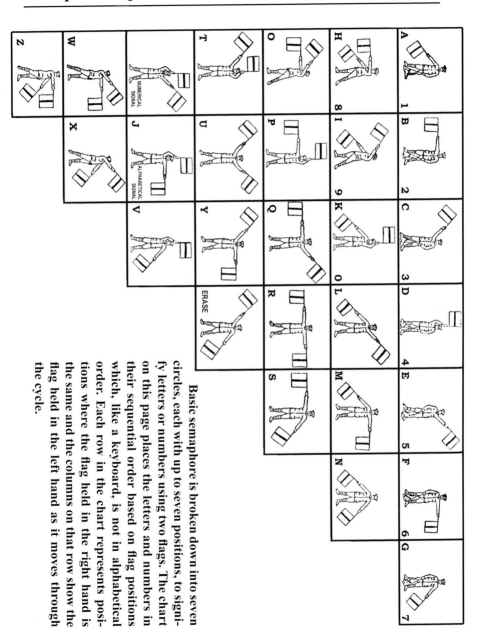

Basic semaphore is broken down into seven circles, each with up to seven positions, to signify letters or numbers using two flags. The chart on this page places the letters and numbers in their sequential order based on flag positions which, like a keyboard, is not in alphabetical order. Each row in the chart represents positions where the flag held in the right hand is the same and the columns on that row show the flag held in the left hand as it moves through the cycle.

. . . . .

Chapter 8 - Anti-Gas Equipment

A soldier ready for training wearing a Mark IV General Service Respirator. Puckapunyal, Victoria, Australia - JUN 1940.

. . . . .

The word *Gas,* in association with munitions during WWI and WWII, applies to any chemical compound that was intended to irritate or kill when released into the air. Gas can take the form of a solid, liquid or vapor and is broken down into two main categories; persistent and non-persistent. Persistent gases include liquid forms of Lewisite and Mustard which slowly vaporize off of sprayed areas and could stay in the air for 30 to 50 hours with the full potential for toxic effects. Non-persistent gases include Chlorine and Phosgene which produced toxic clouds like smoke and would hang in the air until a breeze dissipated them. Gases were also classified into four basic groups that were identified by one of three coloured bands on chemical shells in the case of British munitions, using the first letter for the colour code of that group to identify the compound within. The base colour for all British chemical munitions was gray. Blister Gas was coded yellow and included compounds known as vessicants, which are corrosive and cause blistering. Mustard is one type and it produced intense irritation and blisters on exposed skin. Choking and Nose Gases were coded together as green and included chlorine, phosgene and arsenical compounds. They attacked the lungs and breathing passages and caused death if too much was inhaled. Tear Gases were coded black and were referred to as lachrymators. While their effects were immediate and severe, normally they were not lethal once relief was found.

GAS CHAMBER TEST

Name ROBERTS   Capt.
Personal Number ___ 91471
Facepiece Size ___ Lapp.

Chamber Tests, Dates :- 30.1.43
2 0 AUG. 1943

Certificate of having experienced
D.M.

CERTIFIED that
experienced the effects of D.M.
on _____ at _____
Date _____ Signed _____

2262 / PMED / 2000 / 12.41

A soldier's gas chamber certificate shows training in January and August of 1943

• • • • •

To provide protection in the event of a gas attack, all soldiers, war workers, Home Guard and the rest of the civilian population were issued respirators. The respirators issued to the military were more robust as they were designed for use under combat conditions. Soldiers were also issued a compliment of other anti-gas related items as explained in the pages of this chapter. While there are no documented accounts of lethal gas attack against troops during WWII, most of the major participants on both sides had stockpiles ready for use. The threat of gas attack was very real and all Commonwealth soldiers went through extensive gas training. For the British, this was conducted at the Army Gas School and for the Canadians at the Canadian Small Arms Training Centres. Training included soldiers going into a gas chamber filled with tear gas or DM which was a sneezing gas so they could test the fit of their respirators. They would then remove their respirators to experience the full effects of gas exposure.

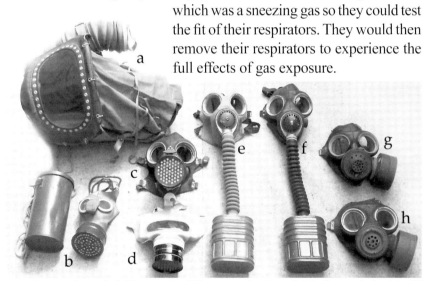

A grouping of civilian and military respirators. (a) is for an infant to fit inside and requires the bellows to be pumped to provide air flow. (b) is one of the multi-coloured variations issued to children complete with carrying tin. (c) is the type issued to British war workers. (d) is one type that was issued to Canadian civilians. (e) is an early Mark IV respirator that was replaced by (f) which is the Mark V, both were designated General Service Respirators. (g) is a British made light respirator which began replacing the General Service Respirator in 1943. (h) is a Canadian made light respirator.

· · · · ·

357

A mother wearing a C.1. General Civilian Respirator holds her baby during a gas preparations test being conducted in London during 1941. The British Ministry of Home Security issued Baby Anti-Gas Helmets for infants and small children that couldn't wear a small child's pattern respirator. The bellows on the side allowed the care taker to pump filtered air into the Anti-Gas Helmet.

· · · · ·

The Anti-Gas Cape was adopted in 1938 and was actually a full length coat with sleeves, produced from a green coloured oilskin fabric. A subsequent pattern introduced in June of 1940 had the same green base colour with the addition of brown camouflage splotches. Both patterns saw service throughout the war. The official army designation for this later pattern garment was *Cape, Anti-Gas, Number 1, Camouflaged.*

It was longer than the standard rain cape, coming down to just past the knees and had a series of snap fasteners to close the front in addition to one for closing up the collar. A flapped pocket with a single snap closure was positioned in the front on the outside near the left hip. It had a grommet at the bottom that served as a drain. This pocket was

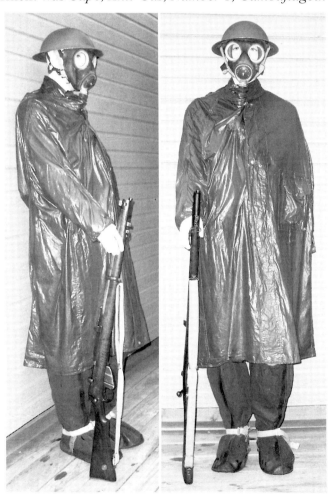

A 1940 dated camouflage Anti-Gas Cape worn with Anti-Gas Boots and General Service Respirator.

• • • • •

intended to hold Anti-Gas Ointment and Cotton Waste. A rectangular hump was built into the rear shoulder area of the cape. This allowed the haversack to be worn underneath and also helped to hold the cape on the wearer while walking and ensured proper coverage. Ventilation holes are located in the armpit area of each sleeve and consist of grommets on early production models or merely stitching reinforced holes on subsequent models. Since normal rank insignia was obscured while the anti-gas cape was worn, gas-detector paint was used to apply rank designation to the sleeves. The gas-detector paint was similar to the type used on vehicles and it reacted and changed colour when exposed to gas. The threat of gas attack diminished as the war progressed and it became common practice for the troops to use the cape as a waterproof during times of inclement weather. Owing to the delicate nature of these garments, most didn't last long in the field and are a very rare collectible today. When not needed by the troops, the anti-gas cape was normally rolled up and carried in the haversack. It was rolled up and secured to the web belt if the haversack was not being carried.

Canadian troops with Anti-Gas Capes rolled and fixed to their web belts. Ortona, Italy – December 1943.

. . . . .

Anti-Gas Curtains & Anti-Gas Hood

The Anti-Gas Curtain Number 1 was introduced in the fall of 1939 and it was produced from green coloured oilskin cloth. It was worn over the brim of the helmet and hung down over the neck enough to overlap the collar of the anti-gas cape. This first pattern anti-gas curtain was found to be flawed because it didn't completely cover the helmet and a tight seal could not be maintained as the soldier moved around. Liquid toxins could run down the crown of the helmet and get under the anti-gas curtain if the seal between it and the helmet was less than perfect. This could allow contaminants to follow the rim underneath the curtain on both sides of the helmet brim where they would then drip down the forehead where the respirator met the head.

A Gas Identification officer, identified by the two diamonds stenciled on the front of his helmet, holds gas detection paper during gas attack preparations. London, England – 1941.

The Anti-Gas Curtain Number 2 was introduced in the summer of 1940 as a replacement for the first pattern anti-gas curtain. It completely enclosed the helmet and an elastic band inside the curtain helped it grasp the rim so a good seal could be achieved. This ensured the helmet would not get contaminated in the event of a gas attack and provided greater protection for the soldier wearing it. A snap fastener provided a means of closing the curtain beneath the chin to complete the head protection after the respirator was in place. The Anti-Gas Curtain Number 2 was produced from the same oilskin fabric as the Anti-Gas Curtain Number 1 but it had the addition of a brown splotched camouflage. Existing stocks of the first pattern curtain were to be used up before the new improved pattern was issued with the exception of operational units which were allowed to use the new pattern at the time they became available.

The Anti-Gas Hood was introduced with the Anti-Gas Cape in 1938. It was worn over the head and had a drawstring to secure it. The length at the rear and sides was sufficient to allow it to cover the neck and overlap the shoulders. Its use for anti-gas protection was discontinued in 1942 in favor of the Number 2 Anti-Gas Ointment which was to be applied to the skin in the event of exposure to gas. While the Anti-Gas Hood provided superior protection for the head, it offered no protection for the helmet which would have to be decontaminated in the event of exposure to gas. Returned stocks of Anti-Gas Hoods to the RAOC were later re-issued to personnel for use as Rain Hoods.

• • • • •

Anti-Gas Overboots and Anti-Gas Gloves were each originally produced from rubber. This was changed to oilskin in September of 1942 due to the need to economize in the use of rubber. The rubber Overboots were soft sided and had a thicker molded sole to provide traction and support. Canvas straps with cinch buckles allowed them to be tightened up at the ankle and at the top, which came to just below the knee. Snaps on the straps helped to keep the ends from swinging around which would have caused them to loosen over time. The later produced oilskin pattern had the same securing straps but these Overboots had the consistency of waterproof surgical scrubs and were not very durable. Both rubber and oilskin patterns of Anti-Gas Gloves had canvas adjustment straps to keep them in place, similar to the Overboots. They were worn with canvas over mittens that protected and extended the life of the Anti-Gas Gloves since they were also delicate and easy to tear. Anti-Gas Overboots and Anti-Gas Gloves were not part of the standard anti-gas outfit issued to soldiers during the war. They were typically reserved for issue to men required to work in gas affected areas in the event of an attack, such as medical orderlies and decontamination teams.

The average soldier relied on Anti-Gas Ointment to decontaminate his exposed hands and Protective Dubbin to keep his boots from absorbing gas and affecting his feet.

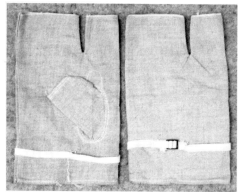

· · · · ·

The General Service Anti-Gas Respirator

The General Service Respirator consists of an assembly of several parts. The main mask made from molded rubber is known as the Facepiece. It has a pair of splinter-less glass eyepieces set in aluminum rims for viewing at the top. An Outlet Value Assembly where the mouth would be vents exhaled breaths out the front and draws inhaled breaths from a Connecting Tube from the bottom. The Connecting Tube is made of corrugated rubber to help prevent its being able to collapse and therefore assures uninterrupted airflow from the Container. The Container is small metal box connected at the end of the Connecting Tube and serves as the filter for air. The Respirator is held in place by the Head Harness on the back which is connected to the Facepiece by a series of elasticized straps. The pattern of respirator is normally identified by the Mark of Facepiece utilized. There were four patterns in use during the war, before the introduction of the Light Respirator. The *Mark IV* can be identified by its hav-

An early production Mark IV Respirator.

· · · · ·

ing a khaki stockinet cover over the rubber body of the Facepiece and Connecting Tube. It was introduced in 1926 and was produced in great numbers. The Facepiece was available in three sizes but there wasn't enough range in sizes to accommodate all troops. Additionally, soldiers couldn't wear glasses underneath it and it had no facility for communications with a microphone. The *Mark IV Special T* was introduced to correct some of the problems in the Mark IV. It was available in four sizes and was shaped to allow for glasses to be worn underneath. The *Mark IV Special T Mic* followed this with the addition of a molded area on the left check that was designed for a special microphone adaptor to connect into. The *Mark V* was introduced in 1939 and is made from black molded rubber which had no outer covering. It incorporated all of the evolutionary changes from the Mark IV series of Respirators and was available in a wide range of sizes.

A standard Mark V Respirator.

· · · · ·

365

Gas training exercises were conducted so the troops could adjust to doing their jobs while wearing protective equipment. At left, four soldiers wearing respirators don their anti-gas capes.

At left, an artillery unit of the A.I.F. carries out respirator drills in England during JAN 1941.

. . . . .

Two soldiers wearing respirators operating a Vickers water cooled machine gun during an exercise conducted at Salisbury Plain, England - 8 AUG 1940.

Two RAAF members practice shooting while wearing respirators in the Darwin area of Australia on 10 MAY 1943.

A "Guinea Pig" takes part in a gas effectiveness demonstration. Soldiers fired on an improvised range and were scored. Then they were subjected to gas and then re-shot the course. The reduction in their scores was taken as an index of the efficiency of the gas. NOV 1942.

. . . . .

Marks V, VI and VII Respirator Haversacks

The **Haversack Mark V** was introduced in the early 1930's and was still in issue when war was declared. It has three divided pockets on the inside that are laid out similar to a small pack. A single flap with a press snap at each corner closes it up at the top and there are three metal drain vents in the bottom. The dimensions of the haversack are 10 inches wide by 9 inches tall by 3.5 inches deep. When worn, the compartment on the left was meant to hold the facepiece. The compartment on the right held the canister and the full width pocket held the anti-gas equipment. A loop of cloth sewn into the bottom was designed to hold the tubular Anti-Dimming Outfit. The Haversack was worn by means of a 2 inch wide webbing strap that had two sliders for adjusting its length. One end of the strap was connected to the top side of the haversack with a D-ring and the other side had a flat metal hook that connected to the opposite D-ring. Normally the haversack was worn slung at the side but when needed for use, it was raised to the alert position which placed everything high on the wearer's chest. The sliders on the strap could be taken up to get to this position or it could quickly be brought up and fastened by means of a metal S-hook that matched to an eyelet placed on a tab extension in the middle of the haversack strap. A piece of twine sewn into the haversack could be passed around the chest of the wearer and tied off to a smaller D-ring on the side of the case. This helped to prevent the haversack from bouncing around when the wearer was running or laying prone.

Haversack Mark V and method of sling strap attachment

· · · · ·

A need for extra pockets on the Haversack came about in 1939 when the Anti-Gas Eyeshields and Anti-Gas Ointment became standard issue. To accommodate this need, another bag was created that had two pockets and a single closing flap with a pair of snaps. This bag was intended to be sewn onto the front of the Haversack and the new designation became *Haversack Mark V-C* for converted.

An example of the special two pocket pouch meant to be sewn to the front of the Haversack Mark V and thus convert it to a Haversack Mark VI pattern.

The *Haversack Mark VI* was introduced around the same time as when the converted Haversack Mark V went into production. It had the same basic layout as the Haversack Mark V-C but the extra pocket was part of the bag and did not have to be sewn on after the fact. The design of the Haversack Strap was simplified and a flat metal hook was placed at each end of the strap for connecting to the D-rings at the top of the bag. This allowed the strap to be interchangeable for replacement if it became damaged.

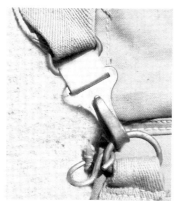

Haversack Mark VI and method of sling strap attachment

· · · · ·

In a further effort to economize production, the Haversack Mark VII was introduced in early 1941. It eliminated the second closing flap for the pair of pockets on the front by moving these pockets into the main bag under a single flap. The number of metal drain vents in the bottom of the Haversack was also reduced to two. A small pocket was added near the top to hold the new pattern Anti-Dimming tin and this allowed it to be accessed easier than the previous models. The Haversack Strap was further simplified by eliminating the flat metal hooks and having each end merely connected to metal rings. A tiny pocket was also added to the outside of the Haversack near the bottom and this held a length of twine for passing around the body as described with the Mark V. The improvement was it connected to a metal disk on the opposite side of the Haversack instead of having to be tied to a D-ring. This made it easier to connect the Haversack to the chest and provided a quick release for removal in an emergency.

An example of a Haversack drain fitting to the left and the new quick release tying disk that was introduced with the Mark VII Haversack to the right.

 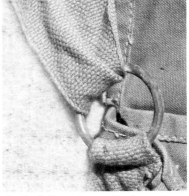

Haversack Mark VII and method of sling strap attachment

• • • • •

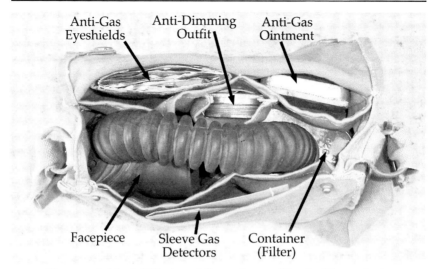

Anti-Gas Eyeshields · Anti-Dimming Outfit · Anti-Gas Ointment · Facepiece · Sleeve Gas Detectors · Container (Filter)

Haversack Mark VII viewed from above with all of its contents

The Container or Filter used with the General Service Respirator was known as the E-Type Container. It was produced in three Marks during the course of the war. The E Mark IV can be identified by its buff colour, the E Mark V by its grey/blue colour and the E Mark VI by its brick red colour. All Marks were made from pressed steel with ribbed reinforcements. A pair of slots in one end near the bottom is where air is drawn in when a breath is taken. When the Container is in the Haversack, these slots should be towards the center of the bag for maximum efficiency. Before the air can get out of the Container, it must pass through cloth and granulated charcoal filters. The difference in the three Marks of Containers is improvements of the internal filter fillings. Typically the date of manufacture and the maker's name or logo will be pressed into the bottom of the Container. The code *No. 4A* will also be found on all three patterns and is considered to be a reference to identify the type of physical metal container as opposed to the Mark of Container or its contents.

· · · · ·

371

The Light Pattern Anti-Gas Respirator

The Light Respirator was introduced early in 1943 and was to gradually replace the General Service Respirator already in issue. The facepiece was similar in design to the Mark V respirator but it had a mounting point on the left side made to receive a filter, designated by the Army as being a container. The outlet valve assembly is situated where the mouth would be located in the front of the facepiece, similar to earlier respirators. It differs in having a recess or shaped protrusion in the center that was designed for the rubber cone on a microphone to fit. Available sizes were *small*, *normal* and *large* and these were molded into the side of the facepiece for easy identification. The head harness for the respirator is typically made of webbing material to save on rubber and it has adjustable elastic straps sewn directly onto it. The container (filter) consists of a metal drum with a threaded neck on one end and a metal

cover on the other end with a one inch inlet hole. Beneath the metal cover is a series of holes that allow air to be drawn inside for filtration into the facepiece. When the container is not fitted to the facepiece, cork or rubber plugs are used to close up the holes on each side to prevent the entry of water. These plugs are each fastened to a length of cloth tape to keep them from getting separated.

· · · · ·

The Haversack for the Light Respirator is made of stiffened waterproof canvas. It has a detachable sling as well as a pair of double hooks on the back for attachment to the web equipment belt. A pocket against the back wall is designed to hold a cardboard sleeve of Anti-Gas Eyeshields. At the bottom there is a cloth covered pocket with a closing snap. Its purpose is to hold the Mark VI Anti-Dimming Outfit. A cloth tape in the bottom with a snap on one end is used to secure the container plugs and haversack sling when not needed. A small pocket on one of the sides is intended for a tin of Anti-Gas Ointment while another on the other side holds Cotton Waste. Sleeve Gas Detectors are carried in the bottom of the haversack when not worn. This pattern haversack was carried over when the Pattern 1944 webbing equipment was produced at the end of the war. Contrary to the method of marking earlier haversacks, a fibre disk like those worn by soldiers with name, number and rank stamped onto it was to be fastened to the container mounting point. Fifteen inches of whipcord was provided for this purpose.

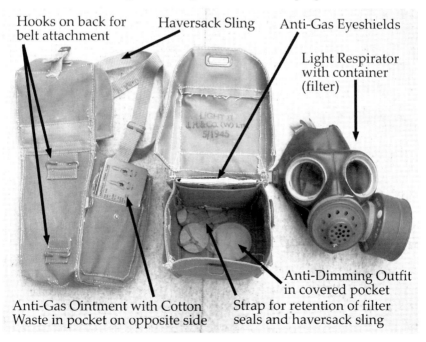

Hooks on back for belt attachment

Haversack Sling

Anti-Gas Eyeshields

Light Respirator with container (filter)

Anti-Dimming Outfit in covered pocket

Anti-Gas Ointment with Cotton Waste in pocket on opposite side

Strap for retention of filter seals and haversack sling

· · · · ·

Two war dated containers for the Light Respirator, with their plugs pictured above them. The one on the right is of Canadian manufacture and was issued with rubber plugs. It also has a more rigid metal screen on the cover to protect the threads of the container and the larger rubber plug presses into it.

The same two containers flipped over, showing the smaller plugs installed. The Canadian container, again on the right, has structural reinforcements in the body of the drum.

An early Number 4 Mark III Head Harness produced in rubber on the left with the later produced canvas type with sewn on straps on the right.

• • • • •

Protective Dubbin Number 1 was used on leather boots as a protective measure against gas. It was rubbed into the leather to provide a waterproof seal and to prevent the boots from absorbing gas. The rubber Anti-Gas Overboots, later oilskin, took too long to put on during a gas attack and problems were found with the Anti-Vessicant treated socks. Issue to the individual soldier was a two ounce refillable tin about the size of a typical boot polish container.

Anti-Dimming compound was used to prevent the lenses of the facepiece from getting fogged up due to formation of condensation from breathing while the respirator was worn. Early issues like the Mark IV and Mark V were in green cylindrical metal containers with a screw off cap on each end. One side held the Anti-Dimming Compound while the other held a small piece of polishing cloth which was used to rub the compound onto the facepiece lenses. These gave way in 1940 to the Mark VI Anti-Dimming Outfit. This tin differed in shape which was in the form of a circular disk with only a single compartment. The polishing cloth for the lenses was inside and it was already impregnated with the Anti-Dimming Compound so it was ready for use.

· · · · ·

Respirator Spectacles

The General Service Respirator could only function properly if a good seal was achieved between the body of the mask and the face of the soldier. Men that wore glasses had to be taken into account so they could still perform their duties while wearing a respirator. In 1939, the R.A.M.C. introduced a set of spectacles that could be worn under the Mark IV Special T, Mark IV Special T Mic and Mark V face pieces without interfering with the seal of the respirator. These spectacles had round lenses and a white metal frame with cable ear pieces to help keep them on. The templates running from the frames against the side of the head were flat and thin and were able to stick out from the sides of the respirator without breaking the seal. They were issued in a hinged fiberboard case that was typical of civilian glasses from that time. An instruction sheet was glued to the bottom of the case with notes on wearing the spectacles with the respirator.

This spectacle frame is designed for ordinary use and for use when wearing a respirator. When the respirator is fitted the spectacle sides are adjusted to the correct setting for the wearer's face Care must be taken to keep the sides at the correct setting, otherwise gas may leak in when the respirator is worn. If in any doubt as to the fitting of the spectacles the matter should be reported to the Medical Officer.

· · · · ·

The *Anti-Gas Eyeshields* were introduced in 1937 and were designed to provide eye protection from liquid gas; either sprayed by aircraft or from the bursting of liquid gas filled artillery shells. The War Office required that eyeshields be inexpensive to produce and disposable so rubber goggles like those issued to U.S. soldiers were ruled out. Three marks were produced during the war and were all constructed from a flat sheet of celluloid. The Mark I pattern had a two piece elastic headband that was stapled to the top edges of the celluloid. Pairs of snap fasteners are near this location. The celluloid is bent at the outer edges so the snaps can be fastened and this maintains a more conforming shape against the head when worn. The Mark II pattern differs by having a one piece adjustable elastic headband. It also has a pressed edge all around the eyeshield for increased strength and to prevent them from tearing when flexed. A green strip of oilcloth is stapled at the top edge and is backed with a piece of white flannel for added comfort and sweat absorption. One part of each fastener pair goes through the oilcloth to increase its strength. The Mark III pattern is very similar to the Mark II in construction but the headband only has a small section that is elasticized in an effort to save on rubber. The green oilcloth is replaced by a similar sized piece of black fabric that serves the same purpose as the oilcloth. The Mark I Anti-Gas Eyeshields were only made from clear celluloid but the Mark II and Mark III patterns offered clear and dark tinted versions. These were authorized for use by troops as anti-dust goggles in 1943 when the fear of gas attack began

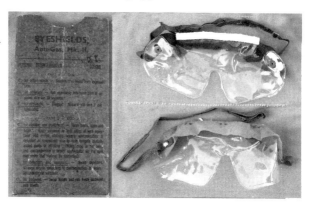

to diminish. Packaging consisted of six eyeshields in either a thin box or cardboard sleeve. They were stored in one of the pockets on the respirator haversack.

· · · · ·

Gas Proof Clothing and Gas Detectors

Clothing impregnated with Dichlorophenylbenzol Chloroinide, an Anti-Vessicant, was considered adequate protection for the wearer from airborne blister agents like Mustard and Lewisite. The process provided a high degree of protection from chemicals while they were in a gaseous form, some protection against exposure to spray, but offered no protection from liquid gas exposure. By 1942, the threat of gas attack was not as imminent and a preventative treatment for the uniform was considered to be a more practical measure of protection for the troops. Treated articles of clothing were marked with an ink stamping of *AV* so they could be easily identified. They could also be identified by the strong smell the Anti-Vessicant treatment left behind, which was disliked by the troops.

Gas detectors for the individual soldier consisted of the ***Sleeve Gas Detector*** and special ***Gas Detector Paint***. The Sleeve Gas Detector was made of paper that had been treated with Gas Detector Paint. It was worn high on the sleeve near the shoulder and had a cloth loop sewn into one end so it could be slipped over the Battledress or Great Coat epaulets. Two pairs were issued to each soldier with one pair being worn while outside and the other pair being kept in the respirator haversack as a spare set. Gas Detector Paint when used alone was normally applied to the sleeve tops of the Anti-Gas Cape. It was also used on fighting vehicles or painted onto metal plaques at command posts. When exposed to sprayed blister gas, the droplets turn the affected areas on the Sleeve Gas Detector or area painted with Gas Detector Paint red, indicating the soldier should carry out personal decontamination.

A Sleeve Gas Detector dated March 1940

· · · · ·

378

Gas Detector Paint was originally produced with a blue tint but was later discovered to still work effectively when tinted with other chemicals that could produce an olive drab colour. The painted surface area of a vehicle or sign would completely dry in about five hours and was effective as a visual detector for up to a month.

Chemical Liquid Detector Paper was produced in small booklets each containing twenty-five sheets. The sheets consisted of small pieces of Bristol board which was treated with Gas Detector Paint. A sheet could be stuck on the end of a bayonet or pole and then used as a probe to test an area for contamination.

Vesicant Detector Crayons were developed as a means of checking stockpiled chemical shells for leaks. These were produced by mixing Impregnite and a Congo red dye into a wax solution which was molded into the form of crayons which were issued in small cardboard cartons. The crayons were to be rubbed on the shells needing to be tested or could be crumbled up and sprinkled onto an area suspected of being contaminated. If mustard agent was present, the pinkish red colour of the crayon would turn blue.

A Gas Identification officer checks a bomb crater during 1941 for signs of a chemical attack in a London park. He uses a Poke Stick with detection paper fastened on one end to see if it reacts and changes colour.

· · · · ·

As part of the training received by Gas Identification officers, **War Gas Smelling Kits** that were developed during the interwar years provided a means of safely learning how the most common chemical weapons of the time smelled. While many were virtually odorless, they could still be detected by people with highly developed olfactory system. The kit contained four vials and a small package of fine papers. The vial for Phosgene had a green label and it contained minute samples of the lung irritant inside glass tubes which were to be broken and sniffed cautiously. The blister agents Mustard (yellow label) and Lewisite (orange label), and the lachrymatory agent Bromobenzyl Cyanide (black label) were contained loose in vials which could be opened and sniffed. The sneezing and vomiting gas Diphenylaminochloarsine was infused on pieces of paper. A small ½" sample was to be heated with a match and the smoke would be cautiously sniffed.

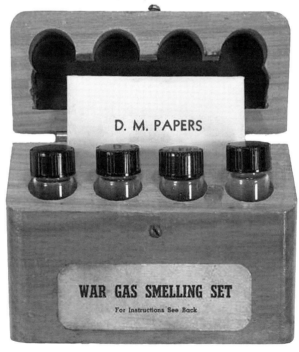

The pictured example was manufactured by Gelatin Products Limited of Windsor, Canada for the Department of Munitions and Supply. These were used for training in Canada, the United Kingdom and in the United States.

· · · · ·

The ***Anti-Gas Wallet*** was made from oilskin similar to the Anti-Gas Cape. Its purpose was to protect documents such as the AB64 and small personal effects such as photographs that would otherwise have to be destroyed if exposed to sprayed gas since there would be no way to decontaminate them. The first pattern produced was 12 ½ inches by 8 inches when opened all the way and folded down to 12 ½ inches by 4 inches or slightly over 6 by 4 inches when folded again to fit in a blouse or trouser pocket. The flap ran the entire length and over-lapped 4 inches where it was fastened shut with a snap at each end. Later produced Anti-Gas Wallets were slightly smaller and dispensed with the snaps since folding the wallet provided a satisfactory seal for the contents.

A 1942 dated Anti-Gas Wallet of Canadian manufacture shown opened all the way above, and folded in the reduced photograph to the left. The AB64 in each picture is for size comparison.

· · · · ·

Anti-Gas Ointment

This was a cream that was applied directly to gas exposed skin. It was squeezed into the palm of the hand and rubbed into the skin as a topical lotion where needed. It was designed to absorb or lift off any blister gas agents and then it was to be wiped off the skin

with a small amount of cotton waste. Prolonged exposure to the Number 2 Anti-Gas Ointment was found to cause skin irritation of its own so it was not to be used repeatedly or for long periods of time. The Number 2 Anti-Gas Ointment was first issued in small glass jars that had a metal screw off lid. This was changed to a hinged tin containing eight individual lead tubes of ointment in April of 1939. The lead tubes were buff in colour and had directions printed onto them. The Number 3 Anti-Gas Ointment that became available in 1941 as well as later issues of Anti-Gas Ointments were improved chemical mixtures and were not as irritating as the Number 2 Anti-Gas Ointment. These later mixtures were packaged in the same way but the lead tubes were not coloured and they had no markings other than their number. The tins they were packaged in changed colour as the Number of the Ointment changed for easy identification.

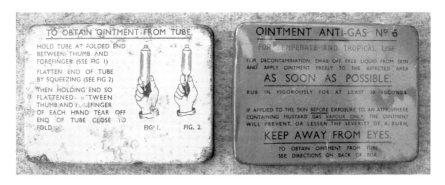

· · · · ·

Davis Respirator

The Davis Respirator was principally developed as an escape device for submariners. The apparatus could provide a limited amount of breathable air for an individual during an emergency. It was small so it would not hinder escape via confining passageways and small hatches. The air tank, hoses and mouthpiece were stored in a special case that was roughly the same size as the general service respirator haversack.

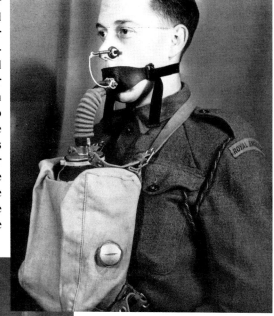

Davis Respirators were provided for use to tank crews of the British duplex drive swimming Sherman tanks during the Normandy landings due to the risk of their rapidly sinking if their floatation system failed. The Sherman crews did not have much time to get out through the commanders hatch once the 32-ton vehicles started to sink. Following the invasion, experiments were conducted for suitability of airborne troops using the Davis Respirator in the event they had to perform a water landing. Many Allied paratroopers had drowned as a result of landing in regions that the Germans had flooded.

. . . . .

383

The respirator typically issued for use by war workers, fire fighters and some A.T.S. units is similar to the Light Respirator. The primary difference is it has a removable container for filtering the air in the front of the facepiece. The left side has a molded plug similar to the type found on the Mark V Facepiece for use with radio microphones. The haversack for this respirator is a simple purse-like bag with one  large flap that covers the single pocket. The flap is kept closed with a pair of buttons. A cotton sling is sewn to the back of the haversack. There are several places where it is folded over and sewn to itself. To make the sling longer, the required number of these sewn sections is released so the sling can be expanded a few inches at a time.

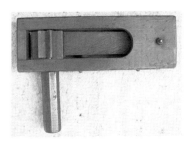

Wooden rattle used to sound the alarm in case of gas attack.

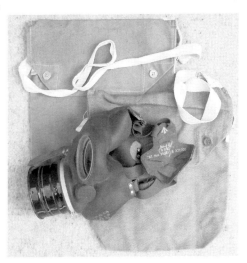

Chapter 9 - Medical Equipment

A wounded Tommy is attended to by stretcher bearers. He and his pal were hit during heavy fighting (10 feet away)…..dead. He is crumpled up, still clutching his sten gun, stretcher bearers have jammed their flags into the ground to show the enemy they were assisting a wounded man, and they placed the stretcher beside him as they bandaged the wounds. Jerries are surrendering, leaving a building in the background of the picture. When our cameraman tried to reassure the wounded man telling him that he wasn't badly hit, he replied "that's right mate – nothing so bad that it couldn't be worse". East of Nimegen during Operation Market Garden – SEPT 1944.

• • • • •

The purpose of this chapter is to provide a basic overview of First-Aid on the battlefield. It does not go into any detail on medical procedures since this would require volumes to cover on its own. What you will find is information about the medical orderlies that went into combat with the troops to assist the wounded until they could be evacuated. This was initially to a Field Ambulance Dressing Station where they would be treated by Medical and Dental officers. The wounded would first have been processed at the Company and Regimental Aid Posts which serve as casualty collection areas were the wounded would receive continued treatment from medical orderlies. These were in more secure areas away from the fighting when possible and served as staging areas for the wounded to wait for evacuation.

The essentials of battlefield first-aid can be broken down into three parts; to prevent immediate death, to prevent the wounded person's condition from getting worse, and to prevent further wounding. The first part deals with keeping any bleeding in check and ensuring the patient can breathe freely. The Surgical and Dressing packs as well as Shell Dressing haversacks were originally stocked full of compresses and bandages for this purpose. The second part entails covering wounds and burns to prevent further contamination, fixing broken bones, treating for shock and reassuring the wounded that they will be fine so they will rest. The third part deals with moving the wounded to shelter. This can range from a slit trench in the immediate battle area to transport back to a Company or Regimental Aid Post. Proximity to the fighting and conditions where the wounded are located will dictate if they should be sheltered prior to treatment. Eventual evacuation of the wounded is carried out on a priority basis. Wounds that continue to hemorrhage despite treatment, sucking chest wounds and open fractures to lower limbs are given highest priority. This is followed by penetrating chest wounds that are not sucking air, open fractures to upper limbs and fractures to the spine and wounds to the jaw. Lastly are the less seriously wounded and the dying. The latter include those with head wounds that are unconscious with a weak pulse and those with abdominal wounds with the bowels exposed.

· · · · ·

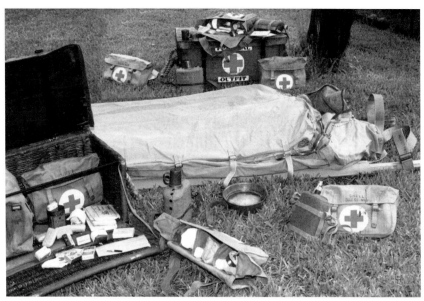

Pictured in the center of the photograph above is a 1942 dated casualty evacuation bag. This consists of a canvas material outer bag very similar to a sleeping bag. Inside is a gray coloured wool inner bag that is laced to the outer bag to keep them together while enabling it to be easily removed for cleaning or disposal as needed. The head portion of the outer bag has a wire frame so it can be formed around the head of the wounded individual for added warmth without having to be laid directly in contact with them. The lower side of the outer bag is reinforced and the long sides each have a channel sewn into them for the addition of poles so the bag can double as a stretcher.

An assortment of British bandages and compresses typical to the WWII period.

· · · · ·

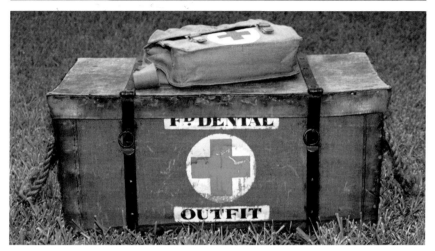

Panniers for medical supplies were made from woven wicker. They had an iron framework inside and were covered with canvas on the outside to make them waterproof and to protect the wicker and the contents inside. The front wall can be lowered to form a shelf, supported by leather straps, once the lid has been raised. Rope handles are at each end to make the pannier easier to carry. The inside of the pannier is merely an empty shell

to contain whatever supplies were needed. Panniers came pre-packed and will have the Geneva cross in a white circle on the front. The pannier designation will be stenciled on the front. These include "Field Surgical Outfit", "Field Dental Outfit", "Medical" and "Gas" as just a few examples.

• • • • •

A stock of field medical, surgical and fracture panniers, medical companions and shell dressing haversacks. 9 APR 1943.

Field Dental and Transfusion Panniers waiting to be loaded onto trucks along with an armload of cotton wool rolled bandages.

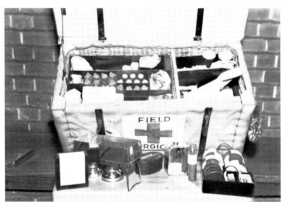

A close-up of a Field Surgical Pannier with some of its contents removed for better viewing.

. . . . .

389

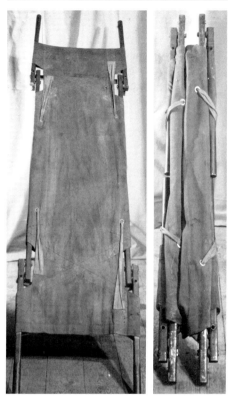

The series of photographs above show a *Folding Stretcher* that can be used as a mobile examination or surgical table with the aid of the *Folding Stretcher Trolley* at the left. The metal framed white disk on one of the stretchers is a shield to block the sun while a patient is being cared for in the field.

· · · · ·

Captain P. G. Costigan of the 1st Canadian Parachute Battalion stands with an airborne folding stretcher. His beret bears the cap badge of the Royal Canadian Army Medical Corps (RCAMC). The side-arm he wears would have been issued for defensive purposes. Brelingen, Germany – 12 APR 1945.

Three glass tubes of surgical catgut produced in June 1942 by Johnson & Johnson in Sydney, Australia.

• • • • •

Body Armour

Individual ***Body Armour*** was being considered for development by the Medical Research Council (M.R.C.) during October of 1940. The idea was to produce a light-weight suit of armour that would not restrict a soldier's movement while providing protection to areas of the body where penetration by a bullet or shell fragment would probably cause death. The Body Protection Council of the M.R.C. made recommendations in February of 1941 for testing to begin with a design consisting of three separate plates produced from 1mm thick manganese steel. The plates were covered in fabric and fastened together with adjustable webbing straps. Two plates were worn in the front and the third plate was worn on the lower back. The top plate in the front was 9 inches by 8 inches and was intended to protect the heart and lung roots. The lower plate in the front was 8 inches by 6 inches and offered protection to the wearer's belly. The plate on the back was 14 inches wide and 4 inches tall with an additional 5 inches sticking up in the center. This plate protected the spinal column, base of the lungs and the liver. Variations in the pattern included the addition of rubber around the edges and then felt pads being added under the fabric covering. Their purpose was to keep the plates from being in contact with the wearer so he would not sweat as much. Sets of body armour were used by glider pilots and some airborne troops during the war. Some elements of the 21st Army group also received sets in early 1944.

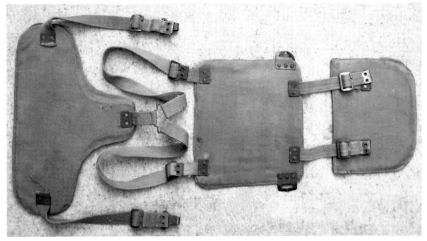

· · · · ·

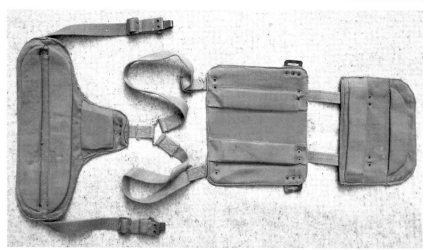

The photograph above shows the rear side of the three plates so the raised sections under the fabric covering are visible. The back plate has a webbing strap with a brass hook at the end on each side. These hooks fasten to slots in the larger plate that hangs on the front and prevents the suit of armour from being able to swing around.

Men of the 56th Infantry Division getting into body armour - 21 MAR 1942.

· · · · ·

Privates Walter Dunn and Bill Butcher of the Queen's Own Cameron Highlanders of Canada hauling surplus kit in a wheelbarrow near Oldenburg, Germany. Of interest is the PIAT on the wheelbarrow and the medic in the rear wears a set of body armor with a Geneva Cross painted prominently on the chest panel.

Stretcher Bearer of an unidentified Regiment of the 9th Canadian Infantry Brigade in the Normandy Bridgehead. 8-9 JUN 1944.

· · · · ·

The large webbing strap pictured here is used to assist in carrying a stretcher. It has loops sewn into each end which are fitted over the handles. The strap is then adjusted to length and worn around the neck on the shoulders to 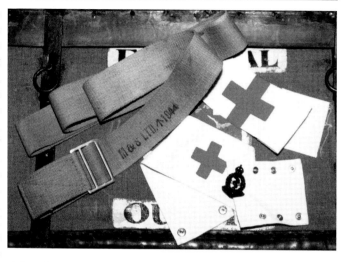 help offset the weight of a wounded man. The brassards are two versions worn by orderlies. One has snap fasteners and the other uses pins. A change was made in early 1945 for medical brassards to be made from a khaki coloured cloth. These were used by front line orderlies so they would not stand out so much, yet would still be easily identified by enemy soldiers that were closer to their positions. The cap badge is one of the economy pattern plastic badges introduced in 1943.

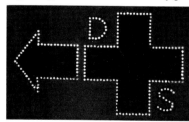

Signs used to indicate how to find the Dressing Station and Wards. The Dressing Station sign consists of a small box that holds a lamp so the pin holes outlining the markings can be illuminated for subdued use at night.

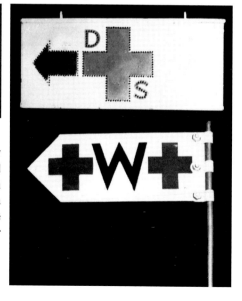

· · · · ·

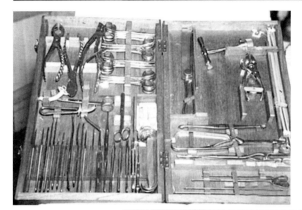

A field surgical case as supplied by Land Headquarters Depot Medical and Veterinary Stores. Melbourne, Australia – 9 APR 1943.

A 1943 dated British army issue field dental instrument roll.

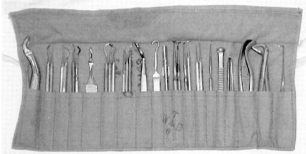

A wounded soldier being carried to the underground regimental aid post of the 2/17 Infantry Battalion in an advanced area. Tobruk, Libya – 30 SEPT 1941.

Canvas camp baths and a 500 gallon water tank in the underground bathing area of the 2/1 Casualty Clearing Station. The facility is a large Dug Out comprised of three tunnels built by the British to serve as a regimental aid post. Mersa Matruh, Egypt – JAN 1941

. . . . .

Lieutenant-Colonel Julien Bibeau, commanding officer, presenting Corporal Lucien Nantel of Le Regiment De Maisonneuve with the Military Medal. Ossendrecht, Netherlands – 17 OCT 1944.

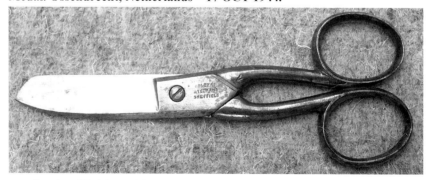

A pair of British military 5-inch Buttonhole scissors made to a standard sealed pattern in May 1940. They were used to make short, straight surgical cuts through the wall of a body cavity.

• • • • •

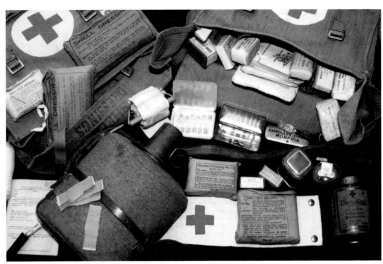

Orderlies were often issued a larger metal water bottle with a removable tin cup stored on the top over the cork stopper. All wounded with the exception of those with stomach and bowel wounds required a large amount of fluids to prevent dehydration. An early form of Band-Aids can be seen lying on the water bottle.

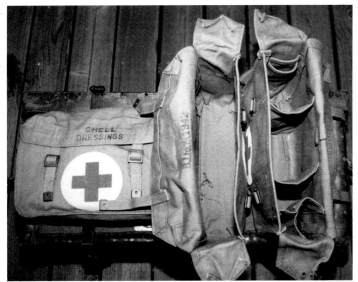

More than one type of Shell Dressing haversack were produced during the war but they all have the same external size and appearance.

· · · · ·

Various bandages, a Morphia injector, and field medical and ID cards to record notes regarding treatment and medications the wounded has received.

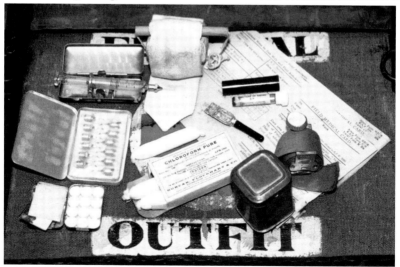

More basic medical equipment including two types of tourniquets, a glass syringe with separate needles each in their own aluminum cases, chloroform ampoules and aspirin tablets.

. . . . .

Large First-Aid kit usually issued with vehicles. Contents included Tubes of Tannic Acid Jelly (2) for burns, Standard Dressings Number 10 (10), Standard Dressings Number 11 (10), Standard Dressings Number 12 (10) and Triangular Bandages (2). The tin case measures 10.75" x 8.25" x 2.75" and this example and its contents are all 1941 and 1942 dated.

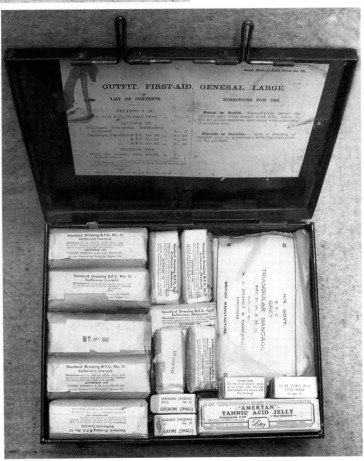

· · · · ·

Pictured at the right is a field surgical haversack. The back folds out to form a tray and has many small pockets in it for forceps, dressing scissors and probes. The main compartment of the haversack is divided to hold various types of bandages, pins, wool gauze and cotton wadding.

The photograph below shows wartime examples of the standardized dressing (D) and surgical (S) packs adopted by the airborne forces. Their contents can be seen on the two pages that follow.

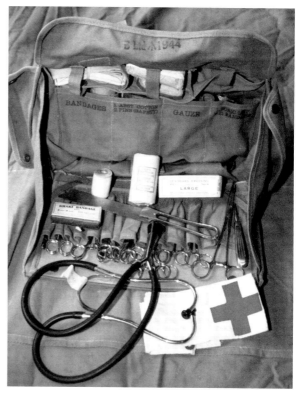

The contents of Dressing Pack, marked with a D and referred to as *Don*, consisted of drugs, anesthetics, dressings and items to comfort the wounded.

5 Grams Tubonic Morphia
40 Tablets Acraflavine
25 Tablets Phenobarbitone
250 Tablets Sulphanilamide
50 Tablets Mepacrine
1 Tube Lysol
1 3-Inch Wide Roll Elastoplast
8 6-Yard Packets Gauze
1 Cramer Wire 8 x 60 cm
1 Tin Safety Pins (20 in Tin)
10 Doses Anti-Tetanus Toxin
1 Spare Battery
20 Form A.F.F. 3118 and 3118A
1 Cube Meat Extract
50 Cigarettes
1 Box Matches
4 Packets Compressed Triangular
   Bandages (2 in Packet)

1 4-Ounce Tube Paraffin Molle
40 Tablets Aspirin
25 Tablets Creta cum ope
50 Tablets Sulphathiazole
50 Tablets Magnesium Sulphate
36 3-Inch Wide Compressed Bandages
1 3-Inch Wide Zinc Oxide Plaster
1 Pound Packet Wool
1 Cramer Wire 10 x 100 cm
1 Lead Pencil
1 Soap Tablet
4 Ounces Crushed Sulphanilamide
12 Tins Tea, Milk and Sugar Powder
4 Candles
1 Bottle Anti-Gas Gangrene Serum
1 Webbing Pack

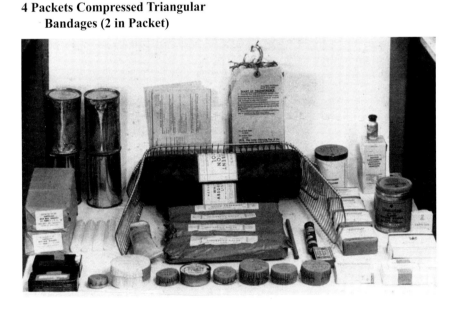

. . . . .

The contents of the Surgical Pack, marked with an S and referenced as *Sugar*, were sufficient for ten operations in the field.

1 Tubes Lysol
1 Bottle Novutox
1 Gauze (6 Yard Packet)
6 4-Inch Wide Bandages
1 Roll Flannelette
1 Tin of Safety Pins (20 in Tin)
6 1-Yard Tins Vaseline Gauze
2 Soap Tablets
2 2-Ounce Tubes Chloroform
1 Pair Operating Gloves
1 Cramer Wire 8 x 60 cm
100 Sterile Swabs
1 3-Inch Roll Zinc Oxide Plaster
1 Packet Compressed Triangular
    Bandages (2 in Packet)

1 Tin 4-Inch Wide Plaster of Paris
1 Tin 6-Inch Wide Plaster of Paris
6 2-Ounce Packets Compressed Wool
16 3-Inch Wide Compressed Bandages
1 3-Inch Wide Roll Elastoplast
1 Jaconet 18 Inches by 19 Inches
1 Yard Cord Extension
12 Ampoules Pentothal Sodium
2 Ounces Sulphanilamide Powder
1 Packet Bard-Parker, Size 22 Blades
1 Cramer Wire 10 x 100 cm
1 Box Opiodene
1 Webbing Pack

· · · · ·

Cylindrical Wicker Panniers were used for transporting eight glass bottles of blood plasma and four Giving Sets. The pannier had a Firth foam-rubber two-part interior with molded sockets to hold individual bottles which prevented them from coming in contact with each other and cracking during rough handling. The Giving Sets consisted of a catheter connected to a length of rubber tubing and a pickup tube that was inserted into a blood plasma bottle so that the fluid could be administered to a wounded soldier. For airborne operations and aerial resupply, three wicker panniers could be packed into a standard C.L.E. Mark III drop container.

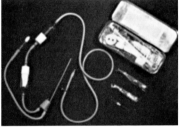

· · · · ·

404

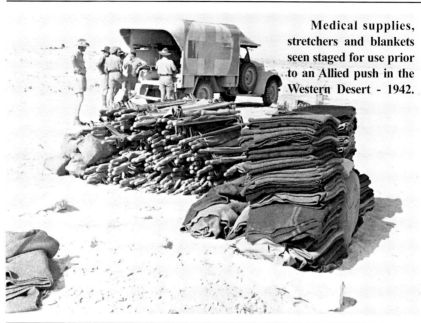

Medical supplies, stretchers and blankets seen staged for use prior to an Allied push in the Western Desert - 1942.

A British 6th Airborne Division soldier who was wounded by sniper fire shortly after landing during Operation Varsity awaits treatment on a stretcher. Near Hamminkeln, Germany - 24 MAR 1945.

. . . . .

Pictured at the left is a Royal Army Medical Corps poster used to seek out volunteers for the parachute medical services.

One of the specially modified airborne jeeps used by the Parachute and Airlanding Field Ambulance units. The jeeps have a special fold-out bracket in the rear designed to support a pair of airborne pattern stretchers. Two brackets similar to the type for mounting rifles on a jeep are fitted to the back edges of each of the front seats to hold the handles of the stretcher on that end. Additional brackets were fitted to the hood for a single airborne pattern stretcher.

Another airborne ambulance jeep used in Operation Varsity - MAR 1945.

Personnel of the Royal Canadian Army Medical Corps (R.C.A.M.C.) loading a casualty into a Willys MB ambulance jeep. Sonsbeck, Germany - 6 MAR 1945.

. . . . .

Jeeps used to transport wounded British paratroopers from the fighting near Ranville, across Pegasus Bridge and into Benouville. Normandy, France – 7 JUN 1944.

Regimental Aid Party of The South Saskatchewan Regiment, North of Laren, Netherlands - 7 APR 1945.

· · · · ·

408

Soldiers of The Loyal Edmonton Regiment rescue Lance Corporal Roy Boyd. The rubble created from a bomb blast pinned Boyd for three and a half days. Remarkably, he survived his ordeal, but others were not so lucky. In fact, the explosion that buried Boyd killed the rest of the platoon. Ortona, Italy – 30 DEC 1943.

· · · · ·

Three photographs showing examples of some of the lorries utilized for medical use during 1941-1943 in the Western Desert of North Africa.

· · · · ·

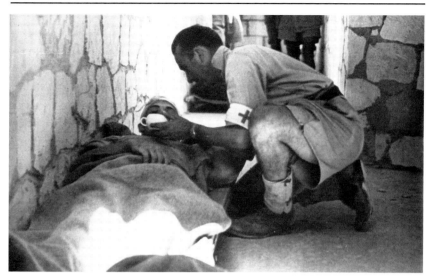

A medical orderly assists a wounded soldier in taking a drink. Tobruk, Libya – 30 SEPT 1941.

A wounded soldier being unloaded from an aircraft of the Royal Australian Air Force's Number 1 Air Ambulance Unit. These air ambulance units first operated in the Western Desert and then later in Italy. Libya – DEC 1941.

. . . . .

The British hospital ship "The Worthing" clearly marked with Red Crosses lying alongside the quay after having been attacked by Nazi planes while returning to England from Dunkirk in June 1940.

Wounded British soldiers being loaded onto trains bound inland to hospitals following their evacuation from France by ship. The roof of each rail car is painted white and bears a Geneva red cross for easy aerial recognition.

• • • • •

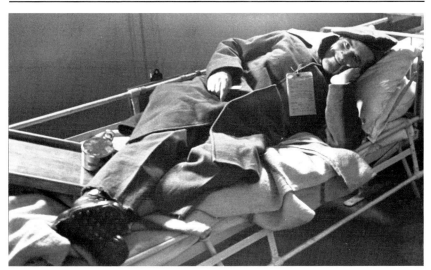

A wounded soldier waiting to be taken off of a British hospital ship.

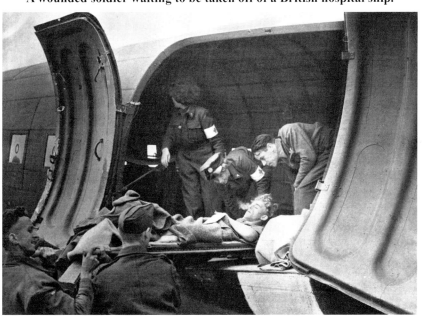

Medical orderlies and W.A.A.F. nurses work with wounded soldiers who will be evacuated from Normandy by air in C-47 Dakota aircraft. The first flights occurred on D+7 as planes began to utilize captured airstrips.

· · · · ·

413

Two armed orderlies with the 224th Parachute Field Ambulance offering water to German prisoners that were employed to assist in digging shelter trenches at a medical dressing station at Bergerfurth during Operation Varsity in March 1945. Photographic evidence indicates it was common for medical orderlies in the 1st and 6th airborne divisions to carry side arms. The central figure in the photograph is wearing one of the rare pouches for two pistol magazines.

A medical officer treats a Canadian with a head wound on the outskirts of Caen.

· · · · ·

414

Major J. W. Forth, Chaplain of the Cameron High-landers of Ottawa (MG), assisting the Regimental Aid Party of the Cameron High-landers of Ottawa in loading a wounded soldier onto a jeep. Near Caen, France - 15 JUL 1944.

Note: Also shown in the photograph at the bottom of the facing page.

An area often overlooked which typically became linked with the medical units during the Second World War is the direct involvement of the military Chaplains. These men assisted the medical orderlies in the field and in many cases assumed a role as an orderly during the fighting. Clergy officers were fully ordained ministers and one was typically assigned to each battalion. Their appointments were made by the Army Chaplains Department (RAChD). These men were part of the non-combatant military forces and in most cases went unarmed. The Geneva Convention stipulates that Chaplains do not have the right to participate directly in hostilities but does not preclude them from being armed. Most references to Chaplains being armed are associated with the fighting that took place against the Japanese in the Far East. Protestant Chaplains were referred to as Padre or Reverend, Jewish Chaplains as Padre, and Roman Catholic and Jesuit Priests were referred to as Father. In addition to perform-ing religious services and providing spiritual leadership, the Chap-lains counseling instilled moral guidance, discipline, and courage and selfness commitment into the troops.

· · · · ·

A medical officer and a chaplain (on the right) prepare a marker for the temporary grave of a casualty during the fighting in Normandy.

Major John W. Forth, Chaplain of The Cameron Highlanders of Ottawa (M.G.), displays his field Communion set. These items would have been packed into the small leather case seen centered against the jeeps windshield frame. A shell dressing haversack and an officer's valise are also on the hood. Near Caen, France – 15 JUL 1944.

· · · · ·

Chapter 10 - Documents and Publications

Men of the British 1st Airborne Division sorting through mail that has finally caught up with them in Italy during FEB 1944. They arrived in Italy by sea near the port of Taranto during Operation Slapstick, which launched on 9 SEPT 1943 in conjunction with the U.S. 5th Army which landed near Salerno as part of Operation Avalanche. The airborne forces were to link up with the British 8th Army which had crossed from Sicily via the Straits of Messina into Calabria, Italy on 3 SEPT 1943 as part of Operation Baytown. The Italians had secretly surrendered in Sicily on 3 SEPT 1943 but it was not announced until the full Allied invasion of Italy was underway on 8-9 SEPT 1943.

· · · · ·

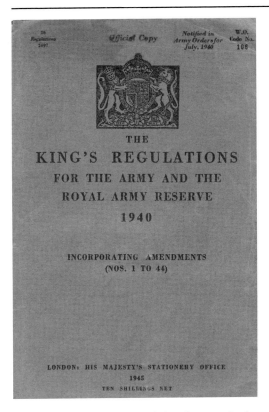

HIS MAJESTY THE KING has been graciously pleased to approve the following revised " King's Regulations for the Army " reprinted with amendments published with Army Orders up to 29th February, 1940, and to command that they be strictly observed on all occasions.

General and other officers commanding will be held responsible for ensuring that these regulations are strictly observed, and that any local instructions or regimental orders that may be issued are guided and directed by their spirit and intention.

Officers are expected to interpret them reasonably and intelligently, with due regard to the interests of the service, bearing in mind that no attempt has been made to provide for necessary and self-evident exceptions.

All previous orders on the subjects to which reference is made in these regulations are hereby cancelled.

The Regulations for the Royal Army Reserve are issued under an Order by His Majesty, a copy of which is contained in Appendix XXIV, and will be amended in accordance with that order.

The *King's Regulations for the Army and the Royal Army Reserve* is the manual that defines procedures of protocol and authority for all matters military. It is often referenced by abbreviation in other manuals by "KR" along with the number of the relevant paragraph. The 1940 edition was reprinted in 1945 with forty-four amendments that had been introduced during the war. There were 815 pages with 1744 paragraphs, spread out over thirteen sections with an additional twenty-nine appendixes. Virtually all topics dealing with military life and its associated duties, obligations, training, procedures and regulations are covered in the manual. A section is also included to cover discipline, courts-martial, military prisons, detention barracks and courts of inquiry.

· · · · ·

418

The **War Office** was the department within the British government that was responsible for the administration of the army until 1963 when this duty was transferred to the Ministry of Defense. Its roots stem from the days in earlier English history when the King and his senior military commanders conducted Councils of War. The Admiralty was the equivalent department for the Royal Navy and the Air Ministry was the equivalent department for the Royal Air Force. The governing board for the army was known as the Army Council and it was composed of nine members, with four of these coming from the military and five being civilian. These members were each the head of a War Office department and they were: the Secretary of State for War, the Military Secretary to the Secretary of State, the Parliamentary Under-Secretary of State for War, the Chief of the Imperial General Staff, the Adjutant-

Flag of the Army Council

General to the Forces, the Quarter-Master-General to the Forces, the Master-General of the Ordnance, the Permanent Under-Secretary of State for War, and the Financial Secretary of the War Office.

For the British military forces, the main source of written training information came from the **Military Training Pamphlet** (MTP) series of manuals. Before the war, most manuals were written by committees and published under the authority of the Army Council. Effective September 1939, the committees were disbanded and manuals were written by individual officers that were assigned to the Directorate of Military Training for that purpose and published under the authority of the office of the Chief of the Imperial General Staff (CIGS). The Small Arms Training (SAT) series of manuals and the weapons Handbook series of manuals are exceptions which continued to be produced under the authority of the full Army Council. In all cases, these were War Office sanctioned publications.

· · · · ·

419

26/GS Publications/998

ROYAL ARMOURED CORPS

Weapons

MILITARY TRAINING PAMPHLET
No. 35

PART 4: VICKERS GO MACHINE-GUN
MARK I

1943

Crown Copyright Reserved

Prepared under the direction of
The Chief of the Imperial General Staff

THE WAR OFFICE,
July, 1943

26/G.S. Publications/500

FIELD ENGINEERING
(ALL ARMS)

MILITARY TRAINING PAMPHLET
No. 30

PART IV: BOOBY TRAPS

1941

Prepared under the direction of
The Chief of the Imperial General Staff

THE WAR OFFICE,
15th *August,* 1941.

The *Military Training Pamphlet* series was developed to teach soldiers how to do specific tasks. These were more detailed than the *Small Arms Training* series and they typically did not focus on individual weapons but rather on skill sets needed to do a job. Weapons that could be encountered for general use were covered such as booby traps, the Vickers "K" Gun and heavy belt fed machine guns since they were not included in the S.A.T. series. Numerous other non-weapons related topics were included and in some cases, pamphlets needed to be broken down into as many as eight parts to cover everything. Examples in this series included camouflage of vehicles and installations, building bridges, crossing water obstacles, stringing barbed wire, use of gas in the field, sniping, building dug-in emplacements, laying mine fields and basic theory dealing with defense, going on an offensive, how to strategically withdraw troops from a fight, drill and structure within a battalion.

· · · · ·

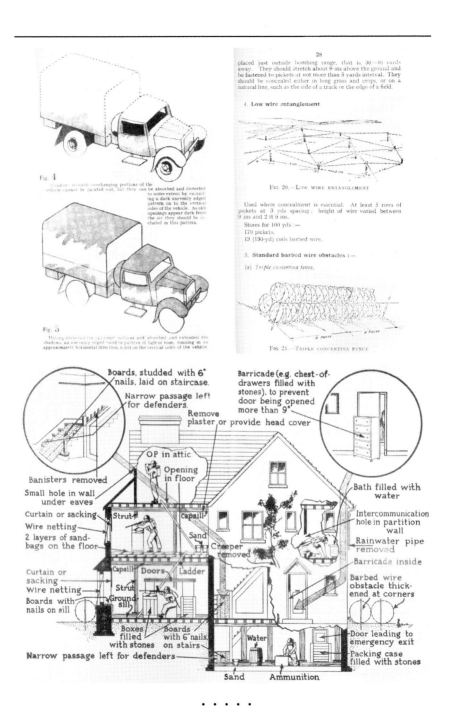

placed just outside bombing range, that is, 30—40 yards away. They should stretch about 9 ins above the ground and be fastened to pickets at not more than 5 yards interval. They should be concealed either in long grass and crops, or on a natural line, such as the side of a track or the edge of a field.

4. Low wire entanglement

FIG. 20.—LOW WIRE ENTANGLEMENT

Used where concealment is essential. At least 5 rows of pickets at 3 yds spacing; height of wire varied between 9 ins and 2 ft 6 ins.

Stores for 100 yds :—
179 pickets.
13 (130-yd) coils barbed wire.

5. Standard barbed wire obstacles :—

(a) *Triple concertina fence.*

FIG 21.—TRIPLE CONCERTINA FENCE

Fig. 4

Fig. 5

Boards, studded with 6" nails, laid on staircase.

Narrow passage left for defenders.

Remove plaster or provide head cover

Barricade (e.g. chest-of-drawers filled with stones), to prevent door being opened more than 9"

OP in attic

Opening in floor

Banisters removed

Small hole in wall under eaves

Curtain or sacking

Wire netting

2 layers of sandbags on the floor

Strut

Capsill

Sand

Creeper removed

Bath filled with water

Intercommunication hole in partition wall

Rainwater pipe removed

Barricade inside

Barbed wire obstacle thickened at corners

Curtain or sacking

Wire netting

Boards with nails on sill

Capsill

Doors

Ladder

Strut

Ground sill

Boxes filled with stones

Boards with 6" nails on stairs

Water

Door leading to emergency exit

Packing case filled with stones

Narrow passage left for defenders

Sand   Ammunition

• • • • •

421

20
G.S. Publications
935

Notified in
A.C. Is.
5th June,
1943.

Small Arms Training
Volume I, Pamphlet No. 24
Projector, Infantry, Anti-Tank
(PIAT)
1943
(Provisional)

By Command of the Army Council,

THE WAR OFFICE,
5th June, 1943.

(Reprinted in Canada (June, 1943), by permission of the Controller,
His Majesty's Stationery Office.)

20
G.S. Publications
750

Notified in A.C.Is.
15th July, 1942

Small Arms Training
Volume I, Pamphlet No. 21
The Thompson Machine Carbine
1942
(This pamphlet supersedes the 1940 edition)

By Command of the Army Council,

THE WAR OFFICE,
15th July, 1942.

Printed under the Authority of HIS MAJESTY'S STATIONERY OFFICE
by Kelther, Hudson & Kearns, Ltd., London, S.E.1.

A series of pamphlets was produced during the war titled *Small Arms Training*. Their purpose was to provide a basic lesson plan for instructors so they could teach the individual soldiers how to use various weapons against the enemy. Each pamphlet covered a single weapon except for a late war publication that combined earlier Sten and Thompson pamphlets into one. Instructors were already proficient with the weapons they were teaching about so the pamphlets do not go into specific details on every little thing. They mostly outline the principal things that should be taught which included the characteristics of a given weapon, field stripping, loading, aiming, firing, etc. Some of the weapons covered include: Rifle, Bren, Lewis, Vickers, Sten, Thompson, P.I.A.T., 29mm Spigot Mortar, 2" Mortar, 3" Mortar, Grenades, Boys A/T Rifle, 6 Pounder A/T Gun, Bayonet Fighting and Pistols. Most of the S.A.T. pamphlets were first printed in the United Kingdom and then were reproduced in Canada, India and Australia as needed.

· · · · ·

12

(*see* Fig. 7), direct the bayonet on to the opponent, deliver the point, withdraw, return " on guard " and pass through.

iv. Instructor with stick outside man's guard, man with rifle and bayonet both in " on guard " position. Instructor makes a *point*, not stepping in; man parries off to the left—makes a *butt stroke*. Instructor places ring for the kill. (*See* Fig. 8.) Man points, withdraws, returns " on guard " and passes through.

v. Explain that should an opponent attack on the right, it will be necessary to parry to the right and point.

Fig. 7.—The Butt Stroke

4. i. Explain use of training stick. Man with rifle and bayonet, instructor with stick.

(a) Pad must be held outside man's guard. (*See* Fig. 5.)
(b) Thrust with stick must be straight and vigorous.
(c) Man using stick must not step in.
(d) Pad will not be placed in position for butt stroke.
(e) Ring placed in correct position for kill. (*See* Fig. 8.)

ii. Practise squad in pairs as master and pupil, instructor exercises any man he may select.

26

Fig 15. Using the bipod from a slit trench.

Fig. 16.

LESSON 11.—HANDLING (BIPOD)

Instructor's notes

Stores.—Gun with sling attached and magazine on. Magazines ; drill cartridges ; utility pouches in the " action " position ; holdall complete
This lesson should be carried out on ground which provides natural and artificial cover.
Realistic targets should be indicated.

1. *Introduction*
Explain that during movement the gunner must be prepared

16

6. *Use of the discharger for the No. 36 grenade*

Explain and demonstrate, squad imitating :—

When the No. 36 grenade is used as a rifle grenade the discharger is attached to the rifle in the way shown above, but the following modifications are necessary :—

i. The rifle must be held at an angle of 45 degrees, heel of butt on the ground (*see* Fig. 10).

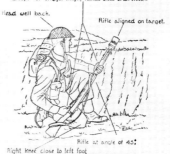

Fig. 10

ii. Ranges are based on the above angle and are obtained by opening or closing the gas port as follows :—

80 yds.	...	...	...	Gas port fully open.
110 „	...	...	...	„ „ ¼ closed.
140 „	...	...	...	„ „ ½ „
170 „	...	...	...	„ „ ¾ „
200 „	...	...	...	„ „ fully closed

21

Dangerous Zone

4. For fire to be effective, the target must be included in the *dangerous zone*, which is the area of *the beaten zone* PLUS *the dangerous space* formed by the lowest bullets of the cone.

5. The bullets are densest in the middle of the beaten zone (Fig. 11).
As the range increases, the depth of the beaten zone decreases (Fig. 12). This is due to the increased angle of descent of the bullets. Beyond 1,500 yards the beaten zone increases again, especially laterally, and at the same time the angle of descent becomes steeper and the dangerous space formed by the lowest bullets of the cone becomes less.
As a result, more bullets have to be fired to obtain fire effect at the longer ranges, and the range has to be more accurately known.

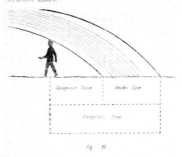

Fig. 11

Ranging

6. Ranging is the process of determining by observation of fire the direction and elevation required to hit a given target. The *permissible error* in ranging is the term applied to the error which can be made in estimating range while still keeping

• • • • •

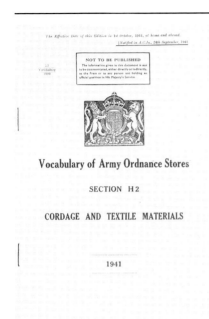

The Effective Date of this Edition is 1st October, 1941, at home and abroad.
[Notified in A.C.Is., 24th September, 1941.

NOT TO BE PUBLISHED
The information given in this document is not to be communicated, either directly or indirectly, to the Press or to any person not holding an official position in His Majesty's Service.

27
Vocabulary
1906

Vocabulary of Army Ordnance Stores

SECTION H 2

CORDAGE AND TEXTILE MATERIALS

1941

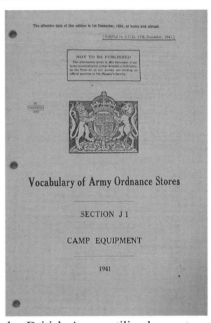

The effective date of this edition is 1st December, 1941, at home and abroad.
[Notified in A.C.Is. 17th December, 1941.]

NOT TO BE PUBLISHED
The information given in this document is not to be communicated, either directly or indirectly, to the Press or to any person not holding an official position in His Majesty's Service.

27
Vocabulary
1906

Vocabulary of Army Ordnance Stores

SECTION J 1

CAMP EQUIPMENT

1941

During the Second World War, the British Army utilized a system for cataloguing equipment, weapons and parts which was known as the ***Vocabulary of Army Ordnance Stores*** (VAOS). This system was introduced following the Crimean War and it remained in service until being replaced in 1956 by NATO Codification. Stores are organized into similar groupings and given the same unique alphanumeric section prefix. Individual items are then given a unique catalog or part number and listed with a text description along with the unit cost at the time the publication was printed. This cataloguing system provided the basis for needed equipment and spare parts to be requisitioned. Illustrated identification and parts lists serve as a cross reference in acquiring the number for a part when it isn't known. Examples of a few sections include: **A1** – Webbing Equipment, Bandoliers and Steel Helmets, **A4** – Airborne Equipment, **C1** – Machine Guns and Accessories (General Service), **C3** – Bicycles, **CJ** – Anti-Gas Clothing, **CM** – Cold Climate Clothing, **D1** – Harness, Saddlery and Packsaddlery, **F1** – Hand Tools, **H8** – Flags, **NN** – Huts and Sheds, **Q1** – Small Arms Ammunition, **M1** – Mortars, Smoke Generators and Flame Throwers.

• • • • •

15

SECTION D 1—HARNESS, SADDLERY AND PACKSADDLERY

Cat. No.				£	s.	d.
DA		GIRTHS—*continued*				
0970	A 3564	**Steadying**	*each*	0	6	0
		P.G.S., worsted web, 26-in. × 4-in., with leather billet $23\frac{1}{2}$-in. × $1\frac{1}{2}$-in. and buckle at each end. For Bags, intrenching tool				
1000		**HALTERS, COMMON**	*each*	0	1	11
	A 3564	Stout jute twine, with brow and throat cords and 7-ft. rope				
1010		**HAMES**	*pair*	1	1	0
	A 3564	H.P.D., with fixed terret rings				
		HANGERS				
	A 3564					
1015		**Gun, sling**	*each*	1	8	6
		P.M.G., wood bearing bar and two felt-lined leather slings, each 3-in. in width				
1016		CAVALRY	*each*	1	5	6
		P.M.G., V-sling leather attachments, with single pad asbestos-covered double pad and two sliding links				
5220	B 2212	**Rifle, anti-tank**	*each*	1	1	0
		With detachable tugs				
1020	A 3564	**Tripod, sling**	*each*	1	17	0
		P.M.G., wood bearing bar, two felt-lined leather slings, $6\frac{3}{4}$-in. and 3-in. respectively and 32-in. × $1\frac{1}{4}$-in. strap and buckling piece				
1021	A 3564	CAVALRY	*each*	1	0	0
		P.M.G., V-sling leather attachment, single pad, and 32-in. detachable strap with tinned lined stop				
1032		**HEADPIECES**	*each*	0	13	9
	A 3564	S.H.C., black leather, with brass scales and eardrops				
1033		**Leathers**	*each*	0	2	3
1034		**Ornaments**	*each*	0	11	6
		HEADS, BRIDLE				
	A 3564					
		S.O.				
1044		SMALL	*each*	0	3	1
		Long side 33-in. × $\frac{7}{8}$-in., short side 7-in. × $\frac{7}{8}$-in.				
1045		LARGE	*each*	0	3	1
		Long side 35-in. × $\frac{7}{8}$in., short side $7\frac{1}{2}$-in. × $\frac{7}{8}$-in.				
		S.U.				
1050		SMALL	*each*	0	3	11
		Long side 36-in. × $\frac{7}{8}$-in., short side 7-in. × $\frac{7}{8}$-in.				
1051		LARGE	*each*	0	3	11
		Long side 39-in. × $\frac{7}{8}$-in., short side 8-in. × $\frac{7}{8}$-in.				
1052		EXTRA LARGE	*each*	0	3	11
		Long side 44-in. × $\frac{7}{8}$-in., short side 10-in. × $\frac{7}{8}$-in.				
		HIDES				
1064		**Bellows**	*lb.*	0	2	0
		Weight 18-lb. to 25-lb.				
	A 3564	**Black**				
		BACKS				
1065		BRIDLE	*lb.*	0	2	7
		Average weight 16-lb.				
1066		COLLAR	*lb.*	0	2	3
		Average weight 23-lb.				

5

SECTION H B—CORDAGE AND TEXTILE MATERIALS

Cat. No.				£	s.	d.
H B		**ASBESTOS AND RUBBER**—*continued*				
		Block, packing—*continued*				
		†WIRE WOVEN, SQUARE				
		Size, $\frac{1}{4}$-in. and upwards				
0190		$\frac{1}{2}$-IN.	*lb.*	0	1	6
0191		$\frac{3}{4}$-IN.	*lb.*	0	1	6
0200	13758	***Rings, wire woven**				
		†SHEETING				
		Thickness, $\frac{1}{32}$-in. and upwards				
0201		$\frac{1}{32}$-in.	*lb.*	0	1	1
0202		$\frac{1}{16}$-in.	*lb.*	0	1	1
0203		$\frac{1}{8}$-IN.	*lb.*	0	1	1
0204		$\frac{3}{16}$-IN.	*lb.*	0	1	1
0205		$\frac{1}{4}$-IN.	*lb.*	0	1	1
0206		$\frac{5}{16}$-IN.	*lb.*	0	1	1
0207		$\frac{3}{8}$-IN.	*lb.*	0	1	1
		WIRE WOVEN				
0220		$\frac{1}{32}$-IN.	*lb.*	0	1	3
0221		$\frac{1}{16}$-IN.	*lb.*	0	1	3
0222		$\frac{3}{32}$-IN.	*lb.*	0	1	3
0223		$\frac{1}{8}$-IN.	*lb.*	0	1	3
0240	13758	**Tape, wire woven**	*lb.*			
		1-in. $\frac{1}{2}$-in.				
		BINDING				
	A 822					
0250		**Cotton**	*doz. yds.*	0	0	5
		$\frac{7}{8}$-in. ; for mattresses				
0255	A 3315	**Upholstery**	*doz. yds.*	0	3	11
		BUNTING				
	A 822	19-in.				
0265		**Black**	*yd.*	0	1	0
		Blue				
0266	A 8873	NAVY	*yd.*	0	1	0
0267		ROYAL	*yd.*	0	1	0
0268		**Crimson**	*yd.*	0	1	0
0269		**Green**	*yd.*	0	1	0
0270		**Red**	*yd.*	0	1	0
0271		**White**	*yd.*	0	1	0
0272		**Yellow**	*yd.*	0	1	0

* To be provided locally.

† Sizes in common demand only are detailed ; other sizes obtainable, if specially required, on demand.

4

SECTION B 1—SMALL ARMS AND THEIR COMPONENTS

Cat. No.				£	s.	d.
		BOTTLES, OIL—*continued*				
		MK. IV.—*continued*				
0055		STOPPERS	*each*	0	0	6
		With spoon				
0056		WASHERS	*100*	0	0	$7\frac{1}{2}$
BA 6320	B 4614	**Mk. V**	*each*			
		Plastic ; with stopper and washer				
BB 6326		WASHERS	*100*			
		CASES				
	A 9120					
0060		**Cattle-killer, ·455-in., Mk. I**	*each*	1	12	6
		Wood				
0061		**Horse-killer, ·310-in., Mk. I***	*each*	0	9	9
		Leather ; with cartridge holder				
BA 0066		**Sight, telescopic**	*each*	1	9	0
		Fibre ; with leather sling and cap ; with Cloth, cleaning and Brush, wire (Section B 2)				
BB 0070		**CATTLE-KILLERS, ·455-IN., MK. I**	*each*	3	8	6
	A 9120	Without Case				
0075		**DIRKS, MK. III**	*each*	2	5	6
	A 9120	With leather washer				
0076		**Ferrules, grip**	*each*	0	4	0
0077		**Grips**	*each*	0	17	0
0078		**Nuts**	*doz.*	0	3	5
0079		**Pommels**	*each*	0	5	9
0080		**Screws**	*doz.*	0	2	10
		Fixing pommel				
0081		**Washers**	*doz.*	0	1	9
		Leather				
BA 0090		**DISCHARGERS, GRENADE, RIFLE**				
	A 2535	**2-in., No. 1, Mk. I**	*each*	1	0	6
		Consisting of barrel with bush, and adjustable shutter ; base ; 2 bolts and 2 nuts. For Rifles, No. 1, Mks. III and III*				
AB 0091		BARRELS	*each*	0	11	9
		With bush				
0092		BASES	*each*	0	4	3
0093		BOLTS	*each*	0	0	4
0094		NUTS	*each*	0	0	2
BA 0100	A 2535	**$2\frac{1}{2}$-in., No. 1, Mk. I**	*each*	2	0	0
		Consisting of barrel with base and adjusting screw. For attachment to Rifles, No. 1, Mks. III and III*. For firing grenades with base gas checks				
0120	23221	SCREWDRIVERS, MK. II	*each*	0	1	9
6630	B 8247	**$2\frac{1}{2}$-in., No. 2, Mk. I**	*each*			
		Consisting of barrel with base complete. For attachment to Rifles, Nos. 1 and 3 (patt. '14)				
6750	B 8247	**$2\frac{1}{2}$-in., No. 3, Mk. I**	*each*			
		Consisting of barrel with locking sleeve complete. For Rifles, No. 4				
BC 0130		**EPÉES, MK. III**	*each*	0	16	6
	A 9120	Fencing				
0131		**Blades**	*each*	0	7	6
		Triangular section ; length of tang $6\frac{3}{4}$-in.				
0132		**Collars**	*each*	0	1	5
		Pommel				
0133		**Grips**	*each*	0	2	0
		$5\frac{1}{2}$-in. long ; wood ; bound with cord				

7

SECTION M 1

Cat. or Part No.				£	s.	d.
		COVERS—*continued*				
		MUZZLE—*continued*				
CM3222	A 9258 B 6676	**3-IN. MORTAR, NO. 1, MK. III**	*each*	0	3	4
		For mortars on Mk. I mtg. and with Harness, mortar, No. 1				
CM2398	B 1082 B 2543	**3-IN. MORTAR, NO. 2, MK. I**	*each*	0	3	8
		For Mks. I and IA mortar barrels				
CM1007	B 6058	**2-IN. MORTAR, MK. I**	*each*	0	1	6
CM2648	B 5648	**RECOIL CASING, MK. I S.B. 3-IN. GUN, MK. I**	*each*	0	3	2
CM2894	B 6088 B 6343	**29-MM. SPIGOT MORTAR, MK. I**	*each*	1	0	0
MR146A	B 8570 B	*DRUMS, CABLE, RIPPLE SWITCH, MK. I*	*each*			
MR2377	B 8570 B	*CABLES, FIRING*	*each*			
MR2598	B 8570 B	*DRUMS, CABLE*	*each*			
MR13GA	B 6058	**FLAME-THROWERS, WHEELED, MK. I**	*each*	23	0	0
MR 595	B 6058	**CONNECTION PIPE**	*each*	0	1	9
HA 5416		**CYLINDERS,** NITROGEN, 40-CU. FT., FILLED	(a)			
MA6615	B 6058	**HOSE,** PETROL, WIRE WOVEN, 2-IN. BORE, 25-FT., WITH CONNECTIONS	*length*	6	15	0
		NOZZLE, HOSE				
MR 696	B 6058	**RODS,** PILOT	*each*	0	1	6
MR788A	B 6058 B 6676	**PIPES, CONNECTING, RESERVOIR**	*each*	0	9	0
MR691	B 6058	**PLUGS,** FILLING HOLE	*each*	0	11	0
		WHEELS, SPECIAL				
		See under Wheels				
		FRAMES, HOUSING SIGHTS, MK. II 2-IN. MORTAR				
CM1008	B 6058	*MK. I*	*each*	0	5	6
CM1600	B 5472	*MK. II*	*each*	0	3	3
		GAUGES, STRIKER, PROTRUSION				
CM5052	B 6386 B	**NO. 27, MK. I**	*each*	0	2	2
		For M.L. 2-in. mortars, Mks. II*, II**, II***, VII, VII*, VII**, VIII and VIII*				
CM3200	B 6873	**NO. 32, MK. I**	*each*	0	2	6
		For S.B. 3-in. Mk. I gun				
CM4023	B 6389 B 7533	**NO. 33, MK. I**	*each*	0	4	3
		For Mortars, spigot, 29-mm.				
		HARNESS				
CM628A	B	**BOMB CONTAINERS, 4·2-IN. MORTAR, MK. I**	*each*			
		MORTAR				
CM215A	A 9258 B 8173	**NO. 1, MK. I**	*each*	0	7	9
		For barrel ; 3-in. mortar				
CM216A	A 9258 B 8173	**NO. 2, MK. I**	*each*	0	12	3
		For base plate ; 3-in. mortar				
CM217A	A 9258 B 8173	**NO. 3, MK. I**	*each*	0	9	0
		For mtg. ; 3-in. mortar				

(a) Demanded under, held and priced in Section H 1.

• • • • •

During the early years of the Second World War, a series of weapons part manuals were produced as ***Illustrated Identification Lists***. Each manual featured a single weapon or class of weapons in some cases such as the Sten Machine Carbines. The manuals were prepared by the Central Ordnance Depot for small arms, machine guns and bicycles at their technical branch located in Weedon Bec, Northamptonshire, England. The format was 5.75 inches by 8.5 inches with approximately 20 pages. Content consisted of drawings of the various parts broken down by assemblies and each was accompanied by its catalog number. The facing page shows the catalog numbers along with their designation or description and any remarks related to the item for each of the parts shown on the illustrated page.

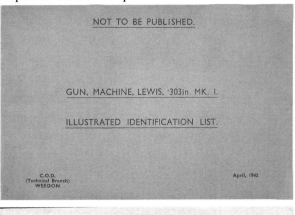

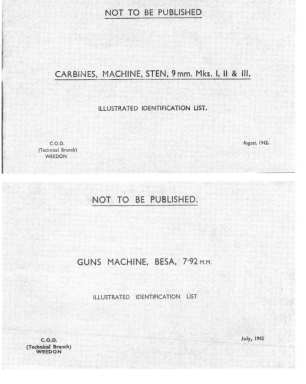

· · · · ·

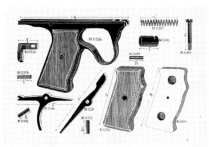

CAT. NO.	DESIGNATION.	REMARKS.
BE 0326	Catches, butt, No. 2	
BE 0336	Guards, trigger, Mk. I* (old pistol grip with wood side pieces and screws).	
BE 0354	Pins, keeper, butt catch.	
BE 0357	Pins, sear.	
BE 0358	Pins, trigger.	
BE 0361	Plungers, spring, trigger.	
BE 0369	Screws, side-pieces, pistol grip.	
BE 0371	Sears, Mk. I.	
BE 0373	Side-pieces, pistol grip, left, Mk. I* (with screw bush).	For trigger guards Mks. I* II. & III.
BE 0375	Side-pieces, pistol grip, right, Mk. I* (with plain bush)	For trigger guards Mks. I* II. & III.
BE 0378	Springs, butt catch.	
BE 0387	Springs, trigger.	
BE 0391	Triggers.	

12

CAT. NO.	DESIGNATION.	REMARKS.
BE 0395	Bottles, oil, butt (with nut, M.G. milled head and M.G. oil brush).	
BE 0396	Brackets, swivel, butt.	
BE 0398	Butts, Mk. II normal (with swivel and swivel bracket ; oil bottle : Mk. I butt plate ; and Mk. I butt cap assembled).	
BE 0399	Caps, butt, Mk. I* (with " U " bracket assembled)	
BE 0404	Nuts, oil bottle (with fixing pin).	
BE 0408	Plates, butt, Mk. I.	
BE 0411	Screws, bracket " U " butt cap	For Mk. I* butt caps.
BE 0413	Screws, bracket " U " butt cap.	1 per set for Mk. I* butt caps.
BE 0414	Screws, butt cap.	
BE 0418	Screws, swivel.	
BE 0420	Swivels	For sling
BD 0102	Brushes, oil M.G., Mk. I (with wood stem).	
BD 2614	Heads, milled M.G., Mk. I (with leather washer).	For milled head.
BD 2696	Washers, leather M.G., Mk. I	
	Screws, butt plate, No. 1	2 each set : to be demanded as " Rifles No. I, Screws, brushes, Section B. I, Cat. No. BB 0735."

2

CAT. NO.	DESIGNATION.	REMARKS.
BE 8387	Tubes, casing, Mk. III	For Mk. III Carbines.
BE 9955	Tubes, casing, Mk. I	For Mk. I Carbines.
BE 9956	Tubes, casing, Mk. II	For Mk. II Carbines.
	Foresights—	
BE 9963	No. 1 (Height of blade from base ·53-in.)	For Mk. II Carbines.
BE 8579	No. 2 (Height of blade from base ·56-in.)	For Mk. II Carbines.
BE 8580	No. 3 (Height of blade from base ·59-in.)	For Mk. II Carbines.

8

CAT. NO.	DESIGNATION.	REMARKS.
BG 4383	Bodies, cover, Mk. III	Not issued separately.

The illustrations opposite show the modification of the Mk. III body to Mk. III* by machining the floor of the body and cutting the recess for engagement of the bolt guide catch.

GUNS MACHINE BESA 7·92 MM. MARK III*.
BM 4550

CAT. NO.	DESIGNATION.	REMARKS.
BG 4089	Distance-pieces, eliminator, flash	For Mks. II and III assembled barrels.
BG 4106	Barrels, assembled, Mk. II (with flash eliminator, locking washer and distance pieces : Mk. II sleeve ; gas cylinder, gas regulator, gas cylinder sleeve and spring ; and Mk. II barrel retainer with carrying handle, plunger, spring and screw)	For Mks. I, II and II* Guns.
BG 4121	Eliminators, flash, Mk. II	For Mks. I, II, II*, III and III* Guns.
BG 4185	Screws, handle, carrying	For Mks. I, II, II*, III and III* Guns.
BG 4186	Retainers, barrel, Mk. II	For Mks. II assembled barrels.
BG 4231	Springs, plunger, carrying handle	For Mks. I, II, II*, III and III* Guns.
BG 4251	Washers, locking, flash eliminator	For Mks. I, II, II*, III and III* Guns.
BG 4270	Barrels, assembled, Mk. III (with flash eliminator, locking washer and distance piece : Mk. III sleeve ; gas cylinder, gas regulator, gas cylinder sleeve and spring ; and Mk. III barrel retainer with carrying handle, plunger, spring and screw)	For Mks. III and III* Guns.
BG 4283	Handles, carrying, Mk. II	For Mks. I, II, II*, III and III* Guns. When fitted to Mk. I carrying handle, pin must be removed from handle.
BG 4286	Plungers, handle, carrying, Mk. II	
BG 4389	Retainers, barrel, Mk. III	For Mk. III assembled barrels.

22

This series of manuals was produced later in the war by the Office of the Chief Inspector of Armaments as an improved replacement for the Illustrated Identification Lists. They continued to show either drawings or photographs of the parts making up an assembly for a given weapon, but they did so as exploded parts diagrams or layouts. This helped to not only identify the individual parts but to show where they went while assembling or disassembling the weapon. The individual parts' drawing number was also referenced in addition to the catalog number, description and remarks shown in the earlier manual series.

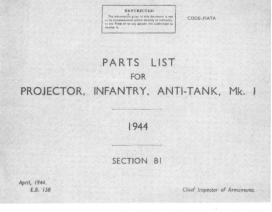

· · · · ·

428

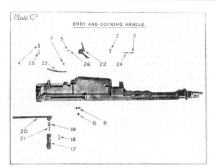

Plate C²

BODY AND COCKING HANDLE.

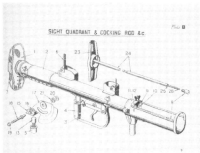

SIGHT QUADRANT & COCKING ROD &c.

Plate B

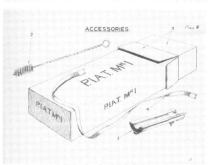

ACCESSORIES.

Plate F

P.I.A.T. Mk1

Plate A BREECH BLOCK AND BARREL ASSEMBLIES, &c.

Identification Lists were another series of parts manuals that were developed during the war by the Office of the Chief Inspector of Armaments. They were slightly expanded editions of their earlier Parts Lists. In addition to the line item information conveyed in the previous parts manual editions, there was a column to show the quantity of a given item that was needed to complete the pictured assembly. Many of the exploded parts diagrams were also laid out in a more precise way to avoid confusion in how the component parts went together. A key plate drawing was also usually included at the beginning of the manual to show an overview of the assembled weapon as a cutaway so that internal assemblies could be seen.

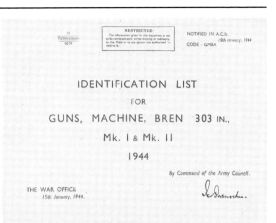

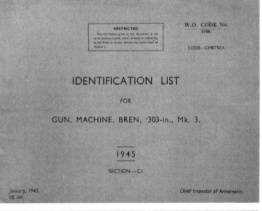

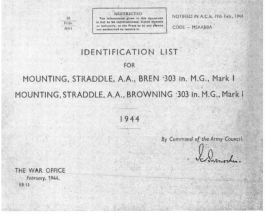

· · · · ·

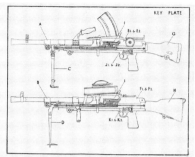

KEY PLATE

A   B₁ & E₂   G
J₁ & J₂   C
B   I   F₁ & F₂   H
D   K₁ & K₂

7

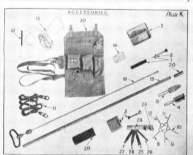

ACCESSORIES   Plate K

15   30
17   16   2   20
18   19   1
4
21   23   3
5   12   11
24   13   6   10
22   14   8   9
29   27 28 25 26

Piece Ref. No.	Designation	Catalogue No.	No. in a set	Drawing No.	Remarks
K					
1	BOTTLE, OIL, MK. 5	BA 6320	1	DD(E)2562	
2	WASHER	BA 6326	1		
3	BOX, SMALL PARTS, M.G., NO. 4, MK. I (empty)	BE 6063	6	DD(E)1897	
4	BRUSH, ROD, CLEANING CYLINDER, .303-IN. M.G., MK. 2	BE 4198	1	DD(E)2904	
5	CAN, OIL, M.G., MK. 3	BE 6167	1	DD(E)1820	
6	WASHER, leather†	BE 6173	1		
7	CLEANERS, GAS REGULATOR, BREN, .303-IN. M.G., MK. 2†	BE 9624	1	DD(E)2376	
8	REAMER, No. 1	BE 9587	1	DD(E)2376	
9	REAMER, No. 5	BE 9591	1	DD(E)2376	
10	REAMER, No. 7	BE 9625	1	DD(E)2376	
11	REAMER, No. 7	BE 9626	1	DD(E)2376	
12	REAMER, No. 8	BE 9627	1	DD(E)2376	
13	MOP, ROD, CLEANING CYLINDER, .303-IN. M.G., MK. 2	BE 9207	1	DD(E)2905	
14	PULLTHROUGH†				
15	CORD, double	BB 0519	1		
16	GAUZE	BB 0521	2		
17	WEIGHT	BB 0522	1		
18	ROD, CLEANING, .303-IN. M.G., MK. 2.B	BD 2553	1	S.A.I.D.1075	
19	ROD, CLEANING CYLINDER, BREN, .303-IN. M.G., MK. 2	BE 4199	1	DD(E)2904	
20	FERRULE	BE 4200	1	DD(E)2906	
21	SLING, BREN, .303-IN. M.G., MK. 2	AA 5663	1	DD(E)3838	
22	TOOL, COMBINATION, BREN, .303-IN. M.G., MK. 1†				
23	HAMMER, copper	BE 9280	1	DD(E)1801	
24	PIN, screwdrivers	BE 9620	1	M.G.D.1543	
25	SCREWDRIVER, fork, large	BE 9282	1	M.G.D.1553	
26	SCREWDRIVER, fork, small	BE 9283	1	M.G.D.1552	
27	SCREWDRIVER, large	BE 9284	1	M.G.D.1551	
28	SCREWDRIVER, small	BE 9285	1	M.G.D.1549	
29	TOOL, MAGAZINE, BREN, .303-IN. M.G., MK. 1	BE 9286	1	M.G.D.1550	
30	WALLET, SPARE PARTS, BREN, .303-IN. M.G., MK. I (Empty)	BE 9316	1	DD(E)2319	
		BE 9342	6	DD(E)1804	

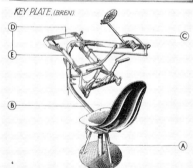

KEY PLATE. (BREN).

D   C
E
B
A

4

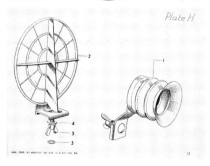

Plate H.

2   I
4
5
3

Plate Ref. No.	Designation	Catalogue No.	No. per set	Drawing No.	Remarks
H					
1	SIGHT, BACK, A.A., UNIVERSAL, M.G., MK. II	BE 9713	1	DD(F)3022	
2	SIGHT, FORE, A.A., UNIVERSAL, M.G., MK. II	BE 9712	1	DD(F)3023	
3	WASHER, ¼-in. Shakeproof, type 12	MTS/9687	2	—	
4	WASHER, ¼-in. B.S.W.	MTS/15348	2	—	
5	WING NUT, ¼-in. B.S.W.	MTS/18262	2	—	

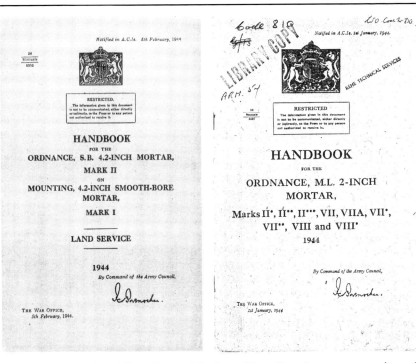

HANDBOOK
FOR THE
ORDNANCE, S.B. 4.2-INCH MORTAR,
MARK II
ON
MOUNTING, 4.2-INCH SMOOTH-BORE MORTAR,
MARK I

LAND SERVICE

1944
By Command of the Army Council,

THE WAR OFFICE,
5th February, 1944.

HANDBOOK
FOR THE
ORDNANCE, M.L. 2-INCH MORTAR,
Marks II*, II**, II***, VII, VIIA, VII*, VII**, VIII and VIII*
1944

By Command of the Army Council,

THE WAR OFFICE,
1st January, 1944.

A series of publications titled as *Handbooks* were produced to cover the specifics of individual weapons used by the British and Commonwealth. These manuals are much more detailed than any of the other weapons-related publications and document the procedures for cleaning and maintenance, assembly, aiming, loading, firing and the types of ammunition available for use. Each topic has a comprehensive text explanation accompanied with diagrams or photographs that assist the reader in understanding what they have read, even if unfamiliar with the actual operation of the weapon or procedure being described. These Handbooks typically have a larger 8.5 inches by 11 inches format with 40-60 pages. The Handbooks exist to teach an individual about every aspect of a given weapon as compared with the Small Arms series which provides a lesson plan for an already knowledgeable instructor to teach the basics to others.

· · · · ·

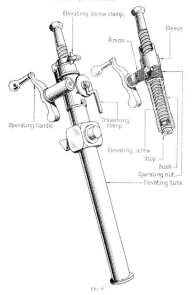

By screwing the wing nut, pressure is applied to the steel band tightening it on the split cap, which in turn, grips the operating nut, and clamps the gear with the mortar at the required elevation.

Elevating screw clamp.

Sleeve.

Pinion.

Operating handle

Traversing clamp

Elevating screw

Stop

Bush

Operating nut.

Elevating tube

Fig. 8

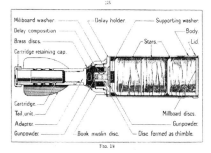

Millboard washer

Delay composition

Brass discs.

Cartridge retaining cap.

Delay holder

Supporting washer.

Body.

Stars.

Lid.

Cartridge.

Tail unit.

Adapter.

Gunpowder.

Book muslin disc.

Millboard discs.

Gunpowder.

Disc formed as thimble.

Fig. 18

BOMB, M.L. SIGNAL, 2-INCH MORTAR
MULTI-STAR, RED

The **Mark I bomb** (Fig. 19) is similar in design to the multi-star white, so far as the delay holder, adapter, closing discs and tail unit are concerned. The filling of the bomb is as follows :—

The bottom of the delay holder contains about 3 grains of gunpowder over which two layers of delay composition are pressed in. This is followed by about 8 grains of gunpowder and a book muslin disc which is secured to the delay holder with shellac adhesive, the whole being surmounted by a millboard washer.

The star container is made of rocket paper formed into a cylinder, the interior of which is coated with shellac varnish. The lower end is strengthened by a tinned plate diaphragm. Two millboard washers, secured together with shellac adhesive, are placed between the star container and delay holder.

The bottom of the container is fitted with a millboard washer, over which a primed muslin disc is placed. This is followed by about 5 grains of gunpowder with a surround of about 50 grains of S.R. composition, over which about 175 grains of gunpowder are placed.

The stars are contained in the case in three tiers, three stars in a tier, each of the latter being separated by a millboard spider. Between each tier of stars and over the top tier, about 175 grains of gunpowder are placed, while the filling space between the stars of each tier and the case, contains about 260 grains of gunpowder.

The star filling is contained in a tube of hard grey wrapping paper, the lower end of which is filled with 10 grains of sulphurless mealed powder, over which about 6 grains of S.R. composition are placed. The star composition, of about 100 grains of S.R. composition, is then inserted and surmounted by a millboard disc, the whole being secured by a strip of white paper and shellac varnish. The letter " R " denoting colour of stars is stencilled on one end of the tube.

KEY PLATE

G TO K

B A E D

C

F

D

· · · · ·

433

Army Council Instructions (ACI) were first issued in January 1916 and were printed and released on a monthly basis thereafter. Prior to 1916 they had been known as War Office Instructions (WOI) which had also been printed and released on a monthly basis. These instructions were assigned a sequential number for reference and would specify new procedures that were intended to supersede a previously documented procedure which would ultimately be released as an amendment for a manual until such time as the manual could be revised and reprinted.

NOT TO BE PUBLISHED

The information given in this document is not to be communicated, either directly or indirectly, to the Press or to any person not holding an official position in His Majesty's Service.

ARMY COUNCIL INSTRUCTION No. 763 of 1939

THE WAR OFFICE,
9th November, 1939.

Care and Cleaning—Guns, Machine, Bren, ·303-inch, Mark I.

It has been brought to notice that wear and damage to certain components of the Bren gun result through excessive cleaning, *e.g.*, it is essential that a good fit is maintained between the bipod sleeve and the gas cylinder, also between the nose of the gas block and the gas cylinder.

The use of abrasives, steel scraping implements or any method which removes metal when cleaning surfaces which are required to fit tightly, is strictly prohibited. In most cases it is necessary only to clean the parts in question with an oily rag leaving the surfaces oiled to prevent rust.

Amendments to Small Arms Training and Instructions to Armourers will be published in due course.

57/S.A./1119 (A. 3).

By Command of the Army Council,

· · · · ·

434

377. Small Arms, - Slings, Bren, .303-inch, M.G., Mark I.

1. The web portion of the above mentioned sling, which is at present 46 inches in length, will be increased to 58 inches by inserting 12 inches of webbing.

2. The modification will be carried out by R.E.M.E. armourers locally or in workshops in accordance with the sketch below.

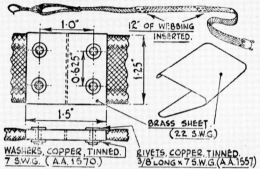

3. The following stores, which are necessary for the modification of each sling, will be demanded from the R.A.O.C. through the normal channels:-

	Section A.I	
Rivets		
Copper, tinned		
AA 1557	3/8-in. x 7 S.W.G.	8
Washers		
AA 1570	7 S.W.G.	8
	Section A.I (N.I.V.)	
Web (as used for sling, Bren Gun)	feet	1
Brass	*Section G.2*	
Sheet		
GB 0078	No. 22 S.W.G. 3-in. x 1-in.	pieces 2

57/S.A./2286 (M.E. 9(c)).

An example of ACI number 377 that authorized lengthening of a rifle sling for use with the Bren machine gun (above). A later ACI number 1327 that cancelled the previously issued ACI number 377 (below).

1327. Small Arms, - Slings, Bren, .303-in. M.G., Mark I.

1. Sufficient stocks now exist of slings 58 inches in length to enable slings 46 inches in length to be replaced. In view of this a modification to the shorter sling by the Insertion of 12 inches of webbing is no longer necessary.

2. Where slings 46 inches in length are held, replacements will be demanded under the following nomenclature: -
Section CI
Slings, Bren Gun (58 inches in length). Cat. No. AA 5663.

3. Replacements will not be demanded for slings which have already been lengthened.

4. Slings replaced will be returned to R.A.O.C. for disposal.

5. A.C.I. 377 of 1944 is hereby *cancelled*.

57/Small Arms/2552 (M.E. 9).

• • • • •

Army Training Memorandum (ATM) were short publications that originated during the interwar years. There were 29 editions printed during the Second World War with most being issued by the Army Council. They were distributed to every officer and conveyed new ideas for training, administration and tactical employment which was usually derived from battlefield experience or extended testing. These were usually quickly written, printed and distributed to ensure the information was received in the field where it could immediately be put to use.

Army Training Instructions (ATI) were more extensive publications than ATMs and they contained similar information to that found in a Military Training Pamphlet. This could include such things as new procedures or training doctrine as a replacement for a previously outlined method described in the earlier official manuals. Like the Army Training Memorandum, they were written and printed fairly quickly and were not as heavily reviewed and edited as the Military Training Pamphlets which could suffer many months or even years or editing revisions until being approved for final release to the troops.

The ***List of Changes*** (LoC) began in 1860 and like Army Council Instructions, each item was assigned a sequential number and they were published on a monthly basis by the War Office and distributed in Army Circulars. The first entry in the original 1860 numbering system was number 1 and it progressed to number 26231 by December 1923. In January 1924 the number series was started over at 1 with an "A" prefix with the intention of limiting the rolling number to four digits. The prefix "B" was started during 1936 and the letter "C" prefix was started in 1944. As a further cross-reference, individual parts mentioned in the List of Changes were given a letter designation to identify their association with one of the services: L for Land, N for Naval and A for Air. Items common to all of the services were given a C designation.

· · · · ·

The text represented in the image at the right is an example of an entry in the List of Changes. It discusses the slings used with the Bren machine gun after taking into account the pair of previously issued wartime Army Council Instructions numbers 377 and 1327 which can be seen two pages earlier in this chapter.

C 2376
SLINGS, WEB, 58-IN., MK. I
For use with
Sling, Bren .303-in. M.G., No. 1, Mk. 2
(Cat. No. AA 5663)   L
1. Introduction.
SLINGS, BREN .303-IN. M.G., NO. 1, MK. 2
Consisting of
Hook, sling, Bren, .303-in. M.G., Mk. 1
(Cat. No. AA 1132)   2
Sling, web, 58-in., Mk. 1 (Cat. No. CA 0737) 1   L
2. New Pattern.
SLINGS, BREN .303-IN. M.G., NO. 1, MK. 1
Consisting of
Hook, sling, Bren, .303-in. M.G., Mk. 1   L
(Cat. No. AA 1132)   2
Sling, rifle, web, (Sect. B 1 Cat No. AA 1657) 1   L
Also for use with
O.M.L. 2-in. mortars, Mks 2 to 2** and 7
(Section M 1)   L
3. Obsolescent.
4. Nomenclature revised.
HOOKS, SLING, BREN .303-IN. M.G., MK. 1
Steel ; for use with
Sling, Bren .303-in M.G., No 1, Mks. 1
and 2   L
5. Nomenclature revised.

1. Design D.D. (E) 3859 has been approved to govern future manufacturing of the above-mentioned sling Cat. No. CA 0737 for use in Land Service.
This sling is similar to the web sling §§ 10442, C 416, but is twelve inches longer.

2. Design D.D. (E) 3838 has been approved to govern the future manufacture of the above-mentioned new pattern sling for use in land service.
The Mk. 2 sling – Cat. No. AA 5663 – differs from the Mk. 1 §§ B 1523, C 415, in that a 58-in. web sling described above is used. The increased length of the sling enables the gunner to adjust the sling in order that the weight of the Bren machine gun is taken on his shoulder, when being carried at the assault position, leaving his hand free for gun control.

3. Consequent upon ¨ 2 ¨ the Mk. 1 sling is hereby declared obsolescent for use with the Bren .303-in. machine gun.

4. The nomenclature of the Mk. 1 sling (§§ B 1523, C 415) has been revised to read as now shown.
These slings have been placed in a numerical series to distinguish them from Canadian pattern slings that have only one hook fitted. Canadian pattern slings have been designated No. 2.

5. The nomenclature of the above-mentioned hooks (§§ B 1523, C 415) has been revised to read as now shown.

8th Nov.,
1944
30th April,
1946
57
Vocab.
1742
C.I.A.
M/125

• • • • •

437

The *M.G.O. Equipment Memorandum* was a periodical printed in Australia by direction of the office of the Master General of the Ordnance. Its purpose was to keep personnel within all branches of the military up to date on improvements to existing equipment and details of new equipment so that they could be employed with maximum effect. Each was broken down into three sections. The first section provided general information related to the structure of operational research divisions, problems with supply and production, history of the Ordnance branch and basic maintenance suggestions. The second and longest section covered equipment and had a format similar to the Military Training Pamphlets, with line drawings or photographs of the items along with a text description of their characteristics and functions. Each edition also had a small third section at the end which discussed Japanese equipment so that it could be operated and maintained should it be required for operational purposes with information provided by the Directorate of Military Intelligence.

. . . . .

13. RIFLE NO. 1 MK III* HT (AUST) AND SIGHTS, TELESCOPIC, PATTERN 18 (AUST)

To overcome the shortage of rifles No. 3 Mk I* T fitted with the Pattern 18 Telescope and used as snipers' rifles, the above rifle is now being fitted with a telescopic sight.

2. Prior to 1939, the Small Arms Factory at Lithgow was manufacturing No. 1 Rifles fitted with a barrel approximately 4-ozs heavier than the standard barrel. These rifles were used by civilian riflemen and, being extremely accurate, compared very favourably with any rifles manufactured overseas. The heavy barrel, unlike the lighter one of the rifle No. 1, does not require the controlling interest of either the inner band, screw and spring, or stud and spring. These items are therefore omitted.

Plate 28—RIFLE NO. 1 MK III* HT (AUST) AND SIGHTS TELESCOPIC PATTERN 18 (AUST)

3. As a large number of these rifles were being held in ordnance depots, it was decided that the Pattern 18 Telescope could be manufactured in Australia and fitted to these rifles after they had been thoroughly reconditioned by the Small Arms Factory.

4. The standard of accuracy laid down for these reconditioned rifles is that each rifle is to be capable of firing a five-round group within a six-inch circle at 200 yards. It is pointed out that, although some of the rifles may not look new, their efficiency is better than that of the Rifle No. 1 Mk III.

5. The Pattern 18 Telescope has been manufactured to UK drawings, modified to suit local manufacture. In order to ensure maximum accuracy, the brackets are fitted to the telescope prior to fitting to the rifle. When fitted to the rifle and zeroed, the Telescope is branded with the serial number of the rifle. It is, therefore, essential that no attempt be made to use a telescope other than on the rifle it was fitted to in the factory. It is equally essential that, if either the rifle or the telescope has to be returned to Workshops, the complete equipment is returned.

42

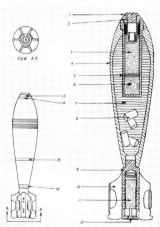

PLATE 61

Japanese Type 94 (1934) 90-mm. Mortar—Incendiary Bomb showing:—

1. Transit Plug.
2. Fuze Holder.
3. Burster.
4. Gas Rings.
5. Cardboard Packing.
6. Wooden Spacing Block.
7. Yellow Phosphorus and Carbon-disulphide filling.
8. Incendiary Rubber Pellets (40)
9. Tail.
10. Fins.
11. Primary Propelling Charge.
12. Percussion Cap.
13. Red Band.
14. Blue Band.
15. Yellow Band.
16. White Band.

78

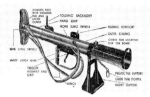

PLATE 8

Ammunition

Four types of ammunition are provided:—
   (i) Bomb H.E./T.A.
   (ii) Bomb Practice Inert/T.A.
   (iii) Bomb Drill/T.A.
   (iv) Shot Practice/T.A.

BOMB HE

PLATE 9

(i) Bomb H.E./T.A.

Colour—Green.
Identification Marks—Filling Band of Red x-x-x-x.
The Bombs consist of:—
   (a) The fuse which when fitted is held in place in the nose of the bomb by a thimble.

46

PLATE 34

Knives, Clasp
(showing newly designed Tin Opener)

23. KNIVES, FORKS AND SPOONS, LIGHTWEIGHT, FS

Experience has shown that troops serving in tropical areas outside Australia require knives, forks and spoons which will be as light as possible without impairing their serviceability, and short enough to fit into Tins, mess, rectangular.

Satisfactory designs have been evolved, the main features of which are:—

   (a) Spoons and forks . . . Each 6" long and made from nickel silver 18% hard.
   (b) Knives . . . 6" long, the blade being made from best cutlery steel and the handle die-cast of aluminium.

There is a saving of over 50% in the weight of Knives, Forks and Spoons, lightweight, FS, compared with standard issues

51

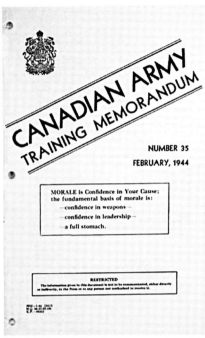

This publication was printed in Canada during the war with the purpose of providing supplemental training to the men and officers serving in the army. It introduced new weapons and equipment that would soon be available for issue and discussed better methods for accomplishing tasks in the field. Acceptable practices being performed in the British army were also discussed as were tactics being employed by the enemy. The first volume of the publication was released in 1941 and a total of 54 volumes ending in September 1945 span the war years.

Ten Commandments of Canadian Parachute Troops

1. You are the elite of the Canadian Army. For you action shall be fulfilment and you must train yourself to stand every test.

2. Cultivate true comradeship, for together with your comrades you will triumph or die.

3. Be shy of speech and incorruptible. The strong act, the weak chatter; chatter will bring you to the grave.

4. Calmness and caution, thoroughness and determination, valour and a relentless spirit of attack will make you superior when the test comes.

5. Face to face with the enemy, the most precious thing is ammunition. The man who fires aimlessly merely to reassure himself has no guts. He is a weakling and does not deserve the name of a "Paratrooper".

6. Never surrender. Your honour lies in victory or death.

7. Only with good weapons can you achieve success. Look after them therefore, on the principle, "First my weapons, then myself".

8. You must grasp the full meaning of each operation so that, even if your leader should fall, you can carry it out coolly and warily.

9. Fight chivalrously against an honourable foe; fifth columnists and civilian snipers deserve no quarter.

10. With your eyes open, keyed up to the highest pitch, agile as a greyhound, tough as leather, hard as steel, you will be the embodiment of a Canadian Paratrooper.

• • • • •

440

YOU STILL CAN'T TALK!

This is as good a time and place as any to warn all ranks that the advent of peace isn't to be taken as automatically removing all restrictions on the communication of military information. Quite true, some of the matters that were hush-hush up to V-J Day, don't matter very much now. But whether you're going to be in the Army for some time yet or whether you are headed for civvy street in the very near future, you still have to keep a tight rein on your tongue.

For one thing, your responsibilities are even greater now. Peace brought an end to censorship of all types in Canada. No longer are there alert press censors, for example, to overtake newspaper items which contain information of value to a foreign power or information which might be prejudicial to the interests of Canada if it were to be published. Anything you say may end up in print—and it may not look as good in print as it sounded in a casual conversation!

The Regulations

Remember, while you're in the Army your dealings with newspaper reporters, radio broadcasters or the general public insofar as communication of military information is concerned are governed by King's Regulations and Orders (Canada), Paragraphs 432, 433, and 434. These paragraphs state quite clearly that an officer or OR **is forbidden** to communicate any military information to any person who is not authorized to receive it, or to publish or communicate either directly or indirectly to the press any military information, or his views on any military subject without special permission of National Defence Headquarters.

Once you are out of the Army, "KR (Can)" doesn't apply to you. But

the Official Secrets Act does, and the Act makes it an offence to obtain or communicate to any other person any information which might be or is intended to be useful to a foreign power or to use any information lawfully or unlawfully obtained or which has been entrusted officially to an officer or soldier in confidence, for the benefit of any foreign power or in any other manner prejudicial to the interest of the State.

So, we'd suggest you play it safe and just don't talk. Whatever information you may have about military weapons and their performance, radar or anything else, may or may not be of value to a foreign power. Let the experts judge that. Just sit on it and you won't get into trouble on **that** count anyway.

MORE JAP BOOBY TRAPS
(U.S. Ordnance Sergeant)

In any discussion of booby traps, it is well to remember that the enemy not only constantly improved his booby trap fuses and devised new ones, but the number of methods of catching the unwary soldier was limited only by the enemy's ingenuity.

A hand grenade and a piece of wire are all that is necessary to booby trap an obstacle (Fig. 3), an item of equipment (Fig. 4) or a corpse (Fig. 1). The purpose of a booby trap is to make an apparently harmless act on the part of one of our soldiers a death trap, and to thus shatter morale and slow up our advance.

Everything from pipes (Fig. 5) to parasols, from fruit to flashlights (Fig. 2) may contain an explosive or be attached to a charge. In fact, it is impossible to

enumerate all the different types of traps which the Japs have left behind.

To understand the Japanese booby trap fuses, it is only necessary to remember how the standard U.S. firing devices operate. Pull, pressure and chemical delay types were employed by the enemy in the same general manner as we employed ours. Besides the chemical delay type, the Japs used their demolition clock (normally employed in demolition work) as a booby trap left behind to go off about the time they thought we would enter an area or building. The clock has delays up to eight days. To set it, the base is turned counter-clockwise, and a small window near

Fig. 1—On a Corpse

Fig. 2—Flashlight Device

Fig. 3—In Obstacles

Fig. 4—In Equipment

Fig. 5—Pipe Device

RIFLE GRENADE EQUIPMENT
(War Office Infantry Bulletin No. 23)

In Infantry Bulletin No. 13 . . . an account was given of the range of rifle grenades intended for the Far Eastern war. Much development has since taken place, and it is thought that a summary of the present position will be of interest.

(a) **Launcher (Fig. 1):** The Launcher, which is a light barrel extension to the rifle, is clipped to the muzzle of the rifle and acts as a spigot for the tail tube of the grenade which slides over it. A photograph of the projector or launcher fitted to the No. 5 rifle is shown at Fig. 1. The launcher for the No. 5 rifle is now in production.

(b) **Sight (Fig. 2):** An open sight suitable for high or low angle firing incorporating a levelling bubble and graduated in yards is in production. The "V" of the backsight can be moved laterally to permit zeroing for line. The sight is rapidly fixed to the barrel of the rifle by means of a cable and screw nut. The sight weighs slightly more than ½ lb.

New Cartridge

(c) **Cartridge:** Some difficulty has been experienced in providing a cart-

Fig. 1. Projector or Launcher fitted to the No. 5 Rifle.

Fig. 2. Sight for use with Rifle Grenade Projector.

TANK AGAINST FLAME-THROWER
(U.S. Tactical and Technical Trends)

The Japanese recognized the flame-thrower as a weapon designed primarily for assault operations against pillboxes and similar fortifications, but, fighting almost entirely on the defensive, they lacked an opportunity for this offensive employment of flame-throwing equipment. As a result the Japs stressed its use as an anti-tank weapon in defensive warfare.

An example of this tank-against-flame-thrower conflict, which usually resulted in defeat for Japanese troops, came from the only Japanese effort to use a flame thrower reported in the Leyte campaign. In this instance, elements of U.S. forces were held up by a Japanese road block during an advance along a Leyte highway. The approach to the road block was protected by groups of foxholes and machine-gun emplacements dug into the bank along the side of the road.

Two Killed

A tank was sent along the road to reduce the Japanese positions. As the tank approached the road block, a single Jap stepped out on the road with a flame-thrower. A Japanese officer, waving his sword and urging the attack forward, followed the flame-thrower operator. It was evident that the flame-

thrower operator had not been properly trained in the use of his weapon. No attempt was made to approach the tank quietly or unobserved, although the ditch along the road could have been used. Both the operator and the officer were killed before the flame-thrower was fired.

Japanese interest in flame-throwers has been evident in the amount of equipment of this type found abandoned in Burma, where they were forced, apparently due to economic and technical limitations, to use inferior substitutes for their standardized flame-throwers. The standard Japanese Army flame-throwers are the Model 93 and Model 100, which are very similar in design and operation.

The standard Japanese flame-throwers do not have a constant pressure regulating valve and as a result only the first burst of flame reaches the maximum range of 30 yards. The pressure drops with each succeeding burst and forces the operator to expose himself to return fire by advancing on the target to deliver successive bursts of flame.

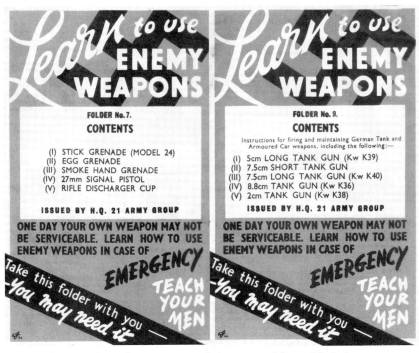

A short series of weapons training pamphlets titled **Learn to use Enemy Weapons** was developed and made available to troops by the 21st Army Group. Unlike the Small Arms Training and Military Training Pamphlet series which were not to be taken to the field, these enemy weapons manuals were intended to be carried by British and Canadian soldiers to the front so they would be available for reference if needed for "on the job" training. The series was printed in April of 1944 and issued prior to the Normandy invasion in June that same year. German weapons were grouped by type into individual pamphlets and only the bare essentials were covered due to space limitations. This included types of munitions, how to load, aim and fire. Examples of individual pamphlets include hand and rifle grenades, igniters and booby traps, magnetic A/T mines and blasting charges, 81mm mortars, PAK howitzers and A/T guns, and instructions for firing and maintaining German tank and armoured car weapons. The pamphlets typically had 8-12 pages with illustrations.

· · · · ·

442

N.B.—There are no special graduations for the hollow charge shell (Gr. 38 H1/A or H1/B). To use this ammunition, use the graduations for the H.E. shell, *adding 50% to the range* (i.e. if you want to open fire with the hollow charge shell at a range of 600 metres (660 yds.), add half the range—300 to the original, making 900 metres. To set any range, rotate the range setting wheel on the left of the eyepiece, causing the range plate to revolve, until the required range marking is opposite the pointer. Then lay on the target through the appropriate triangle. The co-axial machine gun is the normal M.G. 34, described in detail in a previous leaflet. It is fired by operating a foot-pedal on the left-hand side of the 7·5 cm. gun. and is operated by the gunner.

8.8 cm. Kw.K. 36

The 8·8 cm. Kw.K. 36 is the main armament of the Pz.Kw. TIGER. It fires the same ammunition and has the same effectiveness against armour as the 8·8 cm. Flak 18 and 36, but has an electric primer (C/22) instead of the percussion type. It is known to fire :—

Type	Colour of Projectile	Markings
A.P.C.B.C. shell ..	Black, with white tip	Pzgr. 39
A.P. 40 shot (arrowhead)	Black	Pzgr. 40
H.E. shell	Yellow ..	Spgr. (with percussion fuze AZ 23/38)
Hollow charge shell ..	Olive green ..	Gr. 39 H/1

The base of the cartridge case may be stamped 6347, or as shown in the diagram.

The gun is fired by a lever behind the elevating handwheel : the co-axial M.G. is operated by a foot pedal in the normal way.

8

PULL IGNITER ZZ 35

The German Pull Igniter ZZ 35 is used in conjunction with trip-wires to operate S-mines (anti-personnel) and booby traps made up from prepared charges, etc. It is also used as an anti-lifting device, the igniter being screwed into the base and/or side of Tellermines.

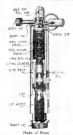

Made of Brass

Operation :
In the armed position the striker is held only by the small cotters or balls, which project into the groove behind the head of the striker. When the cylinder is pulled outwards, a distance of approximately ⅜ in., the cotters or balls are freed and moved outwards, so releasing the striker. The pull required to fire the igniter is 9–13 lb.

To Neutralize :
The igniter is made " safe " by pushing a nail through the hole in the cylinder. The trip-wire may then be cut.

To Disarm :
When the igniter is fitted in a mine or charge :
(i) Unscrew the igniter from the mine or charge, with the nail in place, and secured by string, tape, etc., from falling out.
(ii) Remove the detonator.

GERMAN Z.u.ZZ. 35 IGNITER

The German Z.u.ZZ 35 (Pull and Tension Wire) Igniter is a dual-purpose igniter used in improvised mines and booby traps. It is used in conjunction with a tightly-stretched anchor or trip wire,

2

GERMAN HAND GRENADES

General:
There are two H.E. models in use in the German Army.
(i) The Stick Grenade. (ii) The Egg Grenade.
Unlike the British 36 Grenade, they have a thin metal casing, and rely on blast rather than fragmentation for their effect. They can both be thrown to a greater distance than their effective radius of burst, and consequently can be used by troops advancing in the open.

The Stick Grenade:
Consists of a short cylinder containing the explosive, which is fastened to a wooden handle. Through the centre of the handle runs a double length of cord which is attached at the " explosive " end to the friction igniter system, and at the other, to a porcelain bead, or (in later models) to the screw cap.

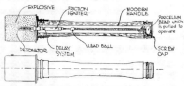

Particulars:

Overall length	..	1 ft. 4 in.
Weight	..	1 lb. 6 oz.
Weight of Explosive	..	7 oz.
Fuze delay ..	..	4½ secs.
Effective range of burst	..	16 yds.

Preparation and Arming:
In the standard metal ammunition boxes, the igniters, detonators and grenades are packed separately.

Preparation:
The explosive head and the screw cap are removed from the two ends of the wooden handle. The cord is lowered through the handle

1

5·9 in. HEAVY INFANTRY HOWITZER
(15 cm. s.I.G. 33)

This standard German infantry support gun fires H.E. or smoke shell. The ammunition is separate. Weight of the H.E. shell is 83½ lb., and of the smoke shell 85 lb. Each is separately packed in a wicker basket. The propellant consists of six removable parts, so that the shell may be fired with any one of 6 charges. Charge 2 consists of parts 1 and 2, charge 3 of parts 1, 2 and 3, etc. The smoke shell is painted field grey, and marked " Nb " in white.

Fire:
1. The firing mechanism is at safe when the safety and fire lever on the right face of the breech block is set at " SICHER ".
2. The breech is actuated by an L.B.M., pivoted on the right upper side of the breech ring.
3. To fire, set the safe and fire lever to " FEUER " and pull the lanyard fully to the rear.

Elevating and Traversing Gear:
The elevating gear is on the right; one turn of the handwheel = 41 mins. (12 mils). The traversing gear is on the left; one turn of the handwheel = 7 mins. (2·2 mils).
The **sight** is of the rocking bar type. All firing data are set on the sight. The gun is then elevated to the total Q.E. and swung round by the appropriate switch from zero.
N.B.—On the angle of sight scale, 300 = angle of sight zero. The scale is graduated in mils; 18 mils are roughly equal to one degree.

Dial Sight:
The Dial Sight (Rbl.F.32) has a slipping scale on the dial, graduated in mils, black from 0 to 32 (anti-clockwise) and red from 0 to 32 (clockwise). The main scale is graduated anti-clockwise in hundreds

5

The *Soldier's Service and Pay Book*, often referred to by its designation A.B. 64, was a small booklet issued to every soldier on enlistment. It contained information pertaining to the individual's description, place of enlistment, type and date of training, inoculations, record of leave and a detachable will. There were minor changes in the A.B. 64 over the course of the war but generally there are twenty-two

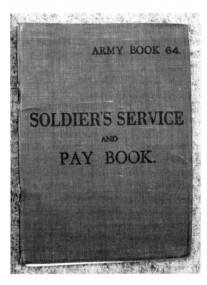

pages in the book. A pair of small paper pockets in the back of the cover provides a place to store passes, identity cards and ration cards. The images on the page at the right are examples from a wartime A.B. 64 that was issued as a replacement to the individual due to loss of his original. In situations were the booklet was lost or destroyed, a replacement was filled out based on service records and then certified by an officer. The two images below show additional pages that were issued and pasted into the A.B. 64.

A.B.64 Part I Slip.

**Casualties, Other Ranks,
Responsibility for Notification**

It is notified for information that the responsibility for notifying casualties affecting other ranks to their next-of-kin rests on the Officer I/c Records of the men concerned, and not on any department or branch of the War Office. All enquiries from next-of-kin or from any organization, etc., regarding casualties of other ranks should be addressed direct to Officers I/c Records, who will immediately take steps to furnish the required information.

The addresses of Record Offices and the units administered by them can be obtained at any Police Station.

Soldiers are, therefore, advised to notify their next-of-kin accordingly. There is no objection to this notice being handed to the next-of-kin.

(4362) 28565/3614 640m 8/44 B & M Ltd 7/8/7

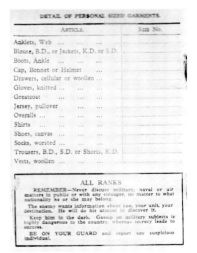

· · · · ·

PYTHON Nov 45 WDayke

(I) SOLDIER'S NAME and DESCRIPTION on ATTESTATION.

Army Number _14877042_

Surname (in capitals) _APPLEBY_

Christian Names (in full) _PAUL_

Date of Birth _19·8·26_

Trade on Enlistment _TYPEWRITER MECHANIC_

Religious Denomination _C.E_

Approved Society _IDEAL BENEFIT_

Membership No. _168760_

Enlisted at _NORTHAMPTON_ On _16·11·44_

For the :— _N.S.A. DURATION OF EMERGENCY._

* Regular Army.   * Supplementary Reserve.
* Territorial Army.   * Army Reserve Section D.
    * Strike out those inapplicable.

For _____ years with the Colours and _____ years in the Reserve.

Signature of Soldier _P. Appleby_

Date _17·11·44_

DESCRIPTION ON ENLISTMENT.

Height _5_ ft. _9½_ ins.   Weight _170_ lbs.

Maximum Chest _40_ ins.   Complexion _____

Eyes _BROWN_   Hair _FAIR_

Distinctive Marks and Minor Defects _____

SCAR BUTTOCK RIGHT

AGE & SERVICE GROUP 64c

CONDITION ON TRANSFER TO RESERVE.

Found fit for _____

Defects or History of past illness which should be enquired into if called up for Service _____

Date _____ 19 _____

Initials of M.O. i/c. _____

PRESCRIPTION FOR GLASSES.

Vision without Glasses.	SPH	CYL	Axis Standard Notation	Vision with Glasses	Optical Centre	Date of Exam.
					Hatfield	11·1·45
R	1·5	+40	105	6/9		Date of Issue
L	1·6	40	75	6/9		D	10·1·45

Signature of M.O.   Optician's Initials

VACCINATION.

Date Vaccinated.	Result.	Initials of Medical Officer.
24·11·44	Immediate	
9·12·46	S.(Acc).	

PROTECTIVE INOCULATIONS.

Nature of Vaccine, "T.A.B." Cholera, Plague, etc.	Date.	Initials of Medical Officer.
T.A.B. T.T. 1st	16·11·44	
T.A.B. T.T. 2nd	22·12·44	
1. Typhus	4·6·45	
2.	22·6·45	
3.	29·6·45	
TYPHUS T.A.B. T.T	27·2·46	9A
TYPHUS	12·9·46	
TAB. TT.	16·5·47	

PARTICULARS OF TRAINING.

Courses and Schools, Specialist Qualifications. Showing result.	Date.	Initials of Officer.
Gas Chamber Test (C.A.P.)	10·12·44	
Rifle War Course Open Range	12·12·44	
Bren	20·12·44	
Completed 2nd Basic Tests	23·12·44	
P.T. Failed 50%		
Completed 6 weeks Primary Training	26·12·44	
Swm X Teams 1 PSP	22 Jan 45	
Attended Pay Duties Course		
Sec 118 at H E.P.D. 20/5/46–2/6/46		
Result A. Pte 20 to 2 June 46		
Passed Swimming Test - 100-yds Sep 46		

PARTICULARS OF NEW ARTIFICIAL DENTURES SUPPLIED.

Particulars.	Dental Centre.	Date.	Initials of Dental Officer.

Date	Nature of Leave	Warrant	Signature
14/5/45 15/5/45	9 days Privilege	yes.	
22/6/45 3/7/45	9 days Priv 12 days/45	"	
3/8/45 18/8/45	14 days Embarkation	"	

O/SERS LEAVE
14 Apt - 19/04/46 Privilege
MARCH - APRIL 46/1AP 32 30 DAYS
8/12/47 - 6/12/47 28 days Rosen

* To include (1) a Skilled, (2) a Specialist, e.g. Signaller a Mt Gunner.

The ***Skill at Arms Record Book*** was similar in construction to the A.B. 64 but it was approximately an inch taller and half an inch wider. There were 66 pages in this book and it served as a log of the particulars

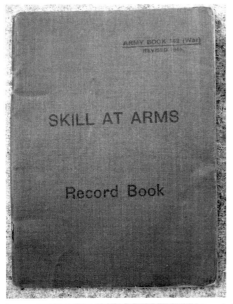

of training an individual solider received. This included a series of shooting proficiency tests under various timed conditions with the Number 4 service rifle, Bren Light Machine Gun and the Sten Submachine Gun. Additional tests were conducted firing the P.I.A.T., 2-Inch mortar and throwing various grenades that were in issue at the time. A record of basic physical training and route marches was in the back section along with logs of gas chamber tests.

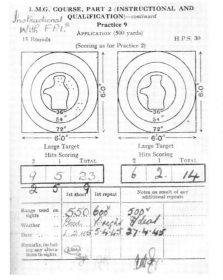

2" Mortar

Date	Rounds Fired H.E.	Smoke	Remarks
7.2.45		2	aiming fair
6.4.45	—	5	Handling. Fair. Gd.
18.4.45	—	4	Average.
26.4.45	4		Handling. Fair. in stops area

P.I.A.T. or 6-Pounder Gun

Date	Distance	Nature of Practice	Rounds Fired	Remarks
6.2.45	75^x	Practice Shot	3	Holding and aiming fair
12.4.45	80^x	PRAC. SHOT	2.	
26.4.45	80^x	LIVE PIAT BOMB.	1	much more practice needed.
4/6/45	80^x	PRAC. SHOT	2.	

Record of Grenades Thrown or Fired

Date	Type	No. Thrown or Fired	Remarks
14/2/44	36	2 THROWN	R gd.
5/2/45	36	2 Thrown	Under service conditions. Very shaky
26.4.45	36	4 Thrown	but not nervous

ANTI-GAS TRAINING

Completed Lessons 1 - 10 18/12/44
Gas Chamber Test C.A.P. 1/2/44

PASSED C.A.P. GAS CHAMBER ON
PASSED D.M. TEST ON 12/1/45
COMPLETED GAS LESSONS 1 - 7
PASSED GAS T's O.E.T. ON 2/2/45

Experienced Mustard Drop

Other Weapons

Date	Distance	Nature of Practice	Rounds Fired	Remarks

SUBJECT	DATE	INITIAL
RIFLE ZEROED	6/7/65	WBa
2" MOR. HE	19.7.65	WBa
" " SMOKE		
PIAT	27.7.45	WBa
36 GRENADE	19.7.65	
77 "		
RIFLE FROM HIP		WBa
STEN PRACTICES		
NIGHT FIRING	24.7.65	WBa
STREET FIGHTING	1.8.65	WBa
PE TESTS	19.7.65	WBa
ASSAULT COURSE	1.8.45	WBa
COMPLETED IRC	11.8.45	WBa

Period	Nature of Training	Remarks
	Completed 9 Weeks Primary Training 16/Nov/44 — 26	
27.12.44	Corps Training	

ROUTE MARCHES

DISTANCE	6	8	10	12	15	17	20	25
DATE								

P.E. TESTS

TEST	1	2	3	4	5	6	7
RESULT	P	P	P	P	P	P	

Endurance Training
Completed 1 to 4 "A" Pack. 2 Div.

Exercise
36 hrs aircraft

Grading
"C" Average

Dogs led
14.

Exercise
13.6.45

· · · · ·

447

A pair of pressed fibre board *Identity Discs* was issued to each soldier along with a length of sturdy string so they could be worn about the neck. Personal information including name, army number and religious denomination was stamped into

each disc. Officers were additionally issued an identity card that had their photograph attached. Several changes were made to the format of the identity cards along with the information they contained as the war progressed. Examples of early and late war identity cards are on this page and the one that follows. Most of the remaining pages in this chapter will have little or no text and feature examples of documents individual soldier's received during their enlistment. Examples of army and invasion currency are also included for reference. Examination of the individual documents should make their purpose apparent without the need of captions and most have been reduced in size and are not to scale with each other.

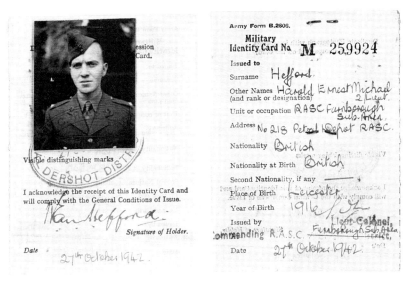

Army Form B.2606.
(REVISED)

MILITARY
IDENTITY CARD No. A 509059

Surname *ARRIL*

Christian Names (and rank or designation at time of issue) *Kenneth James, Lieut.*

Sex *Male*

Personal No.

Height *6' 1"*

Colour of Eyes *GREY*

Colour of Hair *BROWN*

Other Distinguishing Marks (if any) *Scar upper lip and left forefinger*

Date of Birth *27 JAN 1918*

Signature of Issuing Officer

Date *17 MAY 44*

Signature of Bearer

MILITARY IDENTITY CARD No. M

General Conditions of Issue.

1. This document relates only to the identity of the person described. It is not available as a Passport, Pass or Permit.

2. The loss of this Identity Card will be reported at once to the O.C. the Unit to which the holder belongs. The holder should make a separate note of the number of his card.

3. Anyone finding this card should hand it to the nearest Military establishment.

4. Impersonation of the authorised Bearer of an Identity Card or its alteration, destruction or transfer to another person are penal offences.

5. **No indication will be given on this card of the regiment, corps formation or unit to which the holder belongs. In the event of change of name or other particulars, a fresh card will be issued.**

6. An officer ceasing to be employed in a capacity in which the wearing of uniform is permitted, will return his A.F.B.2606 (Revised) to the O.C. Unit.

Army Form B.2606.
(Revised).

· · · · ·

449

NATIONAL SERVICE (ARMED FORCES) ACTS

ENLISTMENT NOTICE

MINISTRY OF LABOUR AND NATIONAL SERVICE DIVISIONAL OFFICE,

NORTH MIDLANDS DIVISIONAL OFFICE.
(M. R. SECTION)
LINDEN HOUSE,
CLUMBER ROAD WEST. **6 - NOV 1940** ......(Date)
NOTTINGHAM.
TEL. No. 41557 EXT. 4)

MR. *T.H Henson*
100 Walgrove Rd
Brampton
Chesterfield

Registration No. *CHN 2221*

DEAR SIR,

In accordance with the National Service (Armed Forces) Acts, you are called upon for service in the .....TERRITORIAL ARMY..................and are required to present yourself on.....................day **14 NOV 1940**.............(date), between 9 a.m. and 12 noon, or as soon as possible thereafter on that day, to :— *Royal Artillery*

236 Searchlight Training Regiment
Oswestry
......*Oswestry*.....................(nearest railway station).

* A Travelling Warrant for your journey is enclosed. Before starting your journey you must exchange the warrant for a ticket at the booking office named on the warrant. If possible, this should be done a day or two before you are due to travel.

A Postal Order for 4s. in respect of advance of service pay, is also enclosed. Uniform and personal kit will be issued to you after joining H.M. Forces. Any kit that you take with you should not exceed an overcoat, change of clothes, stout pair of boots, and personal kit, such as razor, hair brush, tooth brush, soap and towel.

Immediately on receipt of this notice, you should inform your employer of the date upon which you are required to report for service.

Yours faithfully,

G. E. WEAR

| You should take this Notice with you when you report to your Unit. |

for Divisional Controller.

* *Delete if not applicable.*

N.S. 12 (5901) Wt. 18479—4180 1,000M 7/40 T.S. **677**

. . . . .

74190

Army Form X 202B.

CERTIFICATE OF TRANSFER to the ARMY RESERVE

Army No. ...1726067... Rank ...W/BDR...

Surname (Block letters)...HENSON...

Christian Name(s) ...THOMAS HENRY...

Regt. or Corps ...R.A. (H.A.A.)...

The transfer of the above-named to the appropriate Class of the Army

Reserve (see note below) is confirmed with effect from ...30 July 46...

> *The date to be inserted here will be that following the day on which Release Leave terminates, including any additional leave to which the soldier may be entitled by virtue of service overseas.

Note.—The appropriate Class of the Army Reserve is as follows:—

(i) Royal Army Reserve—in the case of a regular soldier with reserve service to complete:

(ii) Army Reserve Class Z (T)—in the case of a man of the Territorial Army, including those called up for service under the National Service Acts:

(iii) Army Reserve, Class Z—in the case of all other soldiers not included in (i) or (ii) above.

Record Office Stamp.

R.A. RECORDS
HEAVY A.A.
6 June 46
RUGBY

for Colonel,
...R.A. Records, Heavy A.A...

Officer i/c .... Records.

Date ....

Warning.—

Any alteration of the particulars given in this certificate may render the holder liable to prosecution under the Seamen's and Soldiers' False Characters Act, 1906.

If this certificate is lost or mislaid, no duplicate can be obtained.

Wt. 37285/90 1,000M 12/45 KJL/1516/16 Gp. 38/3
Wt. 40609/240 1,000M 2/46 KJL/1722/32 Gp. 38/3

· · · · ·

PASS

ARMY FORM B. 295
(pads of 100)

REGT. *R.A.*

No. *1726067*   Rank *BDR.*

Name *HENSON T.H.*

has permission to be absent from his unit

from *AD 24.5.46* to *2359 hrs 26.5.46*

STAMP
(with unit or formation identification
number or letter blanked out).

MAJOR R.A.
C.O. ARTILLERY DEPOT BTY   Commanding

1. From London District	4. Reporting Centre	7. Ration Card Issued
	Sgt A.	*Yes*
2. To London	5. Eire/N Ireland Destination	8. For use of C.M.P.
	Valid only with A.B. 64	
3. Through London	6. Nearest Hospital or Medical Unit	9.
Yes	*Chesterfield*	

* Items not applicable to be deleted and initialled by issuing officer vide A.C.I. 989/42 and any subsequent amendments.   [P.T.O.

If a calling-out of the whole Army Reserve is ordered, every soldier on pass must return immediately to his unit without waiting for instructions.

No ....   Regiment 1 CDN. ARTY. BASE RFT. REGT.

PASS

Army Form B295
(in pads of 100)

No *H20846* (Rank) *L/CPL*   (Name) *SEED*

has permission to be absent from his †quarters/duty, from

1200 hrs 24-3-45 to *2359 hrs 24-3-45*

for the purpose of proceeding to* *SALERNO*

(Station) *FIELD*

(Date) MAR 24 1945

Commanding
1 CDN. ARTY. BASE RFT. REGT.

† Delete whichever is not practicable.
* Destination not required unless absence is to exceed 24 hours, unless notification is desirable owing to local conditions or is necessary to enable purchase of a rail ticket at reduced fare.

CROWN COPYRIGHT RESERVED

If a Calling-out of the whole Army Reserve is ordered every soldier on pass must return immediately to his unit without waiting for instructions.

No ....   Regiment *I C C D.*

PASS

Army Form B295
(in pads of 100.)

No *H20816* (Rank) *L. CPL.*   (Name) *SEED C. O.*

has permission to be absent from his † quarters/duty, from *0800 HRS.*

to *2230 HRS. 17-NOV-44*

CAVA

for the purpose of proceeding to* *FIELD*

(Date) *17-NOV-44*

Commanding

[P.T.O.

*Destination not required unless absence is to exceed 24 hours, unless notification is desirable owing to local conditions or is necessary to enable purchase of a rail ticket at reduced fare.
† Delete whichever is not applicable.

CROWN COPYRIGHT RESERVED

. . . . .

452

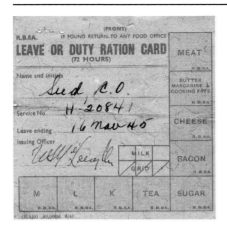

LEAVE OR DUTY RATION CARD
(72 HOURS)

(FRONT)
R.B.SA. IF FOUND RETURN TO ANY FOOD OFFICE

Name and initials *Seed, C.O.*

Service No. H-20841

Leave ending *16 Nov 45*

Issuing Officer

			MEAT	
			BUTTER MARGARINE & COOKING FATS	
			CHEESE	
		MILK GRID	BACON	
M	L	K	TEA	SUGAR

(BACK)
MINISTRY OF FOOD

INSTRUCTIONS

MEAT	
BUTTER MARGARINE & COOKING FATS	
CHEESE	
BACON	
SUGAR	TEA	K	L	M

SA CE 896236

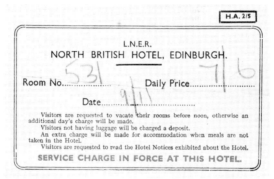

H.A. 2/5

L.N.E.R.
NORTH BRITISH HOTEL, EDINBURGH.

Room No. 531   Daily Price 7/6

Date 9/11

Visitors are requested to vacate their rooms before noon, otherwise an additional day's charge will be made.
Visitors not having luggage will be charged a deposit.
An extra charge will be made for accommodation when meals are not taken in the Hotel.
Visitors are requested to read the Hotel Notices exhibited about the Hotel.

SERVICE CHARGE IN FORCE AT THIS HOTEL.

O. R. LUNCH TICKET

Ristorante **Valiani**
at Central Railway Station

Hand this part and 10 Lire to cashier at Restaurant Entrance

British Army Welfare valid on day of issue only. **15**

O. R. LUNCH TICKET

Hand this part to waiter who serves you at

Ristorante **Valiani**
at Central Railway Station

British Army Welfare valid on day of issue only. **15**

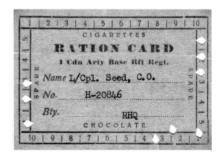

| 1 | 2 | 3 | 4 | 5 | 6 | 7 | 8 | 9 | 10 |

CIGARETTES

RATION CARD
1 Cdn Arty Base Rft Regt.

Name L/Cpl. Seed, C.O.

No.   H-20846

Bty.   RHQ

CHOCOLATE

| 10 | 9 | 8 | 7 | 6 | 5 | 4 | 3 | 2 | 1 |

· · · · ·

A wide range of *Guide Books* and *Language/Phrase Books* were published during the war in the United Kingdom, Canada and America for use by Allied troops bound for unfamiliar territories. These were typically in a small pocket pamphlet form ranging from 50-150 pages depending on the country they dealt with. Contents included monetary currency and rules for marketplaces, weights and measures, local and international road signs, local customs, and Do's and Don'ts. A section for useful words and phrases covered greetings and courtesies, words for basic navigation and phrases helpful when handling prisoners or making military related inquires to civilians.

· · · · ·

A British gunner in Italy assigned to an 8th Army artillery unit reads a copy of *John Bull* magazine during January 1944. Other popular wartime publications that the soldiers could receive overseas were *Blighty*, *Punch*, *Picture Post*, *Parade*, *Union Jack*, *Tobruk Truth*, *Pegasus Goes To It*, *Maple Leaf*, *Springbok*, and *Fauji Akhbar* (The Soldiers' Newspaper) which was an English language magazine for Indian servicemen.

Preparedness—A British Tommy wearing an inflatable life belt reads the "Soldier's Guide to Sicily", while aboard a landing craft approaching the Sicilian coast during Operation Husky, the Allied invasion of Sicily. The Mediterranean – 24 JUL 1943.

. . . . .

2'6 STAMPS 2'6

6 at 2½d. - 6 at 2d. - 6 at ½d.

LETTERS TO THE FORCES

SEND AIRGRAPHS

POSTAGE RATES.
IMPERIAL AND FOREIGN
(except to H.M. Forces and Ships of War abroad).

LETTERS to the British Empire, generally. Territories under British Mandate, Egypt, U.S.A. and British Post Offices in Morocco.	First oz. 2½d. Each additional oz. - 1d.	
To all other destinations - - - -	First oz. - 3d. Each addl. oz. - 1d. tional oz. 7½d.	
POSTCARDS (All destinations) - - - - - 2d.		
PRINTED PAPERS (do.) per 2 oz. - - - - ½d.		

For rates for Commercial Papers, Samples, Small Packets, Magazine Post to Canada and Newfoundland, Literature for the Blind and Parcels—See Post Office Guide.

HARRISON & SONS. LTD., PRINTERS. LONDON.   MARCH, 1945

POSTAGE RATES.
INLAND.

LETTERS—First 2 oz. - - - - - - 2½d.
   Each additional 2 oz. - - - - ½d.
POSTCARDS - - - - - 2d.
PRINTED PAPERS—First 2 oz. - - - 1d.
   Each additional 2 oz. : Max. 2 lb. ½d.
NEWSPAPERS (Regd. at G.P.O.)—
   First 4 oz. (per copy) - - - 1½d.
   Each additional 4 oz. (per copy) : Max. 2 lb. ½d.
Newspapers may be sent as Printed Papers whether registered or not.

PARCELS—

excluding Eire.		Eire.	
3 lb. 7d.	7 l'. - 11d.	2 lb. - 6d.
4 lb. 8d.	8 lb. - 1/-	5 lb. - 9d.
5 lb. 9d.	15 lb. (Max.) 1/1	8 lb. - 1/-
6 lb. 10d.		11 lb. (Max.) 1/3

MARCH, 1945

POSTAGE RATES.
NAVY, ARMY AND AIR FORCE.

H.M. Ships in Home Waters H.M. Army and Air Force stationed at Home	Postage should be prepaid at the ordinary inland rates.
H.M. Ships in Foreign Waters H.M. Army and Air Force abroad (wherever stationed)	Letters, First oz. - - 1½d. Each additional oz. - 1d. Postcards - - - - 1d. Printed Papers, Per 2 oz. ½d. Parcels 3lb. 9d. 11lb. 2s. 0d. 7lb. 1s. 6d. 22lb. 3s. 6d.

MARCH, 1945

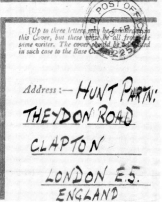

A. F. W3078.

J. D. & Co., Apsley.

ACTIVE SERVICE

[Crown Copyright Reserved.]

This envelope must not be used for coin or valuables. It cannot be accepted for registration.

NOTE :—

Correspondence in this envelope need not be censored Regimentally. The contents are liable to examination at the Base.

The following Certificate must be signed by the writer :—

I certify on my honour that the contents of this envelope refer to nothing but private and family matters.

Signature
Name only

[Up to three letters may be forwarded in this Cover, but these must be all from the same writer. The cover should be addressed in such case to the Base Censor]

Address :— HUNT PARTN:
THEYDON ROAD
CLAPTON
LONDON E.5.
ENGLAND

. . . . .

A.F.A. 2042.
114/Gen.No./5248.

FIELD ⚜ SERVICE

POST CARD.

The address only to be written on this side. If anything else is added the post card will be destroyed.

[Crown Copyright Reserved.]

I am quite well.

I have been admitted into hospital

{ sick } and am going on well.
{ wounded } and hope to be discharged soon.

I am being sent down to the base.

(letter dated _____
I have received your { telegram „ _____
(parcel „ _____

Letter follows at first opportunity.

I have received no letter from you

{ lately
{ for a long time.

Signature }
only }
Date _____

Wt W1566 R1619-18539 8000m. 9-17. C. & Co., Grange Mills, S.W.

Dearest Darling you mentioned a thing in your last letter about a subject I do not wish to have any part of so you can tell your girl friends at work that if they all want a big family, I don't fill I want in this world darling is you, my two boys mam and dad, I would not part with either of you for anything in the universe and now without its charm for this time. I love you "Buida Mia" love them this. Vip
×××××× ×××××××××
FOR. BOYS.   FOR. YOU, DARLING.

`14-5-45.`

SPACE NOT AVAILABLE FOR CORRESPONDENCE—CARD SUBJECT TO WITHDRAWAL IF USED

VERIFICATO
PER CENSURA

Mittente
(Sender's)
(Correspondents)
Cognome DOWDING. A. V.
(Surname)
(Fornavn)
Nome
(Name)
(Navn)
Grado DRIVER. 3907259.
(Rank)
(Grad)
Campo p.g. P.G. 65. SEZ1 3. CAPAN. 5.
(P. of W. Camp.)
(Jlariya. n. n.)
PM 3650. ITALIA.

POSTA. AEREA. VIA. ROMO. LISBONO. E. LONDRA.

POSTE ITALIANE
CARTOLINA POSTALE
PER PRIGIONIERI DI GUERRA
TASSA DI FRANCHIGIA POSTALE

(INGHILTERRA) ENGLAND

BEXLEY. HEATH. KENT.

53. BROADWAY.

Mrs. A. V. DOWDING.

5287

F3
55 049358

COUNTERFOIL.

To be detached and kept by the Sender.

The Postmaster General does not undertake to consider any application respecting an Order which has miscarried, or has been lost or destroyed, unless the counterfoil is produced.

Postal 5|- Order

To whom payable:—
_____
_____
At what Office:—
_____
_____
Whether }
crossed }_____
Date }
sent }_____

NOT NEGOTIABLE.

THE SENDER MUST FILL IN, IN INK, THE PAYEE'S NAME BEFORE PARTING WITH THE ORDER.

F3
55 049 358

BRITISH POSTAL ORDER
To the Postmaster General

5/-

Pay
the
sum
of
5 FIVE SHILLINGS 5
at
Post Office

Three Half-Pence

within Six Calendar Months from the last day of the month of issue.

For Regulations—see back.

RECEIVED the sum due

POSTAL ORDER — FOUNDED

Postage Stamps

not exceeding two: in number may be affixed here but: not elsewhere
(i) up to 5d. for :orders up to 4s. 6d.
(ii) up to 11d. for :orders above 4s. 6d.
Odd halfpennies are: not permissible.

SIGNATURE.

A PAYING OFFICE STAMP WITH DATE

A CANCELLING THIS ORDER

POSTMASTER

ISSUING OFFICE STAMP WITH DATE

THE MANCHESTER LEEDS

21 ARMY GROUP

PERSONAL MESSAGE
FROM THE C-in-C

To be read out to all Troops

1. The time has come to deal the enemy a terrific blow in Western Europe.

The blow will be struck by the combined sea, land, and air forces of the Allies—together constituting one great Allied team, under the supreme command of General Eisenhower.

2. On the eve of this great adventure I send my best wishes to every soldier in the Allied team.

To us is given the honour of striking a blow for freedom which will live in history; and in the better days that lie ahead men will speak with pride of our doings. We have a great and a righteous cause.

Let us pray that " The Lord Mighty in Battle " will go forth with our armies, and that His special providence will aid us in the struggle.

3. I want every soldier to know that I have complete confidence in the successful outcome of the operations that we are now about to begin.

With stout hearts, and with enthusiasm for the contest, let us go forward to victory.

4. And, as we enter the battle, let us recall the words of a famous soldier spoken many years ago :—

> *" He either fears his fate too much,*
> *Or his deserts are small,*
> *Who dare not put it to the touch,*
> *To win or lose it all."*

5. Good luck to each one of you. And good hunting on the mainland of Europe.

B. L. Montgomery
General
C.-in-C 21 Army Group.

1944.

· · · · ·

Soldiers, Sailors and Airmen of the Allied Expeditionary Force!

You are about to embark upon the Great Crusade, toward
which we have striven these many months. The eyes of
the world are upon you. The hopes and prayers of liberty-
loving people everywhere march with you. In company with
our brave Allies and brothers-in-arms on other Fronts,
you will bring about the destruction of the German war
machine, the elimination of Nazi tyranny over the oppressed
peoples of Europe, and security for ourselves in a free
world.

Your task will not be an easy one. Your enemy is well
trained, well equipped and battle-hardened. He will
fight savagely.

But this is the year 1944! Much has happened since the
Nazi triumphs of 1940-41. The United Nations have inflicted upon the Germans great defeats, in open battle,
man-to-man. Our air offensive has seriously reduced
their strength in the air and their capacity to wage
war on the ground. Our Home Fronts have given us an
overwhelming superiority in weapons and munitions of
war, and placed at our disposal great reserves of trained
fighting men. The tide has turned! The free men of the
world are marching together to Victory!

I have full confidence in your courage, devotion to duty
and skill in battle. We will accept nothing less than
full Victory!

Good Luck! And let us all beseech the blessing of Al-
mighty God upon this great and noble undertaking.

Dwight D Eisenhower

. . . . .

During the war, paper currency for use by British military personnel was marked on one side as being issued by the British Military Authority. Following the war, six different series of **British Armed Forces Special Vouchers** were printed and used as paper currency. Currency used by the British Army during the war can be seen in the photo below. The notes with Tripolitania on them are considered to be North African invasion notes. *Allied Military Currency*, also known as invasion notes, was produced as a replacement for the currency issued under the authority of the Axis nations when they were in power. The paper notes were printed in the United

Kingdom, the United States of America and in the Soviet Union. Replacement currency was used in France, Germany, Italy, Austria, Japan and Okinawa. Examples of notes for each nation are pictured on the following page. Japan and Okinawa used the same currency even though they were separate nations. It should be noted that Allied Military Currency was started in 1943 but future issues of notes were still in use in the mid 1950's in some countries.

· · · · ·

Allied Military Currency issued in France (above), Italy (below) and Germany (right).

Allied Military Currency used in Japan and Okinawa (below) and Austria (right).

· · · · ·

461

LES ANGLO-AMÉRICAINS

massacrent nos hommes, nos femmes et nos enfants
détruisent nos villes, ravagent nos campagnes

ET MAINTENANT,

avec ce chiffon de papier sans valeur

ιs prétentent payer les Français
quand ils leur prennent ce qui leur appartient

ILS ONT ATTAQUÉ L'EUROPE
PAR LA FRANCE

parce qu'ils veulent avant tout
se servir de nos enfants en les mobilisant pour
en faire LEUR CHAIR A CANON
parce qu'avant de vaincre l'Allemagne ils veulent

RUINER LA FRANCE

pour assurer sur nos décombres
la victoire de l'Angleterre.

· · · · ·

462

The document below and to the left is the front and back of a flyer the Germans dropped to the French population in Normandy. Essentially it says the Allies are destroying their property and taking their food in exchange for the worthless paper money they brought with them.

Trahie à DUNKERQUE

Poignardée dans le dos à MERS-el-KÉBIR

Attaquée à DAKAR

en SYRIE ⚓

à MADAGASCAR

dépouillée en AFRIQUE du NORD, décimée dans sa population par les pirates de l'air.

LA FRANCE

sera-t-elle définitivement ruinée par les financiers juifs Anglo-Américains ?

The following six pages are examples of British military newsletters printed at the front. News was a morale booster and soldiers would accept a task more readily when they thought they had a basic idea of what was going on around them. The first example is the very first issue of *Pegasus Goes To It* which was printed on D+5 in Normandy. The second example is a more refined and later issue of *Pegasus Goes To It*. The third example is an early issue of another newsletter called *The Cow's Tail*. These newsletters are extremely rare and were printed in very limited numbers and passed from hand to hand so everyone could read them before they became toilet paper or kindling for a fire. At least 119 issues of *Pegasus Goes To It* were printed. The number of issues of *The Cow's Tail* is unknown.

· · · · ·

463

1500 hrs SUNDAY, 11 JUNE 1944.   No. 1.

EDITORIAL.

Gentlemen,

Here is the first issue of YOUR news-sheet. Your Editor wanted to get it out long before this, but he was held up by the bad weather which held up a lot of much more important people and equipment soon after the invasion of France started and has only waited to dig a trench before getting down to this issue.

OFFICERS :

Please see that copies of this news-sheet get round to the men as much as is possible. Paper is limited - especially after one or two vehicles have been drowned ! - and it depends very much on you whether the news-sheet gets round and is any use.

MEN :

Please tell your pals where they can see or get hold of the latest copy of "PEGASUS" if they want the news.

We shall try to get "PEGASUS" to you regularly, but it wont always be possible to be as up to date with news as the B.B.C., and much of the news you will know before this gets out as you are making it yourselves.

If you have any suggestions, rude or otherwise, send them to the Editor (your S.O. Education) through your HQ. In any case, "PEGASUS" may help out the supply of A.F. Blank if it arrives late.

Here's wishing you luck !

The Editor.

AIRBORNE ASSAULT.

The world was thrilled to hear of the opening of the invasion of FRANCE by the use of Airborne troops. On Thursday last the B.B.C. announced that the BRITISH 6th AIRBORNE DIVISION had opened the party with a successful operation and was holding firm and fighting magnificently against repeated heavy attacks by the enemy.

The opening of the invasion was a tactical surprise to the enemy: this must have been helped by your good security which helped before the battle to make the opening phase of the operation so successful.

The Army and Naval personnel your Editor has met in the days since your arrival in FRANCE have been filled with admiration for the courage and skill of the Airborne troops and sens you their good wishes.

NEWS.

Turn over for a short summary of B.B.C. news.

. . . . .

B.B.C. news up to 1300 hrs 11 JUN 44.

THE INVASION OF FRANCE.

The Allied forces in FRANCE continue to make progress everywhere. The main bridgehead is now over 30 miles along the NORMANDy coast and some 10 miles in depth.

On the EAST the BRITISH 6th AIRBORNE DIV is beating off attack after attack by the GERMANS. Between CAEN and BAYEUX fierce fighting is going on against strong GERMAN armoured forces, and considerable losses are being inflicted on the GERMAN armour; fierce tank and infantry battles are still raging round CAEN, but the GERMANS have made no progress there. The GERMANS have not yet launched a major counter-attack. A BRITISH armoured thrust has reached TILLY-SUR-SEULLES more than half way between BAYEUX and the main road from CAEN to BRITTANY. The Allies are 7 miles SOUTH EAST of BAYEUX.

Between TREVIERES and ISIGNY the Americans have advanced south of the flooded ground.

Between ISIGNY and CARENTAN the AMERICANS have also seized valuable high ground.

Further WEST AMERICAN ground forces have linked up with AIRBORNE forces and the railway from CARENTAN to CHERBOURG has been cut. GERMAN communications in this sector are suffering and only a single-track railway along the WEST of the peninsula is left for the GERMANS to communicate with CHERBOURG.

General MONTGOMERY has now set up his Battle HQ in FRANCE.

THE AIR WAR.

Air cover has been resumed in strength in better weather. Yesterday the AMERICANS alone sent out 900 fighters, 20 GERMAN aircraft were shot down, 26 AMERICAN planes were lost.

Allied aircraft is now operating from landing strips on the NORMANDY coast. The first R.A.F. Group HQ is now ashore in FRANCE.

In addition, good shooting by BRITISH guns on land and from the sea has helped considerably in the operations.

Last night BRITISH bombers were over occupied territory and bombed targets at FALAISE, ST LO, LAVAL, LE MANS, AVRANCHES and elsewhere.

In yesterday's early morning attack on BERLIN by MOSQUITOS more than 30 four-thousand lb bombs were dropped.

ITALY.

The FIFTH ARMY has encountered enemy resistance for the first time since passing ROME. Fierce fighting has taken place NORTH EAST of VITERBO. The FIFTH ARMY has reached 10 miles NORTH WEST of VITERBO.

A sector 50 miles deep and more than 30 miles wide has been cleared beyond ROME. PESCARA has been occupied.

PACIFIC.

In the SOUTH WEST PACIFIC Allied warships have beaten off another JAPANESE attempt to reinforce BIAK ISLAND off the WEST of BRITISH NEW GUINEA. 5 JAPANESE destroyers turned and fled when Allied warships opened fire.

BURMA.

On the INDO-BURMESE border Allied troops have kept up the advance on the MANIPUR road.

RUSSIA.

MOSCOW reports no change on the RUSSIAN battlefront.

• • • • •

465

PEGASUS
GOES TO IT.

OVERHEARD IN N.W.EUROPE.
Div HQ Staff Officer:"I suppose that now
the Hun has had a 'plane over here
he'll be bombing Div HQ."
Bde HQ Staff Officer:"What ? Bomb
Div HQ - Hitler's secret weapon ?"

And it must have been the same
Brigade Staff Officer who rang up
Div HQ,and,when somebody replied,
asked:"Is that Hitler's secret
Staff Officer ?"

But,like the Russians,Div HQ
says nothing........

TOO FRIENDLY AND KIND-HEARTED !
This means you !!! And it is
probably true ! One of the things that
sticks out a mile in the Field is the
fact that the British soldier (and,of
course,the Scots,Irish,Canadian and
other Empire soldiers as well as the
Americans),even though he may not know
a word of the language of the country
he is in,gets himself immediately
liked by the locals because he always
manages to be friendly and kind-hearted.
Which is a very good thing in friendly
countries ! But not such a good thing
if you get into Germany.
Why ? Because the Germans despise
people who treat them kindly. They will
laugh at you - they will think you are
'soft' !
Naturally we do not expect you to
believe this. But here are some of the
things said by a well-educated 36-year
old German who gave himself up to the

FAMOUS LAST WORDS:-

"Oh,the buzz-bombs always pass over here !"

Allies.He had travelled all over Germany,arranging supplies from a large Heinkel
factory,where he was the head of a department. He therefore has a wide knowledge of
German opinions and mentality.
"You British and Americans are not awake to the basis of German thought. You are
too friendly and kind-hearted. You judge everybody by your own yardstick.
"My countrymen are all to blame for the war. They will tell you,with tears in
their eyes,that they just had to obey their leaders. Don't be taken in by this attitude;
and don't let your army of occupation be taken in by it either !
"In every German there is the inborn spirit of a soldier. My old father,now 82
years old,even today straightens his back when he hears a military band go by; his eyes
glisten; and you can easily see that he is thrilled at the re-awakening of past
military memories - even though he had only a barrack-room experience of military glory.
"I can still remember the last occupation. In our area a Belgian force made us
feel the consequences of a war were bitter. But,in Cologne,under British occupation,
life was even better than before 1914,and we thought (and spoke) of Cologne as 'paradise'."
Those of you who saw the bodies of Belgian civilians,murdered in cold blood,may
find such 'British kindness' surprising. But will you be just as kind to the same sort
of Germans later on ? Will you be kind and friendly ? Or will you think curfews and
restrictions are a good thing ? We shall tell you more of this German prisoner's views.

• • • • •

466

If you want to write to prisoners or relatives in occupied countries,including
Japan,you can find out how to do so by getting your Post-wallah to ask the Postal
Unit for full details when he collects your unit mail.

We very much want contributions from those of you in the line. We can offer a
small gift of cigarettes to the writers of any stories published. So send your stories
of anything that has happened to you or your friends straight to the Editor,"Pegasus",
c/o Div.Sigs. Any old paper will do. Write in pencil if you like. But send something
if you can,with your name,rank,number and unit. Remember we want stuff which will
interest the greatest number of readers,especially those who are living rough.....

We have run out of paper. There will be no "Pegasus" tomorrow. (N.B. No: we are
not,repeat not,going to Brussels !!!)

B.B.C.news summary up to 2359 hours,Wednesday,14 Feb 45.

- -

The Air War.

On Tuesday night 1,400 heavies went
for an oil-plant at (?) Borna,South of
Leipzig,Magdeburg,Nuremberg,Bonn and
Dortmund. 6 planes are missing. Of these
1,400,800 gave Dresden its first big
attack. 650,000 incendiaries,and both
8,000-pounders and 4,000-pounders were
dropped,causing extensive fires. There
was very little flak. Dresden,the capital
of Saxony,is about as big as Sheffield,
and the centre of a railway network. The
attack was designed to spoil the German
preparations to defend the city against
the advancing Russians,75 miles away.

On Wednesday afternoon 450 heavies
attacked Dresden again. The whole force
of 1,350 heavies with 900 fighters,went
also to Chemnitz,35 miles South West of
Dresden,and to Magdeburg and to Wesel.
Chemnitz has a population of 400,000,is
a rail- and industrial-centre,and its
marshalling-yards handle 3,500 wagons a day.
At Wesel there is a road-bridge over the
Rhine.

2nd TAF,on the Canadian Army front,
had made 1,400 sorties by the middle of
Wednesday afternoon,destroying at least
85 locos,220 railway-trucks and 130 motor
vehicles.

Spitfires attacked V-sites in Holland.
Aircraft from Italy made 2,400 sorties
against rail- and oil-targets in the Vienna
area,the Brenner Pass,harbours in North
Italy,railways in the Po valley and railways
in North Yugoslavia.

Other News.

North East of Mandalay,the 1st Chinese
Army is 55 road miles from Lashio. South
West of Mandalay,the 14th Army took a town
on the Irriwaddy opposite the oilfields of
(?) Chowk,wrecked by us 3 years ago.

In Luzon,the naval-base of Cavite has
been taken; Bataan and Corregidor have been
bombed. In the 5 weeks' fighting Jap casualties are 70,000; American casualties less
than 10,000.

Martial law has ended in Greece.
Sir William Rothenstein,the great British artist,died today in Gloucestershire,
aged 73.

The Eastern Front.

Schneidemuhl,in Pomerania,now 25
miles behind the line,has been taken.
In the Polish Corridor the Russians
are 5 miles from a big junction on the
Danzig-Stettin railway.

In Silesia,the Russian salient
beyond the Oder,and on the Berlin side
of it,has been broadened. 7 big German
towns have been taken: on the North
flank,Nousalz,20 miles from Glogau,
Sprottau,and 2 others; on the South
flank,Streigau,27 miles South West of
Breslau,and 2 other places,35 and 45
miles West of Breslau,have been taken.
Breslau is in a more and more hopeless
position with the Russians flanking
the only escape corridor.

The Germans report fighting in
Sorau,North West of Sagan,5 miles inside
Brandenburg and 70 miles North East of
Dresden.

The Germans have not yet told
their people of the fall of Budapest.
The Russians say that this opens the
road to Bratislava and Vienna,and the
Southern provinces of Germany,where
"the Germans will not be allowed to
remain unmolested." The Russians have
told Vienna to take the fate of Budapest
as a warning.

The Western Front.

The Canadian Army is making slow,
but steady progress against enemy counter
attack,floods and mud. The going is
very heavy. In the North 'waterborne'
Canadians are going North to the Rhine,
and South East to Calcar and Udem. Cleve
is still under shell- and mortar-fire.
The Cleve-Goch road has been cut halfway down. Scottish troops have 2 bridgeheads over the River Nierz,West of Kessel,
and fight in a village 3 miles from Goch.
The whole of the Reichswald Forest is clear.

The 3rd American Army has beaten off
a counter-attack North East of Prum.
In Alsace the Allies now hold the
West bank of the Rhine from North of
Strasbourg to Basle with no German bridge-
heads.

. . . . .

467

THE COW'S TAIL

0900 hours, Tuesday, March 6th, 1945.

No.6.

JOLLY WINTER SPORTS: Moving Div HQ.

Scene: The Planning Room at Div HQ. Furniture as
per G.1098.
Time: Just before any HQ move.
(Two Staff Officers have been sort of thinking
about an HQ shamble to a location where there is likely
to be a more comfortable Officers' Mess).

1st High-Level Offr:"Well,now,is the form about that move clear,old man ?"
2nd High-Level Offr:"I think so,old man. It seems pretty well teed up,old man."
1st H-L O:"Well,lets get back to the mess for a short one,then,old man. I must say it
would have been easier if 'Camp' had been here to do it all,old man."
2nd H-L O:"Rather ! Just a minute,though ! Have you laid on for any food to be left
for the rear party,old man ?"
1st H-L O:"Well,I think it's all laid on. Surely the cooks do that automatically ? I
think you can assume that'll be O.K.,old man."
2nd H-L O:"Good ! Who's looking round the billets after the main body's gone,old man ?"
1st H-L O:"Well,okoherly,we haven't detailed anybody. But the main body will be sure
to have done their stuff,old man."
2nd H-L O:"I must say I hope so. But it seems a pity all the NCOs have already gone
off on the advance party,old man."
1st H-L O:"Oh ! Have they ? Well,you know,there's a lot to do at the other end what
with officers' billets,and the mess,and that sort of thing,old man."
2nd H-L O:"Of course. But on the move here,when you were looking after the rear party,
you kept the NCOs behind because there was always so much to clear up,old man. By
the way,I suppose the billeting forms are all O.K.,old man ?"
1st H-L O:"Good Heavens ! But surely the Town Major or somebody like that does those,
doesn't he,old man ?"
2nd H-L O:"Well,not usually. But I suppose you've laid on a clerk to do all the typing
of these things,old man ?"
1st H-L O:"Well,not okoherly,because I'm not quite In The Picture about the men's
billets,old man."
2nd H-L O:"Pity about that ! The only NCO who really knows all about them has gone on
with your advance-party. And all the others are moving off with the main party in
half-an-hour. But they're not In The Picture,either,old man."
1st H-L O:"I,say,what a bore ! But I expect it'll be O.K.,old man. I'm sure you'll
manage to cope. After all,we can't really be bothered with all that sort of
detail,can we,old man ?"
2nd H-L O:"Heavens,no ! After all,there's a war on,and the civilians must look after
themselves a bit,old man."
1st H-L O:"Well,then,is there anything else,old man ?"
2nd H-L O:"No,except that I think your admin stinks,old man !"
    (Curtain - for reasons of security......)

INSIDE MISINFORMATION.
    It is rumoured that Div HQ,after several day-trips to various North West
European villages,has at last found a location where the curtains in the Officers'
Mess are the right colour. Jolly good show,what !
    It is also rumoured that there will shortly be a vacancy in the Editorial
chair of the "Cow's Tail".

"DEAR HOME" -
Barns are all very well,
But they smell...
Chateaux,I find,are much too big
(Except for a Brig !)
Stables are quite O.K.,of course,
For a horse
In trenches I find the mould
So cold.

In barracks the boss gets mental
(And re-mental).
An unfurnished Officers' Mess
Causes untold distress
In spite of three shillings a day
Paid for living that way.
In short,it would be more fun
Chasing the Hun....."

. . . . .

468

- -

The Western Front.

Tanks of the 1st American Army broke into Cologne on Monday morning at 0700 hrs. Their first objective was the Hohenzollern Bridge, which takes the tram-, railway- and mainroads across the Rhine East of Cologne itself. Other troops moved into Cologne from the West and South West. Light opposition only was met; but it is thought that this may stiffen.

The 1st Canadian Army has cleared the whole of the Hochwald Forest and reached the Rhine North and South of Xanten, East of Goch and South East of Cleves.

The gap East of Venlo and Roermond, and behind the meeting of the 1st Canadian and 9th American Armies, is being filled in, but this is a slow business as the Germans left behind many demolitions.

From Duisberg South to Dusseldorf, only ferry-crossings remain: other crossings have been wrecked. From Dusseldorf South to Cologne, all the Rhine bridges have been destroyed. North of Duisberg the Germans have kept the Rhine bridge at Wesel intact, to supply a German bridgehead now squeezed into an area 10 miles wide and 8 miles deep.

It can now be said that along the whole of the front, from Emmerich, North of Wesel, to Bonn, South of Cologne, the enemy is struggling desperately to evacuate his troops to the far bank of the Rhine.

The 1st American Army has captured Euskirchen, 20 miles South of Cologne and 10 miles West of Bonn: this is an important communications centre on the edge of the Cologne plain.

The 3rd American Army has advanced $3\frac{1}{2}$ miles on a 30-mile front between Trier (Treves) and Prum. They are now 20 miles inside Germany beyond the Luxembourg frontier.

This is important: you have been warned ! The Nazi arrangements for the evacuation of civilians have failed. Many civilians refuse to move. They frequently deny any connection with the Nazis, but, on closer investigation, it is often found that they are either:-

German soldiers who have thrown away their uniforms and put on 'civvies',

or:-

Civilians who have been members of Nazi organisations.

At Krefeld, East of Venlo and Roermond, some hundreds of Allied prisoners have been released by the Allies' overrunning a prison-camp.

In the 10 days of the American offensive 100,000 Germans have become casualties, of which 60,000 are prisoners. It is shortly to be expected that the Germans will be known to have lost 1 million men since D day last June.

The Eastern Front.

The Russians have now reached the Baltic Coast between Stettin and Danzig, thus cutting off German troops in East Pomerania and the Polish Corridor. The trapped Germans are in an area along the Baltic coast 120 miles long and 50 miles deep. The Russians are broadening this salient Eastwards and Westwards: to the East they are making for Koslin; to the West they have taken Stargard and are making towards Stettin. Naugard, 28 miles North of Stettin, has also fallen.

This thrust North to the Baltic was timed to forestall a planned German counter-attack and was started in extremely bad weather. Very heavy German opposition was encountered, including five S.S. divisions.

The Air War.

On Sunday, RAF heavies hit a benzol-plant at Gelsenkirchen. 400 American heavies with 600 fighters went for marshalling-yards at Chemnitz, and oil-refineries at Harburg.

On Sunday night Berlin was attacked by Mosquitos for the 15th successive night. Essen and other N.W. German targets also received attention.

After last Saturday's attack the Dortmund-Ems canal is now dry again.

Far East.

In Burma the 14th Army is making rapid progress from all its bridgeheads across the River Irriwaddy. At the nearest point they are only 18 miles from Mandalay. 80 miles South of Mandalay an Allied group of 40 tanks and 2 battalions of infantry has taken Meiktila, the meeting-place of the 6 most important roads in Burma and puts the Allies across the North-South communication line of the Japs and deep in the enemy rear. The Chinese on the Burma Road are now only 3 miles from Lashio.

Other News.

Invitations to the San Francisco conference on 25 April are being sponsored by USA, USSR and UK. 41 nations have been invited. France is not joining in the sponsoring as she was not present at the Crimea Conference. The nations are going to be asked to consider the Dumbarton Oaks proposals as a basis for world-organisation.

One of the newest German U-boats sank on trials off the Norway coast with important German naval officials on board.

107,000 are now being employed on the repair of damaged houses at home. It is hoped that the target of 719,000 repaired houses will be reached by the end of March.

No change in the strike situation in the London docks.

A British subject who once taught English in Paris has got 12 years' hard for helping Nazi propaganda.

· · · · ·

"NICE LITTLE KIDS, EH HERBIE!"

A Canadian "Herbie" cartoon that appeared in issue number 54 of the Canadian Army Training Memorandum (left) and a rendition of *Mr. Chad* (below) who appeared all over the UK during the war complaining about the lack of nearly everything that was missing or in short supply due to rationing. Mr. Chad later became associated with the "Kilroy Was Here" graffiti.

Mein Early Kampf   by Adolf Hitler

June 5, 1889
I reject milk from Holstein cows as Non-Aryan

A "Dr. Seuss" cartoon created in 1942 for syndication.

• • • • •

Chapter 11 - Folding Bicycles and Lightweight Motorcycles

British airborne troops sit across from a stack of bicycles in the rear section of an Airspeed Horsa glider. More troops can be seen sitting on the opposite side of the glider across from the loading door in the front near the cockpit. Three motorcycles are chained down just behind them in the center of the glider.

. . . . .

Bicycles that folded were not a new concept to the British military during the Second World War. The **_Folding Bicycle_** had been designed and introduced to the military by a British subject named Dursley Pedersen and they were used during the Second Boer War in 1899. They had a compact design which made them easy to carry over the shoulder when needed while traversing rough terrain which was impassable for carts, wagons and the first gasoline powered vehicles of the day. During the Great War, the British army had Cyclist Battalions and maintained in excess of 100,000 rigid-frame and folding bicycles. Bicycles continued in military service between the two world wars but their numbers were greatly reduced as the army became more mechanized. However, a new demand for lightweight folding bicycles came about with the advent of the airborne forces following a memo to the War Office by Winston Churchill. On 22 June 1940, he suggested the need for a Corps of at least 5,000 parachute troops. These troops would go by air to battle and some would have need of traveling quickly once on the ground. Parachute

A paratrooper prepares to drop through the hole in an RAF Albemarle bomber. Note the windshield built into the forward edge of the floor aperture. Its purpose was to divert the air-flow to assist the paratroopers in making a safe exit.

. . . . .

A static line training jump by a paratrooper through the hole in the floor of an RAF Whitley bomber. The floor aperture windshield beneath the bomber can be seen near the center in front of the static lines.

operations by the British military during the first few years of the war were done by jumping through a hole in the floor of existing bombers. Early trials were conducted with folding bicycles which were lightweight but unfortunately of an inconvenient shape. The bicycles were placed in the bomb racks but each one took up three bomb positions. An alternative form needed to be found that would either fit through the hole in the bomber's floor or out one of the aircrafts' side hatches. This lead to new trials for a suitable airborne-specific design using prototypes based on available commercial and military pattern bicycles. These had standard 28-inch diameter wheels, full size rubber or framed metal pedals, and wheel fenders which in some cases even had cargo racks mounted in the rear. They tended to be heavy and presented problems when needing to quickly get them out of an aircraft due to their size.

Jumping from a C-47 with a B.S.A. folding bicycle.

· · · · ·

473

Of the modified folding designs evaluated, one submitted by Birmingham Small Arms was chosen and it would come to be known as the *Airborne Folding Bicycle*. Wartime records related to actual specifications and testing are very scarce so exact dates cannot be pinned down as to when the B.S.A. folding bicycle was selected. But parachuting records from the Central Landing Establishment and the Airborne Forces Experimental Establishment from 1941 through 11 NOV 1942 mention folding bicycles, and as of 26 DEC 1942 they mention B.S.A. folding bicycles. The need for small fold-

ing bicycles diminished as the airborne forces evolved. New aircraft such as the Horsa glider provided a means of delivering bulky items, such as motorcycles, to the battlefield. And the C-47 allowed paratroopers to jump from a standing position out a side door. But folding bicycles continued to be used by the airborne troops as well as by commando and straight leg infantry units. The fact that they folded merely made them easier to transport in bulk by truck, ship or plane.

One of several prototype folding bicycle designs based on existing rigid-frame patterns already being manufactured before the war. These were modified to fold for initial testing and had 28-inch wheels.

· · · · ·

During the Second World War, B.S.A. operated 67 factories producing such items as arms, ammunition, bicycles and motorcycles just to name a few. The company was founded in 1861 by fourteen gunsmiths in Birmingham, England to provide arms to the British Government during the Crimean War. They began to diversify in the 1880s due to a decline in the firearms trade and created a subsidiary bicycle division which later expanded into motorcycles and became B.S.A. Cycles Limited. Subsequently the bicycle division was sold after the war in 1957 to the Raleigh Bicycle Company which was originally based in Nottingham, England.

The Airborne Folding Bicycle was also referred to as the Type G Apparatus or Folding Paratrooper Bicycle in some military manuals. While the military never differentiated between design variations, today collectors classify the B.S.A. folding bicycles into three categories: prototypes, early limited production and later standard production. The length of the bicycle was 44.5 inches folded and 67.5 inches open and assembled. Both production patterns are without fenders and had an elliptical twin tube frame design that could fold in half after unscrewing a pair of large wing nuts. The front

An airborne engineer in battledress watches as men of the 1st Battalion The Border Regiment load folding bicycles into an Airspeed Horsa Mark I glider during a training exercise in the months prior to Operation Market Garden.

· · · · ·

wheel had thirty-two spokes and the rear wheel, which had to bear extra pressure while being ridden, had forty spokes. The wheels had a twenty-six inch diameter and the rear single speed freewheel hub used a coaster brake system. The single chainring had the company's initials B.S.A. spelt out as part of the design, but this was also a feature on their prewar and postwar commercial bicycles. To help reduce the size of the bicycle when folded, the handlebars could be rotated and lowered by unscrewing a Tommy Bar, the saddle could be lowered, and the round metal shafts used for pedals could be pressed inward. For parachute operations, the wheels were strapped together and secured to the rear chain stays to prevent them from rotating. And the saddle was raised so that it would bear most of the shock of landing and thus protect the handlebars from bending. When airdropped, the bicycle had a weight of 32.5 pounds including a Q-Type parachute which had a twelve-foot diameter canopy. Prior to a paratrooper jumping with the folded bicycle, one end of a twenty-foot long suspension line was tied to the wheels furthest from the saddle to ensure it would hit the ground first. The other end of the line was tied to the lower left leg strap on the parachutist's harness. A short quick-release strap going around the back of the parachutist's neck was used to help the parachutist hold onto the bicycle as he exited the aircraft. Once under a fully developed canopy, the quick-release was pulled and he dropped the bicycle which fell to the end of the suspension line until landing.

· · · · ·

Early production B.S.A. folding bicycles can be easily identified by the offset manner in which the saddle is mounted. The saddle tube was a smaller diameter than the saddle post so an additional section of tubing was welded to the back of the saddle tube to accept the saddle post. The tyre inflator was located in front of the saddle tube so it would not interfere with the saddle post and saddle being lowered. It had a pair of tubular reinforcements welded onto the back of the bottom bracket and to the lower elliptical frame tubes, equidistant between the saddle tube and the forward edge of the rear tyre. Another pair of tubular reinforcements was welded onto the back of the saddle post mounting tube, and to the upper elliptical frame tubes, equidistant between the saddle post and the forward edge of the rear tyre. The folding frame hinges were welded on top of the elliptical frame tubes at both locations and all welds on the bicycle were done by hand.

An early pattern BSA folding bicycle shown ready for riding.

· · · · ·

An early production B.S.A. folding bicycle displayed in the process of being folded. The offset saddle mounting design and the tyre inflator situated in front of the saddle tube makes this pattern easy to identify.

Airborne troops and men of the British 50th Infantry Division examine a knocked out German gun emplacement near the coastal village of Asnelles. The late production B.S.A. folding bicycle in the foreground has a bell, tool pouch and tyre inflator among the visible accessories. Normandy, France – 7 JUN 1944.

· · · · ·

The standard production B.S.A. folding bicycles have a much more refined appearance when compared to the earlier pattern. All of the welds are smooth machine processed and the hinged areas on the frame are molded and more robust. The saddle post fits into the saddle tube like most modern bicycles and this added strength while simplifying the design. The tyre inflator was mounted behind the saddle tube which helped to prevent it being accidentally knocked loose while pedaling. It was also out of the way of the canvas wallet which could be strapped inside the perimeter of the bicycle's elliptical frame. There was no longer a need for extra reinforcements behind the saddle post. But a pair of reinforcements was still welded to the bottom bracket, except they were now in the front and running to a point below the lower frame hinge.

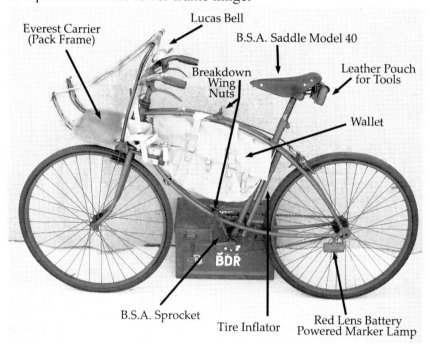

Everest Carrier (Pack Frame)

Lucas Bell

B.S.A. Saddle Model 40

Breakdown Wing Nuts

Leather Pouch for Tools

Wallet

B.S.A. Sprocket

Tire Inflator

Red Lens Battery Powered Marker Lamp

An example of the standard production B.S.A. folding bicycle with optional accessories available during 1943. The Everest Carrier was commonly seen on bicycles issued to Commando groups but infantry units used them as well.

· · · · ·

The photographs on this and the following four pages are from a British wartime report that was classified Top Secret at the time it was prepared during the war. It compares the three main types of folding bicycles that were available for use at the time. Two of these patterns were produced by B.S.A. and the third by Phillips. But undoubtedly other folding patterns were in use during the war along with numerous patterns of rigid frame bicycles. The pattern which is referred to in the report as the Airborne Model is the standard late production folding bicycle produced by B.S.A. The earlier pattern with the offset saddle mounting is also considered to be the same model as far as the military was concerned. For reference, the names of the bicycles in the photo captions are from the original report. Several standard accessories were produced for use on both rigid frame and folding frame bicycles. Variations of each type item exist due to the large number of commercial manufacturers that were pressed into service. Examples of many of these items can be seen throughout this chapter but they were not part of the report. The exception is the rifle mounting clips which can be seen on all three models of folding bicycles in the report.

Airborne Folding Bicycle.

· · · · ·

B.S.A. with folding pedals.

Phillips with folding pedals.

• • • • •

481

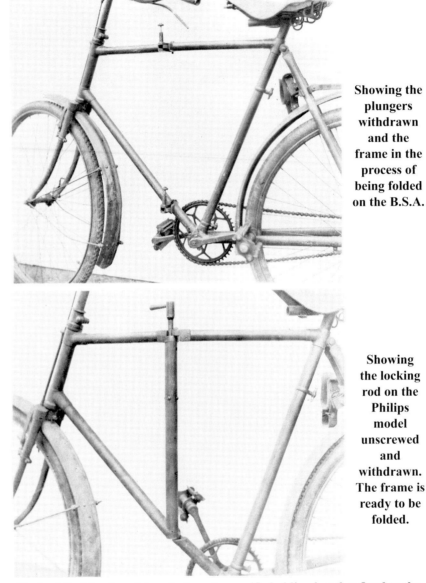

Showing the
plungers
withdrawn
and the
frame in the
process of
being folded
on the B.S.A.

Showing
the locking
rod on the
Philips
model
unscrewed
and
withdrawn.
The frame is
ready to be
folded.

Each of the bicycles pictured above has a rifle holding bracket fixed to the
rear frame support and pegs can be seen near the top and bottom of the
central support for holding a tire inflator.

. . . . .

482

A folding pedal in the normal position. The sleeve that retains the pedal in this position can be seen with its coil spring.

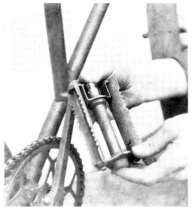

Folding the pedal. The sleeve is pushed back against the spring, allowing the pedal to fold.

The pedal folded. During trials it was found that the spring needed to be strengthened as the pedals tended to fall back into the open position if the bicycle was turned on its side.

· · · · ·

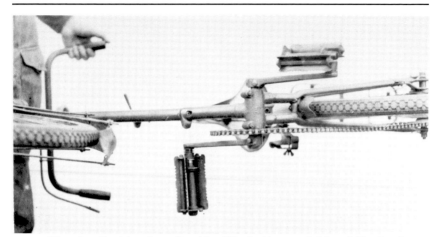

Showing the bicycle on its side. The bottom pedal has fallen back
and locked in the normal position.

The photo above shows the three types of folding bicycles in their folded
positions for comparison. The leftmost bicycle is the B.S.A. model. The
Airborne model is at center. And the Phillips model is at the far right with its
pedals folded out.

. . . . .

Chainrings on the B.S.A. Folding Bicycle have forty-six teeth and the Mark X pattern freewheels have eighteen teeth. With the bicycle having twenty-six inch diameter wheels, this creates a gear inch ratio of 66.44 allowing a speed of 16.80 miles per hour at 85 pedal revolutions per minute. A speed of 22.73 miles per hour could be achieved with 115 pedal revolutions per minute. Seventeen feet is traveled for every complete pedal rotation.

. . . . .

485

Front and back views of the canvas bicycle wallet designed specifically for use on the B.S.A. Airborne Folding Bicycle. Of all the folding bicycle accessories, this is by far the hardest to find and very few wartime photos have been found showing them in use. Several European WWII museums have them in their collections including the British Airborne Museum in England. The wallet has two 1-inch webbing straps that support a cloth carry handle that wraps over the top of the bicycle's upper frame. Three small straps are used to close the flap. Four other small straps around the perimeter of the wallet are used to fasten it to the supports joining the bicycle's twin elliptical frame tubes together.

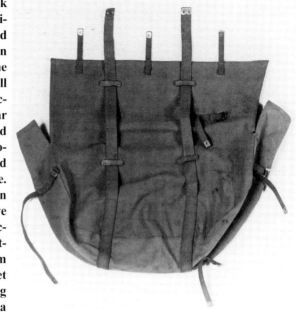

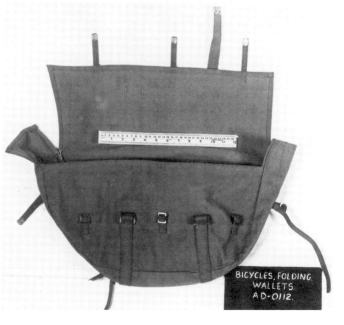

• • • • •

486

Airborne troops with second pattern BSA folding bicycles equipped with web equipment valises. Note the pedal supports which have been fitted with wooden blocks to facilitate easier riding. London, England - JUN 1944.

The folding bicycle handgrips were made from hard celluloid which was formed over a cardboard tube. The grips had a length of 3.25 inches, were black in colour and featured the B.S.A. stacked rifle logo.

. . . . .

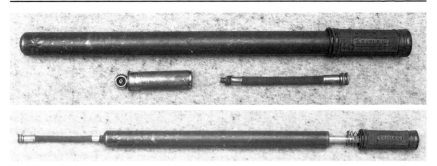

Pictured above are examples of the type of tyre inflator issued with bicycles and motorcycles. This model is made of metal and has "Britannia" in raised letters molded into one side and "British" on the other. The small hose is stored inside one end of the inflator and it screws onto the other end when needed for filling a tyre. The small tube is a "Schrader Balloon Tyre Gauge" made in London, England. It has no date but is typical of a pressure gauge used before the war and well after.

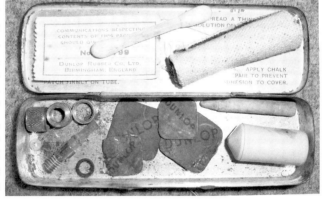

Tyre tube repair kits were issued with the bicycles and carried in the leather tool pouch under the saddle.

• • • • •

The tyres on the B.S.A. folding bicycles had a size of 26 inches by 1 3/8 inches and were produced by many commercial manufactures including Michelin and Dunlop. Various markings were molded into the rubber such as "WAR GRADE", the "/|\" Broad Arrow, manufacturer's name, tyre specifications and the rim size the tyres are for which was B.S. E.A. 3 and F4. Subcontractors were also used by B.S.A. for production of some of the bicycle components. One notable example is the rims which were often manufactured by Dunlop. Markings on the rims will typically read "Dunlop Made In England UK PAT 266486".

The photograph above shows the British War Department stamps found on the inside canvas material used for producing a war grade Dunlop tyre.

Tubes for the bicycle tyres were also manufactured by a variety of companies located in the United Kingdom including Dunlop. A protective Rim Tape made of woven cloth was wrapped around the rim and was held in place by metal clips fitted to the tube stem hole. This tape covered the spoke heads and prevented the tube from rubbing against them and becoming damaged.

· · · · ·

The transfer found on the saddle tube features the B.S.A. "Stacked Rifles" trademark logo in silver. The transfers found on the head tube below the handle bars include the Broad Arrow in black and patent information in silver which reads "PAT. – NO. 543076" and "REGD. DGN. NO. 838413".

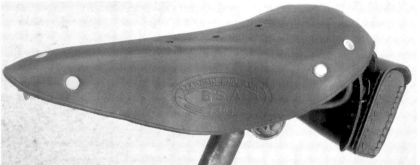

Birmingham Small Arms (B.S.A.) Leather Saddle Model Number 40

The tool pouch pictured at the left has a flap that is secured by a twist fastener and is held to the lower frame of the saddle by a pair of adjustable leather straps. Many variations exist including a type made from canvas material in the same shape as this leather one.

• • • • •

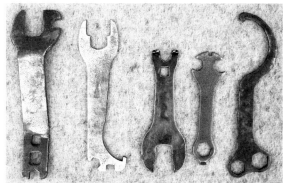

A sampling of combination tools that were typically carried in the leather tool pouch for bicycle repairs in the field. It should be noted that these are variations and depending on the selection, usually two or three could handle any task.

The bracket located at the front of the bicycle between the fork crown and the head tube was intended to be a lamp bracket. It could also be used as a hanger to support other items such as the metal frame of the Everest Carrier. The bracket is marked B.S.A. and bears the stacked rifle logo for the company. The British Electric Lamp Number 1 fits the bracket securely. The early war production Electric Lamp Number 2 will also work but not as well. Examples of each type can be seen in Chapter 4 which covers personal equipment.

Moving bicycles make little noise so they were often outfitted with small bells to warn of their approach when needed. These tended to have a diameter ranging from 1.5 to 3 inches. The example shown here was made by Joseph Lucas Ltd of Birmingham, England and is a Number 50 "Challis" pattern that was produced in nickel covered brass which was painted to reduce its reflective nature.

· · · · ·

491

A small electric torch with a length of 3.5 inches and a diameter of slightly more than 1.5 inches can sometimes be seen mounted to the rear lower frame of British bicycles in wartime photographs. These served as marker lights and had a red lens. The metal housing was made to hold a single D-Size battery and there was no provision for an on/off switch. To turn the torch off, the battery was removed and then reinserted backwards for storage and this also ensured the lens and internal springs would not rattle around. Examples that have been examined had no markings but the design is very similar to the special small and large torches produced by Eveready Battery Company during the war which were used by the S.O.E.

· · · · ·

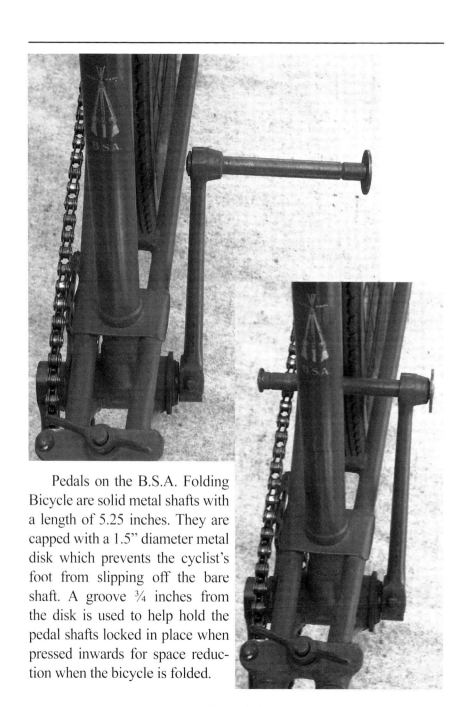

Pedals on the B.S.A. Folding Bicycle are solid metal shafts with a length of 5.25 inches. They are capped with a 1.5" diameter metal disk which prevents the cyclist's foot from slipping off the bare shaft. A groove ¾ inches from the disk is used to help hold the pedal shafts locked in place when pressed inwards for space reduction when the bicycle is folded.

. . . . .

493

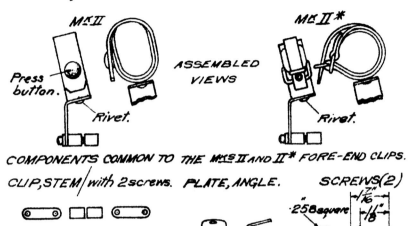

CLIPS, RIFLE, BICYCLE, FORE-END, MᴷˢII AND II *

Mᴷ II

Press button.

Rivet.

ASSEMBLED VIEWS

Mᴷ II *

Rivet.

COMPONENTS COMMON TO THE Mᴷˢ II AND II * FORE-END CLIPS.

CLIP, STEM / with 2 screws.   PLATE, ANGLE.   SCREWS (2)

.258 square

3/16 dia. 32 thᵈˢ per in. RH, C.E.I.

Tapped 32 thᵈˢ per in., 3/16" diam. C.E.I.

An unidentified Bren Gunner, who is securing his weapon onto a special clip mounted at the rear of his bicycle, taking part in a 1st Canadian Infantry Division training exercise. England - 1-3 APR 1943.

Note that this is a rigid frame bicycle with fenders. Accessories include lamps at the front and rear, a tyre inflator and a bell.

. . . . .

CLIP, RIFLE, BICYCLE, BUTT Mᴷ II

ASSEMBLED VIEWS. BODY / Leather lined; with fixed plate.

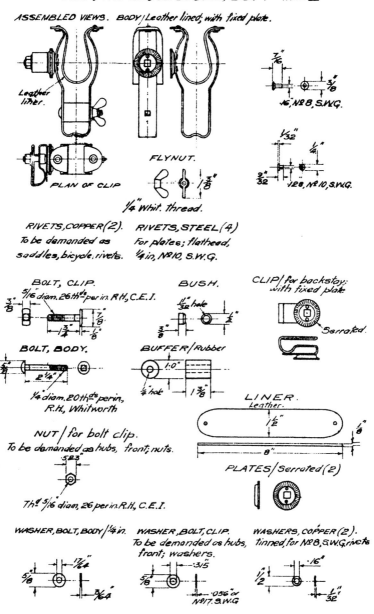

Leather liner.

PLAN OF CLIP

FLYNUT.

¼" Whit. thread.

.16, Nº 8, S.W.G.

¹⁄₃₂" ¼"
⁹⁄₃₂ .128, Nº 10, S.W.G.

RIVETS, COPPER (2).
To be demanded as
saddles, bicycle, rivets.

RIVETS, STEEL (4)
For plates; flathead,
¼ in, Nº 10, S.W.G.

BOLT, CLIP.
⁵⁄₁₆ diam. 26 thᵈˢ per in. R.H., C.E.I.

BUSH.
¹¹⁄₃₂ hole

CLIP / for backstay;
with fixed plate

Serrated.

BOLT, BODY.
2 ¼"
¼ diam. 20 thᵈˢ per in,
R.H., Whitworth

BUFFER / Rubber
1:0"
¼ hole   1 ⅜"

NUT / for bolt clip.
To be demanded as hubs, front; nuts.
.523
Thᵈ ⁵⁄₁₆ diam, 26 per in. R.H., C.E.I.

LINER.
Leather.
1½"
8"

PLATES / Serrated (2)

WASHER, BOLT, BODY / ¼ in.
1⁷⁄₆₄"
⅝
³⁄₆₄

WASHER, BOLT, CLIP.
To be demanded as hubs,
front; washers.
.315
⅝
.056" or
Nº 17. S.W.G

WASHERS, COPPER (2).
tinned, for Nº 8, S.W.G. rivets
.16"
½
¹⁄₃₂"

· · · · ·

495

Private Tom J. Phelan, 1st Canadian Parachute Battalion, who was wounded on 16 June 1944 at Le Mesnil, rides his airborne folding bicycle at the Battalion's reinforcement camp. England - 1944.

A paratrooper with full equipment and Number 4 Mark I rifle quickly pedals off the drop zone on a late production B.S.A. folding bicycle. The weapon is suspended by its web sling in the front, hanging loosely from the handlebars, so that steering would not be impeded.

. . . . .

Infantrymen checking bicycles aboard an LCI(L) of the 2nd Canadian (262nd RN) Flotilla. Southampton, England, 6 JUNE 1944. (L-R): Privates Reg Martin and Rodney Macneill, both of the Lorne Scots (Peel, Dufferin and Halton Regiment); Private George Banning of the Cameron Highlanders of Ottawa (M.G.).

Private R.O. Potter of the Highland Light Infantry of Canada repairing his bicycle. France - 20 JUN 1944.

• • • • •

As the British Airborne Forces continued to evolve, the need was recognized for motorized lightweight, yet reliable, ground transport for use by the frontline troops. These vehicles would need to be delivered by parachute or glider so overall size and weight were crucial factors. They would also be considered expendable pieces of equipment so needed to be cost effective to manufacture. Most motorcycles in British military service at this time were fairly large and heavy. These included the Matchless G3, BSA B30 and M20, the Norton Big 4 and WD16H, and the Triumph Tiger 100. All of these models and more would see service with the army for the duration of the war. And some would find their way into gliders, in spite of their weight and size, as the war progressed. This was due to advancements in glider and tug aircraft that could handle greater payloads and the preference of having the faster and more robust motorcycles in the field.

A Royal Corps of Signals despatch rider on a BSA M20 motorcycle receives a message to relay after it has arrived by carrier pigeon.

• • • • •

498

Associated Motors Limited was the parent company of Matchless during the Second World War and they introduced the ***Matchless G3/L*** in 1941. This was based on the company's prewar G3 design that continued to be produced until 1942. The G3/L was in response to the War Office request for a durable, lightweight, off-road motorcycle, hence the "L" for "lightweight". The motorcycle had a 348cc engine with a 4-speed gear box. Dry weight was 328 pounds and it used 19 inch tyres. The most innovative feature was its *teledraulic* front forks which replaced the girder type front suspension found on all other motorcycles from the time period. The fuel tank had a capacity of three gallons. Top speed was 76 miles per hour and the maximum range was 225 miles. More than 63000 G3/L pattern motorcycles were produced from 1941-1945 and production continued into the postwar years.

Lieutenant G. Murray Williams of Headquarters Company, 1st Canadian Parachute Battalion, riding a Matchless G3/L motorcycle during the battalion's advance from Lembeck through Coesfeld. Germany - 30 MAR 1945.

· · · · ·

The ***Royal Enfield WD/RE*** was developed by the Enfield Cycle Company Limited of Redditch in response to a War Office request for a lightweight airborne motorcycle that could be landed by parachute or by glider. It needed to be rugged and dependable for off-road use and light enough that it could be man-handled over minor obstacles by the rider if necessary. The motorcycle had an Enfield 125cc two-stroke engine and a 3-speed gear box. The dry weight was 137 pounds. Top speed was 40 miles per hour running on 19 inch tyres. The fuel tank had a capacity of 1.5 gallons and the maximum range was considered to be 150 miles. 8000 were produced from 1942-1944 primarily for airborne use. This motorcycle was known as the *Flying Flea.*

A British paratrooper demonstrates that the Royal Enfield WD/RE lightweight 125cc motorcycle can be lifted by one man when necessary. Note the tyre inflator clipped onto the chain guard.
22 APR 1944.

· · · · ·

Airlanding Brigade troops depart a glider landing zone on a lightweight motorcycle and in an airborne modified jeep towing a 10-cwt trailer. (above)

The drop cradle used for parachuting the Royal Enfield WD/RE was built from heavy metal tubing. Production began in December 1942 at Enfield's Calton Hill factory in Edinburgh. The loaded cradle could be hoisted up into a bombers bomb bay and then released over the drop zone where it would descend by static line deployed parachute.

• • • • •

The ***James ML*** (*Military Lightweight*) was produced by the James Cycle Company Limited of Birmingham beginning in 1942. Its design originated in response to the airborne requirement for a lightweight motorcycle. It used a Villiers 9D 125cc two-stroke engine and had a 3-speed gear box. This model was in competition with the Royal Enfield WD/RE but it was twenty pounds heavier, having a dry weight of 157 pounds. A drop cradle was never developed for this motorcycle but it still saw service with the Airborne Forces as a glider landed vehicle and additionally with British and Canadian assault troops who also had need of lightweight motorcycles. The capacity of the fuel tank was 1.4 gallons and it had a top speed of 40 miles per hour. Maximum range was rated at 150 miles. 6040 were produced from 1942-1944 and this model was also known as the *Clockwork Mouse.*

Brigade Sergeant-Major R.M. Cooper of the 9th Canadian Infantry Brigade, wearing wartime censored battledress, sits on a James ML motorcycle. Carpiquet, Normandy France - 12 JUL 1944.

. . . . .

Station IX was one of the Special Operations Executive (SOE) research and development sites during the war, and it was located on the Frythe estate near Welwyn in Hertfordshire, England. It originated as a signals research unit, later to become a special weapons development and production centre, and then in early 1941 transitioned to inter-service research and development. Many of the specialized items to come from this facility had the prefix "Wel" in their name which is derived from Welwyn. These include the silent *Welrod* pistol, the *Welfag* which was a 22LR firing device concealed in a cigarette, the *Welpen* which was a writing pen capable of firing tear gas or a projectile, the *Welpipe* which was a .22LR smoking pipe gun, the *Welman* midget submarine, and probably the most well known of them all, the airborne folding *Welbike* motorcycle.

The design of the **Welbike** is credited to Harry Lester while assigned to Station IX, which was headed up by John R.V. Dolphin. It was proposed initially for use by SOE agents who might have need of a compact and lightweight vehicle to get them quickly off a drop zone. The idea being that the vehicle could be delivered in a currently available 15 inch diameter drop container. And that the vehicle would be easy to hide or dispose of when no longer needed. Six prototypes were built for testing and then marketing to the War

The Excelsior Welbike could be landed by parachute inside a D-shaped Central Landing Establishment Mark I drop container. These were stenciled "MOTOR CYCLE" in white 2-inch tall letters on the side for easy identification on the drop zone.

• • • • •

Office. These were not readily accepted for use by the SOE but interestingly enough, they appear in the American JUN 1944 Office of Strategic Services (OSS) weapons catalog as being available and issued through the SOE. They were also accepted for use by paratroopers as a means to rally on the drop zone after landing, so they could then quickly depart for their intended objective.

One of the six Welbike prototypes is pictured above. These had a black painted finish and a smaller fuel tank than the Mark I production models which were painted Khaki Green Number 3. The later Mark II production models were painted Standard Camouflage Colour Number 4.

The Welbike has a Villiers Deluxe Junior 98cc two-stroke engine. It had 8 inch metal spoke wheels with 12.5 inch tyres. Dry weight was 70 pounds and it had a 6.5 pint fuel tank capacity. Top speed was rated at 30 miles per hour with a maximum range listed as 90 miles.

. . . . .

The manufacturing firm awarded the contract for the Welbike was the Excelsior Motor Company Limited of Birmingham. This initial order for 1200 vehicles was placed 26 AUG 1942. Before production began, minor design improvements were made to the prototype pattern. An unknown number of pre-production Welbikes were built by Excelsior for rigorous load and airdropping tests by the Airborne Forces Experimental Establishment (AFEE) at Sherburn-in-Elmet, near Leeds, Yorkshire, England in SEPT 1942. These test models were most likely all destroyed during or shortly after trials. Official production vehicle frame numbers for the first contract begin at 14 and go to 1213. Frame numbers are noted on each of the official contracts, but they appear to have been added on receipt of goods for inventory purposes as opposed to having been assigned by the contract itself. It is unknown if any of the six Station IX prototypes, or the pre-production Welbikes were numbered. If the prototypes were in fact numbered, then it can be reasoned that pre-production test vehicles were also numbered. This would mean no more than seven pre-production examples would have been built. The first contract was completed and vehicles were delivered on 15 OCT 1942.

Excelsior 98cc "Welbike" Mark I

. . . . .

The second contract was for Mark II pattern Welbikes. 1400 were ordered on 19 NOV 1942 but production was requested to commence in FEB 1943. This contract was completed with vehicles delivered on 15 MAR 1943 with frame numbers 1214 through 2613.

Of interest related to this contract is a note that 302 of the motorcycles were to be boxed for export by 6 MAY 1943. What country received them is unknown. The third contract was also for Mark II pattern Welbikes. It was placed on 27 DEC 1942 with delivery required by May 1943. This contract was originally for 1341 machines but was later reduced to 1241. The original contract shows no date of actual delivery, and frame numbers including the 100 vehicles that were not built run from 2614 to 3954. A fourth contract on 21 JUN 1943 was cancelled and none of the vehicles are known to exist.

The most recognizable difference between the two models of Welbikes is the rear fender used on the Mark II. Modifications were also made to the fuel tanks to further increase their capacity and to make them easier to fill up with the 16:1 fuel oil mixture that was used with both models.

· · · · ·

The Welbike could be unfolded and made ready to ride in a matter of seconds without tools. The steering column was first raised until the diagonal support member is extended and held in place by a spring loaded locating pin. The individual handlebars are then swung outward, if they didn't do so automatically, and these are secured by tightening a large milled hand-screw in the center of the handlebar pivot. The next step is to raise the seat by pulling it straight up until its spring loaded locating pin locks into place. A "Tommy Bar" on the lower seat post is then rotated until tight to ensure the seat will not lower under pressure. Lastly, lower the foot rests until they are at a horizontal position for riding.

Since the fuel tanks are lower than the carburetor, they need to be pressurized using the built in hand pump. To start the vehicle, the fuel tap stop valve needs to be opened and the carburetor flooded by pressing down on a spring loaded knob on the top. Open the throttle but rotating the right handlebar grip and squeeze the clutch lever all the way on the left handlebar grip. The rider then runs alongside the vehicle and jumps onto the seat at the same time he releases the clutch lever. IIis weight and momentum should then roll start the engine.

A Parachute Regiment despatch rider on a Welbike Mark II. The standard tall despatch rider boots, jodhpurs and leather gauntlets seem somewhat out of place in this case.

. . . . .

Wrecked Horsa gliders that were carrying men of the Oxfordshire & Buckinghamshire, Light Infantry lay scattered around the Hamminkeln train station during Operation Varsity. The glider that smashed into the station held an airborne jeep and trailer. Two mangled folding bicycles can be seen still secured to what had been the bottom side of the trailer. Hamminkeln, Germany – 24 MAR 1945.

. . . . .

Chapter 12 - The Art of Deception

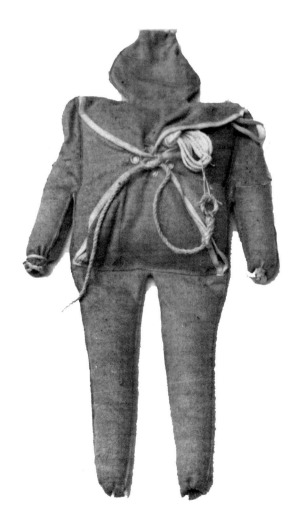

. . . . .

Gingerbread Men

British dummy paratroopers were made from burlap formed into small sacks which were filled with sand and sewn together in the shape of a person 30-36 inches in height complete with a small cotton parachute. The reduced size of the dummy paratroopers wasn't readily apparent when seen in the air since there was nothing else in the sky to serve as a reference of scale.

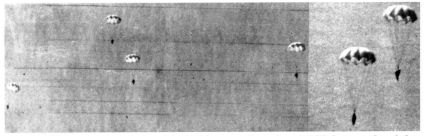

Dummy Paratroopers at roughly 500 feet on the left and 200 feet on the right.

Their first operational use was in September 1942, unsuccessfully, in an attempt to draw the Germans off from a commando raid on Tobruk. Later operations in Europe and the Far East proved to be more successful. Officially they were the **Device Camouflage Number 15** but they had several unofficial names including Gingerbread Men, Paragons and Ruperts. The miniature molded rubber paratroopers depicted in the film *The Longest Day* takes some creative license, but it conveyed the intent of what they were really used for. Most of the dummy paratroopers simply had parachutes to create the illusion of a mass airborne drop. However, some were armed with rifle and machine gun fire simulators that were known at first as Parafexes and later as Bicat Strips. A device known as a Pintail that was invented by Peter Fleming was also used with some of the dummy paratroopers and it fired a signal flare when it struck the ground. All of the armed dummy paratroopers were carried by air in bomb containers and could be dropped remotely by the aircrew. The unarmed dummy paratroopers were lined up on the floor inside the aircraft and dropped manually by air despatchers. A modification

· · · · ·

designed by Douglas Fairbanks, Jr. enabled the dummy paratroopers to self-destruct after landing and firing their pyrotechnic simulators. This helped to delay the deception from being discovering since the remains resembled parachute equipment burned on the ground after use. Conversely, unarmed dummy paratroopers were sometimes used in conjunction with smaller actual parachute operations so that they could be discovered by enemy troops who were investigating sightings of clandestine parachute activity and deduce that it was merely a decoy drop.

Simulator M.G. Fire Mark I with its cardboard cover removed, shown attached to Device Camouflage Number 15.

· · · · ·

The largest use of dummy paratroopers came during the early hours of the Normandy invasion on June 5/6 1944 in the four phases of *Operation Titanic*. Titanic was the overall codeword for the deceptive airborne operations under *Operation Fortitude* in direct support of the *Operation Neptune* landings that were part of *Operation Overlord*. *Titanic I* involved dummy parachutists and small teams of Special Air Service (S.A.S.) troops with portable gramophones that broadcast the sounds of troops calling to each other intermixed with other battle noises. They were dropped 30 miles southwest of Dieppe near Yvetot to simulate an airborne division being dropped north of the Seine. Its purpose was to retain the German forces and reserves in that area. *Titanic II* was cancelled but it originally called for dropping dummy parachutists east of the River Dives to delay German reserve forces from moving west after the real invasion was discovered. *Titanic III* entailed dummy parachutists being dropped southwest of Caen to distract the Germans while the actual 6th Airborne Division was landing closer to the coast near Ranville. And *Titanic IV* had dummy parachutists dropped near the base of the Cotentin Peninsula to draw the German forces west so they couldn't counter attack troops of the U.S. 101st Airborne Division near St. Lo. The combined effect of Titanic served to draw some German units away from their main positions as they launched wasteful counterattacks against an enemy they couldn't find. Because of this, some of the German commanders were skeptical when news of the real Allied drops started coming in and delayed releasing troops and equipment until the attacks could be confirmed.

In addition to Normandy, dummy paratroopers were also used by the British at Arnhem during *Operation Market Garden*. In the Far East, dummy parachutists were used during the deception *Operation Cloak* while General Slims IVth Corps forces crossed the Irrawaddy River during *Operation Capital*, the offensive to destroy Japanese forces in Burma during 1944-45.

. . . . .

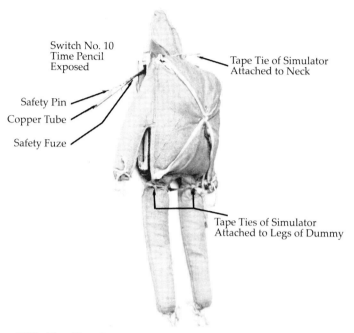

Switch No. 10
Time Pencil
Exposed

Tape Tie of Simulator
Attached to Neck

Safety Pin

Copper Tube

Safety Fuze

Tape Ties of Simulator
Attached to Legs of Dummy

Rifle Fire Simulator Mark I attached to Dummy Parachutist.

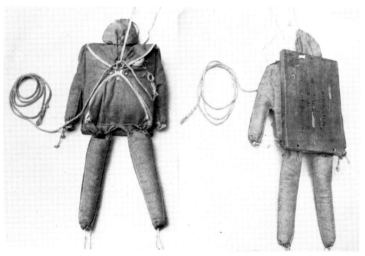

**Front and Back View of Simulator Rifle Fire Mark II (A/B No. 1)
Attached to Device Camouflage Number 15.**

· · · · ·

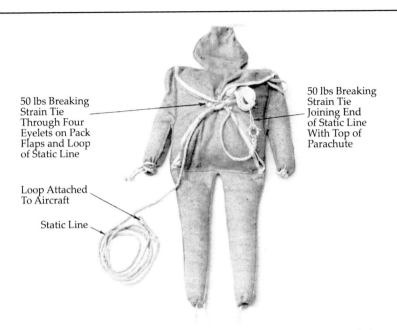

50 lbs Breaking Strain Tie Through Four Eyelets on Pack Flaps and Loop of Static Line

50 lbs Breaking Strain Tie Joining End of Static Line With Top of Parachute

Loop Attached To Aircraft

Static Line

Device Camouflage No. 15 (British Pattern Dummy Parachutist)

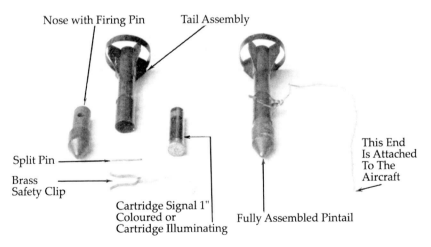

Nose with Firing Pin

Tail Assembly

Split Pin

Brass Safety Clip

Cartridge Signal 1" Coloured or Cartridge Illuminating

Fully Assembled Pintail

This End Is Attached To The Aircraft

Signal Pintail Mark I (Simulator Signal A/B Number 1)

. . . . .

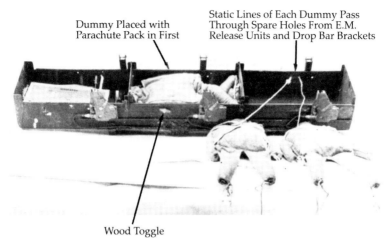

Dummy Placed with Parachute Pack in First

Static Lines of Each Dummy Pass Through Spare Holes From E.M. Release Units and Drop Bar Brackets

Wood Toggle

Method of packing small bomb container Mark IA.

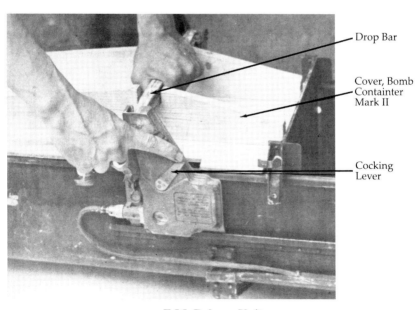

Drop Bar

Cover, Bomb Containter Mark II

Cocking Lever

E.M. Release Unit.

· · · · ·

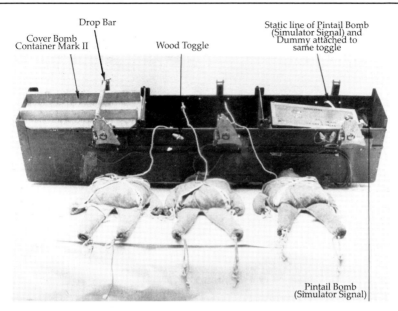

Method of packing small bomb container Mark VA.

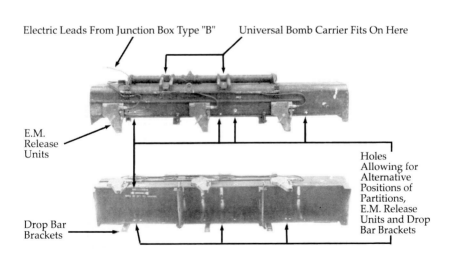

Small Bomb Container Mark IA.
Top view shows position when hung in bomb bays of aircraft.

· · · · ·

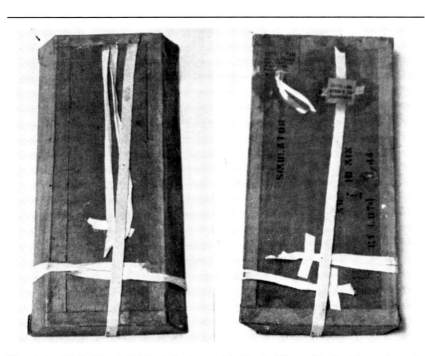

Simulator M.G. Fire A/B Mark I, changed to No. I. View of both sides as issued.

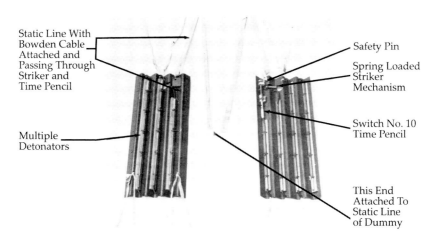

Static Line With
Bowden Cable
Attached and
Passing Through
Striker and
Time Pencil

Safety Pin

Spring Loaded
Striker
Mechanism

Switch No. 10
Time Pencil

Multiple
Detonators

This End
Attached To
Static Line
of Dummy

Simulator M.G. Fire Mark I
Viewed from both sides with the cardboard cover removed.

· · · · ·

517

View of both sides of Simulator Rife Fire Mark II, later changed to A/B No. 1.

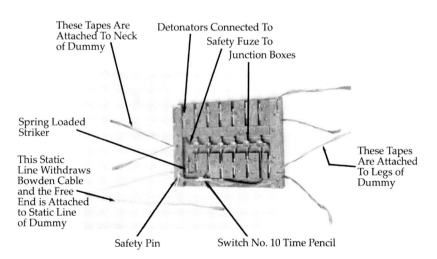

Simulator Rifle Fire Mark II (A/B No. 1) without its packaging.

· · · · ·

Both sides of the Rifle Simulator Mark I alongside one without its package. The detonators and time pencil with safety pin and cord loop can be seen.

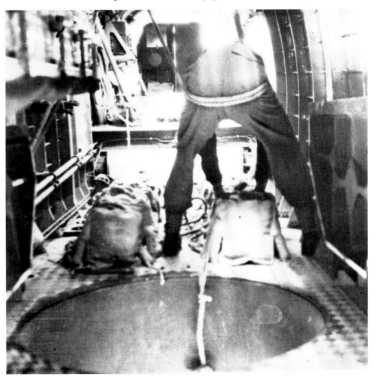

View looking forward on a British Halifax bomber. Number 1 of the dispatching crew is ready to begin dropping dummy parachutists. The number 2 and number 3 dispatchers would be in similar positions further up in the aircraft.

. . . . .

Forty dummy parachutists ready to be manually dispatched through the parachuting aperture on a British Halifax bomber.

View looking forward on a British Stirling bomber. 120 dummy parachutists arranged for manual dispatch from the parachuting aperture.

. . . . .

The art of deception has been practiced on the battlefield for as long as men have been fighting each other. Basic concepts include concealing your plan of attack, the size and location of your forces and what your true objectives are. The British forces under the command of Lieutenant-General Bernard Montgomery conducted *Operation Bertram*, the overall deceptive plans in September and November 1942 for the coming second battle of El Alamein. Part of the deception was to convince Rommel that the British were building up forces for an attack from the south. Tanks and artillery pieces were appearing in great numbers in the south while at the same time tanks and artillery pieces were disappearing in the north. In actuality, the forces in the south were composed of dummy vehicles and guns produced from wooden forms that were bolted together and could be folded up for easy transport. And in the north, equipment was being converted to appear as trucks. In the case of tanks, this was codenamed *Sunshield*. The codename *Cannibal* was used for the concealment of artillery pieces and their trailers so that they also appeared to be trucks.

· · · · ·

Two photographs showing a Churchill tank of the British 8th Army equipped with Sunshield. Egypt – 1942.

A Crusader Tank photographed in the desert equipped with Sunshield on 26 OCT 1942.

· · · · ·

An M3 General Grant Medium Tank being equipped with Sunshield. Part of the British Eighth Army, 7th Armoured Division, 4th Armoured Brigade "Black Rats".

Another Crusader Tank equipped with Sunshield which consisted of painted fabric over a metal framework which could be fitted in a matter of minutes by a few men to change its appearance when viewed from the air.

· · · · ·

A number of special decoy devices were used as part of *Operation Fortitude South* while attempt to convince the Germans that the invasion of France would come in the Pas-de-Calais area. *Quicksilver I* laid out the groundwork for a build up of theoretical troops and equipment in southeast England. *Quicksilver II* entailed deceptive radio traffic for the fake troops in southeast England. *Quicksilver III* provided wireless traffic and road signs related to troop staging areas and dummy landing craft for troop deployment. And *Quicksilver IV* was the air plan which included softening up the beaches and bombing the railroads in the Pas-de-Calais area.

For the *Quicksilver III* operations, *Drybob* was the codename for fake landing craft that were built and left on land. They could also be placed in shallow water with the aid of stilts. A later model codenamed *Wetbob* was an inflatable landing craft. Landing Craft Mechanized (LCM) simulators were known as *Middlebob*. And larger Landing Craft Tank (LCT) simulators were known as *Bigbob*.

· · · · ·

Dummy 160 feet long by 30 feet wide LCTs being set up in England.

. . . . .

In addition to the inflatable landing craft, dummy aircraft, tanks and field pieces were sometimes staged in southeast England as part of the fake army that was supposed to be building up for the Pas-de-Calais crossing. They were not permanently set up because it would have been difficult to keep their true nature from eventually being discovered. They were also susceptible to damage from high winds and general maintenance issues which needed to be addressed quickly since a Sherman tank laying on its side or an LCT in the middle of a field by the shore would not go unnoticed by aerial reconnaissance aircraft. Advancements over the 1942 wooden dummy vehicles were introduced with lightweight metal tubing frameworks that were covered with paint-

ed fabric along the lines of the Sunshield and Cannibal camouflage devices. These were further improved upon with U.S. made dummy vehicles which consisted of inflated tubes with painted fabric coverings over them. These were easier to setup or deflate and transport since they were lightweight and could be collapsed to a smaller size.

A dummy aircraft photographed in England during October 1943.

· · · · ·

Inflatable tube with fabric covering Sherman and Stuart tanks were pro-duced, as were jeeps, trailers and several patterns of trucks and artillery pieces.

· · · · ·

Since the deception of using dummy vehicles as stand-ins for actual vehicles which were relocated and camouflaged was proven to work in North Africa during Operation Bertram, the concept was expanded and put into practice in Europe follow-

ing the successful landings at Normandy. Units that the Germans knew to be in one location could move under cover of darkness while decoy dummy vehicles were set up in their place. And phantom units that the Germans believed existed as part of earlier decep-

tive operations were also simulated since the enemy had to commit resources to their potential movements and threats. An American unit known as the 23rd Headquarters Special Troops was given the unique mission of maintaining the ghost army and its traveling road show until the end of the war.

. . . . .

Four British soldiers carry a dummy Sherman tank that they are shown assembling in the two photographs on the facing page.

A dummy Piper L-4 "Cub" spotter aircraft of the 156 Field Artillery Battalion photographed on 23 FEB 1945. Another dummy aircraft can be seen in the background at the right. Their purpose was to draw enemy fire.

• • • • •

An American 155mm "Long Tom" towed artillery piece and a Sherman tank, both dummies that have been set up and partially camouflaged since this was needed to help convince observers that they were real from a distance.

. . . . .

Chapter 13 - Gliders and Tugs

An American C-47 cargo plane flies over the Pyramids. Egypt - 1943.

A Hadrian (Waco CG-4A) glider on a test flight banks to land. Wilbur Wright Field, Ohio, USA - 1942.

. . . . .

Hotspur Gliders

The *Hotspur* was the first glider adopted by the British military. It originated from the Ministry of Aircraft Production's June 1940 specification X.10/40 calling for an assault glider capable of carrying eight men with light weapons which could be released up to 100 miles from target at an altitude of 20,000 feet to ensure a slow and silent approach. General Aircraft Company Limited of Feltham, Middlesex, England came up with a design that was designated the GAL 48 Hotspur Mark I. Three prototypes were built and the first flight was four months from original conception on November 5, 1940. The glider had a wingspan of 61 feet 10 ¾ inches and a length of 39 feet 3 ½ inches. The empty weight was 1661 pounds and the operational load capacity was 3598 pounds. Seating in the all wood glider was down the center axis with two pilots in the nose and the remaining six men divided between two three-man compartments in front of and behind the wings. The undercarriage had two wheels on the wing struts and these could be jettisoned for rough landings. Skids beneath the fuselage and tail enabled landing without the wheels. The glider was towed from fittings at the front of the keel, and a ring at the rear of the aircraft allowed for a second glider to be tied on and towed in tandem. The top of the fuselage on the Hotspur Mark I was removable and could be thrown off on landing so that the troops could exit quickly. An order of 400 gliders was placed but only twenty-four were produced before the design specifications were changed.

. . . . .

The War Office had a change of view for how assault gliders should be used. In October 1940, a month before the Mark I design flew, specification X.22/40 was issued. It called for a glider that would be towed to target, released at low altitude and take on a steep approach for a fast landing. As it turned out during trials for the Hotspur Mark I, the original Air Ministry specifications could not be met. The Mark I design had proven difficult to handle when fully loaded and it had achieved a maximum glide distance of only 83 miles. As a result, one of the twenty-four production gliders was used as the prototype for the Mark II design. The new gliders had a stronger frame and the wings had inset ailerons. The wingspan was 45 feet 10 inches and the fuselage had a length of 39 feet 8 ¾ inches. The cockpit had the addition of basic instrumentation and the cockpit cover was hinged for access by a first and second pilot. The detachable roof feature of the Mark I design was replaced in favor of a side door on the port side of the fuselage for the entry and exit of the remaining six soldiers. Two sat forward of the wings in-line behind the pilots and the remaining four sat over the center and aft of the wings. A total of 987 Hotspur Mark II gliders were produced during the war.

· · · · ·

The final Hotspur Mark III design was adopted as a result of British government specification X.23/40. It had a slightly increased payload capacity of 3653 pounds and the tow rope mounting was at  the nose instead of the keel as found on previous models. The Mark II which had flight controls for First and Second Pilots shared instrumentation but the Mark III featured duplicated instrumentation for each pilot and dual tow release knobs mounted on the port side of the cockpit. A single lever to jettison the undercarriage continued in use on the starboard side of the cockpit but it was accessible by both pilots. The main fuselage had an added door on the starboard side in front of the wings and the port side continued to have a door aft of the wings. A total of fifty-two Hotspur Mark III aircraft were produced and they were all built on converted Mark II aircraft. An overall wartime total of 1012 Hotspur gliders were produced, including prototypes and conversions. None are known to have been used operationally. This was due to the arrival of the larger Horsa glider so the Hotspur was relegated to training.

. . . . .

Various attempts were made at increasing the payload and troop carrying capacity of the Hotspur gliders until the larger Horsa gliders were available. A prototype twin version was built using a pair of Mark II gliders that were joined together and shared a central twelve foot wing and a common tailplane section. The outboard side of each fuselage retained its original wing making this new aircraft's wingspan 58 feet. The pilots were seated in the port side cockpit and regular troops sat in the starboard cockpit which had no flight controls. The prototype flew in August 1942 but crashed and the project was abandoned. Rocket assisted take-off (RATO) pods were also trialed

in an attempt at helping overloaded gliders to break ground effect, as they could be towed satisfactorily once airborne.

. . . . .

535

Hengist Mark I Glider

The **Hengist** was an attack glider with two pilots and was capable of deploying 15 fully loaded combat troops. The design specification for this glider was X.25/40 and its intended role was for paratroopers to jump from it. Work started on the prototype in January 1941 and an order for 18 aircraft was confirmed in October 1941. The first flight of a Hengist was in January 1942. Delivery of the ordered gliders was scheduled for the summer of 1942 but it actually took place in the summer of 1943. The design is credited to John Carver Frost while working with the civilian glider manufacturer Slingsby Sailplanes Limited. They were constructed from a wooden frame that was covered with plywood. The upper and lower surfaces of the fuselage were curved and the sides were flat. The glider had a length of 59 feet 2 inches and a wingspan of 80 feet. Maxi-

mum payload was rated at 3,721 pounds giving an overall loaded weight of 8,350 pounds. The glider's two wheels could be jettisoned after takeoff and landing was done on a pair of pneumatic skids beneath the fuselage and tailplane section. The fuselage skid housed a twenty foot long air-filled rubber bladder intended to absorb landing stress.

· · · · ·

The men in the main cabin sat facing inwards on upward folding seats which were intended to create a wider walkway when it came time to hook up static lines and move to jump from one of the two doors. The forward door was on the starboard side and aft door was on the port side. In an effort to increase the number of men that could deploy at one time, there was a hook in the tail for pulling a second Hengist glider. Structural weaknesses were said to have been discovered during testing and the design was abandoned in 1943. This was principally because a C-47 could, by then, deploy twice the number of paratroopers and the Horsa glider could land twice as many men. Only 18 aircraft were produced and none saw operational service. None of the wartime Hengist gliders exist today as they were held in strategic reserve until they were all destroyed in 1946. The name for the glider comes from English history as one of the two Saxon leaders that settled people in England, one being Hengist and the other, his brother, Horsa.

Looking forward towards the cockpit in a fully loaded Hengist glider. The photo on the opposite page shows the folding seats in an empty glider.

· · · · ·

Interior of the Hengist glider cockpit as it would be seen from the seats of the First and Second Pilots.

Live ballast used to practice loading and for flight trials.

．．．．．

The two photographs above show the first Hengist glider prototype. This aircraft is serial number DG570 and it flew in January 1942. The other prototypes were DG571, DG572 and DG573. The last two prototypes were delivered to the Airborne Forces Experimental Establishment for flight trials in January and February 1943. The fourth Hengist glider prototype serial number DG573 is shown in the two photographs below and at the top of the first page describing this glider type. These shots were taken in October 1942. Serial numbers for the remaining fourteen production Hengist gliders are DG673 through DG686.

· · · · ·

Horsa Mark I and Mark II Gliders

The *Horsa* was designed by Airspeed Limited as a result of Specification X.26/40 in December 1940. The first official flight was September 12, 1941 by prototype serial number DG597 and the aircraft series became known as the AS.51 Horsa Mark I. Roughly 5000 were produced and this was largely done by subcontracted furniture manufacturers. The original purpose of the Horsa glider was to increase the capacity of bomber aircraft in carrying paratroopers. In addition to the two pilots, twenty-six soldiers could be carried in the central cabin. If they were lightly armed, provisions allowed for the addition of three more men who would be seated across from the port side loading ramp door. The ramp door featured a smaller conventional sized door and a second one was located behind the wings on the starboard side. Each of these doors had a short rail over it for attachment of static lines which paratroopers would connect onto prior to jumping. Eight equipment canisters could be carried inside of wing cells and this provided a means of dropping additional supplies. But four of the cells were located over the undercarriage and could only be dropped if it was jettisoned. This prevented them from being used on large scale glider operations since the wheeled undercarriage was retained so that the aircraft would have a longer landing run and not obstruct the landing zones. When the undercarriage was jettisoned, the glider landed on a wooden, metal-faced skid that had a rubber shock absorber between it and the fuselage. Some Horsa gliders did not have this feature and were designed to only land on their wheels.

· · · · ·

When the glider was first designed, the only vehicles required to be carried and air landed with troops were the solo and combination motorcycles. It was pure luck that a jeep with minor modification could be loaded into a Horsa. They were loaded through a large door on the forward port side that was hinged at the bottom and could serve as a ramp when lowered. To prevent damage to this door, reinforced supplemental ramps were used for loading. After landing, it didn't matter if the door was damaged so it served the purpose of the ramps. To speed the unloading of vehicles after landing and avoid use of the side door, experiments were carried out successfully in early 1944 to remove the rear fuselage with a band of cordtex explosive known as a *surcingle*. At the same time, the R.A.F. Air Transport Technical Development Unit was working out design modifications whereby the tail section of the fuselage would be held to the main fuselage by eight bolts with quick-release nuts. Unmodified gliders were known as White Horsas. Modified gliders were known as Red Horsas and were equipped with a spanner for the bolts and powerful wire cutters to sever the flight control cables. The surcingle charge was still carried onboard for use in an emergency. The Horsa Mark II also retained the removable tail "Red" modification but its primary means of loading and unloading was through the front of the glider as the cockpit was hinged and could swing aside. Before the Mark II designation was adopted, these gliders were known as Blue Horsas.

German prisoners on the landing zone during Operation Varsity – March 1945.

• • • • •

In addition to the side swinging hinged nose, what would be known as the AS.58 Horsa Mark II differed from the original design by having two nose wheels and the tow-cable was fastened to the nose wheel strut. For the Horsa Mark I, the tow-cable was secured to each side of the aircraft at the upper center plane main spar. The Horsa Mark I had an 88 foot wingspan, 67 foot length, 7 ½ foot fuselage diameter, an empty weight of 8,370 pounds and a maximum loaded weight of 15,500 pounds. The Horsa Mark II had virtually identical specification but was 11 inches longer and could accommodate an addition 250 pounds of weight.

Several design modifications were experimented with during the lifespan of the Horsa glider. The AS.52 was in answer to British Specification X.3/41 and was intended to carry bomb loads with a central 25-foot long bomb bay. The AS.53 was intended for vehicle carrying operations but this was superseded by the Horsa Mark II design. Horsa serial number DP749 was used in rocket assisted towed takeoff trials during 1943. and trials were planned for a powered Horsa that would feature a pair of 375 horsepower Siddeley Cheetah X wing mounted radial engines. In May 1944, glider snatch pick-up trials were being conducted at RAF Netheravon, Wiltshire and a while most involved Hadrian gliders, records indicate at least one test involving a Horsa glider.

· · · · ·

An army airborne transport officer checks motorcycles as they are made fast to the floor of a Horsa glider for an upcoming demonstration, April, 1944.

An airborne jeep being manhandled into a Horsa Mark I glider. The special loading ramps can be seen over the open side cargo door.

· · · · ·

Glider assault training exercises conducted in England. Three gliders are visible in this first photograph and men are utilizing both the forward port and aft starboard doors. Note the man in the air and the last man shown exiting the glider each carry Enfield Number I Mark III* rifles fitted with 2.5-Inch Grenade Dischargers.

A second photograph of the same group after taking up a defensive posture.

· · · · ·

Men of the 6th Airlanding Brigade, 2nd Battalion, the Oxfordshire and Buckinghamshire Light Infantry in a Horsa glider. The regimental flashes can be seen on their first pattern airborne helmets.

A second photograph showing men of the Oxfordshire & Buckinghamshire Light Infantry loading into a Horsa glider. This was taken in early 1942 and some of the men can be seen still wearing standard infantry helmets.

• • • • •

Loading vehicles into the AS.58 Horsa Mark II gliders was an easy task since the nose could swing to the side. The photograph above shows an American jeep in British service towing a lightweight 10cwt airborne trailer up ramps and into the glider by men of the British 6th Airborne Division during preparations for Operation Varsity during March 1945.

A jeep still outfitted with windshield and bows for the canvas top, being driven down ramps out of the front of an AS.58 Horsa Mark II glider during a loading exercise. The jeep required no modifications whatsoever when used with this glider pattern.

. . . . .

Wartime gliders and troop carriers were equipped with safety lap belt restraints for the pilots and soldiers being transported. The British pattern was made from webbing material similar to the type found with Pattern 1937 load bearing equipment with a double thickness and a four inch width. The ends each have a pair of heavy steel grommets so they can be cabled to the lower frame of the seats on the glider. The center section has an adjustment buckle so the belt can be tightened to the wearer. A pair of quick release devices located near the center enabled the belt to be removed without need of working the straps loose through the adjustment buckle. The America pattern lap belt used on the Hadrian gliders and on the C-47 troop carriers was produced from an olive drab canvas. It had metal fittings at each end which connected to the aircraft and a pair of size adjusters which were on each side of a central metal quick release device.

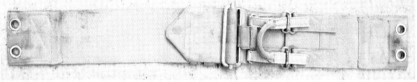

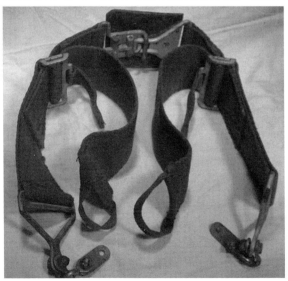

A British pattern safety lap belt made in 1943 with the quick release devices fastened is shown above. The U.S. pattern lap belt shown at the left was produced in 1944.

· · · · ·

Hamilcar Mark I Glider

British Government Specification X.27/40 called for a military glider capable of delivering tanks or other heavy cargo and this challenge was taken up by General Aircraft Limited and the aircraft would have the designation GAL 49 *Hamilcar* Mark I. Two prototypes were ordered in July 1941 and these would be the largest wooden aircraft produced for the British military during the war. Since a design like this had never been attempted before, a single half-scale model was built and flown in the autumn of 1941. This glider was serial number T0227 and the aircraft designation was GAL 50. The first of the full sized prototype Hamilcar gliders flew on 27 March 1942 and was serial number DP206. The cockpit on the Hamilcar was built for two pilots sitting tandem. It was situated on top of the fuselage and was accessible by climbing a ladder found inside the main cabin which led to a hatch in the roof. A unique feature of the Hamilcar was its hydraulic landing chassis. Once landed, the aircraft could be lowered to the ground and the landing chassis would telescope into itself. This made driving vehicles out of the glider extremely quick and easy as no ramps were needed. The nose of the glider swings open and greatly assists in this aspect. The payload was up to 17,500 pounds which gave the glider an overall loaded weight of 36,000 pounds. This enabled it to carry two Daimler Scout Cars, two Universal Carriers, a Locust T.9 (M22) Light Tank, a Tetrarch Mark IV Light Tank, a 25-pounder or 17-pounder field piece with tractor, or up to forty fully armed soldiers.

Hamilcar prototype serial number DP206 photographed in March 1943

· · · · ·

548

    To supplement the lack of sufficient tug aircraft that could tow a loaded Hamilcar, trials were conducted in January 1943 with rocket assisted take-off (RATO) pods mounted to the glider. These consisted of 25 inch diameter steel cylinders that each contained twenty-four 3-inch rockets. The rockets were electrically fired in pairs at intervals of 1.2 seconds. This produced an average thrust rating of 2000 pounds for twenty-nine seconds. After lifting off the ground following the burn of all rockets, the pods were jettisoned and would parachute back to Earth. The overall length of the glider was 68 feet 1 inches with a wingspan of 110 feet. The fuselage had a width of 9 feet 3 inches with an inside cargo space 27 feet long, 8 feet wide and 6 feet 8 inches high. Overall height at the top of the rudder was 27 feet. A total of 344 Hamilcar gliders were built including the prototypes. They were used in airborne operations *Tonga*, *Mallard*, *Market* and *Varsity*. This glider was named after the general that commanded the Carthaginian land forces during the first Punic War against the Romans in Sicily. His name was Hamilcar Barca (275-228 BC) and he was the father of Hannibal.

A practice flight prior to D-Day conducted in May 1944

· · · · ·

Official wartime records indicate that between 18 and 20 Tetrarch Light Tanks were landed by Hamilcar gliders during the Normandy Invasion as part of Operation Tonga. These belonged to A-Squadron of the Armoured Reconnaissance Regiment of the British 6th Airlanding Brigade. Each tank weighed 16,800 pounds. Some were fitted with 2-pounder antitank guns while others had 3-inch howitzers for close support.

The two photographs on this page show a Tetrarch tank in a Hamilcar glider during loading exercises conducted at R.A.F. Tarrant Rushton. The ladder seen at the lower right provided access to the cockpit via a rooftop hatch.

. . . . .

The Armoured Reconnaissance Regiment of the British 6th Airlanding Brigade received seventeen Locust T.9 (M22) Light Tanks in late 1943 which were part of a larger number provided by the United States as Lend Lease. Due to mechanical issues, they were not used operationally until March 1945 when eight were landed by Hamilcar glider during Operation Varsity. These tanks weighed 16,000 pounds and the main armament was a 37mm gun.

A Locust tank exits a Hamilcar after the fuselage has hydraulically lowered.

· · · · ·

A universal carrier of the 6th Airborne Division being loaded into a General Aircraft Limited Hamilcar Mark I glider of the R.A.F. in preparation for Operation Varsity. England – 18 MAR 1945.

Universal Carriers were landed successfully by Hamilcar gliders during wartime operations in Normandy (June 1944), Arnhem (September 1944) and Hamminkeln (March 1945) for use by men of the 1st and 6th airborne divisions.

· · · · ·

British Government Specification X.4/44 called for a powered glider version of the Hamilcar to be used for delivering heavy loads to regions within the Far Eastern theatre of operations. This was needed because the tropical heat reduced the efficiency of the tug aircraft's piston engines and by extension reduced the range and load of the combination. This modified glider design would receive the designation GAL 58 Hamilcar Mark X Air Freighter and the first prototype serial number LA728 flew in February 1945. The experimental design featured twin 965 horsepower Bristol Mercury engines for the purpose of assisting the towing tug on take-off and to increase the operational range of the glider as a tank landing aircraft. Existing Hamilcar Mark I gliders selected for conversion received strengthening to the wings to support the engines and modifications were made to the landing gear. There were two wing tanks that could each hold 195 gallons of fuel and provisions existed for a third 230 gallon fuel tank to be placed in the main cargo hold. A fuel regulator in the cockpit balanced fuel consumption between the wing tanks. Testing was underway with the Airborne Forces Experimental Establishment when the Japanese surrendered in August 1945. At this time, 100 aircraft conversions had been ordered but only twenty-two had been completed, including two prototypes, and the project was cancelled. None were ever used operationally.

· · · · ·

Hadrian (U.S. C.G.-4A Waco) Glider

The Waco Aircraft Company of Troy, Ohio in the United States produced a cargo glider they designated the C.G.-4 and initial flight testing was started in May 1942. The glider had a steel tubing frame which was covered in fabric. The main production version of the glider adopted by the United States Army Air Force (USAFF) was designated the C.G.-4A and in British service it was known as the Hadrian, named after the fourteenth emperor of Rome (AD 117 to 138). The glider was used extensively by the British to supplement the number of Horsa and Hamilcar gliders available for operations. The overall length of the aircraft was 48 feet 4 inches and the wingspan was 83 feet 4 inches. The empty weight was 3,790 pounds with a maximum loaded take-off weight of 7,500 pounds. Two pilots sat side by side in the cockpit and the main cargo cabin could hold thirteen soldiers or a relatively light cargo load consisting of a jeep, a 75mm pack howitzer or a loaded jeep trailer. The nose was hinged at the top and it could be lifted up and locked in place for easy loading and unloading of vehicles and other wheeled equipment.

. . . . .

The first Waco CG-4A glider was delivered to the United Kingdom during Operation Voodoo on 1 July 1943. It was towed from North America over the Atlantic Ocean to the United Kingdom by R.A.F. Ferry Command. The 3500 mile trip had a combined flight time of 28 hours 15 minutes with a route of Dorval, Canada to Goose Bay, Labrador to Bluie West One, Greenland to Reykjavík, Iceland to Prestwick, Scotland. Subsequent gliders were shipped disassembled in crates and of the 14,000 produced during the Second World War, nearly 1,100 were assigned to the R.A.F.

Men of the 1st Battalion The Border Regiment deploy from their Hadrian gliders during a training exercise near Froha, Algeria - June 1943. (both photographs above and on the lower facing page)

• • • • •

The first operational use of the Hadrian glider was by men of the 1st Airborne Divisions Airlanding Brigade during Operation Husky, the invasion of Sicily, which began on 9 July 1943. Hadrian gliders were used after that time for supply and troop deliveries in each Allied air operation that took place in both the European and Pacific Theatres of Operation.

One half of a platoon of men with the 1st Battalion The Border Regiment of the 1st Airlanding Brigade waiting to board their American piloted Hadrian glider the eve of Operation Husky. Near Sousse, Tunisia - 9 JUL 1943.

Glider Snatching was a process employed with the Hadrian gliders operationally, first in Normandy and then later in the Pacific Theatre of Operations during the Chindits long range penetration of the Burmese jungle in 1944. Gliders could be retrieved from areas where powered aircraft couldn't land and this greatly aided in their retrieval since they wouldn't need to be disassembled and moved over land to an airfield. Wounded soldiers were also successfully evacuated inside some of these snatched gliders. The process entailed a 220 foot long tow rope being fastened to the nose of the parked glider. The other end of the tow rope was formed into a triangular loop that was suspended between two 12-foot tall poles which were placed twenty feet apart. A very low flying C-47 rigged with a special winch connected to an extended snatching hook would fly on a diagonal path to the glider at a speed of 125 miles per hour and engage the elevated loop of tow rope. On contact, the cable on the winch would unwind and help offset the snatch shock from the weight of the glider. Once the glider was airborne, the winch cable would be wound back in.

· · · · ·

Two examples of Hadrian gliders being snatched by C-47 tug aircraft. A line of military ambulances can be seen in the photograph at the left, having unloaded wounded for air evacuation back to England.

The photograph at the left was taken in the days following the failure of Operation Market Garden in September 1944. The Germans burned all of the Horsa, Hadrian and Hamilcar gliders on the landing zones that they still controlled to prevent the Allies from recovering them for reuse.

. . . . .

A C-47 flies in low with its tow hook extended about to engage the glider's elevated tow rope during Horsa glider snatching trials.

The tow rope has just been captured but the slack hasn't been taken in yet. The glider used in these trials was an AS.58 Horsa Mark II as can be identified by the pair of front nose wheels and the tow-cable being fastened to the nose wheel strut.

Glider takeoff was relatively smooth but fast, going from 0 to 110 miles per hour in five seconds.

. . . . .

Three photographs taken in April 1944 of a prototype glider serial number NP671 which was designed by General Aircraft Limited. It was designated the GAL 55 and was built in response to the British Government's Specification TX.3/43 for a new training glider. This was a mid-wing two seat glider with a length of 25 feet 6 inches and a wingspan of 35 feet. Air trials were conducted by the Airborne Forces Experimental Establishment and the aircraft was found to be unstable once it reached a 120 mile per hour towing speed. Being deemed unsuitable for use as a military trainer, the project was cancelled.

· · · · ·

Experimental tailless gliders produced by General Aircraft Limited and designated GAL 56 were a research stepping stone in the flying wing concept. One goal was to eventually develop a flying

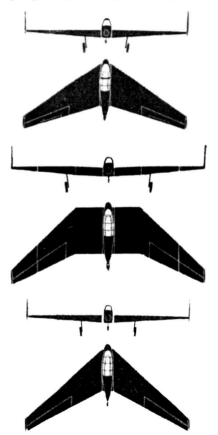

wing which could be attached to tanks and other large and heavy vehicles to give them aerial mobility into battle. Three prototypes were produced during the war and aircraft serial number TS507A shown above was photographed in October 1944. The three prototype variants were a Medium V (pictured above), a Medium U and a Maximum V. The GAL 57 was intended to be a powered version of the GAL 56. The next progression would have been the GAL 61 which was planned as a GAL 56 with a retractable undercarriage and omission of the outboard wing tip stabilizers. The Medium V glider shown in the photograph had a wingspan of 45 feet 4 inches and a length of 19 feet.

· · · · ·

    Hawker Hector was a biplane design by Hawker Aircraft Limited that first flew on 14 Feb 1936 with a total of 178 production aircraft being built. The majority were built under arrangement with the Westland Aircraft Works. The aircraft was powered by a 24-cylinder Napier Dagger IIIMS H-type supercharged and air-cooled engine which was disliked by the maintenance personnel that had to service them. They had a short operational life as army cooperation/liaison aircraft and were replaced by the Westland Lysander as a general purpose aircraft in 1938. When this occurred, they were transferred to the Auxiliary Air Force. The only combat service was with 613 Squadron when they were used to harass the Germans during their advance through northern France before being evacuated from the country in May 1940. They were then assigned the role of towing targets and in late 1940 were assigned the task as tug aircraft for the new Hotspur

gliders which were expected in early 1941. Length of the aircraft was 29.5 feet with a wingspan just short of 37 feet. The Hawker Hart was another biplane used as a tug for the Hotspur gliders, as was the Miles Master II which was a monoplane design.

· · · · ·

Armstrong-Whitworth Albemarle

The *Albemarle* was a medium bomber first used by the R.A.F. in January of 1943. It was employed heavily in airborne operations, being used for paratroopers and as a tug for Horsa and Hadrian gliders. When used for parachuting, ten troops were carried and their exit point was a large dropping hole in the floor. A rail for attachment of the static lines was fitted to the side of the fuselage. Range when used as a glider tug varied depending on the load and type of glider being pulled. In the case of the Horsa, the practical range was 415 miles and slightly more for the Hadrian. Temperature, air density and the number of guns that remained fitted to the aircraft were also considerations in factoring range.

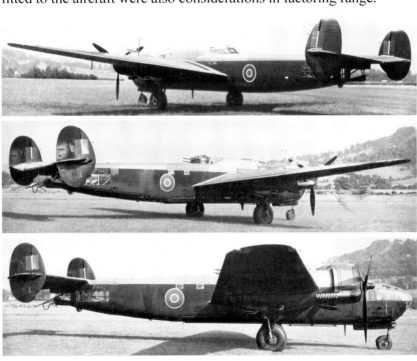

• • • • •

Halifax Mark II

The R.A.F. began receiving the ***Halifax*** heavy bombers in February of 1943 and they were used on every airborne operation until the war ended. The bomber had a great range and was first used for the doomed Operation Freshman in Norway which failed due to bad weather which resulted in several crashes. Survivors were executed under Hitler's standing orders to kill captured commandos. Halifax bombers were used to ferry Horsas from the U.K. to North Africa in July of 1943 and the Halifax was the only aircraft capable of towing a Hamilcar glider. It had a rough range of 395 miles when towing a Hamilcar and a range of 525 miles when towing a Horsa. The range for parachute operations was just over 700 miles.

Halifax Mark III

· · · · ·

Short Sterling & Armstrong-Whitworth Whitley

The **Stirling** was becoming obsolete for bombing towards the end of 1943 and found new life following its transfer from Bomber Command to Transport Command. It was used as a glider tug as well as for parachuting. Paratroopers dropped from a hole near the rear of the aircraft and there was room for 22 jumpers. Twelve drop containers could be carried in the bomb cells and it was used heavily by the S.O.E. in 1944 for supply drops in Europe. It had a radius of action of over 800 miles for parachuting and 525 miles as a Horsa or Hadrian tug.

The **Whitley** was removed from Bomber Command due to being slow and vulnerable to attack. Following this they were found suitable as tugs for gliders as well as being ideal for parachute operations. Ten parachutists could be carried and they dropped through a hole in the floor of the fuselage. The aircraft had a 500 mile radius of action when used for parachuting. Whitley bombers were used over Italy during Operation Colossus in February of 1941. This involved 11th S.A.S. Battalion in the successful attack on the Tragino Aqueduct. It could ferry a Horsa but could not pull one with a combat load.

· · · · ·

Wellington Mark III

The ***Wellington*** was the main British bomber in use from 1939-1943 and could sustain a large amount of damage to itself due to its geodetic internal structure. It had a six man crew and was used predominantly in a night bomber role. It was the first aircraft to drop a ten ton Grand Slam bomb and was used to help initiate the Pathfinder target indicating tactics. When used as a tug for Horsa gliders, it had a range of 424 miles. It was also used for parachuting via a hole in the fuselage towards the tail. The beam guns had to be removed when used for this role. During the war, the nickname for this bomber was *Wimpy*, after the Popeye cartoon character J. Wellington Wimpy.

Wellington Mark IV

· · · · ·

A Whitley Bomber with a Horsa glider drafting in the low tow position.

A Stirling Bomber taking off with a Horsa glider already in its high tow position.

Horsa glider airborne in tow on a training flight.

Paratroopers and gliders share the same field during a training exercise.

· · · · ·

566

The **Dakota** was a general all purpose transport aircraft that saw service in all theatres of operation during the war. It was originally designed as a civilian transport but was found to be easily modified for parachute jumping as well as for towing gliders. It could carry 20-25 fully equipped parachutists and had a practical operating radius of 250 miles in this role. Paratroopers had the luxury of jumping from a standing position with the C-47 as opposed to dropping through a hole on one of the British bombers. Additionally, twice as many paratroopers could deploy together from this aircraft when compared with most others in British service at the time. The C-47 was also used for transporting all types of cargo including jeeps, field pieces, metal drop canisters and wicker supply panniers. Resistance groups as well as airborne and infantry units were often re-supplied by air via the Dakota.

. . . . .

Three wartime photographs showing a Mark III, Class 5 Raft being loaded into a C-47 Dakota. Also known as Assault Boats, they could be folded up and passed through the port side cargo door on the aircraft before being laid out flat inside. The Seagull Mark III 50hp outboard motor set is crated and can be seen in the third photograph towards the front of the cargo area on the plane.

The boats had a wooden floor, canvas sides and a wooden gunwale around the top which was held up by wooden supports. These were used extensively during the war for crossing water obstacles and are best remembered for the river crossings during Operation Market-Garden.

. . . . .

568

One risk in parachuting was becoming a towed jumper. This could happen if the static line was looped through and hung up with the parachute harness or the break cord from the static line to the parachute was too strong and wouldn't separate. U.S. paratroopers were issued a reserve parachute so they could be cut away by a dispatcher. They would then manually deploy their reserve. British paratroopers had no reserve so they had to come up with a procedure to handle this emergency situation.

A special emergency kit was developed and it contained two standard observer type parachutes. These are roughly the same size as a U.S. chest type reserve parachute. The kit also contains a ten foot length of rope, a wire cable with loop on one end and shackle 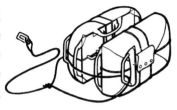 on the other, a hammer, cold chisel and a small metal dolly bar to serve as an anvil. The cable is looped through the d-rings on each parachute to hold them together and then it is passed through all the static line hooks that are still connected to the static cable. This is done since it might be difficult to determine which static line is connected to the towed parachutist. The pair of bundled parachutes is placed near the door with one end of the rope tied to both rip cords and the other end of the rope secured to a cargo lashing point on the aircraft. The static cable is then cut by means of the hammer and chisel, using the dolly as a backing surface against the bulkhead of the aircraft. When the static cable breaks, all of the static lines will fall away,

taking the bundled parachutes with them out the door. The rope will pull the rip cords when it plays out and the towed parachutist should have two canopies over his head.

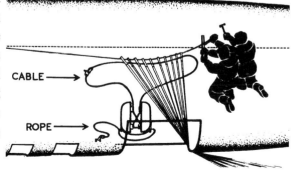

· · · · ·

A navigational aid that was utilized by airborne aircraft in conjunction with Pathfinders and men of the Independent Parachute Companies was the **Rebecca/Eureka** developed in 1941. The first model Eureka was a beacon on the ground that could receive on one fixed frequency and it transmit on another fixed frequency. The Rebecca was carried on an aircraft and it transmitted on the fixed Eureka receiving frequency and received on the fixed Eureka transmitter frequency. Operationally, the Rebecca set would repeatedly transmit a signal and when the aircraft was close enough for the Eureka to receive it, a signal would be transmitted back. The aircraft had an aerial on each wing to receive the Eureka signal and its energy would be measured. An onboard radar screen had a central line with graduated markings ranging from zero to fifty on it. A short vertical line would display on the screen each time a Eureka signal was detected and it would correspond with a marking indicating how many miles away the aircraft was from target. If the signal was stronger on the right side aerial, the line would be displayed farther to the right on the radar screen. The pilot would adjust course as the Eureka signals were received until the displayed line was equally split by the central graduated line. And when they hit the zero mark, they knew that they were over the Eureka unit.

The ground based Eureka sets had a Morse key built in so an operator could transmit his drop zone or landing zone code letter to approaching aircraft. But all of the first pattern devices used the same fixed frequency which could cause a problem for aircraft approaching multiple beacons at different adjacent locations. To resolve this, the Rebecca/Eureka Mark II was introduced in 1943. It had five sets of frequencies so that multiple paired units could be used at one time for a large operation without risk of aircraft following the wrong signal. A lightweight Mark III set was also developed which had the Eureka and battery components small enough to fit into special webbing pouches. The larger Mark I and Mark II Eureka sets required a standard Airborne Kitbag for delivery.

· · · · ·

Under favorable conditions, an aircraft flying at 2000 feet could expect to accurately home in on the beacon from 8-12 miles out. The Mark I sets were used operationally in the failed *Operation Freshman* on the night of 19/20 NOV 1942 in Norway. Mark II and Mark III sets were used operationally for the airborne portions of the Normandy, Arnhem and Rhine Crossing campaigns.

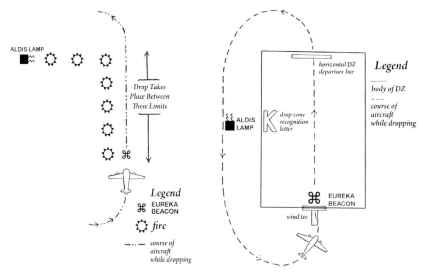

Typical layout of a drop zone by night (left) and by day (right).

During daylight operations, a letter "T" made from white ground strips (red if on snow) will be placed at the approach end of the drop zone. The stem of the "T" should point in the direction of the surface wind. Although stationary, this serves as an airport *Wind Tee* which would rotate with the wind, and resembles an aircraft flying into the wind. A horizontal bar made from ground strips will be laid out at the departure end of the drop zone. The drop zone recognition letter should be sited in the middle of the left hand side and it also will be made from ground strips. The wartime standard ***Ground Strips*** are 12 feet by 2 feet 6 inches. For night operations, the "T" is replaced by an "L" created from lights or fires that are sited 100 yards from one another. Three made up the short leg and five make up the long leg, with one being common to both legs.

· · · · ·

Autogyros

Rotary-wing aircraft, also known as ***Rotacraft***, were the forerunners of the modern helicopter. The development of the helicopter lead to the obsolescence of the glider for military purposes since troops and equipment could be landed and retrieved more safely and efficiently. For this reason, a few rotacraft are briefly covered in this chapter.

An ***Autogyro*** is a wingless aircraft that uses a propeller for forward motion and a freely rotating non-motorized rotor for lift. In some models, the rotor is assisted by the engine to initially get it spinning while rolling down the runway but the rotor is not powered during free flight. How it works: The aircraft is pulled down the runway by the propeller; the forward motion causes the rotor on top to turn automatically. When enough forward speed has been achieved, the aircraft will lift off the ground. Once in the air, the air pressure against the bottom side of the rotor blades causes them to continue to spin and this keeps the autogyro in the air. Helicopter pilots know this phenomenon as autorotation, which is a concept they use for landing if they have lost their engine. In the case of the autogyro, the forward momentum from the propeller allows continued flight as long as the engine is powered. The first Autogyro was developed in Spain in the early 1920s by Juan de la Cierva. The first British-made autogyro to fly was the Weir W-2, powered by a two cylinder Weir Dryad II engine. The flight was during March of 1934 in Abbotsinch.

. . . . .

The **Rotachute** is a type of autogyro developed by Raoul Hafner and the Airborne Forces Experimental Establishment during WWII. The concept originated in 1940 and a contract was placed with the

M.L. Aviation Company 1942. The Rotachute was intended to allow an armed and equipped airborne soldier to land with pin-point precision on the battlefield. It consisted of a tubular framework covered in the back section by rubberized fabric. There were no wings and no engine. A rotor with a pair of wooden blades was intended to create enough lift for a controlled decent by means of autorotation. By design, the Rotachute was to be towed like a glider to the vicinity of the landing zone. The tug aircraft provided the means of forward momentum for the rotors to begin spinning and this created the needed lift for flight. Once the tow line was cast off, the pilot of the Rotachute would pick his landing spot and navigate to during autorotation. The distance he could travel was limited because he would no longer be able to maintain level flight. This is much like a descending parachutist but he would have greater forward momentum as he descended which would allow more options in selecting a landing spot. The length of the aircraft was 7 feet 5 inches and

it had a rotor diameter of 15 feet, 2 inches. While twenty were produced and flown during the war, none were used operationally. The example at the left is from the Museum of Army Flying.

· · · · ·

The Rotabuggy & Rotatank

The **Rotabuggy** took the autogyro concepts employed with the Rotachute to the next level. It entailed mounting a two-blade rotor that had a diameter of 46 feet, 8 inches to a jeep.

The Rotabuggy was first test towed behind a supercharged Bentley and it achieved a gliding speed of 65 miles per hour. The first actual flight was done on November 16, 1943 using a Whitley bomber as a tug aircraft at Sherburn-in-Elmet near Leads. The aircraft had a streamlined tail section with twin fins but it had no rudder. The cockpit had Perspex door panels and an extended front Perspex windscreen to protect the pilot since it could be towed at speeds up to 150 miles per hour. All of the added panels as well as the rotor could be removed from the jeep once on the ground and no longer needed. The Rotabuggy flew during the war but was never used operationally. In late 1943 it became clear that the glider was a more economical and efficient method of landing vehicles and so experiments were to be discontinued. Plans also existed for mounting rotors to trucks as well as to tanks. The **Rotatank** was to be based on a Valentine Tank equipped in a similar way as the jeeps that were used for the Ro-

tabuggy. None were built for testing before the project ended.

· · · · ·

Chapter 14 - Air Dropping

Sergeants J. W. Whawell and John Turl of the Glider Pilot Regiment searching the ruined comprehensive school in Oosterbeek for enemy snipers. A supply container can be seen on the ground in the doorway. The two men were fighting alongside gun crews of the 2nd Battery, 1st Airlanding Light Regiment, Royal Artillery. Turl was killed four days later. Oosterbeek, Netherlands - 20 SEPT 1944

. . . . .

X-Type Parachute

The main parachute used by the British airborne during WWII was the *"X" Type* designed by Raymond Quilter of the G.Q. Parachute Company. It was also known as the *Statichute* because it was deployed by static line. The X-Type harness straps were made of a cotton/linen weave and had a diameter of 1.75 inches. The static line was 12 feet long and made of the same material as the harness but it had a double thickness. The canopy had a diameter of 25 feet which stretched to 28 feet when fully deployed with a load suspended beneath it. The twenty-eight suspension lines were each 22.5 feet long and ran from the edge of the canopy to four "D" rings attached to four risers. Seven suspension lines went to each of the "D" ring/riser combinations. The canopy was first produced from silk like most other parachutes of the time period. After the war started, there was a shortage of silk, since the majority of this material was controlled by the Japanese. Ramex, a type of cotton, was the next material used for

parachutes. This was followed by nylon which was officially adopted in 1944 even though it had been in limited use since 1940. The X-Type parachute was considered to be so reliable that reserve parachutes were not used during WWII by the British and Commonwealth airborne forces. Reserve parachutes were not adopted until 1952 and even then, were not always used on operations including the November 1956 drop to secure the Suez Canal. A low jumping altitude prevented a parachutist from having time to detect a problem with his main canopy and to properly deploy a reserve if he had anything other than a total malfunction which was rare with the X-Type parachute.

. . . . .

The shoulder and leg straps of the harness were held together in front of the parachutist by a metal Quick Release Box. Upon landing, the outer disc was rotated one half turn and pressed inward to  release the straps. This was designed by the Irwin firm in 1929. It was very easy for a man to free himself from the parachute harness since he didn't have a reserve chute to remove first. Two main patterns of X-Type parachute were produced during the war. The Mark I pattern can be identified by the static line being stowed vertically on the back of the container in the center. The Mark II pattern had the static line stowed inside the container beneath the deployment bag at the bottom of the pack tray. The static line was accessible at the top of the container where it passed through a square sewn extraction slot.

· · · · ·

Members of the Oxfordshire & Buckinghamshire L.I. during parachute training.

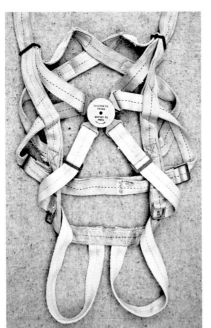

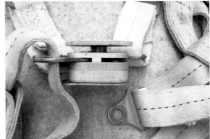

TURN
TO UNLOCK

PRESS
TO RELEASE

The X-Type Parachute Harness with Quick Release Box

· · · · ·

The first aircraft used for British parachute training and operations were bombers. Typically ten parachutists could be carried for deployment with the bulk of their weapons and equipment being stored in drop canisters carried in the bomb cells. The C47 was later adopted for use as it could carry more than twice the men and they could exit quicker and cleaner through a door in the side. Previously jumps were done through a hole in the floor of the bombers. Provisions were made for parachutists to deploy from Horsa gliders up through mid-1944 because of a lack of jump aircraft but this never seems to have progressed beyond the training and planning phase.

· · · · ·

An unidentified paratrooper (right) of the 1st Canadian Parachute Battalion, who wears a Sorbo helmet and an X-Type parachute, receives advice from a British instructor before jumping from a static balloon at the Royal Air Force Parachute Training Center. Ringway, Cheshire, England – OCT 1943.

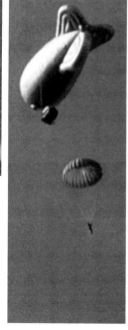

A trainee with parachute canopy almost fully developed, as viewed from the gondola of a balloon. The parachute inner bag, aka deployment bag, hanging from the static line is clearly visible in the photograph above. The photograph at the right shows a trainee with canopy fully developed. The distance between the gondola and the trainee shows how quickly a static line parachute will inflate under good jumping conditions.

. . . . .

British paratroopers in a Whitley bomber wait for the air despatcher to signal they are at the drop zone. They are wearing the first pattern long-sleeved parachutists' jump jackets.

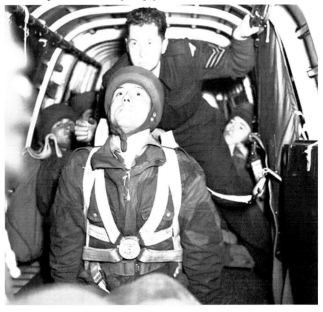

Private L. H. Carter of the 1st Canadian Parachute Battalion, ready to drop through the floor aperture of a British Armstrong-Whitworth Whitley bomber during parachute training. R.A.F. Station, Ringway, Cheshire, England – 4 APR 1944.

. . . . .

British paratroopers (above) with early X-Type Mark I parachutes on-board a C-47 for training jumps. The 12-foot static line on the British X-Type parachutes has a V-Ring at the end. The despatcher would connect each parachutist's static line V-Ring onto a snap hook that could slide on a strong point cable fixed to the aircraft. The American T5 parachute used a static line that had a snap hook at its end. This made it possible for the parachutist to connect his own static line onto the aircraft's strong point cable. In an emergency situation, the snap hook could be fastened to another hard point in the aircraft, or even to the harness of another parachutist, allowing for a daisy chain deployment.

Paratroopers descending with airborne kitbags deployed (left).

. . . . .

The photograph above shows a British paratrooper that has just landed. His canopy is still inflated so he will approach it at an angle while pulling one set of lines so that it will collapse and prevent him from being dragged. Capewell canopy releases were not a feature of the X-Type parachute. The X-Type parachute remained in British service well into the 1960s when it was replaced by the PX-Type. This was a virtually identical parachute system with a larger canopy and it was used with the PR7 reserve parachute. The PX-Type parachute was phased out of military service in 1993.

A British paratrooper with bent knees prepares to land during a training jump that was done at night. (right)

· · · · ·

Knee Pads were issued for use during parachute training. These were worn beneath the trousers so they would stay in place while still allowing the trousers to move freely during tum-

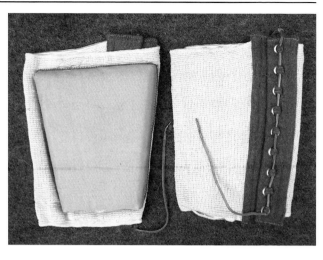

bling and parachute landing falls (PLF). The general design was a knitted elastic sleeve with a thick cotton or wool covered pad being sewn in the front. The knee pads were pulled on over the foot like a sock, and up the leg until they covered the knee. To make it easier to remove them quickly if needed, knee pad could be split in half by pulling up on a leather lace. When assembled, this lace was threaded through a series of loops after they had been inserted through grommets along one side. The end of the leather lace was tightly wrapped with

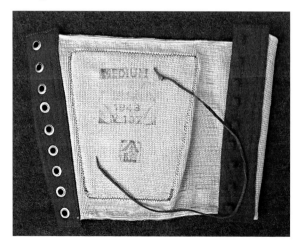

fine wire to make it easier to re-thread it though the loops if the knee pads were ever taken apart. Knee pads were issued in small, medium and large sizes and were produced in the United Kingdom and in Australia during the war.

· · · · ·

At the beginning of the war, there were only two proven methods for dropping supplies. The first was a cylindrical metal container 2.5 feet long by 1 foot in diameter which opened at one end for packing. The other method entailed strapping small packed crates to a wooden beam. This was dropped from the bomb cells of aircraft traveling no faster than 120 miles per hour. The maximum weight of each grouping was 150 pounds and the parachutes used had diameters of 10 and 14 feet. These methods were fine for small supply drops but were not suitable for getting rifles and bulk supplies to troops on the ground. While the Central Landing Establishment (C.L.E.) proceeded with development of alternative drop systems for the army, the S.O.E. made modifications to the small metal cylinders so they could be pre-packed and placed within Type C Containers which were quite suitable to their needs of

supplying only a few men at a time. Pictured at the right are the small and large *Type C Cells* used in the Type C Containers described later. Each was 19 inches tall and had a removable flat topped lid. The diameter on the small cell was 12 inches and the large cell had a diameter of 15 inches.

A large wicker basket known as a *pannier* being loaded onto a Douglas C-47 transport aircraft. Panniers like the one pictured could contain food, arms, ammunition and spare parts of all kinds. They were dropped by parachute whenever needed and were padded with sandbags containing straw to safeguard their contents. Maximum weight of a pannier with a parachute attached is 350 pounds.

• • • • •

Elliot Equipment Company developed one of the first successful methods of air dropping weapons while working with the C.L.E. This consisted of a quilted mat, stiffened with bamboo rods. It had pockets built-in to hold rifles and other equipment as needed.

Once packed, the mat was rolled up and strapped to a steel bar so it could be fitted into the bomb cell of an aircraft. The design had limitations on what could be packed and it wasn't very durable. It was also difficult to unpack once on the ground. The parachute had a similar canopy to the one used with the X-Type parachute, but it was packed into a circular pack the same diameter as the rolled mat, so it could fit into the bomb cell for dropping. This played a major role in the design of parachutes used with later drop canisters.

· · · · ·

The standard **C.L.E. Mark I Parachute** had a 28 foot diameter and was used for most supply drops that were conducted after 1942. The circular pack has six flaps that hold the packed parachute inside after being secured with a break tie that is also fastened to the static line. A second break tie connects the apex of the canopy to a spliced eye loop at the end of the static line. Fol-

lowing deployment of the cargo and the static line being fully extended, the first break tie is snapped which opens the pack. The canopy is then pulled free from the pack, followed by the suspension lines. Once the lines and canopy are completely pulled out, the break tie at the apex snaps and the canopy is free to open.

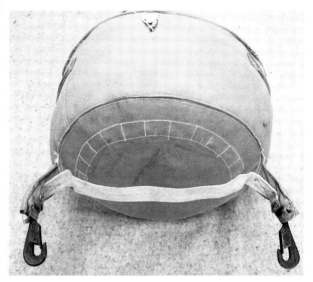

A black container parachute used principally for covert supply drops shown pulled from its pack beside a red container parachute that is packed and ready to go. The photograph above shows the two snap links that connect the parachute to the cargo.

· · · · ·

Before being adapted for use by the airborne forces, the ***Pannier*** was originally used for ammunition storage by units of the Royal Army Ordnance Corps. In their airborne role, they used the C.L.E. Mark I parachute and were deployed via roller conveyors, generally in pairs, by air despatchers. The panniers were made of wicker in a rectangular shape with two halves. The top half fit over the bottom half and it could telescope to a maximum of 30 inches to accommodate the contents in the same way that *revelation* suitcases worked during the pre-war years. A piece of plywood was wired to the bottom of the pannier to make it easier to slide on the rollers for deployment. The top half had a length of rope interwoven into the wicker along the edge which formed a loop at each of the four corners to assist in carrying the load. Empty weight of the panniers was between 25 and 30 pounds and the harness weighed an additional five pounds. Panniers were normally dispatched in pairs because more supplies could be deployed faster and they typically had fairly lightweight contents which one C.L.E. Mark I parachute could handle.

Men of the 1st Airborne Division recover a pannier within the Arnhem perimeter. The majority of resupply containers and panniers that were airdropped there fell into German hands.

· · · · ·

The original C.L.E. metal drop containers had a length of 6 feet and a diameter of 15 inches. They only opened at the end where the parachute was connected. They were developed by G.Q. Parachute Company and designed to fit the bomb cell of the Whitney aircraft. This first pattern was based on the need to hold 12 rifles and 1000 rounds of ammunition. The end-opening containers were adequate for rifles but were not easy to pack and were even more difficult to empty, particularly under fire. The basic design was later changed to have hinges along their length to allow longitudinally opening to facilitate easier loading and un-loading. The Australian Military Forces made their own modifica-tions to the first pattern C.L.E. top loading containers and these were known as ***Storepedos***. Like later cylindrical drop containers, they could be carried in the bomb cells of aircraft or mounted to wing bomb racks on fighters and gliders as long as they were rated to carry 500 pounders.

An Australian Sto-repedo containing an Auster aircraft pro-peller which is to be dropped by Number 5 Tactical Reconnais-sance Squadron to a New Zealand pilot who crash landed in enemy territory. Bougainville Island – 25 DEC 1944.

· · · · ·

The **C.L.E. Mark I Container** has a nearly cylindrical shape, being half an inch wider than it is tall on the hinge edge. It has a metal framework but the outer skin is made of plywood. The maximum weight this container was rated for is 350 total pounds. The empty container with parachute weighs 103.5 pounds which allows for an addition 246.5 pounds of equipment to be packed inside. A percussion head is mounted on one end to absorb part of the landing impact as with the Type E and Type F Containers and the opposite end is recessed for the C.L.E. Mark I parachute. The overall length of this container is 6 feet 2.5 inches.

The **C.L.E. Mark I.T. Container** has the same shape and design as the C.L.E. Mark I Container but it has a metal outer skin instead of plywood. It has an empty weight with parachute of 135.5 pounds. The maximum load it was rated for is 350 pounds allowing for 214.5 pounds of equipment.

The **C.L.E. Mark III Container** is virtually the same as the C.L.E. Mark I and Mark I.T. Containers and they were produced with plywood outer skin as well as with metal outer skin. The shape is exactly cylindrical with a diameter of 14 inches. The length is shorter by eight inches at 5 feet 6.5 inches. This pattern container was intended to replace the earlier two patterns of cylindrical drop containers which were only to be used when the extra length was needed for its contents.

The two C.L.E. Mark III Containers pictured on this page are part of the displayed collection of the Hartenstein Airborne Museum and were salvaged following Operation Market Garden.

. . . . .

Two parachutists fitting a C.L.E. Mark III Drop Container to a bomb release. The packed parachute can be seen on the end of the container with its static line already fastened to the aircraft.

A photograph showing a Mark III container packed but open, next to another that is ready to be mounted for dropping. Examples of padding along with a Number 4 Enfield and a Bren gun can be seen at the far right.

· · · · ·

Experiments were conducted to see how effective it would be for wheels to be added to drop containers. The idea being that mobile, wheeled containers would be easier to recover with their contents if they needed to be moved to another location prior to being opened and emptied. Each wheel was mounted on a spindle on one side of the outer container body along with a carrier and the towing mechanism which were held in place by straps. To assemble the mobile container, the wheels were pulled off the container and the spindles were inserted into each side of a metal tube welded to the bottom of the carrier to create an axle. The towing mechanism was then fitted to the front of the container. Like the airborne Lightweight Trailer, it had multiple mounting points for the handle to compensate for angle needed when pulled by men or by various vehicles. It was found that the mobile container could be maneuvered by two men over rough ground or towed behind a motorized vehicle at speeds up to 30 miles per hour.

Further trials were done with mobile containers to see if a Welbike was capable of pulling the 350 pound maximum weight of a filled container. The container had a length of thin pipe for a handle and this was fastened to a pre-production Welbike using a short webbing equipment strap. Initial tests were a success so the project moved forward and improvements were made to the container's handle and to the method of attachment to a Welbike.

· · · · ·

The improved towing mechanism on the mobile container had a folding T-handle at the top so one or more men could manually pull it. A lunette suitable for attachment to the pintle hook on a jeep was located mid-way down the vertical tube of the towing mechanism. And the lower end of the vertical tube had a quick release Oddie Pin that could mate with a v-shaped Oddie Clip attached at the rear of the modified frame on a Mark I Welbike. This allowed the container to fasten onto the Welbike by simply lining up the Oddie pin and clip. Rotating the T-handle 90 degrees and lifting it would separate the Welbike from the container. The new modifications were successful when conducted on a hard level surface. But when the trials progressed to the field, it was found that the Welbikes light weight and small tyres were not adequate for pulling a loaded container

An Excelsior Welbike Mark I modified for towing a drop container with the revised attachment mechanism.

A pair of C.L.E. Mark I Containers being fastened to the bottom of a C-47. The parachute can be seen at the front of the closest container along with the static line fastened to the aircraft that will deploy the parachute once the container is released.

· · · · ·

593

The *Type E Container* was produced for air deployment of the Number 18 wireless set and its accessories. The loaded container with parachute had a weight of 190 pounds. The shape was rectangular with rounded corners and the outer skin was made of metal. One end had a domed shape percussion head which would collapse on landing to absorb some of the impact. It was also designed to house an identification lighting set, when needed, to assist in locating the landed container during periods of darkness. The opposite end was recessed for attachment and stowage of the C.L.E. Mark I parachute and pack.

The *Type F Container* was produced for air deployment of the Numbers 11, 19, 21 and 22 wireless sets. It had the same shape and features as the Type E Container but was slightly longer.

A Number 18 Wireless Set packed inside a Type E Container. Felt pads were used to cushion the contents. The layer that would cover the area underneath the hinged lid is seen at the upper right corner of the photograph.

· · · · ·

Two photos of the same Type F Container. The top photo shows the container packed and the bottom one with the contents laid out beside it. These include a wireless transceiver with power supply unit, two batteries 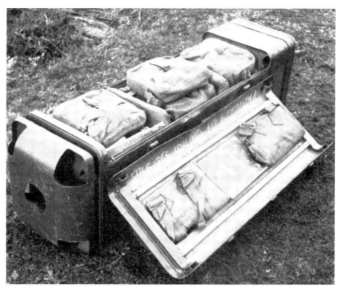 in wooden carriers and two signals satchels that would contain needed ancillaries. The text chalked on the inside of the lid reads "Property of 2 Para Bde Sigs."

. . . . .

The *Type H Container* was used predominantly for dropping supplies to Resistance units, Jedburghs and members of the S.O.E. operating behind enemy lines. It is made up from an assembly consisting of five individual storage sections which are in the center, a percussion head on one end and a parachute stowage section on the other end. The center sections were normally pre-packed and could be ordered by a code designation. H1 contained explosives and related accessories. H2 was packed with Sten submachine gun and accessories. H3 was coded for grenades and other small personal weapons. H4 contained incendiary related materials and H5 was designated for other items related to sabotage. A container could be assembled from one of each of the five types of sections or from any combination of sections including five of the same type depending on the operative's needs. The sections and ends were held together by small tie rods and there are documented instances of the containers separating from the opening shock of the parachute. All parts of the container were painted flat black with white stenciling. Overall length of the container was 5 feet 6 inches and it had a diameter of 15 inches. Each storage section was top loading so the container had to be taken apart to access the contents. A short spade was included on the outside of the container to assist in burying the unneeded container parts and the parachute.

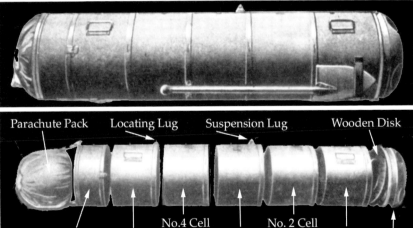

Parachute Pack Locating Lug Suspension Lug Wooden Disk

Parachute
Stowage
Cleeve No. 5 Cell No.4 Cell No. 3 Cell No. 2 Cell No. 1 Cell

Spade

Percussion
Head

· · · · ·

The *Type C Container* was very similar to the C.L.E. cylindrical drop containers used by the regular military forces but they were designed to hold three individual pre-packed *Type C Cells* as described earlier in this section or three 5-gallon cylindrical containers used for petrol or oil. They opened longitudinally and had an overall length of 5 feet 8 inches with an inside diameter of 15 inches. The container could also be used without the internal cells in the event a longer item needed to be packed inside. Special pads were used to wrap the items when this was the case and the types used for rifles and Bren Guns resemble weapons valises without the lacing.

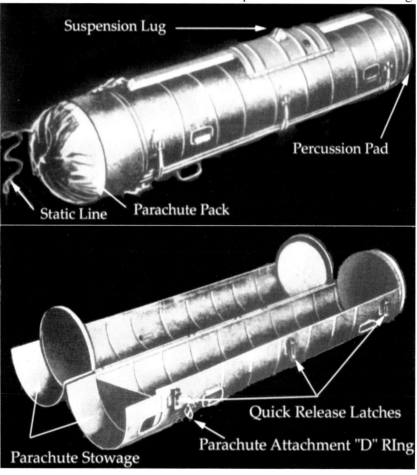

Weapon Valises and Leg Bags

The standard rifle and Bren gun valise were each originally designed for use as protective cases for the weapons when they were packed into drop containers. Valises consisted of thick flat felt of sufficient length and width to cover the entire weapon. The felt was folded in half, lengthwise, and sewn back to itself at one end and on the long edge opposite from the fold. This left one end open and formed a simple sleeve into which the weapon could be slipped into muzzle first. The Rifle Valise was 44 inches by 8 inches and the Bren Gun Valise was 46 inches by 9 inches.

Because drop containers might not always land near the paratroopers, modifications were made to the existing valise designs so they could be carried with the individual soldier when he jumped, thus making his weapon available for immediate action upon landing. An open-ended canvas pocket was added to the outside of the valise to hold a twenty foot suspension line that would be used to lower the weapon once the parachutist was under canopy. One end of the suspension line is fastened to the weapon inside the valise and the other end is pulled through a slit in the side of the felt and is fastened to the parachutist's harness. A webbing strap with a lift-the-dot fastener passes over the open end of the valise once the weapon has been placed inside and this helps to hold it from being able to slide out.

A soldier prepares to extract a Bren gun from its valise inside a drop container that is filled with rifle valises and other equipment. The lack of a visible parachute would suggest this was a staged photograph.

· · · · ·

598

A webbing strap with a quick release device holds the valise to the paratrooper when he exits the aircraft. Once under canopy, the quick release is activated which frees the valise so it can be lowered beneath the parachutist using the suspension line. Other weapons used these patterns of valise as well. The Vickers medium machine gun was inserted into the Bren Valise and a pair of Rifle Valises was used in the case of the 3-inch mortar barrel. The machine gun tripod and the mortar base plate and mounting would be packed into airborne kitbags for aerial delivery.

A solider extracts a rifle valise from a container that has just landed. Weapons for four men were packed inside this container along with the men's haversacks with cased entrenching tools attached to the lower portions of the haversack shoulder straps.

Two soldiers on the drop zone during a training exercise retrieve their rifles from a drop container. The man on the right has already retrieved his weapon and its valise has been tossed away and is still in the air. The man on the left is just beginning to remove his weapon, still in the valise, and the rifle butt can be seen in the open end.

• • • • •

599

It should be noted that the rifle is inserted into the Rifle Valise butt first when used with a parachutist. This is because it is designed to flip over when released due to where the suspension line is passed through its side and secured to the weapon. This ensures it will land butt first where the valise has additional padding. This padding was not a feature of the valise when used in a drop container. Because of this padding, the last 1-2 inches of the muzzle end of the rifle will protrude from the valise. If the weapon is inserted muzzle first, the end of the barrel will work its way around the padding and fit completely inside. But there will be very little to prevent it from tearing out and the parachutist would be at risk while the valise was still attached to his body. And once the quick release was activated, the jolt from the drop would likely cause the rifle to tear through the bottom. It would still be fastened to the parachutist in this case but would be descending unprotected, muzzle first, and subject to damage on striking the ground.

There were two methods of using the Rifle Valise when parachuting and they were known as the Low Position and the High Position. For the Low Position, a webbing bayonet frog is fixed to the upper strap of the parachutist's right anklet and the exposed muzzle of the rifle is inserted into the

A 1944 dated rifle valise is pictured to the right and shows how the weapons muzzle is secured to the parachutist with a bayonet frog. The suspension line can be seen in its pocket with one end entering the valise where it is fastened to the weapon. The single quick release device can be seen near the top where it holds the two pieces of the waist strap together until disconected.

· · · · ·

bayonet frog which holds it in place for easier mobility in the aircraft and while exiting. This places the quick release webbing strap around the parachutists waist and the weapon won't interfere with making a clean exit from the aircraft. Once under canopy, the quick release is activated and the weapon pulled clear of the bayonet frog. It will flip over and drop the length of the suspension line where it will land butt first just prior to the parachutist. The High Position places the quick release strap around the parachutist's neck and he takes up the weight of the weapon with his right hand. When he exits the aircraft, he must hold the valise tightly until under canopy or his neck will take the opening shock due to the strap being wrapped around it. This is also how the Bren Valise is used. The advantage to this position is that a parachutist can sit in the aircraft more comfortably and easily pick up the cased weapon just prior to queuing for the jump.

Parachutists with a Bren Valise (left) and a Rifle Valise (right) which are each shown in the High Position. The webbing strap in the Bren gunners hand is an anti-sear sleeve that helps him to lower the weight of the weapon on the suspension line without getting a rope burn.

· · · · ·

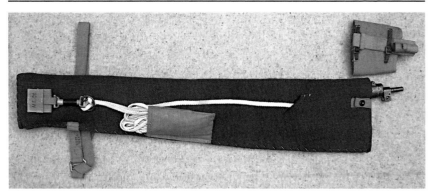

Both sides of a 1944 dated rifle valise are shown above and below. This pattern had a quick-release mechanism that used the cone and grommet format with a light metal wire pull pin/handle.

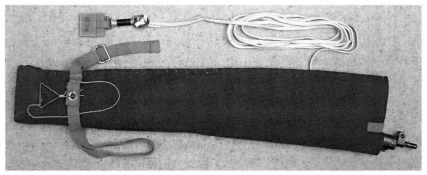

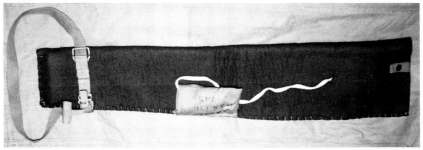

The rifle valise shown above is dated 1945 and features the second style quick-release mechanism that utilized a hasp and staple design similar to that found on a Sten magazine bandolier or the Pattern 1944 Web Equipment components. The pull handle is T-shaped and also made from webbing. This is the pattern shown in the high position on the previous page.

· · · · ·

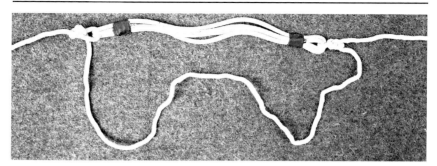

The let down line used with the early Sten and Mortar related leg cases was made from the same cord used for a parachute's suspension lines. Since the cases were designed to drop when released, without the aid of an anti-sear sleeve, a provision was designed to prevent it from breaking from a sudden shock. Two knots with protruding loops were made in the let down line three feet apart. Then a length of elastic cord was folded back on itself four times while being fed through the loops in the suspension line knots. The length of the elastic cord loops were roughly two feet long and bound near the ends with friction tape. This elastic would take the sudden shock of the dropped load and the main let down line would remain intact, even if the elastic section broke under tension.

A sleeve-type quick-release was used with the airborne kitbags and the larger weapons valises. The upper webbing portion formed a loop which allowed a leg strap on the X-Type parachute harness to pass through. The pair of rings at the opposite end were for connecting a rope or heavy let down line that would be fastened to the drop equipment. The example with the black center section can swivel while the one beside it has an emergency jettison feature described on page 613.

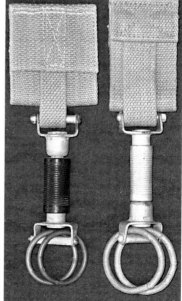

· · · · ·

The **Sten Machine Carbine Leg Case** was developed for airborne use and could hold one Sten Mark II with the stock attached. To do this, the cocking handle had to be pulled to the rear and placed into the safety slot, and the magazine housing needed to be rotated 90 degrees down. This prevented the Sten Mark III from being able to fit in a leg case since its magazine housing was welded in place. The leg case was made obsolete before the Sten Mark V design was introduced. When the weapon is inserted into the case, the stock will stick out from the back. A section of canvas sewn into the end of the leather bag is designed to wrap around the stock reinforcement piece and a draw string closes the canvas tightly around the tube of the stock. This keeps the weapon protected inside the leg bag until it is withdrawn and ready for action. The stock can be removed but it will not fit inside the case with the weapon and separating them would defeat the purpose of the leg bag, since it was designed so a paratrooper would have his weapon immediately available on landing.

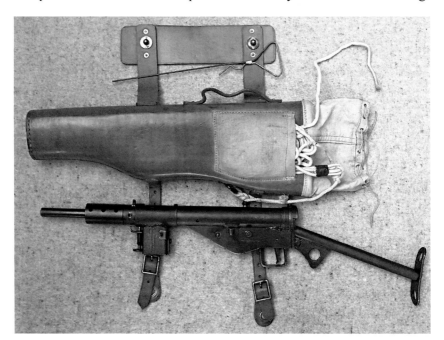

· · · · ·

The Sten leg case is made predominantly from leather with a small about of canvas at the open end as previously described, along with a small canvas pocket sewn to the side for holding the let down rope. Known examples are marked B.H.G. (Barrow Hepburn and Gale Limited) 1942, with an inspector number and a Broad Arrow mark above and below it. The let down rope is made from a length of cotton parachute suspension line. One end is tied to a metal swivel that is riveted to the lower side of the case in the center. The loose end of the let down line would be tied to the parachutists harness. A leather carrying handle is located on the opposite side of the case from where the let down line is fastened. When the leg case is released and hanging from the suspension line, the weapon will be upside down and horizontal with the landing zone so that the handle of the case will hit the ground first.

In practice, the case is worn against the outside of the jumper's leg. Leather straps wrap around the leg and come back to the case. There are four straps with two at the top and two at the bottom. A flat piece of leather is riveted to the top and bottom of one pair of straps and a metal cone is located at these positions. The mates to the two straps each have a large grommet that can be placed over the cones. A metal rod passes through holes in the cones and this prevents the grommet sides of the straps from separating from the cones until the parachutist pulls the pin which releases the leg case from his leg.

· · · · ·

The *Sten Ammunition Leg Case* (Army Stores Reference AA.5333) was produced from webbing material and was intended to hold fifteen filled magazines for the Sten Machine Carbine. Alternatively it could be packed with cartons of ammunition with the quantity being dependant on the rifle or pistol calibre. The case is in the shape of a rectangular box with overlapping fold-out flaps on three sides. A forth flap is sewn in place

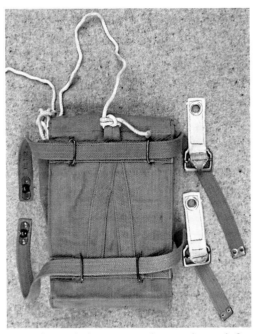

to form a pocket at the lower edge of the case when oriented for hooking up. This prevents the magazines from being able to slip out

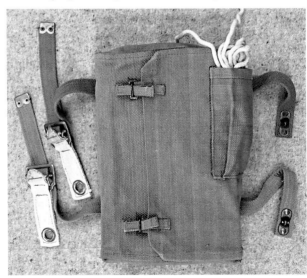

while the case is strapped to a parachutist's leg or after it has been released. When the flaps are folded closed over the magazines, they are held closed by two staple and hasp quick-release fittings. A pocket on one side of the case is designed to hold the let down line. One end would be tied onto a webbing reinforcement loop at the top on the rear of the case and the other end would be tied to the parachutist's harness. The case is held to a parachutist's leg by two webbing straps having pin-and-cone quick-release fasteners. These are held secured by a metal dual release pin, and can be pulled tight once they pass around the parachutist's leg. Each strap is held to the case by being passed through a pair of metal rings on the back. This pattern case, along with Mortar Leg Case and the Mortar Ammunition Leg Case were produced in 1942 and 1943. All of them were initially made obsolescent by the airborne kitbag. And then later in the war they were made obsolete and the quick-release leg straps were cannibalized for use with other items that the soldiers needed to jump with attached to their parachute harness (See page 611).

· · · · ·

The ***Two-Inch Mortar Leg Case*** (Army Stores Reference AA.5380) was developed to hold the Mark VIII Airborne 2-Inch Mortar. This was similar to the infantry 2-Inch mortars, but had a shorter barrel and the base spade was rotated 90 degrees. The webbing case is top loading, as oriented to be worn strapped to a parachutist's leg, and is closed by a flap having a single hasp and staple quick-release in the center. A pocket at the top on the back of the outside of the case is used to store the let down line. A reinforced webbing loop is located at the top back of the pocket and is where one end of the let down line would be fastened to the case. Two webbing straps having pin-and-cone quick-release fasteners are used with this case and each one passes through a web reinforcement on the case, as well as through a pair of metal rings on the back. While not intended for use with a Sten, one can be forced into it if the front sight is removed. See lower photograph on page 265.

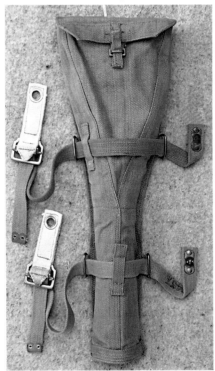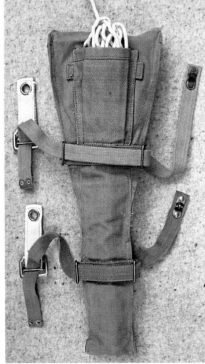

· · · · ·

The **Two-Inch Mortar Bomb Leg Case** (Army Stores Reference AA.5381) is another rectangular box shaped leg case that is similar in design and construction to the Sten Ammunition Leg Case. Its purpose was to hold six fuzed 2-Inch Mortar bombs that were already fitted with launching cartridges. The top and bottom of the case, oriented as worn strapped to the leg, have short flaps that are sewn in place to form pockets. This prevents the bombs from slipping out from either end

when worn or when the case drops after being released. The case is closed by a pair of flaps and these are held closed by three hasp and staple quick-release fasteners. Two webbing straps with pin-and-cone quick-release fasteners each pass through a pair of metal rings on the case and are used to secure the case to the leg of the parachutist. The let down line pocket is on the back and is identical to the one found on the Two-Inch Mortar Leg Case.

• • • • •

The Two-Inch Mortar Bomb Leg Case (above) contains six fuzed H.E. 2-Inch Mortar bombs. The Two-Inch Mortar Leg Case (below) is shown with a Mark VIII Airborne 2-Inch mortar.

· · · · ·

The leg straps with pin-and-cone quick-release fasteners were taken from the webbing leg cases for parts once they were made obsolete. The straps were extended by six inches and the ends with the grommets were each sewn onto a small piece of webbing so they would be parallel to each other 6-8 inches apart. This formed an adjustable length quick-release harness that could be used with virtually any piece of equipment that was durable enough to land undamaged when suspended beneath a descending paratrooper. Typically a heavy let down line would be tied to the item and then wound around it, leaving enough of the free end of the line to tie it onto the parachute harness.

The quick-release harness would be used to hold the piece of equipment to the parachute harness over the parachutist's chest until a metal dual-release pin was pulled. This was possible since the British paratroopers did not have reserve parachutes. Once released, the equipment would descend to the length of the let down line as it unrolled. This type of harness was used for items such as the airborne folding stretcher, folding bicycles, 3-Inch mortar components and the PIAT beginning in 1944.

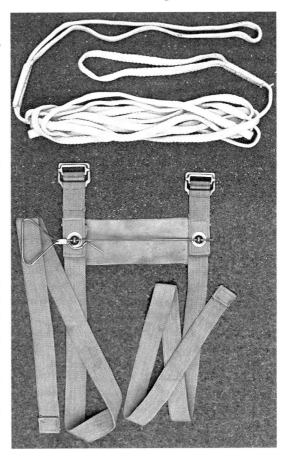

· · · · ·

Airborne Kitbag

The ***Airborne Kitbag*** was specially developed to allow parachute troops to jump with extra equipment they would need once they reached the ground. It is made of waterproof canvas and is generally shaped like a normal kitbag, but it has a slightly larger diameter, and it also opens down the length of one side in addition to the top. The side opening has a series of brass eyelets so it can be laced up to close and to allow the kitbag to be quickly and easily opened when needed. The length of the bag when filled is approximately 30 inches and its diameter is 14.5 inches. A resilient base is sewn to the bottom on the inside and this is

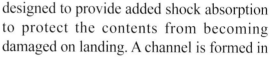  designed to provide added shock absorption to protect the contents from becoming damaged on landing. A channel is formed in

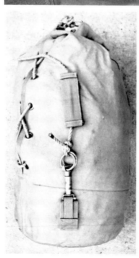

the base from the center to one edge to accommodate the right foot of the parachutist. This assists him in walking around with the kitbag strapped to his leg and makes it easier to keep the bag in a good exit position when he jumps out the door of a C-47 and into its prop wash. The adjustable leg straps are about 11 inches apart and they are used to hold the kitbag in place until a cord is pulled which draws back a pair of pins in the quick release devices. These are each made up from a metal cone that is placed through the center of an eyelet and they cannot separate until the pin is removed. Once released, the parachutist can lower the kitbag via a suspension line so it hangs beneath him during his descent. A sleeve type quick release device was usually part of the webbing that attached the kitbag to the parachute harness. It had a metal cylinder with a central pin that had a pair of "butterfly" wing studs protruding outward. These wings fastened into a swivel base and held the assembly

together. To separate the parts, the metal cylinder merely had to be pulled upward and the kitbag would immediately separate from the parachutist.

Parachutists of the British 1ˢᵗ Airborne Division waiting to take off in a C-47 as part of Operation Market Garden. The men in the foreground are closest to the jump door and alternately have airborne kitbags and Bren Gun valises.

. . . . .

613

Paratroopers stand at inspection prior to boarding a C-47 for a training jump. Each of the men has the end of his static line hanging over his left shoulder so that he can ensure it won't become fouled prior to hooking up for the jump. They are also all equipped with Airborne Kitbags. (above)

An officer with the British 6th Airborne Divisional Engineers explains to His Majesty King George VI the specifics of the specialized equipment his men have been issued. The man being reviewed stands with an Airborne Kitbag containing a PIAT, among other things. England – May 1944.

· · · · ·

Pictured below are two photographs of one type of weapons case that was used inside drop containers. There are two large pockets built into the case. One is on the outside and the other is on the inside in the same location. For demonstration purposes, the case contains a Bren Mark I with a 30-round magazine in each of the pockets. Alternately these cases could contain a P.I.A.T. or an Enfield rifle. This example was made in 1945. Earlier patterns were made from thick felt. Wool blankets were also sometimes used and had to be wrapped around the weapon several times to create a thick enough pad.

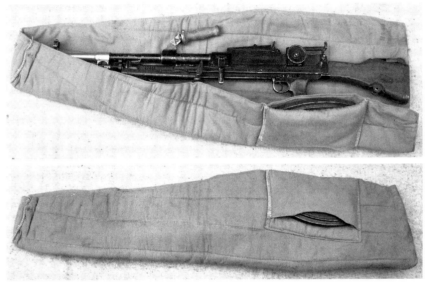

Pictured below is a less common type of WWII British-made parachutists' weapons case and leg strap. The case measures 31 inches long by 12 inches wide. The strap is 1 inch wide webbing with a length of 48 inches.

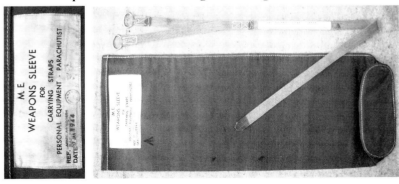

. . . . .

Standard drop containers had a metal percussion head built onto one end that was designed to collapse on landing and absorb some of the landing shock. Panniers, crates, steel drums and other irregular shaped items that could not be delivered via drop container also needed something that would help them survive a parachute landing intact. Following experimental trials, a lightweight design was

adopted that could be tied onto anything being airdropped that needed additional shock protection. These percussion heads were made from canvas that coved a large series of coil springs. One side of the springs was lashed to the board using cords that went through drilled holes. A dense pad was placed on top of the springs to form a dome and then the canvas was pulled over the complete assembly and stapled to the bottom of the board. Four tabs of canvas extended past the board and each had a large grommet in the center which provided tie down points for the percussion head. Like most airborne deployment containers, these generally were only good for one drop which makes complete pads fairly rare to find today.

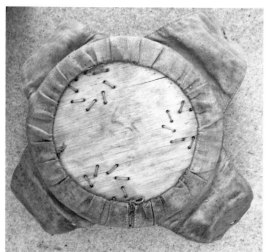

· · · · ·

Rations and stores for units of the 17th Infantry Brigade, supplied by headquarters command, Australian Army Service Corps, 6th Division, being dropped from a 36th Squadron C47 Dakota Transport. The unit was preparing for its big push towards the coast. New Guinea – 6 MAY 1945.

. . . . .

Two photographs of Westland Lysander aircraft on training flights. These planes were often used for dropping equipment containers to S.O.E. and Resistance Units. They were also used for reconnaissance purposes and could carry and drop bombs on targets of opportunity.

Two crates filled with medical supplies and a Field Surgical pannier strapped together and ready to be loaded for air dropping.

· · · · ·

A Type C Container with a black C.L.E. Mark I parachute that was dropped to the French Resistance, now displayed at the Museum of the Order of the Liberation in Paris, France.

Sixteen gallons of petrol prepared for supply dropping from a C47 on 13 DEC 1944. Each container holds four gallons of liquid and they are separated by straw filled sandbags before being lashed together. Small containers like this could also be packed into the C.L.E. Mark III and Type C containers.

A supply drop exercise of bundled food rations on 24 JUN 1943.

· · · · ·

R.A.O.C. Experimental Section, Airborne Forces Development Centre - 26 JAN 45. A crated 3-Inch Mortar Mark II with Base Plate Number 3 Mark I being prepared for a test drop by parachute. The wooden box was 56" x 20" x 11.5" and weighted 195 pounds packed. The test drop was done with a 28-foot cargo parachute.

• • • • •

620

Heavy Dropping was the term for air deployment of loads that were heavier than the standard drop container which was about 350 pounds fully loaded. These drops involved the use of clusters of cargo parachutes, the number of which varied depending on the weight of the item. Some of the larger air dropped items included jeeps, 6-pounder artillery pieces, jeep trailers and even a 6,000 pound midget submarine with a one man crew that required twelve 32-foot parachutes. The principle method of getting these large items to the ground was by glider which normally worked well for large operations, but this was not as practical for covert drops or for small scale operations. As a result, the Ministry of Supply placed an order for 2000 sets of air dropped jeep assemblies in 1944.

· · · · ·

Typically, oversized loads such as jeeps and trailers were mounted on a girder which was slung up underneath or inside the bomb bay of the transport aircraft. In the case of dropping jeeps, it was found that the vehicle's chassis could not take the shock of impact. To resolve this problem, a sub-frame was developed with crash pans that would absorb most of the landing shock. One documented operation using air dropped jeeps occurred on the night of 5/6 July, 1944. Three jeeps were dropped from Halifax bombers to an S.A.S. unit attached to a Maquis group. The drop zone was near Mazignien, France and all three jeeps were recovered without any damage. However, one had landed in a heavily wooded area and forty small trees had to be cut down to unite it with the other two.

. . . . .

A jeep and 6-pounder anti-tank gun are loaded into the bomb-bay on a Handley-Page Halifax Mark IX bomber. This was the last version of the Halifax line of bombers and they were built specifically for the Airborne Forces. The design entered service in November 1945, just after the war had ended, but it still had provisions for towing gliders and for carrying sixteen paratroopers who would exit through a hole in the floor.

Jeep and gun safely under canopy on this test drop that was conducted after the war had ended. While numerous tests had been conducted during the war, the Airborne Forces Experimental Establishment continued such operations with bombers through 1948.

. . . . .

6-Pounder A/T guns, U.S. 75mm Pack Howitzers, normal 25-Pounder A/T guns and Australian short 25-Pounders were all dropped operationally during the war. In most cases, the 75mm guns were disassembled and dropped in multiple loads since they were designed for mountain warfare and could already be easily broken down for loading onto pack mules. The heavier A/T guns were dropped completely assembled but were fitted with extra supports in certain areas. Their frames were much more robust than the jeeps and they held up well.

A standard 25-pounder A/T gun being dropped from a Halifax bomber.

A 25-pounder "short" (Australian) Mark I gun which was parachuted into the Ramu Valley in May of 1944, and used by artillerymen of the 2/4th Field Regiment.

. . . . .

Another photograph of the 25-pounder A/T gun from the previous page, dropped from a Halifax and now safely under canopy.

The barrel of a 25-pounder short gun being dropped from a C47 during a paratrooper exercise by the Australian 1st Parachute Battalion on 24 MAR 1944.

. . . . .

The airborne lifeboat, dropped by parachute, was a new device of Air Sea Rescue. The lifeboat, made of wood with two buoyancy chambers, twenty seven feet in length, complete with sails, had two motors besides rocket life lines which operate when the lifeboat lands on the sea. These were trialed in England during October of 1944 and were dropped from Warwick aircraft.

· · · · ·

A series of photographs showing an airborne lifeboat dropped from an RAF Warwick Air Sea Rescue aircraft to save the crew of an American Catalina flying boat during April of 1945. Five parachutes were required to safely land the airborne lifeboat. The pillar of smoke is coming from a sea marker and other supplies can be seen suspended from the single parachute behind the descending lifeboat. The photograph in the center of this page shows the Catalina crew after they transferred from their dinghy to the airborne lifeboat.

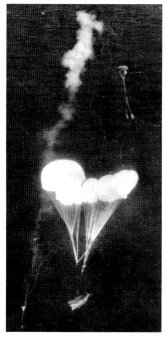

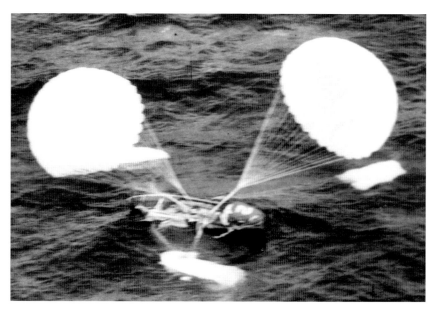

. . . . .

Two mules with parachute equipment strapped to their backs inside an aircraft during supply dropping experiments conducted in Chaklala, India during September of 1943. It is unknown how the two "stable hands" were able to back the animals out of the door of the aircraft while in flight or if the animals survived the trials.

A mule being loaded on board an aircraft of the RAF Transport Command in India during August of 1944. No further references have been found pertaining to air dropping of mules. In all likelihood, air transported cattle, mules and horses were landed by aircraft and then moved by ground transport to their intended destination.

· · · · ·

Free Dropping is the method of air dropping supplies without the benefit of parachutes. A wide variety of supplies could be safely free dropped as long as certain guidelines were followed. The weight of the supplies with their packing needed to be roughly 70 pounds. A danger existed of lighter loads striking the tail of the aircraft and heavier loads were at risk of breaking up when they hit the ground. The load needed to be packed in a way that it would survive impact with the ground and it ideally needed to strike the ground at a 45 degree angle. Through trial and error, the optimal airspeed of the aircraft was found to be 130 miles per hour and the most satisfactory height above

the ground was found to be 100 to 150 feet. Most items were double sacked to prevent the contents from spilling out on landing. Canned goods, tools and spare parts were normally packed into sacks containing rice or straw to help protect them from damage resulting from them striking each other when they made contact with the ground. Ammunition was only to be free dropped during emergency situations and it was preferable that it be dropped into water. In this case, lifebuoys were made up and lashed to the crates to keep them afloat long enough to be recovered.

· · · · ·

Notable dates from some atypical parachuting reports for test drops and jumps conducted in England during WWII by the Technical Development Section of the Airborne Forces Experimental Establishment.

11 SEPT 41 Drop tests with collapsible trolley and mortar base plate.
26 SEPT 41 Packing "Liquitite" containers in AFE Mark I containers.
02 FEB   42 Dropping Everest Carriers from C-47 aircraft.
28 MAR 42 Parachute Dummies.
05 NOV 42 Dropping of Lifebuoy type flamethrower from C-47 aircraft.
11 NOV 42 Dropping of folding bicycle from C-47 aircraft.
18 NOV 42 Dropping panniers from C-47 aircraft.
19 DEC   42 Dropping sleeping bags from aircraft without parachutes.
26 DEC   42 Dropping tests on DKW (pre-war Royal Enfield) motorcycles.
18 JAN   43 Dropping of solo motorcycles in containers.
22 JAN   43 Dropping tests of panniers from Horsa gliders.
05 FEB   43 Dropping tests of Mark II ambulance stretchers.
25 MAR 43 Dropping tests of AED Mark IV compressed paper containers.
19 APR   43 Dropping tests of 75mm American pack howitzer Mark I.
17 MAY 43 Tests of Ramex (cotton) parachute canopies.
29 MAY 43 Dropping tests of Smith Gun from Wellington Mark III.
12 JUL   43 Dropping tests of 4.2" Mortar Mark II.
15 JUL   43 Carriage and dropping of Mark III containers from Hurricanes.
28 JUL   43 Dropping tests on Oxygen and Acetylene cylinders.
07 AUG 43 Dropping of wounded aircrew by parachute.
10 AUG 43 Dropping tests of felt panniers.
03 NOV 43 Dropping tests on flexible petrol tanks.
05 NOV 43 Dropping tests on 6-Pounder A/T Guns by parachute.
08 NOV 43 Tests of paratroopers jumping with Airborne Kitbags.
24 DEC   43 Dropping tests on Willys 5 cwt 4x4 car (jeep) by parachute.
30 DEC   43 Dropping 4.2" mortar as a tactical load with paratroopers.
06 JAN   44 Dropping tests of Bangalore Torpedoes from bomber racks.
19 JAN   44 Tests of paratroopers jumping with Rifle Valise.
21 MAR 44 Tests of paratroopers jumping with 3" Mortar Barrel.
03 APR   44 Free Dropping miscellaneous packages from C-47 aircraft.
27 MAY 44 Trials of paratroop operations from Horsa Mark I glider.
20 JUN   44 Dropping tests on 125cc Royal Enfield Motorcycle.
22 AUG 44 Tests of paratroopers jumping with folding bicycles.
27 OCT   44 Tests of paratroopers jumping with Bren Gun in valise.
29 NOV 44 Dropping of spare barrels for 17-Pounder A/T gun.

· · · · ·

An example of Maintenance by Air can be found in the Top Secret sheets related to Operation Overlord dated 3 JUN 1944 dealing with the 6th Airborne Division. A series of code words were created with a manifest of supplies to be associated with each. The table following deals with the code words "Macintosh" and "Fuller". Macintosh was the standard maintenance for the Parachute Brigade. Fuller was the standard day maintenance for the Airlanding Brigade which included the Armoured Reconnaissance Regiment and two Anti-Tank Battalions. The listings will give you an idea of the magnitude of supplies that were required to sustain just one element of the Allied invasion force.

		Macintosh	Fuller
SAA			
303 in Bandoliers		89256	133884
303 in Cartons		8570 (in mags)	12855 (in mags)
		76000	114000
303 Tracer		18800	28200
303 Mk VIII Z		63086	94629
9mm		34068	51102
38 Revolver		494	741
45 Auto		3420	5130
20mm		364	546
2" Mortar	**HE**	860	1290
	Smoke	1224	1836
	Illumination	304	456
	Signal Red	92	138
	Signal Green	92	138
3" Mortar	**HE**	1168	1752
	Smoke	266	399
PIAT		744	1116
1" Very Illumination		286	429
Red		286	429
Green		286	429
36 M Grenade		544	816
74 Grenade		———	———
77 Grenade		800	1200
82 Grenade		642	963
83 Grenade		32	48

. . . . .

RE Stores	Macintosh	Fuller
28 Pound Coils Barbed Wire	56 Coils	84 Coils
Wire 14 SWG	2 Coils	3 Coils
Nails, Assorted	.01 Tons	.02 Tons
Tapes, Tracing	14	21
Boats, Recce	2	3
Tapes, 100 foot measuring	2	3
Sets C&J Tools in Chest	1 Set	2 Sets
Sets Fitters Tools in Chest	1 Set	2 Sets
Explosives	.8 Tons	1.6 Tons

Breakdown of Explosives		
TNT Slabs	480 Pounds	720 Pounds
808	976 Pounds	1464 Pounds
Ammonal	258 Pounds	384 Pounds
Beehives	44	66
Detonating Fuze	4286 Feet	6429 Feet
Primers 1 cm	1022 Feet	1533 Feet
Detonators No. 27	856	1284
Safety Fuze	1324 Feet	1986 Feet
Igniters SF Striking	102	153
Striker Boards	10	15
Fuze Instantaneous	256 Feet	384 Feet
Switches No. 1 (Pull)	16	24
Switches No. 2 (Pressure)	16	24
Switches No. 3 (Release)	16	24
Switches No. 7 (Electric)	16	24
Switches No. 8 (AW)	16	24
Switches No. 9 (L Delay) Asst A	16	24
Tubes Camouflet	8	12
Points	24	36
Tape, Insulating	4	6
9 (L Delay) Asst B	42	63
Match Fuze Boxes	44	66
Trap Wire .32"	342 Yards	513 Yards
Trap Wire .14"	160 Yards	240 Yards
Clams, Filled	42	63
Limpets	6	3

. . . . .

		Macintosh	Fuller
Medical Stores			
Airborne Panniers Packed		8	12
Stretchers		140	210
Blankets		250	375
Airborne Sleeping Bags		200	300
Ground Sheets		116	174
Kerosene		2.5 Gallons	3.75 Gallons
Splints, Knee Thomas		6	9
Supplies			
14 Man Compo Rations		2000 Rations	4000 Rations
Petrol		285 Gallons	425 Gallons
Oil		28.5 Gallons	42.5 Gallons
Lubricants		24 Pounds	36 Pounds
Wireless Sets	No. 18/68	4	6
	No. 19	——	——
	No. 22	1	2
	No. 38	7	10
	No. 46	——	1
	SCR 536	——	——
Battle Batteries	150/3 Volt	86	129
	162/3 Volt	166	249
	SCR 536	56	84
MT Assemblies and Components			
Car, 5-cwt 4x4	Tyres	——	12
	Rear Springs	——	12
	Radiators	——	12
	Dynamos	——	12
	Carburetors	——	12
	Transfer Cases	——	6
	Front Axles	——	6
	Rear Axles	——	12
	Wheels	——	12
Trailer	Road Springs	——	30
	Tyres	——	24
	Trailer Axles	——	24
	Trailer Wheels	——	24

. . . . .

Specialized airborne forces equipment on display for a *press day*. Royal Ordnance Depot, Greenford, Middlesex - 3 FEB 1943. (a) Airborne Helmet, (b) String Vest, (c) Denison Smock, (d) Denim Oversmock, (e) Wicker Pannier, (f) Airborne Trousers, (g) Lightweight Collapsible Trolley, (h) Folding Bicycle, (i) Ordnance Quick Firing 6-Pounder on Carriage 6-Pounder - Airborne, (j) Sten Leg Case, (k) Drop Container Rifle Valise, (l) 3-Inch Mortar 4-Bomb Pack, (m) 3-Inch Mortar Base Plate Harness, (n) 3-Gallon Canvas Water Bag, (o) Drop Container Type C Cell, (p) Airborne Sleeping Bag, (q) Excelsior Welbike Mark I, (r) 3-Inch Mortar Bipod Harness, (s) 3-Inch Mortar 2-Bomb Pack, (t) Drop Container Bren Valise, (u) C.L.E. Mark I Container Parachute, (v) Everest Carrier, (w) Boys Anti-Tank Rifle, (x) Sten Magazine Bandolier.

The typical contents of a British soldier's small pack circa 1944-45.

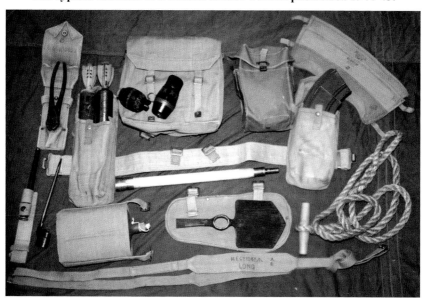

A standard set of Pattern 1937 Webbing Equipment with Toggle Rope.

· · · · ·

635

A selection of equipment normally issued to officers.

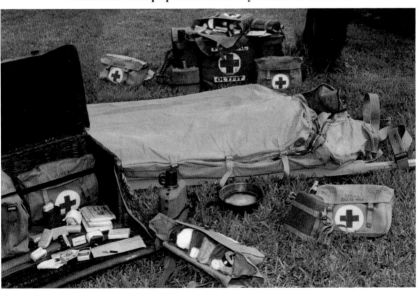

A medical pannier with associated equipment and a casualty evacuation bag.

· · · · ·

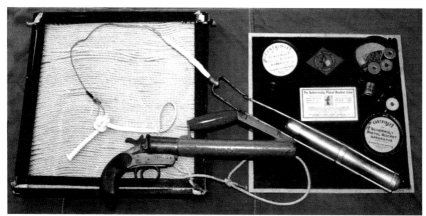

Schermuly Pistol Rocket Apparatus – A British WWII line throwing gun.

Examples of the wire carrier and PIAT round carrier harness with battledress.

. . . . .

Top row from left: 1935 Jubilee Medal, King George VI Coronation Medal, 1939-45 War Medal, Defense Medal, Canadian Volunteer Service Medal 1939-45, New Zealand War Service Medal 1939-45, Australia Service Medal 1939-45, Africa Service Medal 1939-45. Bottom row from left: 1939-45 Star, Atlantic Star, Air Crew Europe Star, Africa Star, Burma Star, Pacific Star, Italy Star, France and Germany Star.

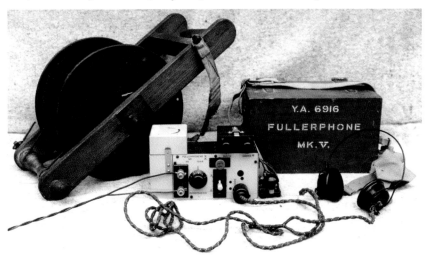

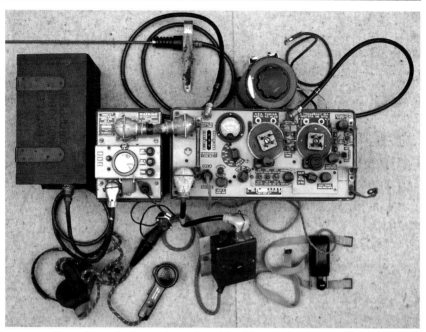

Complete wireless set number 19 with wooden battery box.

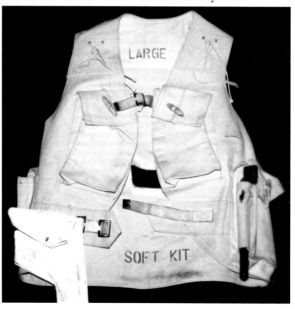

Front side of a 1943 dated battle jerkin with blancoed holster attached.

Fullerphone Mark V with wire spool carrier (opposite page).

· · · · ·

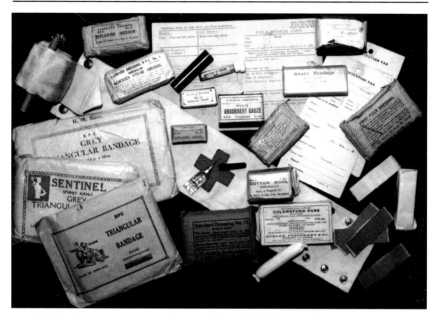

Medical compresses, tourniquets, a Morphia injector and other related gear an orderly might have (above) with a pair of field dressing haversacks (below) along side a larger capacity water bottle typically carried by medical personnel.

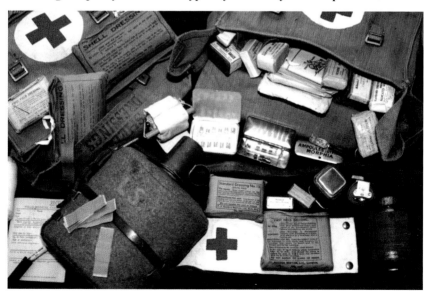

A pair of C.L.E. Mark I Parachutes used with drop containers and panniers.

General Service Blankets (top to bottom) British x 2, Canadian, Australian

· · · · ·

Appendix I - Breakdown of a British Infantry Division

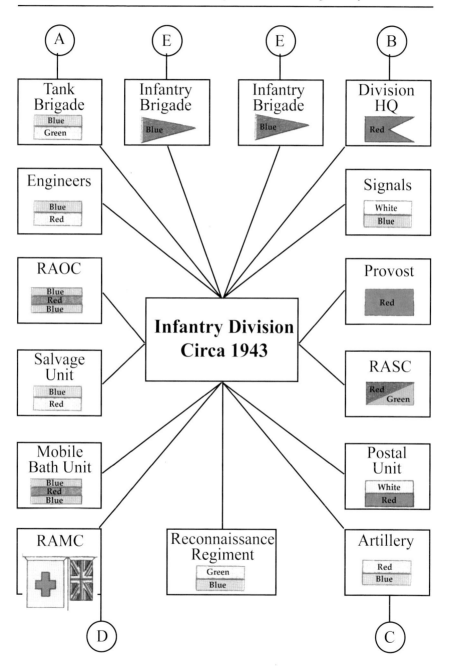

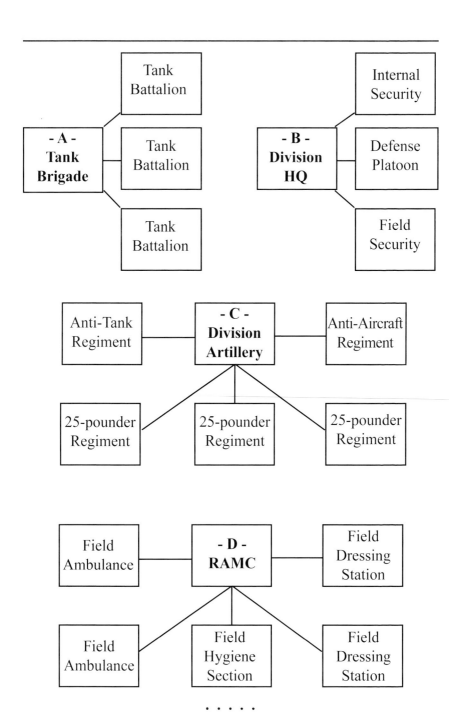

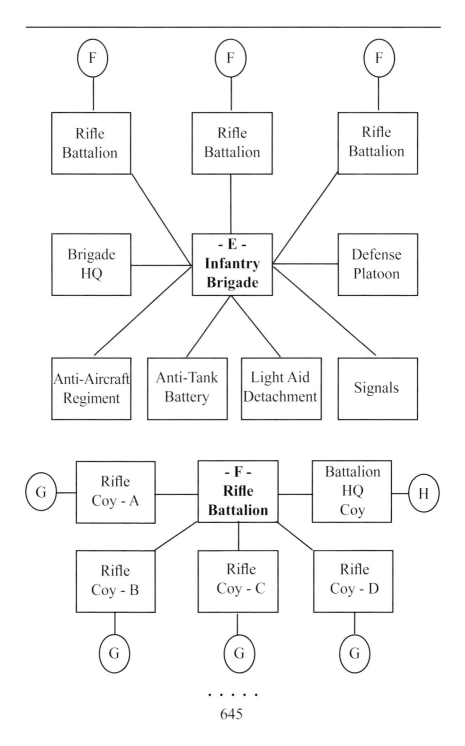

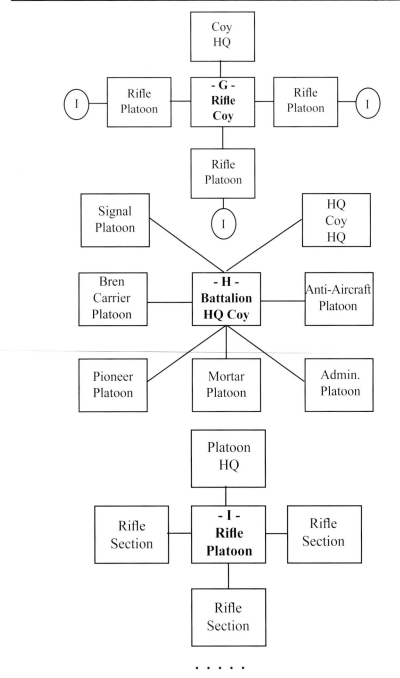

NOTE 1 - Breakdown of Men in Various Formations
    Infantry Division as Diagramed had 757 officers and 16,764 other ranks
    Division HQ had 20 officers and 124 other ranks
    Infantry Brigade had 120 officers and 2824 other ranks
      Brigade HQ had 9 officers and 57 other ranks
      Defense Platoon had 38 other ranks
      Each Rifle Battalion had 33 officers and 753 other ranks
        Rifle Battalion HQ Coy had 13 officers and 277 other ranks
        HQ Coy HQ had 6 officers and 37 other ranks
        Signal Platoon had 1 officer and 35 other ranks
        Bren Carrier Platoon had 2 officers and 62 other ranks
        Anti-Aircraft Platoon had 20 other ranks
        Pioneer Platoon had 1 officer and 21 other ranks
        Mortar Platoon had 1 officer and 45 other ranks
        Administrative Platoon had 2 officers and 57 other ranks
          Each Rifle Coy had 5 officers and 119 other ranks
          Coy HQ had 2 officers and 11 men
          Each Rifle Platoon had 1 officer and 36 other ranks
          Rifle Platoon HQ had 1 officer and 6 other ranks
          Each Rifle Section had 10 other ranks

NOTE 2 - Artillery
Each of the three 25-pounder Regiments had 24 guns
The Anti-Tank Regiment had 48 6-pounder guns
The Anti-Aircraft Regiment had 54 Bofors guns

NOTE 3 - Weapons at the Brigade Level

2240	Rifles
80	Boys Anti-Tank Rifles (Replaced by the P.I.A.T.)
159	Bren Light Machine Guns
15	Twin Bren Light Machine Guns
126	Submachine Guns (Mostly Thompsons, later replaced by the Sten)
18	Three Inch Mortars
48	Two Inch Mortars
154	Assorted Pistols (Gradually standardized with the .38)
114	Signal Pistols

NOTE 4 - Vehicles at the Brigade Level

29	Staff Cars (Mostly Civilian and later replaced by the Humber)
4	8-cwt Trucks
111	15-cwt Trucks (Replaced by the Lend-Lease American Jeep)
40	3-ton Trucks
4	Water Tank Trailers
63	Bren Gun Carriers
88	Motorcycles
93	Bicycles

. . . . .

CONVENTIONAL SIGNS FOR MILITARY FORMATIONS AND DETAIL

Batteries and Gun Emplacements.

General — Nature of Arty:- 6" How, 18 Pdr. 12" etc.

When scale allows individual Emplacements, fixed by photograph, are to be shown.

Anti-aircraft Guns

Artillery / Cavalry or Infantry

Anti-tank

Machine

Trench Mortars

Dumps :-

Supply [S]
Petrol [P]
Ammunition [A]
Engineer [E]

Nutments

Dug-outs

Searchlight

Observation Post — O.P.

Signal Office (Telephone or Telegraph) — O.T.

Wireless Telegraph Station — W/T.

Radio Telephone Station — R/T.

Beam Station — B

Direction Finding Station — D/F.

Visual Signalling Station

Hospital, Clearing Station or Aid Post

Gas :-

Gas Projectors — G.

Mustard

Gassed Areas (shade YELLOW when possible)

SIGNS WILL BE SHOWN IN RED FOR BRITISH (AND ALLIES) AND IN BLUE FOR ENEMY.

Obstacles :-

Abatis

Wire Entanglement { on posts / coiled }

Chevaux de Frise

System of Trenches :-

Old or disused trenches are shown dotted.

Tanks :-

Tank Trap
Road Block
Mine
Mine-field
Areas strewn with Rocks or Boulders of 18 inches or greater Diameter.

Bridges :-

Weight capacity of Bridges and Culverts in tons.

Embankments and Cuttings :-

Height of Embankment in feet — 9
Depth of Cutting — 10

Water :-

Width of Water-way in feet — 15 w.
Depth — 5 ft.

Woods :-

Average diameter of trees in inches — 5 d.
spacing " feet — 10 s.

TROOPS and HEADQUARTERS.

Titles will be written alongside the appropriate sign and the authorized abbreviations will be used.

Troops :- Where necessary (M) will be inserted against mechanized units.

	Cavalry	Artillery	Infantry	Armoured Cars	Transport H.T.	M.T.
Individual						
Units :- General						
Column of Route						

Headquarters :-

G.H.Q.
Army
Corps
Div.

Examples :-

Fd. Bde. R.A. (mechanized)
17 Fd Bde (M)

Thus :-

Bde. (Cav. or Inf.) △ — 5 Inf. Bde
Regt. Bn. or Arty. Bde. ⊞ — 3 R. Tanks
Sqn. Coy. or Bty. ⊞ — B Coy.
Tp or Pl. □ — 5 Pl.

Defended Locality - one platoon. — 6 Pl. L.G.

Unit deployed - one company. — B Coy.

Troops in defence :- showing portions of two battalions.

(Inter Bn. Boundary)

(FORWARD COMPANY) — A COY.

M.G. COY.

(Title of Bn.)

(RESERVE COMPANY) B Coy (Title of Bn)

R.A.P.

Note :- These examples show the use of signs and are not to be taken as standard dispositions.

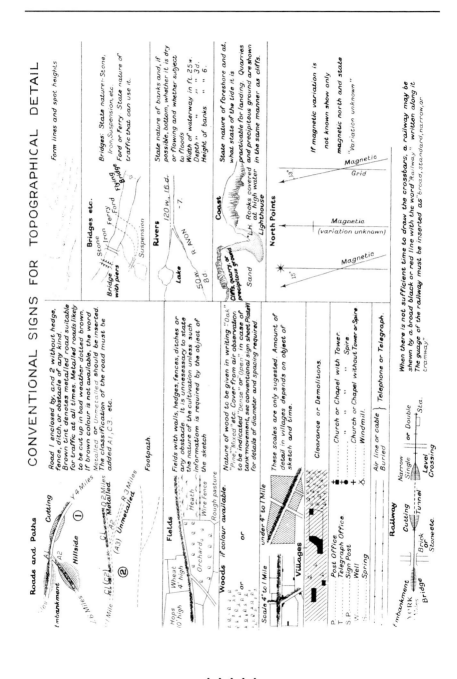

CONVENTIONAL SIGNS FOR TOPOGRAPHICAL DETAIL

Roads and Paths

Road, 1 enclosed by, and 2 without hedge, fence, ditch, or obstacle of any kind. Brown tint denotes metalled road suitable for traffic at all times. Metalled roads likely to be cut up in bad weather dotted brown. If brown colour is not available, the word Metalled or Unmetalled should be inserted. The classification of the road must be added A1, C3, etc.

Footpath.

Fields

Fields with walls, hedges, fences, ditches or any obstacle. It is unnecessary to state the nature of the cultivation unless such information is required by the object of the sketch

Woods if colour available.

Scale 4" to 1 Mile   under 4" to 1 Mile

Villages

These scales are only suggested. Amount of detail in villages depends on object of sketch and time.

Nature of wood to be given in writing "Oak" "Pine" "Mixed" etc. Cover from air observation to be indicated "Dense" or "Open." In case of tank movement, see conventional sign sheet. Plate IV for details of diameter and spacing required

Clearance or Demolitions.

P .... Post Office.
T .... Telegraph Office
S.P. ...... Sign Post
W. .... Well
S. .... Spring

■ + ● + Church or Chapel with Tower.
+ .... " " " Spire
× .... Church or Chapel without Tower or Spire
X .... Windmill.

--- Air line or cable } Telephone or Telegraph.
... Buried

Railway

Narrow   or Double
Single

Level Crossing   Sta.

Embankment   Cutting
Bridge   Brick or Tunnel Stone etc.

Bridges etc.

Bridges: State nature:- Stone, Iron, Suspension, etc.
Ford or Ferry State nature of traffic that can use it.

Stone
Iron Ferry
Ford
Suspension
Flying Bridge

Bridge with piers

Rivers

120 w. 16 d.
- 7.
R. AVON
50 w.
8 d.

State nature of banks and, if possible, bottom, whether it is dry or flowing and whether subject to floods
Width of waterway in ft. 25 w.
Depth "   "   "   3 d.
Height of banks "   "   6.

Lake

Coast

State nature of foreshore and at, what state of the tide it is practicable for landing. Quarries and precipitous ground are shown in the same manner as cliffs.

Cliffs, quarry, or precipitous ground
Lh
Rocks covered at high water
Lighthouse
Sand

North Points

Magnetic
Grid
13°

Magnetic
(variation unknown)

Magnetic
15°

Form lines and spot heights

If magnetic variation is not known show only magnetic north and state "Variation unknown"

When there is not sufficient time to draw the crossbars, a railway may be shewn by a broad black or red line with the word 'Railway" written along it. The guage of the railway must be inserted as "broad, standard, narrow, or tramway".

Cutting
Hillside ①
Embankment
A1
A2
Class ... C1 (C2) ... A2 Metalled
(A3) Unmetalled ②
¼ Mile
Y 4 Miles
Q 2 Miles
R 3 Miles

Hops 10 high
Wheat 4 high
Orchards
Heath
Wire Fence
Rough pasture

· · · · ·

649

Index

• • • • •

• • • • •

Index

• • • • •

• • • • •

Index

• • • • •

• • • • •

Index

Data on Devices, Headquarters A.T. & D. Centre Technical Branch
    Top Secret as of October 1944. Reference Copy No. 61 of 100
Descriptive Catalog of Special Devices and Supplies, M.O.1. (S.P.)
    Top Secret as of 1944. Reference Copy No. 46
Maintenance by Air – 6th Airborne Division Code Sheets - Overlord
    Top Secret as of 3 JUN 1944. Reference Copy No. 3
Airborne Forces – The Second World War - 1939-1945, Air Ministry (Restricted) 1951
Army Council Instructions and *List of Changes* entries spanning 1935-1948
Vocabulary of Army Ordnance Stores – Various Sections 1940-1944
King's Regulations for the Army and the Royal Army Reserve, 1940 Amended thru 1945
U.S. War Department TM E-30-451: *Handbook on German Military Forces*, 1945
U.S. War Department TM 30-410: *Handbook on the British Army with*
    Supplements on the Royal Air Force and Civilian Defense Organizations, 1943
Gas Training – 1942, with Amendments No. 1 – July 1943
Royal Army Medical Corps Training Pamphlet Number 3, 1944
Working Instructions: Wireless Set (Canadian) No. 19 Mark III
Field Service Pocket Book, 1932
Royal Engineers Pocket Book Pamphlets I – XIV – Revised Through 1944
The Pattern 1937 Web Equipment, 1939
Army Air Warfare Pamphlet: No. 1 - Air Support General, 1944
                                                        No. 4 - Airborne Air Transported Operations, 1945
                                                        No. 5 - Maintenance By Air, 1945
Military Training Pamphlet: No. 23 - Parts I - X – 1939, 1942
                                                        No. 30 - Parts I - V – 1941, 1942, 1944
                                                        No. 37 - The Training of an Infantry Battalion
Canadian Army Training Pamphlet: No. 1 in Seven Parts - 1940
Airborne Operations Pamphlets: No. 1 - General, 1943 (Provisional)
Signal Training Volume III, Pamphlet No. 2, Heliograph, 5-Inch, Mark V – 1922
Signal Training Pamphlet No. 2, Visual Signaling - 1942
Commercial Reference Books
    RAF Airborne Forces Manual Vol. 8, Museum Series – 1979
    WWII Troop Type Parachutes: Allies – Guy Richards, 2003
    SAS with the Maquis – Ian Wellsted – 1994
    Quarter Ton – Pat Ware – 1996
    British Uniforms & Insignia of WWII – Brian Davis – 1983
    Tommy: Airborne Uniforms, Weapons, Equipment – David Gordon - 1998
    Saddle Up – Rick Landers – 1998
    Tangled Web – Jack L. Summers -1992
    British and Commonwealth Military Knives – Ron Flook - 1999
    British & Commonwealth Bayonets – Ian Skinnerton – 1986

· · · · ·

David Gordon has had a life-long interest in the history of the Second World War. As an amateur historian, his military studies and pursuits have included living history events, parachuting, research and restoration of WWII arms and armaments, and the restoration of several WWII military vehicles. Producing the books in this series has provided an outlet for sharing some of his accumulated knowledge with fellow enthusiasts. Additional information can be found at the following web site.

http://www.visualcollector.com/

End of the road: Shell misses occupants but destroys jeep motor. – Two 5th Army soldiers escaped injury when a German shell that had penetrated the rear of their jeep passed through the vehicle, missing them, but destroying the motor. Here a soldier looks over the damage to the front of the jeep which was hit when the 5th Army patrol withdrew after coming under shellfire on the road to Piscolella, Italy. 8 NOV 1943.

. . . . .

Cigarettes, matches and lighters.

Anti-Gas related equipment (above) and a rifle valise (below).

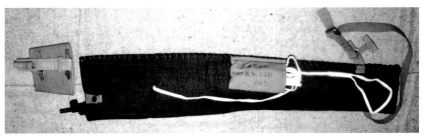

· · · · ·